# Stories
## OF
# Faith

**Other Books by Ruth A. Tucker**

365 DAILY DEVOTIONS
_____

# Stories
## OF
# Faith

*Inspirational Episodes from the
Lives of Christians*

# RUTH A. TUCKER

Daybreak Books

Zondervan Publishing House
Grand Rapids, Michigan

STORIES OF FAITH
Copyright © 1989 by Ruth A. Tucker

Daybreak Books
are published by
Zondervan Publishing House
1415 Lake Dr., S.E.
Grand Rapids, MI 49506

**Library of Congress Cataloging-in-Publication Data**

Tucker, Ruth, 1945–
   [Sacred stories]
   Stories of faith : 365 daily devotions / Ruth A. Tucker.
     p.  cm.
   Originally published under title: Sacred stories.
   ISBN 0-310-51621-8
   1. Devotional calendars.  I. Title.
  BV4811.T83  1990
  242′.2–dc20
                                                 90–39455
                                                  CIP

*Printed in the United States of America*

90  91  92  93  94  95 / AF / 10  9  8  7  6  5  4  3  2

# PREFACE

*Since we are surrounded by such a great cloud of witnesses, let us throw off everything that hinders and the sin that so easily entangles, and let us run with perseverance the race marked out for us.*

*Hebrews 12:1*

This oft-quoted verse reflects on Hebrews 11, the 'Hall of Faith' chapter, but it is equally appropriate as we reflect on the "great cloud of witnesses" that have become part of our glorious Christian heritage in the generations since the days of the biblical saints. The inspirational stories of men and women through the centuries and from around the world serve to challenge us to "run with perseverance the race marked out for us."

These stories of historical and contemporary Christians blend with biblical narratives and admonitions. Indeed, the selected biblical passages are essential and should be read first, as an introduction to the story narrative. And on completion of the book, the reader will have sampled God's Word from all sixty-six books of the Bible.

All the stories included in the book are referenced, and a subject and Scripture index further aid the reader in seeking specific information. The subject index not only includes persons, denominations, and mission organizations, but also includes such entries as "Persecution," "Doubt," "Forgiveness" "African Christians," "Native-American Christians," and "Physically Handicapped."

It is my prayer that this book will be a powerful source of encouragement and inspiration to you who may feel frustrated and overwhelmed by the disconnectedness and the demands of modern society. Here you will find friends and role models—ordinary people struggling with doubts and feelings of inadequacy who have sought God's guidance in their journeys of life. Their messages are for you, whether you are a youth, a young adult, or a senior citizen—and whether you are a mature Christian or an unbeliever seeking to discover who God is.

I wish to thank the many people who have encouraged me in this project and those who have given me story ideas, especially my students at Trinity Evangelical Divinity School.

# "BROTHERS, STAND FIRM AND HOLD TO THE TEACHINGS"

At the age of sixteen, George Williams left his home in the English countryside and took a job working for a dry goods dealer as one of more than a dozen clerks. As was the custom, he lived with the other clerks in the home of his employer. During this period of employment he became a Christian, and immediately he began sharing his faith with the other clerks, several of whom also professed faith in Christ.

When he was nineteen, Williams moved to London, where he found employment at a larger firm with more than one hundred clerks. Again, through his quiet witness, he led some of his fellow clerks to faith in Christ. But he was not satisfied with simply professions of faith. He was concerned about discipling these young men and helping them to reach out to others. He started small prayer meetings. "At first it was necessary to persuade the other clerks to stay away, and not to interfere with them. Soon, however, they pleaded for a chance to attend the meetings. The room was crowded, and there were many conversions."

Williams kept a record in his diary of those who did not profess faith, and he prayed for them regularly. "On December 23, 1844, he mentioned a number of men for whom he was praying, and on the first of January of the following year six of these gave evidence of the work of grace. His own employer was of the number thus prayed for and converted."

One young man for whom he was praying was particularly unreceptive to the gospel, but Williams had an idea. "Learning that he was very fond of oysters, an invitation was sent him to an oyster supper given by a company of Christians. Surprised, he accepted. And he enjoyed himself. . . . Feeling himself in honour bound, he attended a prayer meeting, and was, soon after, converted."

This young man later became a charter member of an organization that Williams founded for the purpose of reaching young men for Christ and discipling them in the faith—the YMCA (Young Men's Christian Association).[1]

But we ought always to thank God for you, brothers loved by the Lord, because from the beginning God chose you to be saved through the sanctifying work of the Spirit and through belief in the truth. He called you to this through our gospel, that you might share in the glory of our Lord Jesus Christ. So then, brothers, stand firm and hold to the teachings we passed on to you, whether by word of mouth or by letter.

May our Lord Jesus Christ himself and God our Father, who loved us and by his grace gave us eternal encouragement and good hope, encourage your hearts and strengthen you in every good deed and word.

*2 Thessalonians 2:13–16.*

# A HYMN OF INVITATION, WRITTEN OUT OF DESPAIR

One of the greatest evangelistic hymns of all time was written by a woman who knew well the release and peace that comes from confessing one's sins and failures to God. "Just As I Am," a hymn frequently sung at the close of evangelistic meetings, was written by Charlotte Elliott, who at one time had been very bitter with God about the circumstances of her life.

Charlotte was an invalid from her youth and deeply resented the constraints her handicap placed on her activities. In an emotional outburst on one occasion, she expressed those feelings to Dr. Cesar Malan, a minister visiting in her home. He listened and was touched by her distress, but he insisted that her problems should not divert her attention from what she most needed to hear. He challenged her to turn her life over to God, to come to him just as she was, with all her bitterness and anger.

She resented what seemed to be an almost callous attitude on his part, but God spoke to her through him, and she committed her life to the Lord. Each year on the anniversary of that decision, Dr. Malan wrote Charlotte a letter, encouraging her to continue to be strong in the faith. But even as a Christian she had doubts and struggles.

One particularly sore point was her inability to effectively get out and serve the Lord. At times she almost resented her brother's successful preaching and evangelistic ministry. She longed to be used of God herself, but she felt that her health prevented it. Then in 1836, on the fourteenth anniversary of her conversion, while she was alone in the evening, the forty-seven-year-old Charlotte Elliott wrote her spiritual autobiography in verse. Here, in this prayer of confession, she poured out her feelings to God— feelings that countless individuals have identified with in the generations that followed. The third stanza, perhaps more than the others, described her own pilgrimage:

> Just as I am, though tossed about
> With many a conflict, many a doubt,
> Fightings and fears within, without
> Oh Lamb of God, I come.

Many years later, when reflecting on the impact his sister made in penning this one hymn, the Reverend Henry Venn Elliott said, "In the course of a long ministry I hope I have been permitted to see some fruit of my labors, but I feel far more has been done by a single hymn of my sister's, 'Just As I Am.' "[2]

[Jesus said] "Come to me all you who are weary and burdened, and I will give you rest. Take my yoke upon you and learn from me, for I am gentle and humble in heart, and you will find rest for your souls. For my yoke is easy and my burden is light."

*Matthew 11:28–30.*

# "IF ANYONE IS THIRSTY, LET HIM DRINK"

Seventeen forty-four had been a tough year for David Brenard. It was his second year as a missionary to the Susquehanna Indians of the middle Atlantic states. He had seen little success in the work, and his health was poor. But 1745 would be a fresh, new year, and he committed it to God. On January 3, he set aside the entire day for prayer and fasting, asking God to pour out the Holy Spirit on him and on his work among the Indians. As he prayed, he sensed that Jesus was inviting him to come to him, if he were thirsty, and drink.

In the following weeks, he preached from this text in John, and each time he felt God quenching his thirst in a greater way. He continued to have health problems, and traveling through the forested mountains and ravines and across raging rivers was often very difficult, but that verse propelled him on, and he preached it over and over again as he traveled.

This year proved to be the most fruitful year of his ministry. An important breakthrough occurred during the summer of that year when his interpreter, Moses Tinda Tautamy and his wife professed belief in the Lord and asked for baptism. Moses was a notorious drinker, and sometimes he had been drunk when he was interpreting. But David did not know the Indian language, and had no choice but to depend upon Moses.

The change in Moses was dramatic. "Immediately there was a difference in the way he interpreted. There was a new rapport between them, and Moses seemed to have the same anointing and expressions as David himself. Furthermore, frequently when David had finished preaching, Moses would carry on preaching himself and exhorting his fellow Indians to come to Christ." In his preaching, David repeatedly returned to his favorite text, John 7:37, and wherever he went revival broke out.

"This marvelous season of blessing continued throughout August. Indians who but shortly before this were hallooing and yelling in their idolatrous feasts and drunken frolics, were now transformed by the power of God. . . . This continued with but little abatement to the end of the memorable year of 1745. On the last Sunday of the year (December 29th) as he preached, many white people as well as Indians were in tears, and after the service many followed to his house and asked with tears in their eyes, what they must do to be saved."[3]

On the last and greatest day of the Feast, Jesus stood and said in a loud voice, "If anyone is thirsty, let him come to me and drink. Whoever believes in me, as the Scripture has said, streams of living water will flow from within him." By this he meant the Spirit, whom those who believed in him were later to receive. Up to that time the Spirit had not been given, since Jesus had not yet been glorified.

On hearing his words, some of the people said, "Surely this man is the Prophet."

Others said, "He is the Christ."

*John 7:37–41.*

# "BLESSED BY THE LORD—THEY AND THEIR DESCENDANTS"

David and Svea Flood, a young Swedish missionary couple, were on fire for God when they arrived in Africa in 1921. They were determined that they would do pioneer work among unreached people, but the Africans were hostile and the climate was deadly. Soon after the birth of their second child, Svea died. The pain was too much for David. Doubts consumed him. Why had God let them down when they had sacrificed everything for Him? Had God forgotten them? Were they on a fool's errand? For all their work they had only one convert, and he was a child.

David was in this mindset when he left Africa with his young son, leaving behind his baby girl who was too weak to travel. A missionary couple took her in, and when they subsequently died, she was passed on to another missionary couple, who later raised her in America. In the meantime, David, who was living in Sweden, turned his back on the church and his thoughts were far from the spiritual realm. After his second marriage dissolved, he began living with a mistress. He thought little about the daughter whom he had not seen since infancy.

His daughter Aggie, however, thought about him often. She had learned about the work he and her mother had begun in Africa, and she wanted to talk about it with him. After high school and further study at North Central Bible College, she married Dewey Hurst and together they served in various ministries with the Assemblies of God. But she longed to visit her father and her homeland of Sweden.

Finally, she was able to make the trip to Stockholm, where she found her seventy-three-year-old bed-ridden father in a run-down apartment with liquor bottles lining the window sills. She took him in her arms and told him she loved him and that God had taken care of her through the years.

Indeed, God had done far more than that. There in his grimy bed with tobacco juice running down his unshaven face, her father heard for the first time that the little boy who had been converted through his and Svea's ministry had won his village of 600 people to Christ, and had gone on to be a great leader in the church. It was an emotional moment for him, and through his daughter's urging, he recommitted his life to God. There was joy in that tiny apartment that day, and neither of them could know that David had only six months more to live.[4]

> They will not toil in vain or bear children doomed to misfortune; for they will be a people blessed by the Lord, they and their descendants with them. Before they call I will answer; while they are still speaking I will hear.
>
> *Isaiah 65:23–24.*

# "WHEN I AM WEAK, THEN I AM STRONG"

Festo Kivengere, the great Anglican Bishop from Uganda, is remembered for his dedication to the work of the Lord and his spirit of humility. He became an internationally-known Christian leader, but he never forgot his meager heritage or his obligation to serve others.

This was evident during the ritualistic and formal ceremony of "enthronement" that marked his promotion to the office of bishop. He spoke of the potential dangers of adulation associated with the rite and the office. He recognized that such exaltation "can make one very high and dry," and then he reiterated the words of his friend, Yohana Omari, the first African bishop in Tanzania: "I want to be like the little donkey our Lord chose to ride on to enter Jerusalem. They laid their robes on it and shouted, but the shouting was all for the Lord Jesus whom he was carrying."

These words foreshadowed the path his own life would follow and the often lowly position he would be required to fill as a servant of the Lord. It was during times of insults, hardships, and persecutions that he found strength in God.

Festo was a product of the revival fires that began sweeping through East Africa in the 1930s, and he himself fanned those flames through his own evangelistic and missionary outreach. But by the early 1970s there were storm clouds threatening to quench those fires. The bloody dictator Idi Amin had come to power through a military coup and Christians became the target of brutal atrocities. Amid the terror, rumors were rampant that Festo either had been or would be the target of a death squad. Yet he continued to preach, and churches throughout Uganda were filled to capacity.

By 1977, however, Festo's home, family, and personal activities were under constant surveillance, and then suddenly Archbishop Janani Luwum and two other prominent Christians were arrested and killed— killed in what the government claimed was an accidental automobile collision. Time was running out, and Festo was convinced he must flee with his wife, although she was not well. They crept out of their home in the middle of the night and stumbled along an unmarked path through the mountains. They lost their way and feared for their lives, but they miraculously found their way to the border.

Though Festo did not have the strength to stand against a ruthless dictator, through his weakness he was made strong. In the years that followed, he preached the gospel worldwide through the power of the Lord.[5]

Therefore I will boast all the more gladly about my weaknesses, so that Christ's power may rest on me. That is why, for Christ's sake, I delight in weaknesses, in insults, in hardships, in persecutions, in difficulties. For when I am weak, then I am strong.

*2 Corinthians 12:9b– 10.*

# "FORGIVE AS THE LORD FORGAVE YOU"

Corrie ten Boom became famous through the book and film "The Hiding Place," that tells how her family, in Holland, hid Jews from the Nazis and how they later suffered in a Nazi death camp. The camp was a place of terror, cruelty, and anguish—a place that would forever remind her of the painful death of her dear sister, Betsie, who was incarcerated with her.

In 1947, two years after she had been released, Corrie returned to visit that death camp in Germany. There she gave a message of forgiveness to a group of German people who had come to hear her, and it was at that time that she was confronted with the most difficult moment of sharing Christ's love that she would ever face. She had come to Germany to reach out in love with the gospel of Christ to those who had wronged her, but she could not have anticipated the challenge the Lord would require of her.

The place was Ravensbruck and the man who was making his way forward had been a guard—one of the most cruel guards.

"Now he was in front of me, hand thrust out: 'A fine message, Fraulein! How good it is to know that, as you say, all our sins are at the bottom of the sea!'

"And I, who had spoken so glibly of forgiveness, fumbled in my pocketbook rather than take that hand. He would not remember me, of course—how could he remember one prisoner among those thousands of women?

"But I remembered him and the leather crop swinging from his belt. I was face-to-face with one of my captors and my blood seemed to freeze.

" 'You mentioned Ravensbruck in your talk,' he was saying. 'I was a guard there.' No, he did not remember me.

"But since that time,' he went on, 'I have become a Christian. I know that God has forgiven me for the cruel things I did there, but I would like to hear it from your lips as well. Fraulein,'—again the hand came out—'will you forgive me?'

"And I stood there—I whose sins had again and again to be forgiven—and could not forgive. Betsie had died in that place—could he erase her slow terrible death simply for the asking?

"It could not have been many seconds that he stood there—hand held out—but to me it seemed hours as I wrestled with the most difficult thing I had ever had to do."[6]

Therefore, as God's chosen people, holy and dearly loved, clothe yourselves with compassion, kindness, humility, gentleness and patience. Bear with each other and forgive whatever grievances you may have against one another. Forgive as the Lord forgave you. And over all these virtues put on love, which binds them all together in perfect unity.

*Colossians 3:12–14.*

# "THIS SON OF MINE WAS DEAD AND IS ALIVE AGAIN"

The story of the prodigal son that Jesus told has been played out in different versions again and again over the centuries in every culture and on every continent. Pastor Peter Dabieh's autobiographical version, however, has an ironic twist that uniquely portrays God's faithfulness in bringing a lost son home.

Peter grew up in the poor back country of Liberia where his father was a village pastor who served several tiny remote churches. It was a difficult life for Peter, and he was excited when he had the opportunity to attend school in Monrovia. He scorned his former life, convinced that now he could rise above the poverty and hardship of his childhood. As soon as he graduated he found a job and began enjoying the pleasures the city had to offer. He spent his money as fast as he earned it in the bottomless pit of Monrovia's night life. He enjoyed the night clubs and beautiful women and times of carousing with friends. It was all so very different from the dull life in the village. His occasional visits to his family were an annoying reminder of how far he had strayed from the things of God, but not enough to change his course. Life was to be spent on fun and pleasure! There was no time for reflection.

But Peter's fast-paced life came to a screeching halt when a messenger came with the news that his father had died. Until that moment he had not realized how much he loved that old man—a man who had sacrificed so much to follow the call of God to preach in villages where the gospel of Christ was not heard. Peter was heartbroken as he began the long day's journey home. The grief was overwhelming as he focused on his own loss and on his widowed mother.

But God was preparing Peter's heart. During the funeral message for his dead father, Peter was reborn. He committed his life to God and to Christian ministry. He returned to Monrovia and became actively involved in a church and then went on to Bible college. After his graduation, he became the pastor of a church in the city of Buchanan and in two years saw that church grow from two hundred to six hundred people, with outreach ministries in the neighborhoods as well as at the hospitals and the prison. Yet, while he tended to the vast needs of the city, he could not forget the commitment of his father to the villages. In his own city church in Buchanan, Peter opened a Bible school to train village pastors.[7]

The son said to him, "Father, I have sinned against heaven and against you. I am no longer worthy to be called your son."

But the father said to his servants, "Quick! Bring the best robe and put it on him. Put a ring on his finger and sandals on his feet. Bring the fattened calf and kill it. Let's have a feast and celebrate. For this son of mine was dead and is alive again; he was lost and is found." So they began to celebrate.

*Luke 15:21–24.*

# "BELIEVERS FROM OUT OF NOWHERE"

Throughout the history of Christian missions there have been those rare incidents when missionaries have been baffled by the discovery of believing Christians whose origins are a source of mystery. This was true in Korea. Both Roman Catholics and Protestants had met with heavy persecution when they sought to bring the gospel to that peninsula nation. By the late nineteenth century, however, the Catholic church was growing and Protestant missionaries were beginning to establish a permanent presence in the country. But progress was slow. After two years of joint efforts among the Presbyterians and Methodists, there was only one convert.

It was positively astonishing, then, when Sang-Yoon Suh, a Korean from an isolated coastal town of Sorai, suddenly appeared at the door of missionary Horace Underwood's home, requesting that he return with him and baptize the believers located there. *How could there be believers in Sorai when no missionary had ever traveled to that region?* the missionaries wondered. They were amazed and exhilarated by the news, but none of the missionaries was free to travel such a distance before the winter chill set in.

The following spring Sang-Yoon Suh arrived again, but this time with more realistic expectations. If the missionaries would not come to his church, he would bring his church to the missionaries. This prompted the missionaries to convene a council at which time they found three of the believers fit for baptism. After further instruction, the group returned to Sorai, and some months later Underwood visited them and baptized seven more.

"This obscure little hamlet has been rightly called 'the cradle of Protestant Christianity in Korea,' by Dr. George L. Paik. Its tiny church, first in the peninsula, gave a distinctive stamp to the amazing growth of the Protestant church that followed. Started by the Korean Christians themselves, it was self-supporting from the beginning."[8]

While Apollos was at Corinth, Paul took the road through the interior and arrived at Ephesus. There he found some disciples and asked them, "Did you receive the Holy Spirit when you believed?"

They answered, "No, we have not even heard that there is a Holy Spirit."

So Paul asked, "Then what baptism did you receive?"

"John's baptism," they replied.

Paul said, "John's baptism was a baptism of repentance. He told the people to believe in the one coming after him, that is in Jesus." On hearing this, they were baptized into the name of the Lord Jesus.

*Acts 19:1–5.*

# "A GIFT OPENS THE WAY FOR THE GIVER"

Joni Eareckson Tada, who became a quadriplegic following a diving accident in 1968, has since become very actively involved in ministry to disabled people. Her vibrant testimony has been the source of comfort and inspiration to others who have suffered similar pain and discouragement—pain that is sometimes, unfortunately, further magnified by well-meaning but misguided efforts of kindness. She strongly encourages people to be aware of opportunities to reach out to the handicapped, but she also warns would-be helpers to avoid answering before listening to disabled peoples' needs.

Giving a gift to a disabled person certainly would seem like a kind gesture that would not have a negative fall-out, but such is not always the case—especially if the gift contains a message the individual is not prepared to receive. This happened to Joni herself, when she was deluged with copies of the inspirational book *The Other Side of the Mountain*, written by Jill Kinmont, an Olympic skier who was paralyzed in a skiing accident. Joni was not ready, at that point in her recovery, to hear and accept the fact that she too could turn tragedy into victory. That assurance would only come gradually. And when it did come, she realized she could not force it onto others prematurely.

That lesson was painfully brought home to her again years later when she began receiving letters and clippings sent from people from all over the country who had heard about a boy from Illinois who had suffered a spinal injury. With good intentions, these individuals had all sent copies of her book *Joni* to this unfortunate young man. As the letters kept coming, Joni, in her own words, "began to get desperate." Through her own resourcefulness she was able to contact the boy's mother and apologize, suggesting that all the books but one be given to libraries or charities. And the one remaining copy? "Put it up on a shelf somewhere and maybe in a year or two, you could brush the dust off and flip through it. Perhaps it will be encouraging then."[9]

He who answers before listening—that is his folly and his shame.

A man's spirit sustains him in sickness, but a crushed spirit who can bear?

The heart of the discerning acquires knowledge; the ears of the wise seek it out.

A gift opens the way for the giver and ushers him into the presence of the great.

The first to present his case seems right, till another comes forward and questions him.

*Proverbs 18:13–17.*

## "UNLESS SOMEONE EXPLAINS IT"

Walter L. Wilson was a medical doctor from Kansas City who later became a preacher and Bible college president. He was known for his passion for winning souls for Christ. He was convinced that there were people ready and willing to hear the gospel and that he simply must be willing to be the agent in the process of their conversion, even as Philip was with the Ethiopian eunuch.

On one occasion Wilson was in New York City, about to leave his hotel room for a business appointment. Before he left, however, he prayed that God would lead him to someone, as he had so many times before. "My Lord," he implored, "this is a large city of seven million people, and I am just a weak, unknown servant of Thine with no knowledge of the city and no acquaintance with the hungry hearts that may be there. . . . Here is my body—my feet and my lips. Will you take them today to some troubled heart and speak through me Thy Words of light and life? Thank You Lord, I believe You will do it."

As Wilson walked out on Thirty-Second street, he passed by a stationery shop, where he noticed a small notebook displayed in the window—just the kind of notebook he needed for his daily prayer reminders. He entered the shop, purchased the book, commenting to the shopkeeper that it was just the kind of prayer book he needed. Bewildered, the shopkeeper unwrapped the notebook, explaining that it contained blank pages and was not a prayer book.

"That was just the opening Dr. Wilson needed. He explained that he made his own prayer book, using the left-hand pages for the petitions and the right-hand pages for the answers. Then he added his testimony of knowing the Lord Jesus as his Saviour, and invited the shopkeeper to do the same."

The reply was not surprising. "Mister, I have tried to find Gott for many years. I have gone around Manhattan and Brooklyn and the Bronx, night after night, attending many services, but failed always to find Gott. Can you tell me how to get to Him?" Once again God had answered Wilson's prayer, and he was able to lead his newfound friend to Christ.[10]

Now an angel of the Lord said to Philip, "Go south to the road—the desert road—that goes down from Jerusalem to Gaza." So he started out, and on his way he met an Ethiopian eunuch, an important official in charge of all the treasury of Candace, queen of the Ethiopians. This man had gone to Jerusalem to worship, and on his way home was sitting in his chariot reading the book of Isaiah the prophet. The Spirit told Philip, "Go to that chariot and stay near it."

Then Philip ran up to the chariot and heard the man reading Isaiah the prophet. "Do you understand what you are reading?" Philip asked.

"How can I," he said, "unless someone explains it to me?" So he invited Philip to come up and sit with him.

*Acts 8:26–31.*

# "THE GIFT OF HOSPITALITY"

Hospitality is a gift that manifests God's grace on a very human level, but unfortunately, it has often been neglected in our modern fast-paced culture. Hospitality requires time and emotional strength, and too often, people are not willing to make the necessary sacrifices.

Hospitality is sometimes confused with entertaining, but the two are very different, as Karen Mains has pointed out in her book *Open Heart, Open Home*. Entertaining is an exercise that often serves to flatter the host and hostess—to show off their home, their fine furnishings, their elegant table setting, and their delectable dinner. It is a courtesy that repays a favor or that seeks to win a favor.

Hospitality, on the other hand, is a gift—a giving of oneself. It is not self-serving. Rather, it seeks to focus the attention on the guest—to meet the needs of an individual who may never be able to return the favor. The etiquette of hospitality is not found on the glossy pages of women's magazines. It is not concerned with precise color coordinations, a polished silver service, or the choicest cuts of meat. Its guidelines are found in the Bible and Jesus is the ultimate role model.

Karen Mains, whose husband for many years was a Chicago inner-city pastor, has not only written about hospitality, but she practices it as a gift. Her ministry of hospitality has been focused on people who are very often unable to reciprocate. "For ten years my husband and I have lived in Chicago's inner city or close to it," she writes. "We have immersed our lives in the needs and problems of its inhabitants. Ours is a fractured society much in need of healing. . . Christ's ministry to this impoverished, captive, blind and oppressed world must, in one way or another, also be ours."

It has been largely through this gift of hospitality that Karen and David Mains have served so effectively in the inner city. They have selflessly opened their home and reached out in love with the message of Jesus to those who most needed their attention, and in doing so have been repaid by the satisfaction that they were properly exercising their God-given gifts.[11]

**Above all, love each other deeply, because love covers over a multitude of sins. Offer hospitality to one another without grumbling. Each one should use whatever gift he has received to serve others, faithfully administering God's grace in its various forms.**

*1 Peter 4:8–10.*

# "GOD CHOSE THE FOOLISH AND THE LOWLY"

John Sung, the great evangelist of China has an amazing testimony of how the power of the gospel changed his life. He was born into a Christian family in China, the son of a Methodist minister. As a youth he traveled with his father and became known as a boy preacher with exceptional talent. He was brilliant and won scholarships that paid for his college and graduate studies in American universities. He focused all of his energies on his education, and earned honors in physics and chemistry. In 1926 he received a doctorate from Ohio State University.

But with all this prestige, he was not happy. He could not forget his Christian heritage and God's claim on his life. He sought advice from a minister who urged him to enroll at Union Theological Seminary—a school not known for encouraging warm evangelical ministry.

While at the seminary, John became so confused about his relationship with God that be began immersing himself in Buddhism and Taoism and other ancient religions of the East. He even began chanting Buddhist scriptures in his search for God It was a depressing time for him, as he later recalled: "My soul wandered in a wilderness. I could neither sleep nor eat. My faith was like a leaking, storm-driven ship without captain or compass. My heart was filled with the deepest unhappiness." Then very suddenly, John's life began to change.

In his search for God, he agreed to attend an evangelistic campaign with some fellow students. A brilliant and eloquent preacher was the featured speaker—a man who had challenged many intellectuals through his powerful messages. But John had no more than arrived when he learned that the program had been changed. Instead of this well-known orator, the pulpit would be filled by a fifteen-year-old girl.

What could a Ph.D. learn from a mere child? But it was too late to walk out, so he stayed and listened. Her message was simple, but her words were penetrating. Indeed, so moved by her message was he that he returned for the next four nights to hear her preach.

After that, John Sung began reading the Bible and Christian biographies, and rededicated himself to God. So exuberant was he that he began singing and praising the Lord to the point that seminary officials were convinced he was insane. Indeed, they committed him to a mental institution, during which time he immersed himself in the Bible. When he returned to China he was flooded with offers to teach science at universities, but he was determining rather to pursue the gospel ministry. In the years that followed he earned a reputation as one of China's greatest evangelists.[12]

But God chose the foolish things of the world to shame the wise; God chose the weak things of the world to shame the strong. He chose the lowly things of this world and the despised things—and the things that are not—to nullify the things that are, so that no one may boast before him.

*1 Corinthians 1:27–29.*

# "THE MULTIPLICITY OF LANGUAGES"

Marilyn Laslo's work with Wycliffe Bible Translators was among a remote tribe in Papua, New Guinea has been a ministry that is in many ways a showpiece of missionary outreach. Yet, it has been a ministry that has often been characterized by discouragement and difficulties—especially in the area of communicating cross-culturally.

The most frustrating aspect of ministry for Marilyn was the arduous task of breaking down the very difficult language. Indeed, the difficulty and variety of languages in this region had caused missionary James Chalmers a century earlier to lament that "this country must be the authentic site of the Tower of Babel," and Marilyn echoed his frustration.

Marilyn spent long days walking through the village pointing to objects that a villager would identify and copying down the phonetic sound of the words. Nouns were easy. Verbs were in a different category altogether. "Take, for instance, the verb *to cut*," she wrote. "Cutting down a tree to build his house, the Sepik Iwam will use one word; if he's cutting it down for firewood, he will use another and very different one. The vocabulary goes on endlessly. Cutting bananas off the stalk, or whiskers off his face, or sago palm leaves for his roof—whatever the action or its reason, he uses words that sound like no other."

Marilyn quickly discovered that learning a language involved far more than simply learning words. As she began to communicate with the people, she realized that "the center of life and seat of emotions was the *throat*." Thus, in the tribal tongue one would never say, "I've asked Jesus to come into my *heart*," but rather "into my *throat*.'" The more words she wrote down on her notebook, the more ignorant she realized she was. In her discouragement she often needed to be reminded why she was in Papua, New Guinea.

One day an old man asked her why she was carving with a thorn on a banana leaf (translated: *writing in her notebook*). She explained that she was learning the language so she could write God's Word on a banana leaf. "Incredulous" . . . the old man said, "You mean to say, Mama Marilyn, that God's talk and our talk can be carved on the banana leaf for us to see and understand?" Hardly believing what he was hearing, he shook his head and said, "Marilyn, oh, Marilyn, why did it take you so long to come?"[13]

Now the whole world had one language and a common speech. As men moved eastward, they found a plain in Shinar and settled there. They said to each other, . . . "Come, let us build ourselves a city, with a tower that reaches to the heavens, so that we may make a name for ourselves and not be scattered over the face of the whole earth."

But the Lord came down to see the city and the tower that the men were building. The Lord said, "If as one people speaking the same language they have begun to do this, then nothing they plan to do will be impossible for them. Come, let us go down and confuse their language so that they will not understand each other."

*Genesis 11:1–7.*

# "I CAME TO YOU IN WEAKNESS AND FEAR"

When Ann Hasseltine Judson, the wife of Adoniram Judson, initially contemplated foreign missionary service to women "in heathen darkness," she was consumed by fear. Indeed she agonized over the decision. "For several weeks past, my mind has been greatly agitated. An opportunity has been presented to me, of spending my days among the heathen, in attempting to persuade them to receive the Gospel." She knew she would be leaving her family in America, never to see them again, and she realized her very life would be in jeopardy. "I have felt ready to sink," she wrote, "being distressed with fears about my spiritual state, and appalled at the prospect of pain and suffering, to which my nature is so averse, and apprehensive, that when assailed by temptation, or exposed to danger and death, I should not be able to endure, as seeing Him who is invisible."

Finally after many weeks of indecision, she felt peace about going. "Yes, I think I would rather go to India, among the heathen, notwithstanding the almost insurmountable difficulties in the way, than to stay at home and enjoy the comforts and luxuries of life. Faith in Christ will enable me to bear trials, however severe."

When Ann arrived in Burma with her husband, many of her fears were realized. Tropical fever ravaged their already weakened bodies and threats on their lives were an ever-present reality. Yet, Ann proved to be one of the most dedicated missionaries of all time. After she arrived in Burma she wrote of her desire to have a fruitful ministry: "I aspire to no higher enjoyment in this life, than to be instrumental in leading some poor, ignorant females to the knowledge of the Saviour. To have a female praying society, consisting of those who were once in heathen darkness, is what my heart earnestly pants after, and makes a constant subject of prayer. [I am] resolved to keep this in view; as one principal object of my life."

Ann served faithfully in Burma, reaching out to people in her neighborhood and translating portions of the Bible. But her ministry was cut short during the time that her husband was tortured for nearly two years in a Burmese death prison. She herself was severely weakened by the ordeal, and soon after that she died. Her ministry lasted only fourteen years, but it was one that displayed a powerful "demonstration of the Spirit's power."[14]

When I came to you, brothers, I did not come with eloquence or superior wisdom as I proclaimed to you the testimony about God. For I resolved to know nothing while I was with you except Jesus Christ and him crucified. I came to you in weakness and fear, and with much trembling. My message and my preaching were not with wise and persuasive words, but with a demonstration of the Spirit's power.

*1 Corinthians 2:1–4.*

# "IT WAS NOT WISE TO TAKE HIM"

Although John Mark was perceived as a failure by Paul at this time, it is clear from other Scripture that he went on to serve faithfully and was later commended by Paul. There is no evidence that John Mark denied the faith or was guilty of misconduct. Rather, he may have become discouraged or homesick, or he may have simply felt he was not cut out for the work. Christians down through the ages have encountered similar experiences of failure and like Mark have later gone on to great success.

During his early adult years, Phillips Brooks never could have imagined that he would one day become the Episcopal Bishop of Boston and be regarded as one of America's most celebrated preachers. Nor could he have imagined he would be asked to deliver his *Lectures on Preaching* at Yale Divinity School or be invited to preach at Westminster Abbey and in the Royal Chapel at Windsor before Queen Victoria. Brooks knew he was a failure and he saw little hope for the future.

After university training, Brooks became a teacher, and soon after, he wrote to a friend about it. "In all my experience of schoolboys and schoolmasters, I cannot recall a single teacher who was honoured with such an overwhelming share of deep, steady, honest unpopularity." Soon after this he resigned because he simply was unable to maintain control of the class. A friend spoke of him as "humiliated, discouraged, utterly broken down, indeed, by his complete failure at the threshold of life, not seeing well or at all in what direction to turn or to apply his hand." The headmaster only added to his despair. When Brooks left, the headmaster told him that he had "never known any one who had failed as a schoolmaster to succeed at any other calling."

After reading a book about an "attic philosopher," Brooks contemplated living a secluded life with his books, supporting himself as a clerk and being forced to live on the edge of poverty. But his lethargy was not permanent. Six months after he resigned his teaching position, he entered seminary. As one writer commented, "What a blessing it was that Phillips Brooks was not permitted to be successful in Latin School! If he had been able to manage the boys in his class, the brilliant, soul-winning, character-building minister might have been lost to the world."[15]

Some time later Paul said to Barnabas, "Let us go back and visit the brothers in all the towns where we preached the word of the Lord and see how they are doing." Barnabas wanted to take John, also called Mark, with them, but Paul did not think it wise to take him, because he had deserted them in Pamphylia and had not continued with them in the work. They had such a sharp disagreement that they parted company. Barnabas took Mark and sailed for Cyprus, but Paul chose Silas and left, commended by the brothers to the grace of the Lord. He went through Syria and Cilicia, strengthening the churches.

*Acts 15:36–41.*

# "LET HIM HAVE YOUR CLOAK AS WELL"

Confronting highway robbers and beggars was not an uncommon occurrence for travelers in the Roman Empire, and the typical reaction was aggressive self-defense in the case of a bandit or to simply ignore the nuisance of begging. That would have been the normal response for any fourth-century Hungarian cavalry officer who was leading a regiment of his troops, but this day was different. Something prompted the officer to stop when he came upon a poorly clad beggar. It was a blustery winter day, and the man was noticeably suffering from the frigid temperatures.

So moved was he by the man's pain and misery that the officer removed his own warm cape and wrapped it around the poor beggar. It was a gesture that he hoped would ease his conscience. But just as he was about to leave, he was stunned by what he saw. In a visionary appearance that was a startling reality to him, he saw the beggar was Jesus. Indeed, for a fleeting moment that shivering, ragged, disheveled beggar was incarnating Jesus Christ.

It was this visionary miracle that led to the conversion of this Hungarian cavalry officer who later became the Bishop of Tours—St. Martin, as he is generally remembered. Soon after that incident, Martin resigned his position in the military and became a monk. He founded a monastic community and became known for his healing miracles and good deeds to the poor. Indeed, whenever he encountered poor and needy people, he was reminded of Jesus' admonition to "give to the one who asks you."[16]

Martin never forgot his powerful vision. He was convinced that Jesus had called him in a very special way in order that he might compassionately sacrifice his life for others to further the kingdom of God. So popular was he among the people that he was later chosen to be bishop, an office that he reluctantly accepted.[16]

And if someone wants to sue you and take your tunic, let him have your cloak as well. If someone forces you to go one mile, go with him two miles. Give to the one who asks you, and do not turn away from the one who wants to borrow from you.

*Matthew 5:40–42.*

# "I COMMIT YOU TO GOD"

January 17, 1970, was an exciting day for the Chuj people of Guatemala. It was the day they celebrated the completion of the New Testament in their language. Ken and Barbara Williams had lived with them and studied their language for eleven years, all in preparation for this memorable day. But the day was marked with sadness, too. Their translation work completed, Ken and Barbara were making preparations to move on to another tribe to begin work on another language into which God's Word had not been translated.

It was a painful departure—"such incredible wrenching and tearing feelings," demonstrated by tears streaming down the faces of men who had never cried before. Ken had agonized over the decision to leave. Many of the people were Christians, but were they mature enough to stand alone? Then he remembered Paul's words to the Ephesian church leaders, "Now I commit you to God and to the word of his grace." He would trust the Holy Spirit to lead them in his absence.

In the years that followed the Chuj people endured painful struggles. "Guerrilla warfare swept through their region like a searing fire. For three years no word got in or out because guerrillas had killed the bus drivers and burned the buses and trucks. The area was completely cut off." Finally, when word did reach Ken and Barbara, the message was "We are bones." Crops and homes had been destroyed and the people were utterly impoverished.

Finally in 1986, it was once again safe enough for Ken and Barbara to return. Fearing that the church might not survive such devastation, they were astonished that the church had grown. They were moved by the testimonies of courage, and by the numbers of people, who had given their lives rather than deny their faith. Four pastors who had teamed up to share the gospel at a refugee camp had been brutally murdered by the guerrillas; others had been terrorized. Yet, the church grew to the point that half the Chuj people—nearly sixteen thousand people—had professed faith in Christ. Even more remarkable was the news that the Chuj church had sent out seven of their own families as cross-cultural missionaries.[17]

Keep watch over yourselves and all the flock of which the Holy Spirit has made you overseers. Be shepherds of the church of God, which he bought with his own blood. I know that after I leave, savage wolves will come in among you and will not spare the flock. Even from your own number men will arise and distort the truth in order to draw away disciples after them. So be on your guard! Remember that for three years I never stopped warning each of you night and day with tears.

"Now I commit you to God and to the word of his grace, which can build you up and give you an inheritance among all those who are sanctified."

*Acts 20:28–32.*

# "GO OUT AND MAKE THEM COME IN"

One of the most effective evangelists, church planters, and preachers in modern times has been Malla Moe. She was a pioneer missionary who served in Swaziland in Southern Africa for fifty-four years with The Evangelical Alliance Mission (TEAM). That mission was founded by Fredrik Franson—the man who gave Malla Moe a powerful vision for foreign missions.

Franson believed that most people in America had the opportunity to hear the gospel—and to reject it. But most people in Africa had not even been invited to the "master's feast." Thus it was a solemn obligation of the Christian church to go abroad with that invitation.

Malla had immigrated to Chicago from Norway in the 1880s, and was soon recruited personally by Franson. She had previously met Dwight L. Moody, and became convinced that she should take two years of training at Moody Bible Institute before launching into Christian ministry. Franson believed otherwise. "God says 'go,' and the heathen say 'come.' You must go *now*," he admonished her.

Within days she enrolled in his Bible school—a two-week course "filled with Bible study, exhortation, and practical suggestions." There were no educational requirements for the course, but there were spiritual prerequisites: to be "filled with the Spirit" and to "know how to trust God." The candidates, three men and five women, were given one week to set their affairs in order. They would then leave for New York for their commissioning and then sail to South Africa.

Despite her brief training, Malla was a very effective missionary. She had a passion for lost souls, and was determined to compel them to come to the Lord—to the master's banquet. Indeed so forceful was she in her evangelistic methods that some of her "victims" were unable to escape. A friend later told a story of how she had confronted an African man with physical force. "The day before she told him [a Swazi] she was going to pray till he got saved." Then, when she unexpectedly met him on the trail, "she shouted to him to come back, and grabbing him by the arm, pulled him down into the grass and prayed mightily to God to save him from Satan and hell. It was more than he could stand. He wept and prayed and got saved."

Malla truly loved the Africans and they loved her. As a result of her ministry hundreds—perhaps thousands—of Africans were brought to Christ.[18]

Jesus replied: "A certain man was preparing a great banquet and invited many guests. At the time of the banquet he sent his servant to tell those who had been invited, 'Come for everything is now ready.'

But they all alike began to make excuses. . . .

Then the master told his servant, 'Go out to the roads and country lanes and make them come in, so that my house will be full.'"

*Luke 14:16–17, 23.*

# "WOUNDS FROM A FRIEND CAN BE TRUSTED"

It was before dawn on the morning of January 19, 1981, when the most feared and dreaded nightmare became a reality for a young missionary family in Colombia—a family who, as Wycliffe Bible Translators, had dedicated themselves to translating the Bible for a tribe of Indians.

That day the doorbell to the mission compound rang before 6:30 A.M., and before anyone realized what was happening, Chet Bitterman was taken hostage by M-19 terrorists, leaving his wife Brenda and two young daughters behind. Time suddenly stood still. For the rest of the world, Chet's kidnapping was overshadowed by another hostage story. The following day, as President Jimmy Carter left the White House to return to private life, fifty-two American hostages were released after 444 days in captivity.

That joyous news brought little consolation for the Bittermans, who were just beginning their terrifying ordeal. They waited, not knowing what another day would bring. The days turned into weeks, as family and friends raised their hopes, only to have them dashed as the terrorists made new demands and death threats, and as rumors of Chet's execution repeatedly surfaced. Finally on March 5, the long ordeal came to a tragic end when Chet's body was found in a bus, where it had been dumped by the terrorists.

Amid the brutality and anguish of the prolonged violence, however, neither Chet nor Brenda could forget why they were in Colombia. They loved the people and wanted nothing else but to share the gospel of Christ. These people were their friends, including, in a strange sense, the terrorists. This was evident in the communication between Brenda and Chet during the weeks of captivity.

To the terrorists, Brenda wrote, "As you are living with Chet in these days you will have the opportunity to get to know him and I am sure that you will be friends. The only thing Chet wanted in life was to be dedicated to God, his family, and a group of Colombian Indians."

In a tape to Brenda, Chet, too, spoke of friendship. "Our relationship is like a two-sided wall. On the one side is our personal relationship and on this side of the wall we have no problems at all. You could say that we are friends. They like me and I like them and we have not had any difficulty. . . . On the other side of the wall there is the ideological problem. . . ." Chet hoped that this "friendship" could prevail, but in the end he found that "wounds from a friend can be trusted, but an enemy multiplies kisses." He died their friend.[19]

Anger is cruel and fury overwhelming, but who can stand before jealousy? Better is open rebuke than hidden love. Wounds from a friend can be trusted, but an enemy multiplies kisses.

*Proverbs 27:4–6.*

# "GREATER LOVE HAS NO ONE THAN THIS"

The Simba Rebellion that raged in the Congo (Zaire) in 1964 is often remembered in the West for the loss of missionaries' lives. But in the Congo it was a time of devastation and loss of life for thousands of Africans. Indeed, as the Simbas moved from village to village, it was their practice to kill someone simply to show that they were in control—and that the villagers dare not defy their authority.

The victims were often chosen at random, as was the case when the Simbas entered the village where the Udubre family lived. The Simbas decided that one of the two Udubre brothers should face the firing squad. The decision was a crushing blow to their elderly father Lazaro. He begged the rebel leader to allow him to die in his son's stead. "If someone must die, let it be me," he pleaded. "I am old and I have lived my life. I am a Christian and I know that when I die I shall go to heaven to a life that is far better than anything here on earth. Don't take the lives of any of our villagers. Kill me!"

After they led Lazaro away to where the firing squads were doing their dastardly deeds, one of the commanders suggested as a cruel joke to allow Lazaro to preach to the men before they were shot. Despite the horror of the moment and the revulsion at the massacre that was about to take place, he accepted this mockery as an opportunity to share the gospel of Jesus Christ—the way of salvation—to these men in their final moments. He sensed a positive response in some of the faces of these terror-stricken men even as the blast of the rifles sounded.

Others were brought before their executors, and again Lazaro had a few moments to share the gospel, always certain that he himself would be in the next line-up, but for some reason the rebels either forgot their threat to kill him or purposely avoided gunning down a man who obviously had such a deep walk with his Lord. When the Congolese Army moved into the area some time later, Lazaro was rescued. He returned to his village with a renewed love for God and an even greater commitment to sharing the gospel.[20]

My command is this: Love each other as I have loved you. Greater love has no one than this, that he lay down his life for his friends. You are my friends if you do what I command. I no longer call you servants, because a servant does not know his master's business. Instead, I have called you friends, for everything that I learned from my Father I have made known to you. You did not choose me, but I chose you and appointed you to go and bear fruit—fruit that will last.

*John 15:12–16a.*

# "KNOWING CHRIST JESUS MY LORD"

Kari Torjesen Malcolm served as a missionary to the Philippines for fifteen years after growing up in China as the daughter of missionaries. As a teenager, she was confined for a time during World War II in an internment camp, and there she discovered a deep truth that changed her life.

In the camp she was number sixteen, and only one of many Westerners who sought self-identity and comfort from others behind the walls and the electric fence that separated them from the outside world. There were other missionary kids in the same predicament, and often they managed to get together for a few moments of prayer—prayer for freedom.

But as time passed, Kari began to feel uneasy about these times of prayer. Freedom was becoming the ultimate goal in life, and God seemed to become less and less important—except for his answer to their prayers for freedom. She knew God was more than simply her ticket to freedom. She began to pray and search the Bible. "Gradually it dawned on me that there was just one thing the enemy could not take from me. They had bombed our home, killed my father, and put my mother, brothers and me into prison. But the one thing they could not touch was my relationship to my God."

Kari had a new outlook on life, and she no longer desired to join the others in their prayers for freedom. Her absence was immediately noticed, and she was confronted by her friend Debbie who rebuked her. "I cannot even remember trying to defend myself," Kari later recalled, "but Debbie must have surmised something of what had occurred in my thinking. Her reproof ended with the final taunt, So we aren't good enough for you anymore, eh? Getting holier than the rest of us, I can see.'"

It was a hard lesson for her: "As I walked away, I felt lonelier than I had ever felt in my life. My last bit of security was peeled off. This was the climax to the peeling process that had been going on through the war years with the loss of my father, my home, my education, my freedom. Now I no longer belonged to my peer group.

"It was only then that I was able to pray the prayer that changed my life: 'Lord, I am willing to stay in this prison for the rest of my life if only I may know You.' At that moment I was free."[21]

But whatever was to my profit I now consider loss for the sake of Christ. What is more, I consider everything a loss compared to the surpassing greatness of knowing Christ Jesus my Lord, for whose sake I have lost all things. I consider them rubbish, that I may gain Christ and be found in him, not having a righteousness of my own that comes from the law, but that which is through faith in Christ—the righteousness that comes from God and is by faith. I want to know Christ and the power of his resurrection and the fellowship of sharing in his sufferings, becoming like him in his death, and so, somehow, to attain the resurrection from the dead.

*Philippians 3:7–11.*

## "MAY GOD SANCTIFY YOU THROUGH AND THROUGH"

As a missionary, the apostle Paul realized that his work entailed more than persuading someone to accept Christ as Savior. Once an individual had taken that initial step of faith, it was crucial that it be followed by a holy life. Sometimes this aspect of salvation is neglected by missionaries and evangelists.

It was Francis Asbury, more than anyone else, who made the doctrine of sanctification an integral part of American Methodism. He was converted in England at the age of fifteen. Although he had a very limited education, he immediately began preaching while continuing to work his regular job. In 1771, at age twenty-six, he began his ministry in America. The following decade, in 1784, John Wesley appointed him, along with Thomas Coke, to be joint American superintendents.

Asbury's *Journal* indicates his concern for personal sanctification in himself and others. On March 19, 1779, he wrote: "I fear I have been too slack in urging both myself and others to diligently seek the experience of this great and blessed gift. May the Lord help me from this time, to live free from outward and inward sin, always maintaining the spirit of the Gospel in meekness, purity, and love!"

Despite such commitments, he continually found it more difficult to preach sanctification than salvation. In 1793, during a time of sickness, he wrote: "I have found by secret search, that I have not preached sanctification as I should have done: if I am restored, this shall be my theme more pointedly than ever, God being my helper."

Apparently, he kept that promise. In 1803, while an itinerant preacher in North Carolina, he wrote: "I find the way of holiness very narrow to walk in or to preach; and although I do not consider sanctification-Christian perfection, commonplace subjects, yet I make them the burden, and labour to make them the savour of every sermon. I feel, I fear for my dear lowland brethren—so much of this world's wealth: so much fullness of bread, and idleness, and strong drink. Lord, help!"[22]

Do not put out the Spirit's fire; do not treat prophecies with contempt. Test everything. Hold on to the good. Avoid every kind of evil.

May God himself, the God of peace, sanctify you through and through. May your whole spirit, soul and body be kept blameless at the coming of our Lord Jesus Christ. The one who calls you is faithful and he will do it.

*1 Thessalonians 5:19–24.*

## "YOU MUST BE BORN AGAIN"

The Declaration of Independence, which proclaimed that all men are created equal, had no bearing on Lott Carey, who was born into slavery on a Virginia plantation some four years after the declaration was signed in 1776. He had little hope as he was growing up that he would ever enjoy the freedom won through the Revolutionary War.

As a young adult Carey was sent to Richmond by his master to work as a hired slave. There in 1807 his life was transformed. Still a slave, he found freedom in Christ when he heard a sermon at the First Baptist Church on the story of Nicodemus. Here was a man who had everything, but it amounted to nothing because he did not have eternal life.

From that point on, Carey was determined to serve the Lord. He could not forget his early memories of his grandmother Mihala telling him as a young child that one day it might be his privilege to go across the seas and tell his own people about Christ. With that inspiration and the encouragement of Christian friends, Carey enrolled in classes and took on added employment. By 1815, he was able to purchase his freedom. Soon after, he was licensed to preach by the First Baptist Church, and then set about fulfilling his commitment to missions—motivated in part by his distaste of living in a country where there was no racial equality:

"I am an African, and in this country, however meritorious my conduct, and respectable my character, I cannot receive the credit due to either. I wish to go to a country where I shall be estimated by my merits, not by my complexion, and I feel bound to labor for my suffering race."

Although Carey's employer offered to raise his salary if he would stay on, he was resolute in his decision to leave. When he and his family sailed for west Africa on January 23, 1821, they became America's first black missionaries to Africa.

Life in Africa was not easy for this freed American slave. His wife died, leaving him to care for three children. Conflicts often developed between him and tribal and colonial leaders. But there were successes as well—especially in his mission outreach with a tribal group known as the *Mandingoes*. Many years later the *Mandingoes* became the focus of media attention through Alex Haley's book, *Roots*.[23]

"How can a man be born when he is old?" Nicodemus asked. "Surely he cannot enter a second time into his mother's womb to be born!"

Jesus answered, "I tell you the truth, no one can enter the kingdom of God unless he is born of water and the Spirit. Flesh gives birth to flesh, but the Spirit gives birth to spirit. You should not be surprised at my saying, 'You must be born again.'"

*John 3:4–7.*

## "PEACE I LEAVE WITH YOU"

Henri Nouwen, a widely acclaimed author, educator, and Roman Catholic priest, has a view of Christian ministry that differs radically from most popular perceptions of that term. In the 1980s, after having lived and taught at Harvard University, he moved to a community near Toronto called Daybreak. It is a "family" comprised of six individuals who are mentally handicapped and four who are not, all seeking to live by the beatitudes of Jesus.

In this setting, Nouwen discovered a deeply fulfilling ministry of not only giving to those who are handicapped but also allowing them to give to him. It is a community where each one is recognized as an individual who is unique, while at the same time bound together with the rest into a cohesive unit. "All have their gifts, all have their struggles," he writes. "We eat together, play together, pray together and go out together. We all have our own preferences in terms of work, food and movies, and we all have our problems getting along with someone in the house, whether handicapped or not. We laugh a lot. We cry a lot too. Sometimes both at the same time."

In this life of mutual sharing, it has been Adam who has had the deepest impact on Nouwen. "He is a 25-year-old man who cannot speak, cannot dress or undress himself, cannot walk alone, cannot eat without much help. He does not cry or laugh. . . . He suffers from severe epilepsy and, despite heavy medication, sees few days without grand-mal seizures."

To many people Adam is a virtual "vegetable," but not to Nouwen. "As my fears gradually lessened, a love emerged in me so full of tender affection that most of my other tasks seemed boring and superficial compared with the hours spent with Adam. Out of his broken body and broken mind emerged a most beautiful human being offering me a greater gift than I would ever offer him. . . . The longer I stayed with Adam the more clearly I saw him as my gentle teacher, teaching me what no book, school or professor could ever teach me."

Adam, the priest discovered, could offer him the gift of peace—"a peace rooted in being." Nouwen had been caught up in his prestigious career—one "so marked by rivalry and competition, so pervaded with compulsion and obsession, so spotted with moments of suspicion, jealousy, resentment and revenge." But with Adam he discovered there was more to life and ministry. "Adam's peace, while rooted more in being than in doing, and more in the heart than in the mind, is a peace that calls forth community. . . . Adam in his total vulnerability calls us together as a family.

"In Adam's name, therefore, I say to you: Do not give up working for peace. But remember that the peace you seek is not of this world."[24]

All this I have spoken while still with you. But the Counselor, the Holy Spirit, whom the Father will send in my name, will teach you all things and will remind you of everything I have said to you. Peace I leave with you; my peace I give you. I do not give to you as the world gives. Do not let your hearts be troubled and do not be afraid.

*John 14:25–27.*

# "MY SOUL THIRSTS FOR GOD"

The Reformation brought spiritual renewal to many parts of Europe, but in the century that followed the church in many areas was cold, and the church leaders often showed little evidence of spirituality. This was not always true among the common people, as Madame Jeanne Guyon found as she traveled about the French countryside during the latter years of the seventeenth century.

Madame Guyon was a widow who had attained her title by marrying a wealthy Frenchman. For a time, she had enjoyed the high living and lavish parties that Parisian society offered, but not without a sense of guilt. Deep down she was very unhappy, knowing that true happiness came only from serving God. After her husband died, she was consumed with the responsibility of caring for her little children, but still she could not escape the sense of God's call on her life. She visited a priest, hoping that he would absolve her of her duty, but instead he further confirmed that God had a special ministry for her.

In the years that followed, she became a self-appointed Catholic evangelist who went from village to village challenging people to renew their faith in Christ. She wrote of her experiences, and her writings have deeply influenced Christians ever since, including the great revivalist and churchman John Wesley. Of her, he wrote, "We may search many centuries before we find another woman who was such a pattern of true holiness."

On one occasion, as she was conducting her itinerant preaching, she encountered a woman, who had been physically abused by her husband and threatened by church officials for sharing her faith publicly. The church authorities insisted it was the business of the educated priests to pray and preach, but her neighbors were longing for more than the superficial words of the local priests. They were thirsting for God and they continued to seek her out, convinced that "God had taught her inwardly by the Holy Ghost."

Sometimes Madame Guyon was overwhelmed by the spiritual hunger she encountered. This was true in the town of Thonon: "I have never in my life had so much consolation as in seeing in that little town so many good souls who vied with each other in giving themselves to God with their whole heart. There were young girls of twelve and thirteen years of age, who worked all day in silence in order to converse with God, and who had acquired a great habit of it. As they were poor girls, they joined in couples and those who knew how to read, read out something to those who could not read. It was revival of the innocence of the early Christians."[25]

As the deer pants for streams of water, so my soul pants for you, O God.

My soul thirsts for God, for the living God. When can I go and meet with God?

*Psalm 42:1–2.*

Blessed are those who hunger and thirst for righteousness, for they will be filled.

*Matthew 5:6.*

## "WHAT I WANT TO DO I DO NOT, BUT WHAT I HATE I DO"

This personal testimony of the apostle Paul is one common to all men and women, especially those who suffer from addictions. It is a testimony that could be given over and over again by alcoholics, and it is one that illustrates the story of Mel Trotter.

Mel began drinking in his teens and continued after he had a wife and family. He knew that he had a serious alcohol problem, and he repeatedly promised his wife he would mend his ways, but time after time he went back on his word. On one occasion, "after a record-breaking period of eleven and one half sober weeks, Mel succumbed to his vice again, possibly encouraged by a suspended court sentence hanging over him. He went into the country, drove up to a saloon, put the horse in the shed and said, 'There's an old nag out there with the buggy. Everybody have something to drink. Drink up the horse!'

"For six years I tried to quit," he later recalled. "Every time after promising my wife and my boy and myself that I'd never take it again, I'd fall. . . . I hated myself. Finally after a drunk I just wouldn't go home any more. I got to staying away for three or four days at first, then a week, and gradually longer and longer. I even committed burglary to satisfy the awful craving for drink.

"God gave us only one baby. When the little fellow was hardly two years old I went to our little home one day . . . and found him dead in his mother's arms. I'll never forget that day. I was a slave, and I knew it. . . . Over the body of our dead baby, lying in the little white casket, she made me promise that I'd never take another drop. I promised, put my arms around her, and told her I'd never touch liquor again as long as I lived. The funeral hadn't been over two hours before I staggered home so drunk I couldn't see. I couldn't help it; the devil had me."

Convinced there was no hope for him, Mel decided to end it all. On a frigid January night in 1897, after too many drinks, he vowed he would throw himself into the icy water of Lake Michigan. Instead, he staggered into the Pacific Garden Mission where he was converted. This time his commitment was real; he stopped drinking and he went on to establish his own rescue missions.[26]

We know that the law is spiritual; but I am unspiritual, sold as a slave to sin. I do not understand what I do. For what I want to do I do not do, but what I hate I do. And if I do what I do not want to do, I agree that the law is good. As it is, it is no longer I myself who do it, but it is sin living in me. I know that nothing good lives in me, that is, in my sinful nature. For I have the desire to do what is good, but I cannot carry it out. For what I do is not the good I want to do; no, the evil I do not want to do—this I keep on doing. Now if I do what I do not want to do, it is no longer I who do it, but it is sin living in me that does it.

*Romans 7:14–20.*

# "NO HELP FROM THE PAGANS"

Life in Phnom Penh, Cambodia, was routine for Socheth Na, his parents, and seven brothers and sisters until 1975. In April of that year the Communist Khmer Rouge took control of the country and terror reigned for the next three years, eight months, and seven days. Socheth was twenty-two years old and had completed a year of college, which was a factor that made him a target for the bloody new regime. Young men with education were regarded as a threat, and most were systematically killed.

Socheth's family was split up and he was taken to a work camp. There, while living on a starvation diet, he spent long days in hard labor under the eye of the guards. Soup made with water and one spoon of rice was served to dozens of hungry men. Survival meant sneaking moments when the guard wasn't looking to forage for leaves or bark or grasshoppers or rodents—anything to keep from starving.

The most terrifying facet of the death camp atmosphere was the constant fear of execution. Socheth lied, claiming that he had only a third grade education. But the guards were suspicious and he shuddered at the thought that he would be led away for execution. There was safety in numbers, but when, on two occasions, he was taken by a guard into the forest alone, he was certain he would never come back out alive. For some reason he was spared. He pondered the reason for his narrow escapes, and for his surviving a treacherous fall over a rocky gorge. Indeed, as he was plummeting to what he thought was his death, he could hear someone calling his name. Who was it? he wondered, after he regained consciousness.

Socheth's indescribable horror ended in January of 1979, when the Vietnamese Communists gained control of the country. Socheth and his brother were able to escape to a refugee camp on the border of Thailand, where they were later joined by other family members. Here they came in contact with Baptist missionaries. Socheth listened to the gospel message, but was a Buddhist and was not ready to change his religion. Yet, he was overwhelmed with the love the Christians showed him.

In 1981, Socheth and his family, along with other refugees, came to the United States. Life was difficult in this strange land, but once again it was the Christian community—and particularly one businessman, Robert Reitsma—who reached out in love. It was not so much the doctrine of Christianity that eventually brought Socheth to Christ, but the love of Christians.[27]

**Dear Friend, you are faithful in what you are doing for the brothers, even though they are strangers to you. They have told the church about your love. You will do well to send them on their way in a manner worthy of God. It was for the sake of the Name that they went out, receiving no help from the pagans. We ought therefore to show hospitality to such men so that we may work together for the truth.**

*3 John 5–8.*

# "REACHING OUT TO THE RICH"

Jesus set an example that is rarely followed today; he ate with and reached out to the wealthiest people in society. There is legitimate and well-placed concern for the poor and the need to reach them for Christ, but fewer efforts are made to reach out to the rich.

For Nancy DeMoss and her late husband, Art, however, reaching out with the gospel by means of dinner invitations to wealthy acquaintances seemed only natural. God had allowed them to attain great wealth through Art's National Liberty insurance business, and it seemed only proper to use the wealth and the personal contacts they had made to further God's kingdom.

Their dinner parties not only featured fine food but also a gospel message from a prominent Christian, such as Charles Colson, Pat Boone, or Washington Redskins' coach Joe Gibbs. They personally greeted each guest at the door and sent personal follow-up letters encouraging each one to prayerfully consider the claims of Christ. Small group Bible studies also became a part of the ministry.

When this ministry became too large for the DeMosses alone, they obtained help from Campus Crusade for Christ through their Executive Ministries program.

After Art died suddenly of a heart attack in 1979, at the age of fifty-three, Nancy continued on with the work. She expanded it far beyond what she and Art had ever imagined when they hosted their first evangelistic dinner party years earlier.

"Probably the most rewarding part of this ministry for Nancy is seeing those who become Christians also grow and become disciples who reach out in the same way to others," one author writes. There is truly a mission field among the wealthy. "These people know little or nothing about the Lord," Nancy writes, "and they are so hungry for Him."[28]

Jesus entered Jericho and was passing through. A man was there by the name of Zacchaeus; he was a chief tax collector and was wealthy. He wanted to see who Jesus was, but being a short man he could not, because of the crowd. So he ran ahead and climbed a sycamore-fig tree to see him, since Jesus was coming that way.

When Jesus reached the spot, he looked up and said to him, "Zacchaeus, come down immediately. I must stay at your house today." So he came down at once and welcomed him gladly.

All the people saw this and began to mutter, "He has gone to be the guest of a 'sinner.'"

*Luke 19:1–7.*

# "I WILL HELP YOU SPEAK AND TEACH YOU WHAT TO SAY"

At the age of forty Moses fled to the "far side of the desert" after killing an Egyptian, and then after another forty years God spoke to him through the flames of a burning bush. God called him to deliver his people from bondage in Egypt (Acts 7:23–34).

For most people, God's timing does not allow for forty years on the "far side of the desert." But it was true for Carl F. H. Henry. As a forty-year-old Fuller Seminary professor, he was visiting London in the summer of 1953 when he came upon a father/son team of street preachers. Perhaps with a tinge of guilt for his own reluctance to so brazenly preach the gospel, he commended their boldness. Their immediate response was to invite him to step up on the soapbox. "I somewhat reluctantly mounted the ladder to give my testimony about God's forgiving my sins and saving me," he writes. His message was timid and brief: "Right now, if you will repent and receive Christ as Savior, God will forgive your sins, too, and give you new life."

The response was not surprising but nonetheless unnerving: "At that a chorus of contraries erupted. 'What God?' 'What sins?' 'What Christ?' 'What life?' In mockery one man threw himself on the ground at the base of the ladder and mimicked, 'God be merciful to me, a sinner.'"

Henry was humiliated. "I disengaged myself from my lofty perch as discreetly as possible and listened to the father and son a bit longer until I could saunter away unobserved. I paid no attention to two men walking nearby until I overheard one of them remark, 'That blooming American didn't have very much to say, did he?'"

That experience made a deep impression on Henry, and he went on to become America's leading evangelical thinker and theologian. As the founding editor of *Christianity Today* and the author of more than thirty books, he has challenged Christians to make their presence known in the world. Their place is not on the "far side of the desert" but rather in the public forum, leading a nation out of bondage.

In his book *The Uneasy Conscience of Modern Fundamentalism*, Henry criticizes the fundamentalist mentality. "Whereas once the redemptive gospel was a world-changing message, now it was narrowed to a world-resisting message." This message ought rather to be a biblically-based "world-life view."[29]

---

Moses said to the Lord, "O Lord, I have never been eloquent, neither in the past nor since you have spoken to your servant. I am slow of speech and tongue."

The Lord said to him, "Who gave man his mouth? Who makes him deaf or mute? Who gives him sight or makes him blind? Is it not I, the Lord? Now go; I will help you speak and will teach you what to say."

But Moses said, "O Lord, please send someone else to do it."

*Exodus 4:10–13.*

# "A SERVANT GIRL BRINGS GOD'S MESSAGE"

Some mission strategists would argue that the best way to reach lower levels of any population is to reach the higher levels first so that they can then reach the poorer elements of society. But that is not necessarily God's strategy of evangelism.

Sandra Contreras found this to be true as she was growing up in a large city in a middle-class home in Honduras. Her father employed a maid—a Honduran Indian named Argentina from the Mosquito tribe of the remote northern tropical coastal region of Honduras. He knew she would be a good worker in the home and be a tremendous help to his wife in the care of their children. What he did not know was that she would be a Christian witness who felt compelled by God to share her faith.

Except for her deep faith in Christ and her insights on spiritual values, Argentina did not have any credentials to be an evangelist. Yet, she made a powerful impact on this family and especially on Sandra. "She did not have a college degree; she never even went to high school or elementary school; in fact she could hardly read and write, but yet, she seemed to have just the right answer for everything and anything. Sometimes I noticed that even my mother was somehow struck by this woman. My little brothers loved her, too."

It was Argentina's quiet testimony and patience that caused Sandra to begin to question her own faith. She had grown up in a religious home and in a church environment, but God was remote: "He loved the good people and punished the bad ones." A deep personal faith and regular Bible reading was not expected—or even desired—of the ordinary lay Christian. But now she discovered a different kind of religion. "Argentina's life witnessed to me that Jesus was real today. It also showed me the need I had for Jesus. I knew Argentina prayed for me a lot but I was somehow struggling within myself."

Finally, after four years, Sandra committed her life to Christ. It was not an easy decision. Family and friends rejected her, but Sandra could say confidently, "I knew that no matter how high the price I had to pay would be, Jesus was worth it." Since Sandra has committed her life to Christ, her three brothers have also professed their faith in him and her parents are no longer hostile and, indeed, are more open to the gospel.[30]

Now bands from Aram had gone out and had taken captive a young girl from Israel, and she served Naaman's wife. She said to her mistress, "If only my master would see the prophet who is in Samaria! He would cure him of his leprosy."

Naaman went to his master and told him what the girl from Israel had said. "By all means, go," the king of Aram replied. "I will send a letter to the king of Israel." So Naaman left, taking with him ten talents of silver, six thousand shekels of gold and ten sets of clothing. The letter that he took to the king of Israel read: "With this letter I am sending my servant Naaman to you so that you may cure him of his leprosy."

*2 Kings 5:2–6.*

# "HAVE PITY ON US"

Father Damien was distressed when he heard of the wretched condition of the people on the island of Molokai, a tiny island in the Hawaiian Island chain. He was a priest from Belgium, who could have had a pleasant life ministering with his fellow priests among the carefree Hawaiian islanders. But his heart went out to Molokai, and in 1873 he began to live on that desolate, rocky, barren island, inhabited by the lepers who were banished from the other islands.

He knew that the moment he set foot on land he would never be allowed to leave the island again. The residents were dumbfounded by his sacrifice, and he was shocked by the deplorable conditions in which they were living. He immediately challenged those who had given up hope to help him rebuild the old hospital and to reach out and minister to those who were worse off than they were.

Before Father Damien had arrived on the island, the atmosphere was hostile. No one cared for the lepers, so why should they care for each other? When residents were gravely ill they were ignored, and when the person died, the body was thrown on the rubbish heap. And sometimes the two procedures were mixed up. One day when he was passing the dump, Father Damien saw some movement in a pile of rags, and then he heard a cry, a cry not unlike the lepers who called to Jesus, "Have pity on us." There in the rubbish was a man sent to his grave while he was yet alive.

With Father Damien's compassionate leadership, the residents developed medical programs, agricultural ventures, a sanitation policy, and set aside land for a burial ground. But as benevolent as it was, the ministry was not without controversy. When the Protestant leaders learned of what was happening—of the many converts and of church services being conducted—many of them were upset. They sought to deport Father Damien, but he refused to leave. He vowed he would stay with his people the rest of his life, although he did not realize, at the time that he was becoming one of them.

One day in 1884, after a long, arduous horseback ride, he asked that water be heated so that he could soak his feet. He tested the water and put his feet in, only to be told it was boiling hot. He had not felt it, for his nerve endings were dead. He too was a leper. For the next four years he wasted away like those around him. He lived to the very end with a heart of compassion for those like himself who were considered the refuse of the world.[31]

Now on his way to Jerusalem, Jesus traveled along the border between Samaria and Galilee. As he was going into a village, ten men who had leprosy met him. They stood at a distance and called out in a loud voice, "Jesus, Master, have pity on us."

When he saw them, he said, "Go show yourselves to the priests." And as they went, they were cleansed.

*Luke: 17:11–14.*

## "HOW GREAT THOU ART"

"How Great Thou Art," one of the best loved hymns in America—and perhaps the world—found its way into the hearts of Christians in a very roundabout way. Written in the 1880s in Sweden by a well-known minister, Carl Boberg, it was translated into German in 1907, and from German into Russian in 1912. Finally it was translated into English by a British missionary, Stuart K. Hine, who distributed it in leaflet form in the 1950s. Although it had touched hearts all along the way, it remained relatively obscure until one of the leaflets fell into the hands of George Beverly Shea, whose voice was known by millions who listened to Billy Graham's radio broadcasts and attended his crusades.

During the great Madison Square Garden crusade of 1957, Shea and the choir sang that song a total of ninety-nine times—sealing its destiny in Christian hymnology. Shea played a crucial role in the longevity of that hymn. He was a man uniquely qualified in a spiritual sense to offer such a tribute to God; from personal experience he knew that praise must go to God alone.

Born the son of a Wesleyan minister on February 1, 1909, Shea was give opportunities to perform musically as he was growing up, but was self-conscious and plagued by feelings of insecurity—these feelings were only magnified at age seventeen when he sang a solo at a tent meeting.

"Before going to the platform to sing, I stood outside the tent doing a last-minute repair job on my hair. Naturally, I had no idea the entire congregation was watching a silhouette struggling with his stubborn cowlick. As I combed and recombed, the smiles of the audience turned into a chorus of giggles. When I finally got my locks in place, I parted the flap and paraded into the tent—into a crescendo of laughter."

Later the same evening, his voice cracked on a high note, and he vowed that night would mark not only the beginning but the end of his singing career. The experience was appropriate for one who went on to become an internationally acclaimed musician whose baritone voice was recognized by millions. In a profession that can so easily foster false pride and egotism, he was able to turn the attention away from himself and to focus on God. This ability was nowhere more evident than in his rendition of "How Great Thou Art."[1]

I will exalt you, my God the King, I will praise your name for ever and ever. Every day I will praise you and extol your name for ever and ever. Great is the Lord and most worthy of praise, his greatness no one can fathom. One generation will commend your works to another, they will tell of your mighty acts. They will speak of the glorious splendor of your majesty, and I will meditate on your wonderful works. They will tell of the power of your awesome works, and I will proclaim your great deeds.

*Psalm 145:1–6.*

# "GOD IS NOT A GOD OF DISORDER BUT OF PEACE"

The apostle Paul's concern about disorder in the church has been perplexing to many Christians. Women are admonished not to ask questions in church, but in most churches men do not ask questions either. In Sunday school they do, but rarely is this verse applied to Sunday school. How then should it be applied?

Interestingly, there is much insight to be gained through an understanding of Middle Eastern and Eastern culture, and missionaries have been able to make significant contributions to the understanding of this passage through their observations of religious customs.

Olive Rogers observed women during her years in India, and she relates that there are many similarities between these Indian women today and Palestinian women of the first century. She tells of her visit to the golden temple of the Sikhs in Old Delhi. "Suddenly, as so often happens in the East, the Scriptures became alive," she writes. "We were high above the main body of the temple. The worship—intoning of the Sacred Book, and instructions for salvation—being carried on down below was pertinent only to the men, for they alone have souls to save. I tried in vain to hear what was going on, but the women were sitting around in groups gossiping, amused at the play of their children, careless of the fact that they were in a place of worship."

That the Sikh women would behave in this manner was not surprising to Olive. The Sikh religion had so little to offer women. But Christianity was different— or so she thought.

"Not many months later I attended one of the Christian conventions held annually in South India. Day after day thousands of men and women sat under the large leaf shelter. The men's section of the 'pandal' was quiet and orderly as they listened to the Word, taking notes with assiduous care. The women's half was another matter. All the children were there, restless, demanding and noisy, and many of the women were sitting in groups chattering."

Indeed, it was in this setting that the Bible became utterly relevant and Paul's admonitions applied very literally. The women needed to be admonished to be quiet. But simply quieting them was not enough. They needed to realize that they were precious in the eyes of God, and that his message applied to them as much as it did to the men.[2]

For God is not a God of disorder but of peace.

As in all the congregations of the saints, women should remain silent in the churches. They are not allowed to speak, but must be in submission, as the Law says. If they want to inquire about something, they should ask their own husbands at home; for it is disgraceful for a woman to speak in the church.

*1 Corinthians 14:33– 35.*

## "WHEN YOUR WORDS CAME, I ATE THEM"

This passage portrays Jeremiah as a man suffering persecution and yet finding joy and delight in "eating" the words of the Lord. These words express the sentiment of another saint of God who lived many centuries later, the great sixteenth-century reformer and Bible translator William Tyndale.

William Tyndale, himself a highly educated man, was deeply concerned that his fellow Englishmen were ignorant of the Bible. He loved the Scriptures and deplored the fact that the parish priests were not preaching the Word, and that lay people had no access to the Bible in their own language. To one of these clerics he said, "If God spare my life, ere many years pass, I will cause a boy that driveth the plough shall know more of the Scriptures than thou dost."

Tyndale finished translating the New Testament into English in 1525, but was forced to leave England because of political pressure and threats on his life. While living in Brussels, and prior to completing the Old Testament translation, he was arrested and imprisoned. While in prison, he wrote the following letter to the prison governor:

"I believe, right worshipful, that you are not unaware of what may have been determined concerning me. Wherefore I beg your lordship, and that by the Lord Jesus, that if I am to remain here through the winter, you will request the commissary to have the kindness to send me, from the goods of mine which he has, a warmer cap; for I suffer greatly from cold in the head, and am afflicted by a perpetual catarrh [runny nose], which is much increased in this cell; a warmer coat also, for this which I have is very thin; a piece of cloth too to patch my leggings. My overcoat is worn out; my shirts are also worn out. He has a woolen shirt, if he will be good enough to send it. I have also with him leggings of thicker cloth to put on above; he has also warmer night caps. And I ask to be allowed to have a lamp in the evening; it is indeed wearisome sitting alone in the dark. But most of all I beg and beseech your clemency to be urgent with the commissary, that he will kindly permit me to have the Hebrew Bible, Hebrew grammar, and Hebrew dictionary, that I may pass the time in that study."

Tyndale loved the words of the Lord. More than anything else, he desired to finish the translation of the book he loved. That wish did not come true. He was burned at the stake the following year. Reportedly, his last words were: "Lord, open the king of England's eyes."[3]

You understand, O Lord; remember me and care for me. Avenge me on my persecutors. You are long-suffering—do not take me away; think of how I suffer reproach for your sake. When your words came, I ate them; they were my joy and my heart's delight, for I bear your name, O Lord God Almighty.

*Jeremiah 15:15–16.*

# "BEATING SWORDS INTO PLOWSHARES"

The Lord's promise that in "the last days" there will be peace symbolized by turning weapons into productive tools has been a hope of many Christians through the centuries including Toyohiko Kagawa, who was born in Japan in 1888.

At the age of fourteen, he enrolled in an English class taught by a Presbyterian missionary. Although he had been warned by relatives not to be influenced by Christianity, he could not resist. One year later he confessed his faith in Christ and was baptized. The first real test of his faith came when Japan declared war on Russia. He was conscripted into the military along with other students, but his conscience would not permit him to train with a rifle. "All he could hear in his mind were the words of Jesus, 'Love your enemies,' and all he could see was Christ dying without resistance on the cross." His stand created an uproar. His instructor physically assaulted him, and he was attacked by fellow students.

Following his college years, Kagawa took seminary training. But he soon left his studies in order to reach out with the gospel to the impoverished and destitute slums in the city of Kobe. He lived with the people in a tiny hut with a dirt floor and bamboo walls, and quickly became known among the people as "the Christian." But despite all his sacrifice, Kagawa realized that what the impoverished people in the inner-city needed most was not hand-outs but organizational strength. After studying for a time in America, he returned to Japan and organized labor unions and relief programs. Then "in 1928 he initiated the 'Kingdom of God Movement,' a daring, nationwide evangelistic campaign to win a million Japanese to Christ."

Once again, however, Kagawa's faith was tested by nationalism and militarism. When Japan attacked Manchuria in 1931, he made a public apology: "To my brethren in China, Forgive the sin of Japan. Though Japanese Christians have not the power to oppose military force, some of them regret the sin of Japan. I wish the day of reconciliation may soon come." He was even more distressed by the bombing of Pearl Harbor in 1941 and the U.S. retaliation—a retaliation that seemed incomprehensible to him because it was coming from a "Christian" nation.

Kagawa lived out his life seeking to beat swords into plowshares. He wanted to stop the senseless killing and to raise the standard of living of the poor. He seemed to meet with little success in light of the military build-up in both the East and the West. At times he seemed to be one lone Christian against the rest of the world—a man whose motto was the hymn, "Jesus Keep Me Near the Cross."[4]

He will judge between many peoples and will settle disputes for strong nations far and wide. They will beat their swords into plowshares and their spears into pruning hooks. Nation will not take up sword against nation, nor will they train for war anymore.

Every man will sit under his own vine and under his own fig tree, and no one will make them afraid, for the Lord Almighty has spoken.

*Micah 4:3-4.*

# "THE JUG OF OIL WILL NOT RUN DRY"

During their agonizing imprisonment at the Nazi death camp of Ravensbruck, Corrie ten Boom and her sister Betsie suffered from the ill-treatment and lack of medical care. They were treated worse than common criminals, though their only "crime" had been sheltering Jews who were seeking to escape the murderous tyranny of Nazism.

The prison they were confined in was overcrowded, and the living conditions in the barracks were atrocious. Disease and malnutrition were rampant, and they feared that they, like so many of the prisoners around them, would soon be languishing in death. In their misery, they often were forced to depend wholly on God. And God heard and answered their prayers, sometimes demonstrating his miraculous protection in the times of their deepest need.

When Betsie was desperately ill on one occasion, Corrie realized that the tiny bottle of Davitamon was down to the very last drops. "My instinct," she wrote, "was always to hoard—Betsie was growing so very weak! But others were ill as well. It was hard to say no to eyes that burned with fever, hands that shook with chill. I tried to save it for the very weakest—but even these soon numbered fifteen, twenty, twenty-five. . . ." Corrie's heart went out to them, but she desperately feared that sharing those precious drops with all the others would rob Betsie of the only chance she had for survival.

Betsie recognized her need for the medication, but she reminded Corrie of the account of the widow of Zarephath who shared with Elijah and whose handful of meal and small amount of oil lasted as long as there was a need. Betsie was convinced that God could perform a similar miracle for them. Corrie initially belittled the idea of such a miracle in modern times, but she soon was a believer: "Every time I tilted the little bottle, a drop appeared at the top of the glass stopper. It just couldn't be! I held it up to the light, trying to see how much was left, but the dark brown glass was too thick to see through."

Each day she continued to dispense what she thought was the very last drop, until one day when a female guard who had shown kindness to the prisoners before, smuggled a small quantity of vitamins into the barracks for the prisoners. Corrie was thrilled, but she determined to first finish the drops in the bottle. "But that night, no matter how long I held it upside down, or how hard I shook it, not another drop appeared."

God had proven himself to her no less than he had thousands of years before to the widow of Zarephath.[5]

Sometime later the brook dried up because there had been no rain in the land. . . . So he [Elijah] went to Zarephath. When he came to the town gate, a widow was there gathering sticks. He called to her and asked, "Would you bring me a little water in a jar so I may have a drink? . . . And bring me, please, a piece of bread."

"As surely as the Lord your God lives," she replied, "I don't have any bread—only a handful of flour in a jar and a little oil in a jug. I am gathering a few sticks to take home and make a meal for myself and my son, that we may eat it—and die."

Elijah said to her, "Don't be afraid. Go home and do as you have said. But first make a small cake of bread for me from what you have and bring it to me, and then make something for yourself and your son. For this is what the Lord, the God of Israel, says: 'The jar of flour will not be used up and the jug of oil will not run dry until the day the Lord gives rain on the land.' "

*1 Kings 17:7, 10–14.*

# "TEACHER, TEACH THYSELF"

God does teach through his creation as this passage in Job confirms, and sometimes the animals can teach us more than our human teachers can. Teaching is a gift, as the apostle Paul emphasizes in his epistles. It is a gift that requires understanding of those being taught, and sometimes the teacher's seemingly best efforts come to nought because the teacher's method has relied on human wisdom rather than the wisdom and power that belongs to God.

Thomas Hale, a missionary medical doctor to Nepal, tells the story of a community health nurse who sought to educate the local villagers on the subject of communicable diseases. "Western professionals have implicit faith in the triumph of knowledge over ignorance," he writes. "All we have to do, we suppose, is *teach* the people, and the scales will fall from their eyes." But experience confirms that is not true. Speaking of this nurse, he continues:

"Employing the finest product of our Western educational system—the visual aid—she presented her eager learners a large poster showing a hugely magnified common fly, its great bulbous eyes and long hairy legs graphically displayed in lifelike detail. Wide-eyed with amazement, her listeners gathered around in awed silence as she described the evils of this monstrous insect. She explained how these flies picked up harmful germs and deposited them on food, on plants and glasses, and on sores and cuts. Encouraged by their attentiveness, she described the diseases flies carry, how quickly they reproduce, and how they lay eggs.

"When she finished, an animated discussion began among her listeners. It seemed they had been truly impressed by her account of these gigantic British flies (she was from Britain) and they were greatly relieved that such creatures were not to be found in Nepal. Did they entertain the notion, too, that she had perhaps come to their country to escape those dreadful flies? Ah teacher, teach thyself."[6]

But ask the animals, and they will teach you, or the birds of the air, and they will tell you; or speak to the earth, and it will teach you, or let the fish of the sea inform you.

Which of all these does not know that the hand of the Lord has done this?

In his hand is the life of every creature and the breath of all mankind. Does not the ear test words as the tongue tastes food? Is not wisdom found among the aged? Does not long life bring understanding?

To God belong wisdom and power; counsel and understanding are his.

*Job 12:7–13.*

## "THE GIFT OF SINGLENESS"

Singleness is often associated with loneliness, and perhaps in some instances with good reason. But singleness can be a tremendous advantage to an individual, especially someone who is involved in an all-encompassing Christian ministry. Single missionaries have found this to be true, and sometimes they have been almost the envy of their married counterparts.

J. Herbert Kane testifies to this in reflecting on his years in China as a missionary. "During the Sino-Japanese War and later during the civil war between the Nationalists and Communists," he writes, "I was separated from my wife and two boys on three occasions for a total of twenty-seven months. On each occasion they were on one side of the battle line and I on the other."

This was a very trying time for him and his family. "During two of those separations letters did not get through for three months. My last thought at night and my first thought in the morning were 'I wonder how Winnie and the boys are.' When our city at Fowyang was surrounded, first by the Japanese and later by the Communist armies, and everything on wheels had been commandeered by the military, evacuation with a wife and family was a nightmare."

For both Herb and Winnie, life would have been less complicated, as the apostle Paul warned, without marriage and family. "I couldn't help but think enviously," writes Herb, "of the Roman Catholic missionaries in the Jesuit mission in the same city. When the enemy was banging on the north gate of the city they could hop on their bicycles and escape through the south gate. Things weren't that simple for us.

"The single missionaries have only their own safety to consider and half the time they don't bother about that. The older ones especially insist on remaining at their posts regardless of the danger. . . . If worse comes to worst and they get caught in the crossfire of the contending forces, or they are killed by an exploding bomb, or shot, accidentally or otherwise, by a drunken soldier, so what? They go home to heaven in a blaze of glory!"[7]

Now for the matters you wrote about: It is good for a man not to marry. But since there is so much immorality, each man should have his own wife, and each woman her own husband. . . . I wish that all men were as I am. But each man has his own gift from God; one has this gift, another has that. . . . But those who marry will face many troubles in this life, and I want to spare you this. . . .

I would like you to be free from concern. An unmarried man is concerned about the Lord's affairs—how he can please the Lord. But a married man is concerned about the affairs of this world—how he can please his wife—and his interests are divided.

*1 Corinthians 7:1–2, 7, 28b, 32–34a.*

# "GOD'S COMFORT IN TIME OF NEED"

This passage in Isaiah depicts Jerusalem in her millennial glory, symbolized as a nursing mother and climaxed with the portrayal of God as a comforting mother. It is a passage that has brought comfort to many people over the centuries, not the least of whom was Evelyn Brand, a missionary to India. In 1923, after she and her husband Jesse had worked tirelessly among the remote hill people, they returned with their two children to the United States for their first furlough.

Evelyn had dreaded the furlough because it meant leaving her children behind for their education when she and Jesse returned to India. "The year was blessing . . . and it was torture. Everywhere the message was well received. . . . But as the sands of the year ran low the constant dread of parting turned into agony," one author writes to her biographer. "To leave her children, even in capable and loving hands, for five or six whole years! Why, Paul would be almost a man, and Connie, her precious golden-haired treasure, now scarcely out of babyhood. . . ."

Finally Evie succumbed. "I can't do it," she tearfully pleaded with her husband. "Paul, yes, he's old enough to stand the separation, and he must have his school now. But Connie, my little darling . . . Jess, I must take her." Jesse was sympathetic and finally agreed that if Connie wanted to return with them to India, he would consent to separate the two children. But when Evie asked Connie, she reluctantly declined. She could not bear to leave her brother behind by himself.

The rapidly-approaching farewell was agonizing for Evie, but she relieved her pain by painting plaques with Bible verses that she hung over her children's beds. One read "I will be a father unto you" and the other in similar fashion expressed the promise of God that she would be clinging to in the years ahead: "As one whom a mother comforteth, so will I comfort you."

When the dreaded day arrived, "Paul and Connie hugged their parents tightly, seized their school satchels, and ran down the steps. Evie stood by the gate looking after them, eyes so blurred with tears she could scarcely see the waving of their hands before they ran around the corner." She was clinging to God's promise, but the pain was no less real. "As I stood watching them," she later related, "something just died in me."[8]

"Rejoice with Jerusalem and be glad for her, all you who love her; rejoice greatly with her, all you who mourn over her. For you will nurse and be satisfied at her comforting breasts; you will drink deeply and delight in her overflowing abundance."

For this is what the Lord says: "I will extend peace to her like a river, and the wealth of nations like a flooding stream; you will nurse and be carried on her arm and dandled on her knees. As a mother comforts her child, so will I comfort you; and you will be comforted over Jerusalem."

*Isaiah 66:10–13.*

# "HAND THIS MAN OVER TO SATAN"

Expelling a member from a church fellowship and turning that person "over to Satan" is by any standard a drastic procedure, but it is necessary at times in order to maintain the purity of the church. Temple Gairdner, a missionary to the Muslims in Egypt in the early twentieth century, found it necessary to take such action in his tiny Christian assembly in Cairo.

Gairdner was known for his unwavering love for the Muslims—Muslims whose hostility toward him was not disguised. But the love and tenderness that he expressed toward unconverted Muslims was only exceeded by the even deeper devotion he had for his converts—courageous followers of Christ who had sacrificed so much to take their stand.

This passion for his followers was demonstrated during a time of persecution when a convert fell away and was seeking to influence the others. Gairdner poured out his grief in a letter to his wife: "I believe I would have felt it less even if one of our own little ones had been taken." His reaction to the betrayal of faith, however, was swift and severe. He met with the small band of Christians in a desert cave, where he implored the name of Christ "to deliver such a one unto Satan for the destruction of the flesh, that the spirit may be saved in the day of Jesus Christ."

He reported that the faithful Christians "agreed with trembling," and he later described the meeting: "We invoked divine power. There was a rallying, and only one or two fell away." It was a painful time for Gairdner, and he later referred to the ordeal as "Black Holy Week." Yet he was philosophical as he reflected on the situation: "We're not the first to cope with this. The men who *really* had a hard time were the people in the first centuries when there was no Church history. We have only to look up the Early Fathers to see that our troubles have been survived before. Blessed be God for History!"[9]

It is actually reported that there is sexual immorality among you, and of a kind that does not occur even among pagans: A man has his father's wife. And you are proud! Shouldn't you rather have been filled with grief and have put out of your fellowship the man who did this? Even though I am not physically present, I am with you in spirit. And I have already passed judgment on the one who did this, just as if I were present. When you are assembled in the name of our Lord Jesus and I am with you in spirit, and the power of our Lord Jesus is present, hand this man over to Satan, so that the sinful nature may be destroyed and his spirit saved on the day of the Lord.

*1 Corinthians 5:1–5.*

## "MY GUILT HAS OVERWHELMED ME"

"One tiny nut left unturned." A mistake that any aviation mechanic could potentially make, especially if his attention were momentarily distracted by what seemed to be a more pressing concern. Yet, that "little" mistake resulted in a crash of a twin engine Piper Aztec in New Guinea in 1972. Seven people were killed in that fiery crash, including Doug Hunt, the chief pilot for JAARS (Jungle Aviation and Radio Service, an arm of Wycliffe Bible Translators) and Darlene Bee, a brilliant linguist and Bible translator who had earned her Ph.D. at Indiana University.

An inspection of the wreckage at the crash site indicated that the mid-air explosion had resulted from a fine spray of gasoline escaping where a nut had not been properly tightened. The individual responsible for tightening that B-nut on the fuel-line was a mechanic who was reaching remote villagers with the gospel of Christ. Indeed, he had made great sacrifices to serve in the disease-infested jungle of New Guinea.

For him—this guilt-ridden JAARS mechanic—the pain was almost unbearable. "The funeral was a ghastly ordeal," he later confessed. "The sight of those caskets lined up in the little opensided tropical church hit me like a blow to the stomach. I wanted nothing but to get out of there. . . . How could I face my friends? How could I face myself? I was over-whelmed with guilt. I was a failure."

It took time before this mechanic could accept himself and the love that was bestowed upon him by surviving family members and co-workers. "I felt forgiveness from everyone around me—my co-workers, and most importantly, the pilots who contin-ued to entrust themselves to my skill and workman-ship. I knew their total, loving acceptance. Praise God, the body of Christ was showing love and forgiveness to a member who was hurting."

It also took time for him to realize that God, too, loves, forgives, and accepts us when we make mis-takes. "Except for God's Grace," he later wrote, "I'd be somewhere cowering in a corner in guilt-ridden despair—the eighth fatality of that Aztec crash. That would really be failure. . . . Praise God, it isn't so!"

This mechanic, however, realized that he could not simply depend on God and others to deal with his guilt and bring something good out of a terrible tragedy. "I knew then I should share my experience of God's comfort and support to help others and to glorify the Lord Jesus Christ. That's why I write this." Perhaps by sharing his guilt openly, even as the psalmist did, he prevented others from making the same tragic mistake he did.[10]

My guilt has overwhelmed me like a burden too heavy to bear. My wounds fester and are loathsome because of my sinful folly. I am bowed down and brought very low; all day long I go about mourning. My back is filled with searing pain; there is no health in my body. I am feeble and utterly crushed; I groan in anguish of heart. All my longings lie open before you, O Lord; my sighing is not hidden from you.

*Psalm 38:4–9.*

## "ENDURING FALSE ACCUSATIONS"

The gospel of Matthew offers perspective on persecution that points to the past—"in the same way they persecuted the prophets"—and to the future—"great is your reward in heaven." As difficult as persecution is to endure, this perspective can be of great consolation in the midst of persecution and false accusations. This passage was no doubt a comfort to Jennie Adams in 1983, when her accusers charged her with the most modern of crimes—drug-running.

Miss Adams had served in Peru as a missionary with Baptist Mid-Missions for thirty-four years. She had ministered faithfully as a teacher at the mission's Bible school in Trujillo and in remote villages. She drove her own van, and often picked up passengers who needed rides into town or back to their homes in the villages. Her willingness to give a young woman a ride one day was routine. The young woman had previously attended a mission school and her father was a village pastor, and she frequently asked for rides. Little did Miss Adams know that the young woman's brother processed cocaine, and used his sister to transport the drug.

Peruvian law views a person guilty until proven innocent. In Jennie's case the newspapers were quick to exploit the story in an obvious attempt to discredit foreign missionary endeavors. "A North American Protestant woman pastor has discovered without any doubt," one reported, "that there is not a better or more rapid way 'to get to heaven' than with cocaine, a drug which is able to trigger a 'divine high.' Jennie Adams was captured by the National Guard with three kilos and 900 grams of cocaine."

The reporter went on to say that "no one suspected what her true activities were as a drug trafficker" and that "the 'pastor of souls' could not give any coherent explanation." She was gleefully dubbed "the cocaine missionary," and authorities arrested her with no consideration of her long years of service as a missionary.

After twenty days of imprisonment, Miss Adams was released, but not until after she and the work of the mission had suffered humiliation at the hands of false witnesses. While other people ridiculed her, she could be comforted by the Scripture, "Great is your reward in heaven."[11]

Blessed are those who are persecuted because of righteousness, for theirs is the kingdom of heaven.

Blessed are you when people insult you and persecute you and falsely say all kinds of evil against you because of me. Rejoice and be glad, because great is your reward in heaven, for in the same way they persecuted the prophets who were before you.

*Matthew 5:10–12.*

## "IN THE BEGINNING GOD CREATED"

Shimeta Neesima was born into a Shinto family in Japan on February 12, 1843. He went often to the temple—offering sacrifices to the god who would be his lifelong guardian.

When Neesima was in his teens, he was chosen by a prince to attend a military school, where he had the opportunity to study and later teach Chinese. While there he came upon a copy of the Chinese Bible. He opened it and began reading the most remarkable message he had ever heard: "In the beginning God created the heavens and the earth."

Later he reflected on the experience: "I put down the book and looked around me saying . . . Who made me, my parents? No, my God. God made my parents and let them make me. Who made my table? A carpenter? No, my God. God let trees grow upon the earth, although a carpenter made up this table, it indeed came from trees, then I must be thankful to God, I must believe Him, and I must be upright against Him." Shimeta then prayed a simple prayer: "Oh! if you have eyes, look upon me, if you have ears, listen for me."

So compelling was this book that told of the Creator God that Neesima vowed he would search until he was satisfied that he understood the full meaning of the message. At the age of twenty-one, he took temporary leave from the military school, and under cover of night he took refuge in an American ship, where he found his way to Shanghai. Here he obtained passage to Boston on a ship owned by a Christian businessman, who offered to help him obtain a Christian education—first at Phillips Academy and then Amhurst College and Andover Theological Seminary, where he graduated in 1874.

The following year, Joseph Hardy Neesima (having taken the names of his benefactors) returned to Japan where he founded the Dashia Christian College in Kyoto. In the quarter-century that followed, some one hundred of the graduates became ministers of the gospel—despite heavy opposition from the Japanese authorities.

Neesima's health failed and he had to turn the leadership of the school over to others, but he continued to be a mighty source of inspiration until his death with his motto: "Let us advance on our knees."[12]

In the beginning God created the heavens and the earth. Now the earth was formless and empty, darkness was over the surface of the deep, and the Spirit of God was hovering over the waters. . . . So God created man in his own image, in the image of God he created him, male and female he created them.

*Genesis 1:1–2, 27.*

## "BY PERSEVERING PRODUCE A CROP"

Eusebius, the prolific church historian of the early centuries, records many accounts of persecution and martyrdom. In one account he tells of the horrors that befell Christians in the North African city of Alexandria, a one-time stronghold of the faith, when the Emperor decreed that everyone must worship at pagan altars. It was a decree that separated the nominal Christians from those who retained the gospel and persevered.

When the officials began to interrogate people, "many of the more eminent immediately gave way to them . . . and when called by name, they approached the impure and unholy sacrifices . . . pale and trembling. . . . But some advanced with greater readiness to the altars, and boldly asserted that they had never before been Christians."

Eusebius emphasizes what a trying time this was for those who wanted to follow Christ, but whose faith was too weak: "some fled, others were taken, and of these some held out as far as the prison and bonds, and some after a few days imprisonment abjured [Christianity] before they entered the tribunal. But some, also, after enduring the torture for a time, at last renounced."

But the story does not end with those who faltered. Among those who stood firm for their faith were two women: Quinta and Apollonia. Officials tried to force Quinta to worship an idol, "but when she turned away in disgust, they tied her by the feet, and dragged her through the whole city, over the rough stones of the paved streets, dashing her against the millstones, and scourging her at the same time, until they brought her to the same place, where they stoned her. . . . But they also seized that admirable virgin, Apollonia, then in advanced age, and beating her jaws, they broke out all her teeth, and kindling a fire before the city, threatened to burn her alive, unless she would repeat their impious expressions. She appeared at first to shrink a little, but when suffered to go, she suddenly sprang into the fire and was consumed."

The seed had fallen on good soil and these women with a "good and noble heart" witness to us, of their faith through the ages.[13]

"This is the meaning of the parable: The seed is the word of God. Those along the path are the ones who hear, and then the devil comes and takes away the word from their hearts, so that they may not believe and be saved. Those on the rock are the ones who receive the word with joy when they hear it, but they have no root. They believe for a while, but in the time of testing they fall away. The seed that fell among thorns stands for those who hear, but as they go on their way they are choked by life's worries, riches and pleasures, and they do not mature. But the seed on good soil stands for those with a noble and good heart, who hear the word, retain it, and by persevering produce a crop."

*Luke 8:11–15.*

## "I WILL POUR OUT MY SPIRIT"

Revival—the pouring out of God's Spirit—often comes through the ministry of those who would be considered the least likely candidates for greatness. It is then that the power of God can be separated from the power of a charismatic personality. God was able to use one of these "least likely candidates" in 1927, as the prelude to a great revival that swept the churches deep inside China.

A well-known Chinese evangelist was scheduled to be the featured speaker at a major regional conference. The day before the meetings began, however, word came that he was unable to attend. Emil Jensen, the senior missionary, was devastated. He had been praying fervently for the meetings, convinced that God would bring a mighty revival. He was the logical replacement as a speaker, but he declined. Instead he asked Marie Monsen, a single missionary who had served faithfully in China for many years, but was not known as a revival speaker.

Miss Monsen was stunned by the request, but after spending the night in prayer, she reluctantly agreed. She knew that she, in herself, had nothing to offer the large number of people who had congregated. Revival, she was convinced, depended entirely on the Spirit of God moving in their midst. In the days that followed, as the meetings continued, the Spirit moved mightily in the conference, and beyond—out into cities and villages.

Referring to this revival, Leslie Lyall of the China Inland Mission wrote: "the pioneer of the spiritual 'new life movement,' the handmaiden upon whom the Spirit was first poured, was Marie Monsen of Norway. Her surgical skill in exposing the sins hidden within the church, and lurking behind the smiling exterior of many a trusted Christian—even many a trusted Christian leader—set the pattern for others to follow."

Indeed, Miss Monsen "began a movement which swept through the churches of China like a cleansing gale of wind. This continued through the 1930s and 'gave an impetus to the transference of full authority from the missionaries to the churches.' That God was behind this strategic and timely move was soon to become evident when the Japanese invasion occurred shortly thereafter, to be followed later by the communist takeover."[14]

And afterward, I will pour out my Spirit on all people. Your sons and daughters will prophesy, your old men will dream dreams, your young men will see visions.

Even on my servants, both men and women, I will pour out my Spirit in those days.

*Joel 2:28–29.*

## "ONCE DARKNESS, BUT NOW YOU ARE LIGHT"

As a young Navaho Indian growing up in Arizona, John Peshlakai "worshiped many sacred gods." They were all around him. Indeed, the belief in spirits was an all-pervasive aspect of his life. Both of his grandfathers were medicine men and one of his grandmothers was a medicine woman, and John followed in their footsteps. "I was involved in many cleansing and purification rituals," he recalls. "I carried many sacred medicine tools for protection and learned sacred songs to keep evil spirits away."

As a young adult, John delved deeper into spiritism and was trained to communicate with spirits through a crystal stone, and he became even more involved in the native American church known as Peyotism, which uses a cactus plant for its various rituals. In this environment, he contacted spirits who served as his guides and gave him messages relating to his own life and to the lives of others.

John's wife Sylvia was a Christian, and her influence had a positive effect on him after they were married, but he continued on in his spirit worship. He was trying to be both a Christian and a medicine man at the same time. It was a dream, more than anything else, that suddenly turned his life around. "An angel spoke to me saying that I was going about it in the wrong way, in serving the Lord, and that I would be afflicted with a pain and that through this pain, I would be drawn closer to the Lord."

"The months passed and finally in 1982, I ended up in the hospital in New Mexico. It was here that I made my decision to give myself to God. Late one night, I gathered all my sacred belongings and took them up to one of our sacred mountains. I recall how frightened I was. I was prepared to face death because of what I was about to do. I was thinking to myself, *What if I was wrong doing this?* The gods would take my life, like many who have gone to their graves. It was here that I buried all my sacred tools."

"It was at this point that I confessed to God that I didn't fully understand the meaning of my medicine tools and that I wanted instead to take the Bible as my power and strength, and that no more would I look to the gods I once served." In the weeks that followed, John was tormented by evil spirits. He endured terrifying nightmares and "would wake up choking, sweating, or yelling in the middle of the night." But "then one morning," he recalls, "God released me from the bonds of Satan and there came upon me a peace I can't explain." In the years since, John has studied at Reformed Bible College and has served in mission outreach to other native Americans in Nebraska, New Mexico, Arizona, and Oklahoma.[15]

**For you were once darkness, but now you are light in the Lord. Live as children of light (for the fruit of the light consists in all goodness, righteousness and truth), and find out what pleases the Lord. Have nothing to do with the fruitless deeds of darkness, but rather expose them. For it is shameful even to mention what the disobedient do in secret. But everything exposed by the light becomes visible, for it is light that makes everything visible. This is why it is said: "Wake up, O sleeper, rise from the dead, and Christ will shine on you."**

*Ephesians 5:8–14.*

## "GIVING THE LAST COIN"

J. Hudson Taylor, the great missionary statesman and founder of the China Inland Mission, prepared himself for missionary service by doing "gospel work" in London among the people "in the lowest part of the town." On one occasion, as he was finishing up his work late at night, he was stopped by a man who asked if he would come and pray with his sick wife. The man explained that he had sought to find a priest, but was told that he would need a payment of eighteen pence, which the man did not have. Indeed the man confessed that he did not even have money to buy food for his starving family.

Taylor agreed to go to his home, but immediately his conscience was stricken. He too was living on virtually a starvation diet, but he had money—a half crown—in his pocket. It was all the money he had, and his own food was running out. "If only I had two shillings and a sixpence," he contemplated, "instead of this half-crown, how gladly would I give these poor people a shilling!" But to give all his money to a stranger—that was unthinkable.

Finally they arrived at the tenement. "Up a miserable flight of stairs into a wretched room he led me, and oh, what a sight there presented itself! Four or five children stood about, their sunken cheeks and temples telling unmistakably the story of slow starvation, and lying on a wretched pallet was a poor, exhausted mother, with a tiny infant thirty-six hours-old moaning rather than crying at her side."

Taylor spoke to them, trying to bring comfort and encouragement, but the words stuck in his throat. "Something within me cried, 'You hypocrite! telling these unconverted people about a kind and loving Father in heaven, and not prepared yourself to trust him without half a crown." With nothing to say, Taylor determined to get the visit over quickly so he offered to pray as the man had initially requested. "But no sooner had I opened my lips with, 'Our Father who art in heaven,' than conscience said within, 'Dare you mock God? Dare you kneel down and call him "Father" with that half-crown in your pocket?' "

When Taylor got up from his knees he was so distraught that the man asked him what was wrong. The man could never have understood, but Taylor himself knew what was wrong and there was only one remedy. He dug deep into his pocket for his half-crown and gave it to the man. "And how the joy came back in full flood tide to my heart! . . .Not only was the poor woman's life saved, but my life as fully realized had been saved too."[16]

As he looked up, Jesus saw the rich putting their gifts into the temple treasury. He also saw a poor widow put in two very small copper coins. "I tell you the truth," he said, "this poor widow has put in more than all the others. All these people gave their gifts out of their wealth; but she out of her poverty put in all she had to live on."

*Luke 21:1–4.*

## "UTTERLY FORSAKEN"

In the hour of his deepest anguish, Jesus felt utterly forsaken by God. Others have shared this feeling of suffering—suffering to the point that they were no longer able to comprehend God's compassion. This was true of Helen Roseveare, a missionary medical doctor to the Congo, who was caught in the throes of a bloody civil war in 1964.

Helen had been placed under house arrest during the summer of 1964, continuing to live and work in her own home, but late that fall the medical compound came under rebel attack. It was a night of terror. She tried to escape, but with no success. "They found me, dragged me to my feet, struck me over the head and shoulders, flung me on the ground, kicked me, dragged me to my feet only to strike me again— the sickening searing pain of a broken tooth, a mouth full of sticky blood, my glasses gone. Beyond sense, numb with horror and unknown fear, driven, dragged, pushed back to my own house—yelled at, insulted, cursed."

But the beating was only the prelude to what would come. According to Helen's biographer, the soldier "forced her backwards on the bed, falling on top of her. . . . The will to resist and fight had been knocked out of her. But she screamed over and over again. . . . The brutal act of rape was accomplished with animal vigor and without mercy."

"My God, my God, why have you forsaken me?" rang over and over again in her numbed consciousness. How could God have allowed her to endure such unspeakable torment? She could not have understood at the time that the terrible, personal violation that night would allow her to have a ministry that she otherwise never could have had.

When later she was incarcerated in a convent with other expatriate prisoners, including nuns, she encountered a young nun who had lost the will to live. She was convinced that God had utterly rejected her because the ruthless act of rape had deprived her of her virgin purity. Helen was able reassure her that God's concept of purity was a purity of the heart and that her faith in him is what would count for eternity.

Such opportunities for ministry, and her subsequent release and return to the mission field, confirmed to Helen that indeed God had not forsaken her. He allowed her to endure testing for a time, and she responded in a way that would bring encouragement and inspiration to people the world over.[17]

From the sixth hour until the ninth hour darkness came over all the land. About the ninth hour Jesus cried out in a loud voice, *"Eloi, Eloi, lama sabach-thani?"*—which means, "My God, my God, why have you forsaken me?"

*Matthew 27:45–46.*

## "A NEW CREATION"

In reflecting on his work in Nepal as a missionary medical doctor, Thomas Hale was very aware that his service as an ambassador for Christ involved far more than simply giving medical treatment. It involved the ministry of reconciliation. "Though communicating love through medicine may discharge our responsibility as medical workers," he wrote, "it does little for the sick person coming for treatment if all he has to look forward to after recovery is a life of continuing unhappiness and hopelessness. . . . We know from personal experience that God's love changes lives; the faith we share with our Nepali friends is not a hand-me-down or merely theoretical faith. His love changed our lives and sent us to Nepal; His love has kept us here. . . . We share *His* love, not our own, and His love never runs dry."

It was through this ministry of reconciliation that Thomas witnessed the remarkable "new creation" in the life of Chandra Bahadur. Chandra reached out—not with a "hand-me-down" faith, but with a vibrant ministry of reconciliation of his own. Chandra was a boy who had dropped out of school to care for his widowed mother and to keep up the family farm. While stripping leaves from a tree for his cattle one day, apparently this epileptic boy had a seizure. He fell some sixty feet. Amazingly, he was not killed. He was, however, paralyzed from the waist down.

After a time of hospitalization, Dr. Hale realized he could do no more for the boy and asked the family to take him home. The family resisted, and Chandra was left to waste away at the hospital. "As the months wore on, every remaining flicker of hope for Chandra's recovery was extinguished. He entered long periods of despondency. . . . He could seen no reason to continue living."

But suddenly Chandra's life began to change. In his boredom he had picked up a Nepali New Testament, and his life was revolutionized. "In short, Chandra Bahadur became a new person: usually cheerful, often joyful, and always different from what he was before. And what he has found is so much greater than what he had that if you asked him today, he would tell you he is thankful he fell out of that tree."

Chandra learned to type and to do accounting and then became a cashier at the hospital. He also became a leader in the local church, causing people—especially his non-Christian countrymen—to marvel at his changed life. That changed life—far more than theoretical faith—demonstrated the power of God. [18]

Therefore, if anyone is in Christ, he is a new creation; the old has gone, the new has come! All this is from God, who reconciled us to himself through Christ and gave us the ministry of reconciliation: that God was reconciling the world to himself in Christ, not counting men's sins against them. And he has committed to us the message of reconciliation. We are therefore Christ's ambassadors, as though God were making his appeal through us.

*2 Corinthians 5:17–20.*

## "IF I PERISH, I PERISH"

When Esther determined that she would stand for her people, she knew that her decision was one that went beyond the law and even her instinct for self-preservation. She was courageous and God used her mightily. Her words "If I perish, I perish" symbolize the courage of another individual who defended the Jews in the face of appalling injustice.

Dietrich Bonhoeffer was born in 1906 into a nominally Lutheran family in Germany. As a young man it would have been easy for him to take the safe course, which would have been to follow along with church leaders during the time of turmoil in the 1930s. Indeed, the German Lutheran bishops declared: "We German Protestant Christians accept the saving of our nation by our leader Adolf Hitler as a gift from God's hand."

Bonhoeffer was well aware of the diabolical nature of Hitler and of his wretched anti-Semitic policies. What was the purpose of Christianity, he reasoned, if it did not take a stand in a time like this? Bonhoeffer wanted no part of a church without a soul. He had studied at Union Theological Seminary in New York, where his faith was challenged—in a negative way. "Union students," he observed, "intoxicate themselves with liberal and humanistic expressions, laugh at the fundamentalists, and basically they are not even a match for them. . . . I never heard the Gospel of Jesus Christ . . . of the cross, of sin and forgiveness, of death and life [while] in New York . . . only an ethical and social idealism which pins its faith to progress."

Bonhoeffer knew that it was this kind of teaching that could allow a church such as his own in Germany to slip into the hands of Hitler. He vowed he would be different, and he joined with those Christians who opposed Hitler to form the Confessing Church. Here he could freely confess that it was not Hitler, but the "Bible alone is the answer to all our questions . . . that is because in the Bible God speaks to us."

Bonhoeffer developed a small seminary and took a leading role in the Confessing Church, all the while publicly deploring Hitler's increased attacks on the Jews. As time went on, he secretly began working with others to remove Hitler from power. When that scheme was uncovered, Bonhoeffer was imprisoned and hanged. He was a martyr to his faith. Such was *The Cost of Discipleship*, which was the title and subject of his classic and penetrating book.[19]

When Esther's words were reported to Mordecai, he sent back this answer: "Do not think that because you are in the king's house you alone of all the Jews will escape. For if you remain silent at this time, relief and deliverance for the Jews will arise from another place, but you and your father's family will perish. And who knows but that you have come to royal position for such a time as this?"

Then Esther sent this reply to Mordecai: "Go, gather together all the Jews who are in Susa, and fast for me. Do not eat or drink for three days, night or day. I and my maids will fast as you do. When this is done, I will go to the king, even though it is against the law. And if I perish, I perish."

*Esther 4:12–16.*

# "MY SALVATION WILL NOT BE DELAYED"

Though God may send a man from "a far-off land" to fulfill his purpose, it still might seem as though his salvation is delayed. But what seems like delay in the eyes of humanity may be perfect timing for God. So it was for Mokwae, the Queen of Nalolo, who lived and reigned in southern Africa in the late nineteenth and early twentieth centuries.

Mokwae first heard the gospel through the ministry of a French Protestant missionary, Francois Coillard, who began his missionary work in 1878 in what is today called Zambia. A powerful queen, she enjoyed relishing in victory over her enemies. When Coillard visited her after a series of battles she exuberantly boasted: "We have utterly destroyed Mathaha and his gang, and their bones are bleaching in the sun. And the insolence of these sorcerers to beg for mercy! Mercy indeed! We threw them out on the veldt to the vultures. That was our mercy!"

Although Mokwae listened to Coillard's gospel message, she showed no eagerness to accept it for herself. Indeed, she was not above blaming the missionaries for disease and death. But slowly things began to change. When his wife died in 1892, she sent a delegation to the funeral, and two years later she requested that a missionary come to Nalolo—though Coillard questioned her motives: "Do not imagine that the inhabitants of Nalolo . . . are yearning for the Gospel. No, it is only a question of dignity. Lewanika [her ruling brother] has his missionary, a European missionary, and why not Mokwae? In their estimation, a white missionary is a good milch cow!"

It was important for African tribal leaders to gain the influence of a European, and "the Queen may well have been tempted to 'convert' simply to show her appreciation for Coillard's support. Yet still she held off." By 1907, she had become a regular at worship services, but was still uncommitted. Then one Sunday in 1916, she asked if she could speak at the end of the service. The queen testified that she was not a Christian, but that she was coming closer and closer.

Finally, on February 20, 1920, after thirty-five years of "delay" she stood up at the end of a service and testified: "It is enough. I believe. I am God's. I am of the Kingdom. May God forgive me my sins, they are many and they are great. And you—believe!" The matter was settled.[20]

I make known the end from the beginning, from ancient times, what is still to come. I say: My purpose will stand, and I will do all that I please. From the east I summon a bird of prey, from a far-off land, a man to fulfill my purpose. What I have said, that will I bring about, what I have planned, that will I do. Listen to me, you stubborn-hearted, you who are far from righteousness. I am bringing my righteousness near, it is not far away, and my salvation will not be delayed.

*Isaiah 46:10–13a.*

## "O UNBELIEVING AND PERVERSE GENERATION"

Millie Larson has served as a missionary with Wycliffe Bible Translators among the Arguaruna people living in the tropical rain forest of Peru. She tells of her reluctance to accept the reality of demonism and of her lack of faith in seeking God's help in dealing with it. "We had believed medicine to be the all-powerful force that would overcome superstition and sorcery," she writes. "If we could prove that all sickness had a natural cause, people would be free from their terrifying fears of it. . . . Whenever someone claimed to be sick because of *tunchi*, we would try to show how it wasn't actually sorcery. It must be parasites, or some germ—and usually it was."

But the longer she worked among the people, the more Millie realized that she could not simply continue to disbelieve in demonism. There was too much evidence all around her. But even when she did observe individuals who she felt certain were possessed, she "felt no power to save these people from Satan's attack."

Her inability to deal with demonism became frighteningly clear to her late one night when she was called out to a "dimly lit thatched hut, where Elsa was believed by her neighbors to be dying of *tunchi*. 'She's been cursed; she's going to die; it's *tunchi*,' they insisted. Her moods swung from violent writhing on the floor to chanting, 'There are many of you. don't come any closer'—apparently referring to the demons.'"

It was then that Nelson, Elsa's brother and a Christian, took charge. He sang his song of exorcism, "and eventually Elsa quieted down and fell asleep." Millie realized that this man, who had far less knowledge of the Bible than she did, was accepting the reality of demons more than she was. "For the first time in my life, I knew that demons were real and powerful. Did I have the courage to cast them out, as Jesus gave his disciples power to do. . . . I am translating the Scripture into their language, but do I truly believe it myself?" she asked herself.

Millie did experience God's strength as she confronted demonism in the years that followed. She came to realize that the message these people wanted was not so much that there was a Savior who would provide them a heavenly home in the future, but "that there was a Savior who had power to free them in this life from demons, to protect them from sorcery and to heal them of constant sickness." As her message focused on these issues, she saw an increased response to the gospel among the people.[21]

When they came to the crowd, a man approached Jesus and knelt before him. "Lord, have mercy on my son," he said. "He has seizures and is suffering greatly. He often falls into the fire or into the water. I brought him to your disciples, but they could not heal him."

"O unbelieving and perverse generation," Jesus replied, "how long shall I stay with you? How long shall I put up with you? Bring the boy here to me." Jesus rebuked the demon, and it came out of the boy, and he was healed from that moment.

*Matthew 17:14–18.*

# "TO THE JEWS I BECOME LIKE A JEW"

When a Jew becomes a Christian, usually it is a traumatic experience for the family. The family immediately suspects that the individual is no longer Jewish. To an extent this is true, because the person significantly changes his or her religious faith. Most Jewish Christians, however, do not turn away from their Jewish customs. Indeed, many observe Jewish holidays and seek to maintain closer cultural bonds to their heritage than do many Jews who claim a nominal religious faith. Keeping close ties to the Jewish religious heritage is imperative when reaching Jews with the gospel of Christ, as the apostle Paul realized.

Stan Telchin tells of the anguish he felt when his twenty-one-year-old daughter told the family that she had put her faith in Jesus as the Messiah. It was shocking news that jolted their tranquility, but in the weeks and months that followed, as they observed her newfound happiness and peace, they began to inquire about Jesus Christ for themselves. Stan initially studied the Bible in an effort to refute all that his daughter believed, but as time passed he became a believer, as did his wife and other daughter. And they all came to faith independent of each other.

Did they lose their Jewishness? Stan spoke to that issue: "I am a Jew. I was born a Jew, and I will die a Jew. Even if it were possible for me to reject my Jewish identity and heritage, I would never do so. I am a Jew by birth and by desire. As a matter of fact, I am so comfortable and so secure in my Jewish identity that I am not threatened by the fears and anxieties of some who would question it. My Jewishness was not conferred upon me by public opinion or by government edict. It was not given to me by men, and it cannot be taken away from me by men.

"As a Jew," writes Stan, "I am even more sensitive to the teachings of Jesus, who was born a Jew, lived as a Jew, chose other Jews as His disciples and loved the Jewish people. As His disciple today, I know that He is more concerned about the attitudes of our hearts than the actions we perform. . . . In relations with members of my family and friends I am to remain consistent, never turning my back on my heritage, on my ancestry, on Israel, or upon them."[22]

Though I am free and belong to no man, I make myself a slave to everyone, to win as many as possible. To the Jews I became like a Jew, to win the Jews. To those under the law I became like one under the law (though I myself am not under the law), so as to win those under the law. To those not having the law I became like one not having the law (though I am not free from God's law but am under Christ's law), so as to win those not having the law.

*1 Corinthians 9:19–21.*

# "OUT OF THE DEPTHS I CRY"

It is sometimes tempting to think that we are the first generation to deal with a contagious life-threatening disease such as AIDS. In the time of Jesus, however, lepers were the disease-ridden outcasts of society who were kept away from public exposure. This treatment continued through the centuries, and often the public expressed very little sympathy for these unfortunate people.

One individual who stands out for her caring concern for lepers is Katherine Zell, an outspoken pastor's wife and reformer in her own right in Reformation Germany. She wrote tracts and edited a hymnbook, but she also used her gift of writing in more personal ministries. When a city official, who was a longtime acquaintance of hers, was quarantined from Strasbourg because he had contracted leprosy, she visited him and spoke to local magistrates about improving his situation.

The most enduring aspect of her ministry to this man, however, was her letter writing. These letters not only expressed her tender words of consolation, but they included Scripture passages. In the sixteenth century, the Bible was not readily available, and these copied verses may have been the only Scripture this disease-ridden and disconsolate man had available. One of the passages she meticulously copied was Psalm 130—a psalm of anguish with which he could readily identify.

In her letter she explained why she had included the portions of Scripture: "My dear Lord Felix . . . I have not been able to come as often as I would like, because of the load here for the poor and the sick, but you have been ever in my thoughts. We have often talked of how you have been stricken, cut off from rank, office, from your wife and friends, from all dealings with the world which recoils from your loathsome disease and leaves you in utter loneliness. . . . Because I know that your illness weighs upon you daily and may easily cause you again to fall into despair and rebelliousness, I have gathered some passages which may make your yoke light in the spirit, though not in the flesh."

Katherine made brief comments on these Scripture passages. They were designed not to be scholarly commentary, but a practical source of encouragement to a downcast soul.[23]

Out of the depths I cry to you, O Lord; O Lord, hear my voice. Let your ears be attentive to my cry for mercy.

If you, O Lord, kept a record of sins, O Lord, who could stand? But with you there is forgiveness; therefore you are feared.

I wait for the Lord, my soul waits, and in his word I put my hope. My soul waits for the Lord more than watchmen wait for the morning, more than watchmen wait for the morning.

*Psalm 130:1–6.*

# "NO SECOND CHANCE"

Those who advocate capital punishment as a biblical principle applicable today generally would not advocate the Levitical law as it was set up for sins other than murder—particularly in its death penalty for blasphemy and its injunction to injure the one who has injured you. And sometimes those who favor the death penalty fail to take into account the words of Jesus: "You have heard that it was said, 'Eye for eye, and tooth for tooth.' But I tell you, Do not resist an evil person" (Matthew 5:38–39).

Those who oppose capital punishment today not only point to such statements of Jesus but also to the fact that an innocent person could be executed without being given an adequate time to overturn a guilty verdict. They also state that one of the goals of the criminal justice system is to seek to rehabilitate criminals.

Can violent criminals be rehabilitated? Billy Graham tells the story of Velma Barfield and how she had an impact on his own family. In 1978 she was arrested for the murder of four people including her fiancé and her own mother. She admitted her guilt and did not seek to excuse it, though she had been a victim of violence and sexual abuse and had become a drug addict after a doctor had prescribed powerful pain-killers for her.

After her conviction, she was sent to prison and it was there that her life changed. "One night the guard tuned in to a twenty-four-hour gospel station. Down the gray hall, desperate and alone in her cell, Velma heard the words of an evangelist and allowed Jesus Christ to enter her life.

"Her conversion was genuine," writes Billy. "For six years on death row she ministered to many of her cell-mates. The outside world began to hear about Velma Barfield as the story of her remarkable rehabilitation became known. Velma wrote to Ruth and there developed a real friendship between them. In one letter Ruth wrote to Velma, "God has turned your cell on Death Row into a most unusual pulpit. There are people who will listen to what you have to say because of where you are. As long as God has a ministry for you here, He will keep you here. . . ."

Prior to her final date of execution, Velma wrote to Ruth: "If I am executed on August 31, I know the Lord will give me dying grace, just as He gave me saving grace, and has given me living grace." She was executed; she was the first woman in twenty-two years to suffer that penalty in the United States. "On the night she was executed," writes Billy, "Ruth and I knelt and prayed together for her till we knew she was safe in Glory."[24]

"If anyone curses his God, he will be held responsible; anyone who blasphemes the name of the Lord must be put to death. The entire assembly must stone him. Whether an alien or native-born, when he blasphemes the Name, he must be put to death.

"If anyone takes the life of a human being, he must be put to death. Anyone who takes the life of someone's animal must make restitution—life for life. If anyone injures his neighbor, whatever he has done must be done to him: fracture for fracture, eye for eye, tooth for tooth."

*Leviticus 24:15–20.*

# "PROTECT THEM FROM THE EVIL ONE"

This passage in John 17 was Jesus' prayer for his disciples before he left them to return to his Father. It is a powerful and passionate prayer that parents can readily identify with—especially the plea that God will "protect them from the evil one."

Amy Carmichael, a single missionary to India who had no children of her own, founded and directed Dohnavur Fellowship, a ministry that offered a secure home for hundreds of Indian children who had been rescued from temple prostitution. Her love for children was boundless, and that love is illustrated in a prayer that she wrote in poetic form.

> Father, hear us, we are praying,
> Hear the words our hearts are saying,
> We are praying for our children.
>
> Keep them from the powers of evil,
> From the secret, hidden peril,
> From the whirlpool that would suck them,
> From the treacherous quicksand pluck them.
>
> From the worldling's hollow gladness,
> From the sting of faithless sadness,
> Holy Father, save our children.
>
> Through life's troubled waters steer them,
> Through life's bitter battle cheer them,
> Father, Father, be Thou near them.
> Read the language of our longing,
> Read the wordless pleadings thronging,
> Holy Father, for our children,
> *And wherever they may bide,*
> *Lead them Home at eventide.*

God answered Amy's prayer, and hundreds of the children she cared for went on to live faithful Christian lives and to reach out to others with the gospel.[25]

Jesus prayed] "I am coming to you now, but I say these things while I am still in the world, so that they may have the full measure of my joy within them. I have given them your word and the world has hated them, for they are not of the world any more than I am of the world. My prayer is not that you take them out of the world but that you protect them from the evil one. They are not of the world, even as I am not of it. Sanctify them by the truth; your word is truth. As you sent me into the world, I have sent them into the world. For them I sanctify myself, that they too may be truly sanctified.

*John 17:13–19.*

# "I WILL WALK ABOUT IN FREEDOM"

The early Quakers were known for their boldness in demanding religious liberty, sometimes appealing their cases to the King of England or before powerful magistrates. Often their pleas were ignored, and like other religious minorities they immigrated to America in search of freedom.

Many of our Colonial forefathers did not practice religious toleration, however. Although the Puritans had themselves faced harsh persecution for their religious beliefs, once in power, they showed no mercy to minority religious groups. This was particularly true in Boston. There the Puritans often banished people in order to clear the area of heresy, and when that failed, the offenders were hanged.

One of those who struggled the hardest to force a change in this brutality perpetrated in the name of religion was Mary Dyer. She was a Quaker who immigrated to Boston in 1659. Her story, according to historian Daniel Boorstin, is "one of the most impressive in all the annals of martyrdom." She was brought to trial only weeks after she arrived in the Bay Colony, and she was sentenced to hang, along with two Quaker men. The execution was scheduled for the following week, and on that fateful day she "marched to the gallows between the two young men condemned with her, while drums beat loudly to prevent any words they might preach on the way from being heard by the watching crowd. . . . The two men were executed, and Mary Dyer was mounted on the gallows, her arms and legs bound and her face covered with a handkerchief as the final preparation for hanging. Then, as if by a sudden decision, she was reprieved from the gallows."

The magistrates had no intention of hanging her. They forced her to go through the terrifying ordeal to intimidate her and perhaps force her to recant. "She refused to accept the reprieve unless the law itself was repealed. But the determined judges sent her off on horseback in the direction of Rhode Island." Less than a year later she returned, determined that they could not take away her God-given right to "walk about in freedom." Once again she was led to the gallows and offered a reprieve if she would simply leave the colony. She refused, convinced that the laws of God were above the laws of men. "Nay," she insisted, "I cannot. . . . In obedience to the will of the Lord God I came and in his will I abide faithful to death." With those final words, she was hanged.[26]

May your unfailing love come to me, O Lord, your salvation according to your promise; then I will answer the one who taunts me, for I trust in your word. Do not snatch the word of truth from my mouth, for I have put my hope in your laws. I will always obey your law, for ever and ever. I will walk about in freedom, for I have sought out your precepts. I will speak of your statutes before kings and will not be put to shame, for I delight in your commandments because I love them.

*Psalm 119:41–47.*

## "BURIED ALIVE"

These are dismal words coming from Job, who was being sorely tested by his "friends," but they offer a profound truth that is very closely tied to the underlying motive for missions. Death is real, and indeed, "the dead are in deep anguish"—those who have never accepted the redeeming love of Christ. To save people from an eternity without Christ, missionaries have sacrificed their families, their health, their wealth, and sometimes their very lives.

Death was a frequent companion to the Sepik Iwam people of Papua, New Guinea, as Marilyn Laslo quickly realized when she arrived in 1969 to work among them as a Wycliffe Bible Translator. To battle their health problems, the villagers had developed superstitions, and blamed evil spirits for various maladies. In the village of Hauna alone there were more than fifty witch doctors. Each had individualized remedies for every ailment known among them, and each remedy had a different degree of effectiveness.

Marilyn wanted to introduce more humane treatment for sickness. In her struggle against some of the most disturbing practices of the witch doctors, she began practicing a simplistic form of medicine. She began dispensing medicines, lancing boils, and pulling teeth, but what she found most effective and gratifying were the preventive health measures she took. "Convinced that many of the illnesses came from the polluted river water, she launched one of her most ambitious projects: the installation of four 2,000-gallon tanks to catch the rain water and pipe it to locations convenient to all villagers."

Like all members of Wycliffe Bible Translators, Marilyn was expected to observe tribal customs. But some customs were painfully difficult to accept. This was particularly true when her friend Neemau was buried.

Marilyn had known Neemau was sick, but was perplexed when she received the news that Neemau had been buried. Marilyn hurried to the grave site only to find that Neemau was still alive. "That's my good friend Neemau!," she cried. "She's not dead. Can't you see she is still breathing? You can't bury her! Let me take her to my house and revive her!" But the people ignored her pleas. Neemau was not talking. Her throat had died. Therefore she was dead.

Marilyn was distraught. She had sacrificed so much to save people—dear people like Neemau—from physical death and spiritual death, and now she could only watch as Neemau was buried alive.[27]

Then Job replied: "How you have helped the powerless! How you have saved the arm that is feeble! What advice you have offered to one without wisdom! And what great insight you have displayed! Who has helped you utter these words? And whose spirit spoke from your mouth?

The dead are in deep anguish, those beneath the waters and all that live in them. Death is naked before God; Destruction lies uncovered."

*Job 26:1–6.*

# "IN THE SHADOW OF THE ALMIGHTY"

Reading this psalm in church, where parishioners are sitting sedately in rows of pews, might not have the powerful impact that it would have if read in other circumstances—especially if the setting were a gymnasium turned into a makeshift prison, surrounded by gun-toting gestapo guards. The man reading the psalm was not a chaplain or clergyman. He was an ordinary layman who loved the Lord. His name was Casper ten Boom, and he would be lost in the annals of history were it not for his daughter whose stories of suffering in a Nazi death camp became famous the world over.

It was February 28, 1944. Only hours before Mr. ten Boom and his daughters and grandson were herded into the gymnasium, they had been quietly going about their business at home. Strangers had come to the door. When grandson Peter answered, they claimed they were friends of his grandfather. He was suspicious and told them they could not see his grandfather. The next moment a gun was pointed in his face. Terror gripped him as the guards came into the home and forcibly took their prisoners. The crime was serious. The ten Booms had been hiding Jews from the Nazis.

Psalm 91 gives assurance that "no harm will befall you . . . For he will command his angels concerning you." Young Peter felt disillusioned, as he later reflected on the incident.

"But tragedy *had* struck. Where was the host of angels we had prayed for so often? Had God forgotten us? Then I glanced over at Grandfather sitting in the corner. There was such an expression of peace on his pale face that I could not help marveling. He actually *was* protected. God had built a fence around him. Suddenly I knew: The everlasting arms are around all of us. God does not make mistakes. He is at the controls."

Casper ten Boom died in a prison hospital within weeks of that incident. The others, except for Corrie and Betsie, were released soon after. For all of them, however, Psalm 91 became a source of consolation. As Corrie and Betsie languished in the Nazi death camp, they were comforted by their certainty that they were resting in the shadow of the Almighty.[28]

He who dwells in the shelter of the Most High will rest in the shadow of the Almighty. I will say of the Lord, "He is my refuge and my fortress, my God, in whom I trust." Surely he will save you from the fowler's snare and from the deadly pestilence. He will cover you with his feathers, and under his wings you will find refuge; his faithfulness will be your shield and rampart. You will not fear the terror of night, nor the arrow that flies by day, nor the pestilence that stalks in the darkness, nor the plague that destroys at midday. A thousand may fall at your side, ten thousand at your right hand, but it will not come near you.

*Psalm 91:1–7.*

# "WE SEEMED LIKE GRASSHOPPERS IN OUR OWN EYES"

This familiar story of Caleb in Numbers 13 has been a source of inspiration for Christians down through the centuries, especially during times when courage was needed to stand up against the consensus of opinion. Without such courage it is difficult to imagine how the modern missionary movement that began with William Carey would have transformed the world as it did.

One modern-day missionary who is heralded for her courage in overcoming obstacles was Gladys Aylward, who became the subject of Alan Burgess's book *The Small Woman* and the film *Inn of Six Happinesses* starring Ingrid Bergman.

After being turned down by China Inland Mission, Gladys began her mission career by saving her money and traveling to China alone. Though the mission board did not deem her fit to serve, this one woman proved to have more fortitude than many who had gone before her. She traveled by rail across Europe, Russia and Siberia. It was a harrowing journey that she completed only because of her relentless determination. The train was packed with Russian troops on their way to fight an undeclared border war with China, and at one point—more than half way into the journey—Gladys was informed she would have to get off the train. She refused, fearing she would be denied reentry onto the train. Several miles later, the train stopped, the troops were ordered off, and Gladys found herself alone on an empty train in the remote wasteland. She had no choice but to trudge back to the station where she had been ordered to disembark in the first place. Her biographer tells the story:

"The Siberian wind blew the powdered snow around her heels, and she carried a suitcase in each hand, one still decorated ludicrously with kettle and saucepan. Around her shoulders she wore the fur rug. And so she trudged off into the night, a slight, lonely figure, dwarfed by the tall, somber trees, the towering mountains, and the black sky, diamond bright with stars. There were wolves near by, but this she did not know. Occasionally in the forest a handful of snow would slither to the ground with a sudden noise, or a branch would crack under the weight of snow, and she would pause and peer uncertainly in that direction, but nothing moved. There was no light, no warmth, nothing but endless loneliness."

Gladys would encounter more frightening episodes and towering obstacles before she reached China, and many times she felt like a grasshopper up against giants. She was determined, however, that nothing would deter her from following God's call to share the gospel with the Chinese people.[1]

Then Caleb silenced the people before Moses and said, "We should go up and take possession of the land, for we can certainly do it."

But the men who had gone up with him said, "We can't attack those people; they are stronger than we are." And they spread among the Israelites a bad report about the land they had explored. They said, "The land we explored devours those living in it. All the people we saw there are of great size. We saw the Nephilim there (the descendants of Anak come from the Nephilim). We seemed like grasshoppers in our own eyes, and we looked the same to them."

*Numbers 13:30–33.*

## "KEEP IN STEP WITH THE SPIRIT"

Patience is a fruit of the Spirit and is essential for cross-cultural evangelism. Often missionaries become discouraged because people do not readily respond to their preaching or because their expectations are not met by those who do profess faith in Christ. This was true in the life of James O. Fraser who served as a missionary for many years among the Lisu tribe of northwest China. He shared his frustrations regarding his Lisu converts with his supporters back home.

"I am not painting a dark picture; I only wish to tell you the real position of things as candidly as possible. In some ways they are ahead of ordinary church-goers at home. They are always hospitable. They are genuinely pleased to see me when I go to their villages. They are sincere, as far as they go; we see very little among them of the ulterior motives commonly credited to 'rice Christians.' They will carry my loads for me from village to village without pay. . . . But with the exception of a few, very few, bright earnest young people, there are not many who wish to make any progress or are really alive spiritually. . . .

"I have often in time past given way to depression, which always means spiritual paralysis, and even on this last trip have been much downcast, I admit, over the state of the people. When at a village near Mottled Hill, a month or more ago, I was much troubled over all this, but was brought back to peace of heart by remembering that, though the work is bound to be slow, it may be none the less sure for all that. My mistake has too often been that of too much haste. But it is not the people's way to hurry, nor is it God's way either. Hurry means worry, and worry effectually drives the peace of God from the heart.

"Rome was not built in a day, nor will the work of building up a strong, well-constructed body of Lisu Christians in the Tengyueh district be the work of a day either. Schools will have to be started when the time is ripe. There will be need of much visitation, much exhortation, much prayer. It will not be done all at once. The remembrance of this has cast me back upon God again. I have set my heart upon a work of grace among the Tengyueh Lisu, but God has brought me to the point of being willing for it to be in His time as well as in His way. I am even willing (if it should be His will) not to see the fullness of blessing in my life-time."[2]

But the fruit of the Spirit is love, joy, peace, patience, kindness, goodness, faithfulness, gentleness and self-control. Against such things there is no law. Those who belong to Christ Jesus have crucified the sinful nature with its passions and desires. Since we live by the Spirit, let us keep in step with the Spirit. Let us not become conceited, provoking and envying each other.

*Galatians 5:22–26.*

## "SPREADING SLANDER"

These rules for living in Leviticus 19 that God gave Moses thousands of years ago are as applicable today as they were then, and they are as applicable today as they were during John Wesley's life in eighteenth-century England.

Wesley's evangelical revival movement in England was not a movement focused so much on a charismatic leader as it was a movement that was centered in organizational work, with lay people actively involved in the ministry. It was through the laity and the organizational network that Wesley was able to have such a powerful influence. But no matter how efficient any organizational structure is, in the final analysis its success depends on the faithfulness of the people, and how well they are able to work together.

In his *Journal*, Wesley recorded the sad story of a woman whose ministry had been destroyed because of malicious gossip: "She found peace with God five and thirty years ago, and the pure love of God a few years after. Above twenty years she has been a class and a band leader, and of very eminent use. Ten months since she was accused of drunkenness, and of revealing the secret of her friend. Being informed of this I then wrote to Norwich (as I then believed the charge) that she must be no longer a leader, either of a band or of a class. The preacher told her further that, in his judgment, she was unfit to be a member of the society."

With this judgment, the woman was severed from her ministry and the fellowship of other Christians. Indeed, as is sometimes the case in Christian circles today, "Immediately all her friends (of whom she seemed to have a large number) forsook her at once."

The real tragedy of the situation was that a reputation was ruined on unfounded charges. "On making a more particular inquiry," Wesley wrote, "I found that Mrs. W. (formerly a common woman) had revealed her own secret, to Dr. Hunt and to twenty people besides. So the first accusation vanished into the air. As to the second, I verily believe the drunkenness with which she was charged was, in reality, the falling down in a fit [presumably an epileptic seizure]. So we have thrown away one of the most useful leaders we ever had, and for these wonderful reasons."[3]

"Do not pervert justice; do not show partiality to the poor or favoritism to the great, but judge your neighbor fairly.

"Do not go about spreading slander among your people.

"Do not do anything that endangers your neighbor's life. I am the Lord.

"Do not hate your brother in your heart. Rebuke your neighbor frankly so you will not share in his guilt.

"Do not seek revenge or bear a grudge against one of your people, but love your neighbor as yourself. I am the Lord."

*Leviticus 19:15–18.*

# "HE WILL BEAR THEIR INIQUITIES"

Who is spoken of in this passage? That was the question young Solomon Ginsburg put to his father, a Jewish rabbi, when he was reading through the book of Isaiah. When his father did not respond, he asked a second time. So angry did his father become that he grabbed the book away from him and slapped his face. "I felt quite chagrined," Ginsburg later wrote, "but in the providence of God it served its purpose, for, when the Jewish missionary asked me to go and hear him explain that very chapter, I went out of curiosity to see if he had a better explanation than the one my father had given."

Ginsburg was born in Poland in 1867. By the time he was a teenager he had become disillusioned with the strict rules and regulations of his family's faith, and he was determined not to be pushed into rabbinic training and an arranged marriage by his domineering father. At fifteen, he fled his home and eventually found his way to London, where he worked for his uncle, also an orthodox Jew.

In London Ginsburg was stopped one day on the street by a converted Jew, who invited him to come and hear him preach—on the fifty-third chapter of Isaiah. Immediately Solomon remembered the angry outburst of his father years earlier, and his curiosity was piqued.

"He listened with fascinated interest as the speaker called attention to the wonders of the life of Jesus and showed how every Old Testament Messianic prophecy was fulfilled in Him. He could not grasp it all, but he did understand that Isaiah 53 was a divinely given picture of the coming Messiah and that its prophecies had their exact and revealing fulfillment in the drama that took place on Golgotha's brow."

Ginsburg began to study Scripture, and when he came to the story of the crucifixion, he confessed, "I realized that I must cast in my lot with Jesus and plead for forgiveness *for the part I had in that great crime at Calvary.*" Not surprisingly, his uncle and other relatives were infuriated by his conversion—so much so that they physically drove him out of their home. But "the story of his conversion and persecutions spread widely and a crowd of over three thousand attended the service when he was baptized. He eagerly became involved in lay ministries and later served effectively in Brazil as a Baptist missionary."[4]

By oppression and judgment he was taken away. And who can speak of his descendants? For he was cut off from the land of the living; for the transgression of my people he was stricken. He was assigned a grave with the wicked, and with the rich in his death, though he had done no violence, nor was any deceit in his mouth. . . . After the suffering of his soul, he will see the light of life and be satisfied; by his knowledge my righteous servant will justify many, and he will bear their iniquities.

*Isaiah 53:8–9, 11.*

## "GREATNESS IS SERVANTHOOD"

We sometimes think that power comes only through aggressive self-promotion, but Jesus made it clear that this was not so when the mother of James and John asked Jesus for a special place for her sons in his kingdom. He explained to his disciples very bluntly that power and authority in his kingdom is based on servanthood.

Dee Jepson who served as an assistant to her husband, a U.S. senator, quickly became aware of the power-hungry atmosphere of Washington, D.C. Political wheeling and dealing was the name of the game—always with an eye on gaining influence with high-ranking officials. Jesus' message of servanthood seemed entirely out of place, until one day when Dee observed an honored guest's visit to the city.

"The unimportance of sophistication was brought home to me," she writes, "at a Capitol Hill luncheon for Mother Teresa. . . . In came this tiny woman, even smaller than I had expected, wearing that familiar blue and white habit, over it a gray sweater that had seen many better days, which she wore again to the White House the next day. As that little woman walked into the room, her bare feet in worn sandals, I saw some of the most powerful leaders in this country stand to their feet with tears in their eyes just to be in her presence.

"As I listened that afternoon, I thought, 'Don't forget this, Dee. Here in this little woman, who doesn't want a thing, never asked for anything for herself, never demanded anything, or shook her fist in anger, here's *real* power.' It was a paradox. She has reached down into the gutter and loved and given. She has loved those the world sees as unlovable—the desolate, the dying—because they are created in the image of the God she serves. Ironically, seeking nothing for herself, she has been raised to the pinnacle of world recognition, received the Nobel Peace Prize, and is a figure known to most people, at least in the Western world, and revered by many. She has nothing, yet in a strange way, she has everything."[5]

Then the mother of Zebedee's sons came to Jesus with her sons and, kneeling down, asked a favor of him.

"What is it you want?" he asked.

She said, "Grant that one of these two sons of mine may sit at your right and the other at your left in your kingdom." . . .

When the ten heard about this, they were indignant with the two brothers. Jesus called them together and said, "You know that the rulers of the Gentiles lord it over them, and their high officials exercise authority over them. Not so with you. Instead, whoever wants to become great among you must be your servant, and whoever wants to be first must be your slave—just as the Son of Man did not come to be served, but to serve, and to give his life as a ransom for many.

*Matthew 20:20–21, 24–28.*

# "SHUNNING THE SAMARITANS"

In the time of Jesus the Samaritans were looked down upon by the Jews. They were regarded as inferior, and even though the Jews were neighbors, they had very little interaction. Jesus, to the surprise of his disciples, ignored that social restraint and freely conversed with a Samaritan woman. To him people were people, and there was no place for such artificial barriers. The situation is not so entirely different from the racial barriers we often erect in our modern world.

While white Christians in the pews are admonished to support and become involved in missionary work in Africa, those same Christians often ignore blacks in the neighborhood and even those next door to the church. This is the testimony of Michael Haynes, a black pastor who has served the Twelfth Baptist Church in Boston.

"My entire lifetime was spent just a few yards from a great evangelical church. I had lived two-thirds of my life before I ever received an invitation to come in. As a child whose family had just moved into a fast-changing white neighborhood on the edge of a Negro ghetto, I sat on the stairs of this church and played. I looked into the downstairs window as white face upon white face sat around tables at church suppers. I can vividly recall one day that I, a poor black child whose family was on welfare, yelled into the window of this church, 'We're hungry. Give us something to eat!' only to have a beautiful white lady come out and tell my brother and me how rude we were."

This woman may not have realized the message she was conveying to this child. Her values were such that scolding a child for "rudeness" took precedence over concern for his well-being and for his eternal destiny. Indeed, it was a message that may have forever turned him away from church. But that was not the case. Even as Jesus broke convention and reached out to the Samaritan woman, there were those who were willing to reach out to youngsters such as this boy.

"Thank God, His love found me," writes Haynes. "And . . . it was not through the church that I was lifted from sinking sands of misdirection and degradation. It was through a . . . settlement house that I was lifted high enough to be able to catch a breath of air in this society."[6]

When a Samaritan woman came to draw water, Jesus said to her, "Will you give me a drink?" (His disciples had gone into the town to buy food.)

The Samaritan woman said to him, "You are a Jew and I am a Samaritan woman. How can you ask me for a drink?" (For Jews do not associate with Samaritans.)

Jesus answered her, "If you knew the gift of God and who it is that asks you for a drink, you would have asked him and he would have given you living water."

*John 4:7–10.*

## "SHOPWORN FAITH"

Helen Barrett Montgomery, who was the first woman to translate the New Testament from the Greek and the first woman to serve as the head of a major Protestant denomination (American Baptist), was a well-known missions and ecumenical leader of the early twentieth century. She wrote books and lectured on the subject of foreign missions, pleading for the cause that was very dear to her.

During her youth and early years at Wellesley College, she was a doctrinaire Baptist, and as such refused to join in fellowship with her classmates from other denominations. "Stiff little Baptist that I was," she wrote, "I used to walk to Natick and take communion in the church there." She wrote home lamenting her lonely course of action: "Oh, you don't know how it seems to feel that you are an outset, that you are regarded as narrow, bigoted."

As time went on, however, Helen slowly began to recognize that there was a better path to follow. She began to see the value of other points of view and the futility of arguing over minor points of doctrine. She expressed her feelings on this after she had been in the company of a dogmatic Baptist who was convinced he was orthodox on every doctrinal point.

In reflecting on him, she was philosophical about her own religion: "I tell you this Christian faith of ours is all shopworn being handled over the counter and mussed and creased and discussed. We want to get it off the counter and cut into coats to cover the naked. My own soul is sick with theory—I'm getting so I don't care how or when or where or whether the Pentateuch wrote Moses or Moses, the Pentateuch. There is good news, the gospel, the love of God, the life of Jesus, and here am I, sinful and selfish and blind as a bat—for the secret of the Lord is with them that fear him. I know enough things now to make me a saint if I lived 'em. I'm going to live more and talk less."

Helen put her philosophy of faith into action as she went on to become the foremost leader of the Women's Missionary Movement during the first decades of the twentieth century.[7]

It was he [Christ] who gave some to be apostles, some to be prophets, some to be evangelists, and some to be pastors and teachers, to prepare God's people for works of service, so that the body of Christ may be built up until we all reach unity in the faith and in the knowledge of the Son of God and become mature, attaining to the whole measure of the fullness of Christ.

Then we will no longer be infants, tossed back and forth by the waves, and blown here and there by every wind of teaching and by the cunning and craftiness of men in their deceitful scheming. Instead, speaking the truth in love, we will in all things grow up into him who is the Head, that is, Christ. From him the whole body, joined and held together by every supporting ligament, grows and builds itself up in love, as each part does its work.

*Ephesians 4:11–16.*

# "PRAYER FOR A SON"

Hannah has been an inspiration for many Christian mothers over the centuries who have dedicated their children to the Lord for ministry. Achiamma Yohannan is one such mother. She raised six sons in her native village in South India, and challenged them to listen for the call of God. But despite her encouragement, they seemed to be drawn in other directions and she feared that they would all seek secular employment.

One day, as Achiamma was bending over the open cooking fire with the spicy aroma of breakfast filtering through the morning air, she was reminded of the longing in her heart and right then stopped and "vowed to fast secretly until God called one of her sons into His service. Every Friday for the next three and a half years, she fasted. Her prayer always was the same." One by one her sons turned to other vocations, until only the "scrawny and little baby of the family was left." He had made a profession of faith at the age of eight, but he was "so shy and timid" that he "trembled when asked to recite in class." But his mother refused to forsake her dream, and when he was sixteen, her youngest son answered God's call—a call not so unlike that of Samuel's. It came in the night after he had heard a powerful challenge from missionary statesman George Verwer of Operation Mobilization.

"Alone that night in my bed, I argued with both God and my own conscience. By two o'clock in the morning, my pillow was wet with sweat and tears. I shook with fear. What if God would ask me to preach in the streets? How would I ever be able to stand up in public and speak? What if I were stoned and beaten?" This would be impossible, he reasoned, knowing he "could hardly bear to look a friend in the eye during a conversation, let alone publicly speak to hostile crowds on behalf of God." But suddenly he sensed he "was not alone in the room." He "felt the presence of God" and fell on his knees, responding to the call of God, in answer to his mother's prayers.

Little could K. P. Yohannan have realized that night that God would raise him up to be a great evangelist. He became a leader among his people and the president of Gospel for Asia, with influence worldwide.[8]

In bitterness of soul Hannah wept much and prayed to the Lord. And she made a vow, saying, "O Lord Almighty, if you will only look upon your servant's misery and remember me, and not forget your servant but give her a son, then I will give him to the Lord for all the days of his life, and no razor will ever be used on his head.". . .

The Lord called Samuel a third time, and Samuel got up and went to Eli and said, "Here I am; you called me."

Then Eli realized that the Lord was calling the boy. So Eli told Samuel, "Go and lie down, and if he calls you, say, 'Speak, Lord, for your servant is listening.' " . . .

The Lord was with Samuel as he grew up, and he let none of his words fall to the ground. And all Israel from Dan to Beersheba recognized that Samuel was attested as a prophet of the Lord.

*1 Samuel 1:10–11; 3:8–9a, 19–20.*

# "WHERE YOU DIE I WILL DIE"

The decision to be a missionary in the eighteenth century was a lifetime decision that was often seen as irreversible and, frequently, one without furlough. Some wives opposed going abroad, but then reluctantly agreed to go, acquiescing in their husbands' call. This was initially true of Giertrud Rask, the wife of Hans Egede, a Norwegian pastor who left his homeland in 1718 to serve in Greenland.

Giertrud's initial opposition to her husband's rash decision was natural. She was not a young woman—especially considering the normal lifespan in the eighteenth century. Hans was thirty-two at the time of their departure, and she was thirteen years his senior. She had four children, the youngest barely a year old. When Hans first disclosed his plans, "his own and his wife's friends wrote to express their severest reprobation. . . . His mother-in-law further inflamed the feeling against him, and even his wife began to hint that she repented having attached herself to a man who by such plans was going to ruin himself and those belonging to him."

Hans did not ignore his wife's feelings. He wanted her to concur in his decision. He did all he could "to make his wife see the will of God . . . and to regard it as their bounden duty to show a more resolute self-denial by leaving their home and going forth to preach the Gospel among the heathens," and then "they both laid the matter before God in prayer." The result was "the bending of her will, so that she confidently promised to follow him wherever he went."

Before they set sail, however, Hans had misgivings. "He was assailed by doubts as to whether he really had been justified in jeopardizing his and his family's welfare." It was then than Giertrud rallied his spirits: "My dear wife gave a proof of her great faith and constancy by representing to me that it was too late to repent of what had been done. I cannot say how much she encouraged me by speaking in this way and by the fact that she, a frail woman, showed greater faith and manliness than I."

During the many years of their ministry in Greenland, Giertrud was by his side helping in the ministry. In 1733, during a smallpox epidemic, she opened her home to the sick and nursed them in her own bedroom. It was a gesture of kindness that deeply impressed the Greenlanders, who had been reluctant to listen to the Lutheran preacher. But it was a heavy price to pay. "Not only I," wrote Hans, "but also my beloved wife after that time suffered greatly in strength and health . . . until God in his mercy called her to him." She lived and died vowing to remain always with her husband.[9]

But Ruth replied, "Don't urge me to leave you or to turn back from you. Where you go I will go, and where you stay I will stay. Your people will be my people and your God my God. Where you die I will die, and there I will be buried. May the Lord deal with me, be it ever so severely, if anything but death separates you and me." When Naomi realized that Ruth was determined to go with her, she stopped urging her.

*Ruth 1:16–18.*

# "A GIFT FROM THE FATHER"

Oswald Chambers, the well-known Bible teacher and author of the devotional classic *My Utmost for His Highest,* has been a deep source of encouragement to people who struggle to yield themselves entirely to God. He was born and raised in Aberdeen, the son of a Baptist preacher, and was converted under the preaching of Charles Haddon Spurgeon. During his adult life he became an itinerant evangelist for the Pentecostal League of Prayer and served as the principal of a Bible college. His final service to God was rendered in desert military camps in Egypt, where as an administrator of the YMCA he shared his faith with troops.

The process of moving from one stage in his life to another might have seemed natural to those who assume that a youth with his background and environment would become a great spiritual leader, but the evangelist tells otherwise. During his Bible college training, F. B. Meyer visited the campus and gave powerful messages on the subject of the Holy Spirit. After one of the meetings, Chambers was so moved by the challenge that he returned to his room and asked God for the baptism of the Holy Spirit, but nothing happened. "From that day on for four years," he wrote, "nothing but the overruling grace of God and kindness of friends kept me out of an asylum. . . . The Bible was the dullest, most uninteresting book in existence, and the sense of depravity, the vileness and bad-motiveness of my nature, was terrific."

Chambers came face to face with the fact that on his own he could not attain spiritual power and he even doubted his own salvation. "Then Luke 11:13 got hold of me—'If ye then, being evil, know how to give good gifts unto your children: how much more shall your heavenly Father give the Holy Spirit to them that ask him?' "

It was only by claiming that gift and sharing that claim with others that Chambers' life changed. It was a difficult change for him. At first, "I was not willing to be a fool for Christ's sake," he later related, until "I got to the place where I did not care whether everyone knew how bad I was.

"It is no wonder that I talk so much about an altered disposition," he wrote. "God altered mine; I was there when He did it."

During his exhausting final years in Egypt, he shared the gospel with British troops patrolling the Suez Canal region and became ill and died. He was buried in a cemetery in old Cairo, beneath a headstone that read "How much more shall your heavenly Father give the Holy Spirit to them that ask him?"[10]

"Which of you fathers, if your son asks for a fish, will give him a snake instead? Or if he asks for an egg, will give him a scorpion? If you then, though you are evil, know how to give good gifts to your children, how much more will your Father in heaven give the Holy Spirit to those who ask him!"

*Luke 11:11–13.*

# "GIVE YOURSELVES NO REST"

The challenge from Isaiah for "you who call on the Lord" to "give yourselves no rest" is a difficult one to carry out. Indeed it is far easier to fulfill the challenge to take no rest when actively engaged in active and arduous work for the Lord. It is easier to rest, perhaps even neglect, the inactive ministry of praying.

An individual who became known worldwide for his involvement in prayer was John Hyde, a missionary to India who has often been referred to as "Praying Hyde." His first twelve years in India saw very little fruit from his labor. All that time he was actively engaged in missionary work, but his prayer life was lacking.

In reflecting on those years, he became convinced that earnest prayer would have made a difference. He determined in his heart that he would become a watchman for the Lord and that he would give himself no rest in his prayer life. Then in 1904, he met with fellow missionaries and together they formed the Punjab Prayer Union, based on five principles that each member was required to affirm.

1. Are you praying for quickening in your own life, in the life of your fellow workers, and in the Church?
2. Are you longing for greater power of the Holy Spirit in your own life and work, and are you convinced that you cannot go on without this power?
3. Will you pray that you may not be ashamed of Jesus?
4. Do you believe that prayer is the great means for securing this spiritual awakening?
5. Will you set apart one-half hour each day as soon after noon as possible to pray for this awakening and are you willing to pray *till the awakening comes*?

An awakening did accompany Hyde's ministry, but it was not one that was a result of prayer alone. It depended also on his faithful proclamation of the gospel. "He received assurance in prayer that at least one soul would come to the Saviour each day during 1908. There were more than 400 converts added that year. The following year the Lord laid two souls a day upon his heart, and prayer was fully answered; the following year his faith was enlarged to claim four a day."[11]

I have posted watchmen on your walls, O Jerusalem; they will never be silent day or night. You who call on the Lord, give yourselves no rest, and give him no rest till he establishes Jerusalem. . . .

Pass through, pass through the gates! Prepare the way for the people. Build up, build up the highway! Remove the stones. Raise a banner for the nations.

The Lord has made a proclamation to the ends of the earth: "Say to the Daughter of Zion, 'See your Savior comes! See his reward is with him, and his recompense accompanies him.'" They will be called the Holy People, the Redeemed of the Lord; and you will be called Sought After, the City No Longer Deserted.

*Isaiah 62:6–7, 10–12.*

# "WORK WITH YOUR HANDS"

Christian ministers are sometimes referred to as parasites. In the minds of their detractors, they live off other people and have nothing of value to contribute. To counteract such perceptions of Christian workers in his own day, the apostle Paul admonished his followers to "work with your hands . . . so that your daily life may win . . . respect."

William P. Nicholson was an Irish evangelist who traveled through the British Isles conducting tent revivals during the early years of the twentieth century. He was often a target of scurrilous criticism. His constituency consisted of rough coal miners who worked long arduous days and had little tolerance for a preacher without dirty fingernails. Nicholson relates a story that challenged him about the need to work with his hands.

"During the summer we held our missions in a big tent. At one place, while erecting the tent, a big strong miner came and helped me to get the tent up. He held the pegs while I hammered them in with a 14 lb. hammer. It was sunny and hot, and I was wearing dungarees and singlet. The man said, 'The way you are working would put to shame the preacher. I suppose Nicholson will come all dressed up and begin preaching after you have done all the hard work.' I never let on who I was, but let him talk away about the well-fed, fat, lazy preacher. He would do no good, he said; and for his own part, the miner wouldn't come near a meeting! I didn't contradict him."

Nicholson went on to tell that the man actually did attend the first meeting—perhaps to scoff. But when he saw who the preacher was, he was ready to listen, and after Nicholson finished preaching, "he was soundly converted." This experience and others impressed upon Nicholson the necessity of being able to identify with his audience in their work and in their spiritual struggles.

Following these early years of preaching among coal miners in small towns and villages, Nicholson went on to be an internationally-known evangelist. He traveled to Australia and later to America, where one Sunday morning while preaching in a church in Los Angeles a stranger walked in off the streets. This stranger later testified that the preacher "preached on hell and heaven and sin, and told me Christ was the one I needed. He seemed to pick me out of that huge congregation, and speak directly to me." This young man was Percy Crawford, and he was converted that Sunday and later went on to become a leading radio and television youth evangelist and the president of The King's College.[12]

Now about brotherly love we do not need to write to you, yourselves have been taught by God to love each other. And in fact, you do love all the brothers throughout Macedonia. Yet we urge you, brothers, to do so more and more.

Make it your ambition to lead a quiet life, to mind your own business and to work with your hands, just as we told you, so that your daily life may win the respect of outsiders and so that you will not be dependent on anybody.

*1 Thessalonians 4:9–12.*

## "WHEN YOU REMEMBER SOMEONE"

Charlotte "Lottie" Moon was a Southern Baptist missionary appointed to China in 1873, who, soon after her arrival, was soon accused by the wife of one of her colleagues of being mentally unbalanced because of her "lawless prancing all over the mission lot." Actually, what Lottie was involved in was church planting, but that was not deemed proper for a woman. Nor was her assertiveness in other matters. But if some of her qualities were not perceived as feminine enough, there should have been no doubt about the motherly compassion she demonstrated during times of famine and hardship in China.

When a smallpox epidemic and severe drought struck in 1911, she pleaded with the churches back home to share their wealth with the starving and homeless people all around her. Churches contributed money, but not nearly enough to alleviate the critical situation that eventually developed. She pleaded for more, hoping that those with an abundance of food would share with those who were starving, but her pleas went unanswered. All that remained for her to do was to give from her personal account, and when that fund was exhausted, there was nothing more she could do. Yet, there were people all around her begging for food to stay alive.

Lottie did have food in her cupboards for her own sustenance—food that seemed to taunt her every time she ate. How could she eat food and at the same time turn away starving children who were begging at her door? She could not. That she was starving along with her Chinese friends was not discovered by her colleagues until she was critically ill. In hopes of saving her life, her colleagues made arrangements for her to return home in the company of a nurse, but it was too late. She died aboard ship while at port in Kobe, Japan, on Christmas Eve, 1912.

The compassion that characterized her life had a deep impact on the women of her church back home, and the following year they initiated a Christmas offering in the name of Lottie Moon for needs on the mission field. In recent years this offering has netted over twenty million dollars annually.[13]

Is not this the kind of fasting I have chosen: to loose the chains of injustice and untie the cords of the yoke, to set the oppressed free and break every yoke? Is it not to share your food with the hungry and provide the poor wanderer with shelter—when you see the naked, to clothe him, and not to turn away from your own flesh and blood?

*Isaiah 58:6–8.*

# "I AM COMPELLED TO PREACH"

Dawson Trotman, the founder of the Navigators, was a strong believer in setting goals and rules for daily living, especially with regard to his spiritual life. He developed this practice while he was in his twenties. He kept track of his record meticulously in a notebook, and he banded together with others for mutual accountability. One particular group was known as the Minute Men. They had a rigorous commitment to Scripture memorization, prayer, and witnessing.

The commitment to witnessing was simple: "Touch a life a day for God." Every day, without fail, each member was to share the gospel with another individual. The rule was not God's rule, but it was one established by Dawson and upheld by the group; it was a rule that Dawson felt obliged to strictly observe.

*"Touch a life a day for God."* Dawson had just climbed into bed when he realized he had not talked to anyone about Christ. Well, what if he spoke to two tomorrow? It wouldn't do, he decided. Rather than fail his week's assignment, he dressed and clattered off in his Model-T to find a listener. After several miles he saw a man with a briefcase who had just missed the train to Long Beach, and Dawson offered him a ride.

" 'You may not believe this,' he began after introductions, 'but I got out of bed to come down here. It's a rule of my life never to end the day without sharing with someone the most wonderful thing in life. I am a Christian.'

"The passenger heard the story of God's love in Christ, then said thoughtfully, 'Son, twenty years ago I started to search for God. I've gone to church nearly every Sunday for twenty years. Tonight you have told me about what I've been looking for.' "

Dawson's motivation for witnessing that night could certainly be categorized as legalistic, and he did not wish to fail in the eyes of those to whom he was accountable. Is such a motivation God-honoring? "If going out to witness that night instead of the next day merely to check off his daily chart was legalistic," writes his biographer, "it was legalism in the providence of God, for the next day he would not likely have crossed the path of the man who that night ended his long search for peace with God."[14]

Yet when I preach the gospel, I cannot boast, for I am compelled to preach. Woe to me if I do not preach the gospel! If I preach voluntarily, I have a reward; if not voluntarily, I am simply discharging the trust committed to me. When then is my reward? Just this: that in preaching the gospel I may offer it free of charge, and so not make use of my rights in preaching it.

*1 Corinthians 9:16–18.*

## "THE SONG OF THE LAMB"

As "The Song of the Lamb" indicates, all nations will worship God, and each nation will no doubt have its own songs of praise. These songs may not seem like songs of worship to Christians from the West who have been raised on the standard hymn books in the pews.

Bruce Olson had to expand his definition of worship as he worked with the Motilone Indians of Colombia, South America. He tells about how his friend Bobby shared his faith in Christ through a song, and how that song was sung according to tribal custom, with other Motilone men joining in.

"Bobby's song was about the way the Motilones had been deceived and had lost God's trail. He told how they had once known God, but had been greedy and had followed a false prophet. Then he began to sing about Jesus. As he did so, the other men who were singing stopped. Everyone became quiet in order to listen.

"'Jesus Christ was incarnated into man,' Bobby sang. 'He has walked our trails. He is God yet we can know Him.' . . . People were straining their ears to hear."

But the eagerness to hear was not shared by Bruce. "Inside me a spiritual battle was raging. I found myself hating the song. It seemed so heathen. The music, chanted in a strange minor key, sounded like witch music. It seemed to degrade the Gospel. Yet when I looked at the people around me, and up at the chief swinging in his hammock, I could see that they were listening as though their lives depended on it. Bobby was giving them spiritual truth through his song.

"Still I wanted to do it *my* way. . . . Then I saw that it was because I was sinful. I could love the Motilone way of life, but when it came to spiritual matters I thought I had the only way. But my way wasn't necessarily God's way. God was saying, 'I too love the Motilone way of life. I made it. And I'm going to tell them about my Son in *my* way.'

"I relaxed, able at last to find real joy in Bobby's song. It continued for eight hours, ten hours. . . . That night a spiritual revolution swept over the people. No one rejected the news about Jesus."[15]

I saw in heaven another great and marvelous sign: seven angels with the seven last plagues—last, because with them God's wrath is completed. And I saw what looked like a sea of glass mixed with fire and, standing beside the sea, those who had been victorious over the beast and his image and over the number of his name. They held harps given them by God and sang the song of Moses the servant of God and the song of the Lamb: "Great and marvelous are your deeds, Lord God Almighty. Just and true are your ways, King of the ages. Who will not fear you, O Lord, and bring glory to your name? For you alone are holy. All nations will come and worship before you, for your righteous acts have been revealed."

*Revelation 15:1–4.*

## "HIS UNFAILING LOVE"

Deep depression is a condition that is not entirely uncommon among the great saints of the church. Indeed, some of the greatest missionaries, preachers, and musicians have suffered from black spells of utter dejection. One such individual was William Cowper, a hymn writer and close friend and parishioner of John Newton, the eighteenth-century sea captain turned preacher, who is known for penning the words of "Amazing Grace."

Cowper was a well-educated, cultured, affluent gentleman who eagerly became involved in lay ministry. But his desire to serve God was marred by his bouts of despair. On one occasion John Newton was called to Cowper's home only to find that he had made an unsuccessful attempt to commit suicide by cutting his throat with a knife. He was utterly convinced that God had rejected him.

On another occasion, when Cowper was suicidal, John brought him to his own home and kept him under surveillance for several months. "During this period when Cowper's mental health was at its worst, John Newton's burden was heavy. Cowper's condition demanded almost constant attention. In his fits of depression Cowper insisted God had marked him for eternal damnation, that he had been cut off from mercy and was hopelessly undone. For months Cowper's obsession that God had cast him off persisted despite all Newton's best efforts to convince him otherwise. His despair and woe were beyond words to describe.

"Finally under John's leadership, prayer groups were formed to pray for Cowper's mental health. As these groups continued to pray, his condition began slowly to improve. After many months the gloom began to lift from his spirit, and William Cowper became his normal self. . . . Had not Newton stood by him during this critical time, Cowper's beautiful hymns, that have blessed thousands all over the world might never have been written. . . . Cowper's famous hymn, 'There Is a Fountain Filled With Blood,' was from this period as well as others of his most beautiful works."[16]

I am the man who has seen affliction by the rod of his wrath. He has driven me away and made me walk in darkness rather than light; indeed, he has turned his hand against me again and again, all day long. . . .

For men are not cast off by the Lord forever. Though he brings grief, he will show compassion, so great is his unfailing love. For he does not willingly bring affliction or grief to the children of men.

*Lamentations 3:1–3, 31–33.*

## "SHARE IN HIS SUFFERINGS"

The assurance that we are heirs of God, if we share in Christ's sufferings, is a comfort to those who truly do suffer for the cause of Christ. When we contemplate Christ's suffering and death on the cross, we are graphically reminded that there is nothing we can do to repay the debt. Yet, Christ's willingness to suffer and to be a sacrifice can be a powerful model for his followers. Dr. Eleanor Chestnut's life illustrates this.

During the years before and after China's Boxer Rebellion of 1900, foreigners were viewed with hostility—even those who were there in the front lines to offer sacrificial service. Indeed, many gave their lives to minister to the needy people of China. One of those was Dr. Chestnut, a missionary serving with the American Presbyterian Board.

Soon after she arrived she built a hospital, buying the bricks with her own money. But even before the hospital was completed, she was performing surgery in her own bathroom—for want of a better place. "One such operation involved the amputation of a coolie's leg. Complications arose and skin grafts were needed. Later the doctor was questioned about a leg problem from which she herself was suffering. 'Oh, it's nothing,' she answered, brushing off the inquiry. Later a nurse revealed that the skin graft for the 'good-for-nothing coolie' had come from Dr. Chestnut's own leg while using only a local anesthetic."

During the Boxer Rebellion, Dr. Chestnut remained on her post longer than most missionaries, and she returned to China the year after the rebellion was over. Then in 1905, while she was busy working at the hospital with four other missionaries, a mob stormed the building. Although she got away in time to alert authorities, and in fact could have escaped, instead she returned to the scene to help rescue her colleagues. It was too late. Her colleagues had been slain. But there were others who needed her help. Before she herself was killed, her final act of selfless service to the Chinese people was to rip a piece of material from her dress to bandage the forehead of a child who had been wounded.

She could never repay the debt she owed for her sins, but she could share in Christ's sufferings. In gratitude to him, she took up her cross and followed him to China to endure a life and death of suffering in order to further his kingdom.[17]

**For you did not receive a spirit that makes you a slave again to fear, but you received the Spirit of sonship. And by him we cry, "*Abba* Father." The Spirit himself testifies with our spirit that we are God's children. Now if we are children, then we are heirs— heirs of God and co-heirs with Christ, if indeed we share in his sufferings in order that we may also share in his glory.**

*Romans 8:15–17.*

# "DID GOD REJECT HIS PEOPLE?"

Frank Gaebelein is remembered as a "giant of Bible interpretation." He was a self-made scholar with no seminary training who borrowed books from others, but he nevertheless became one of America's most respected biblical scholars and the author of the multi-volume set *Annotated Bible* and many commentaries on individual books or passages of Scripture. His book, *The Jewish Question*, on Romans 11, according to Warren Wiersbe, "is a classic study of this critical chapter."

But Gaebelein did not simply write devotional commentaries of Scripture. He put his words into action by reaching out in ministry in a demonstration of his written expressions. Early in his ministry he was challenged one day by Samuel Goldstein, a Hebrew Christian who was a member of his church. Noting the pastor's many Hebrew books in his study, he commented, "It is a shame that you do not make greater use of your knowledge. You should go and preach the Gospel to the Jews. I believe the Lord made you take up these studies because He wants you to go to my brethren, the Jews."

"That was the beginning of a remarkable ministry in New York City. Hundreds of Jewish people crowded into halls to hear Gaebelein expound their Old Testament Scriptures, and many found Christ as their Savior. For five years (1894–99) Gaebelein superintended the Hope of Israel Mission, wrote books and tracts, edited two magazines, and sought to win both Jews and Gentiles to Christ."

After his book *Studies in Zachariah* was published, Gaebelein sent a copy to every rabbi in New York City. There was no response from any of the rabbis. "However, some time later, a young Hebrew Christian began to attend one of Gaebelein's meetings regularly, and it turned out he had been secretary to a well-known rabbi. The rabbi had thrown *Studies in Zachariah* into the wastebasket, but the secretary had rescued it, read it and trusted Christ!"

In 1889, Gaebelein began an itinerant Bible conference ministry that took him to cities throughout the United States, Canada, and Europe. When asked in later life how he managed to travel so much, write books, and edit a magazine, he summed up his philosophy in four words: "I never waste time."[18]

I ask then: Did God reject his people? By no means! I am an Israelite myself, a descendant of Abraham, from the tribe of Benjamin. God did not reject his people, whom he foreknew. Don't you know what the Scripture says in the passage about Elijah—how he appealed to God against Israel: "Lord, they have killed your prophets and torn down your altars; I am the only one left, and they are trying to kill me"? And what was God's answer to him? "I have reserved for myself seven thousand who have not bowed the knee to Baal." So too, at the present time there is a remnant chosen by grace.

*Romans 11:1–5.*

## "HE MUST MANAGE HIS FAMILY WELL"

For a father to have a child follow in his footsteps can be a source of great joy, especially if the father is a minister and has paved the way for his child by managing his family well. Reflecting on his childhood home, evangelist Mordecai Ham testified, "We had a family revival every evening. Father (a preacher himself—pastoring as many as six Kentucky country churches at one time) would give us a Bible reading and a sermon, then ask his children to confess any ill conduct of which they had been guilty that day."

From a very early age it seemed only natural that Mordecai would follow in his father's footsteps. So zealous was he to emulate his preacher father that he reportedly preached to neighborhood dogs and cats. The story is told that he tried to "immerse an old tomcat in a rain trough, and when the subject vented all its feline ferocity in objecting to the 'baptism,' little Mordecai threw him down with the disgusted exclamation, '*Go on, get sprinkled and go to Hell.*'"

Mordecai's early motivation to preach came not only from his father but also from his preacher grandfather. When the old man died in 1899, twenty-two-year-old Mordecai "knew his grandfather's mantle had fallen upon him." But despite this clear call to the ministry, he continued to work as a traveling salesman.

It was his father's presumptuous announcement at a district meeting more than two years later that suddenly thrust him into the ministry. He was startled when, with no warning, his father announced, "the next message will be given by Rev. Mordecai F. Ham, Jr." His mind in a daze, he walked up to the pulpit and preached a sermon from Matthew 11:12. "That day he was not preaching to cats and dogs, but pastors and messengers from the association: and preaching not on some street or alley, but from the pulpit where his grandfather had preached for forty years! God's blessing was upon him—the congregation was stirred, invitations to preach in other churches were extended and that day Mordecai F. Ham, Jr. entered the ministry."

Mordecai went on to conduct very successful evangelistic campaigns. In Raleigh, North Carolina, some five thousand people were converted, and in Macon, Georgia, thirteen houses of prostitution were closed, due to the mass conversion of the prostitutes.[19]

Here is a trustworthy saying: If anyone sets his heart on being an overseer, he desires a noble task. Now the overseer must be above reproach, the husband of but one wife, temperate, self-controlled, respectable, hospitable, able to teach, not given to drunkenness, not violent but gentle, not quarrelsome, not a lover of money. He must manage his own family well and see that his children obey him with proper respect. (If anyone does not know how to manage his own family, how can he take care of God's church?)

*1 Timothy 3:1–5.*

# "THE INEVITABILITY OF PERSECUTION"

Christians who live in countries where there is freedom to openly practice their faith have difficulty comprehending the courage required of believers who live under oppressive political regimes. In such countries as Nepal, it has been illegal to convert to another religion, and as a result Christians have been heavily persecuted for their faith.

Brother Prem, sometimes referred to as the "Apostle to Nepal," is a native-born Nepali who was incarcerated in some fourteen different prisons in the 1960s and 1970s. His imprisonments began after he baptized five men and four women who were also imprisoned; those people served one year each for changing their religion, and he was imprisoned for six years for his part in their conversions.

"Nepali prisons are typically Asian—literally dungeons of death. About 25 or 30 people are jammed into one small room with no ventilation or sanitation. The smell is so bad that newcomers often pass out in less than half an hour." Lack of heat in the winter and no ventilation in the summer added to the discomfort, as did cockroaches, lice, and rats that gnawed on the prisoners' toes while they slept.

Amazingly, all nine of the new converts survived the first year, as did Brother Prem. But, while the others were granted freedom, he was placed in even worse conditions in an attempt to "break" him.

"In the damp darkness, the jailer predicted Prem's sanity would not last more than a few days. The room was so small he could not stand up, or even stretch out on the floor. He could not build a fire to cook, so other prisoners slipped food under the door to keep him alive.

"Lice ate away his underwear, but he could not scratch because of the chains, which soon cut his wrists and ankles to the bone. It was winter, and he nearly froze to death several times."

He was kept in solitary confinement and total darkness, but still he did not break. His Bible was taken away, but he miraculously saw the pages of Scripture that he had become so familiar with when he had held that cherished volume in his hands. He was transferred to other prisons, and wherever he went he shared his faith—with both prisoners and guards. When he was released he refused to stop witnessing or organizing secret churches, and he was arrested again. "How can a Christian keep silent?" he insisted. "How can a church go underground? Jesus died openly for us. He did not try to hide on the way to the cross. We also must speak out boldly for Him regardless of the consequences."[20]

**You, however, know all about my teaching, my way of life, my purpose, faith, patience, love, endurance, persecutions, sufferings—what kinds of things happened to me in Antioch, Iconium and Lystra, the persecutions I endured. Yet the Lord rescued me from all of them. In fact, everyone who wants to live a godly life in Christ Jesus will be persecuted. . . .**

*2 Timothy 3:10–12.*

# "FROM THE LIPS OF CHILDREN AND INFANTS"

Sometimes the Christian witness of children has a more powerful influence on adults than the witness of other adults. An example of the truth of this is the testimony of Mr. Tamba, a well-educated Indonesian intellectual who was a member of the largest church in that country. It had been founded by missionaries, and Tamba, as the choir director, was a prominent figure in the congregation.

"My pride was nurtured by the fact that I thought I was the only Christian in Palembang with a university degree," Tamba later reflected. "I was not only a lecturer at Sriwidjaja University but also the chairman of the Association of Lawyers in Palembang. And, as if that were not enough, I was elected president of the town's Christian Intellectuals Club. With all my titles and offices therefore, and with the large salary I earned, it was no wonder that I began to look down on all the Christians I met."

He was confident about his religion, and it had never occurred to him that he was not a true believer—not until an evangelist, Pak Elias, came to his city to hold meetings. Tamba attended the meetings, but was furious when Pak challenged those assembled to make a personal commitment of faith. When young people from his church responded, he was angry. "You didn't have to do that," he argued. "You've already been born again through baptism and confirmation."

Yet, it was the courageous stand of these young people that prompted him to return to the meetings the following nights, and through Pak's personal counselings Tamba committed his life to Christ. "I felt a burden come upon my own soul. My past sins and my unimaginable pride loomed up before my eyes. For the first time in my life I asked the Lord that night to forgive my sins, and I was wonderfully saved."

Despite his profession of faith, Tamba still struggled, but what was initiated by youth was carried on by a little child. "A few months after the campaign had ended . . . I found myself once more bogged down in a mass of problems relating to my work. I hardly had enough time even to pray. It was then that the Lord sent me a tutor in the form of my two-year-old nephew. I had told the boy that a Christian ought always to pray to the Lord Jesus before he goes to sleep at night. He was visiting us at the time and we had allowed him to sleep in the same room as myself. When we went to bed my little nephew asked, 'Uncle, why aren't you saying your prayers? Have you quarrelled with Jesus?' This childlike question brought me to my senses. The Lord had chosen to use a two-year-old boy to be his witness and my counsellor. 'By the mouths of babes and infants . . .' (Psalm 8)."[21]

O Lord, our Lord, how majestic is your name in all the earth! You have set your glory above the heavens. From the lips of children and infants you have ordained praise because of your enemies, to silence the foe and the avenger.

*Psalm 8:1–2.*

# "THE ONE WHO IS IN YOU IS GREATER"

"The Tiger spoke!" Those words were enough to send a chilling frenzy through the little jungle village in Colombia, South America, where Bruce Olson served as an independent missionary among the Motilone Indians. Bruce was puzzled. During the months he had spent becoming acquainted with these tribal Indians, he had not before encountered such fear and superstition. He hurried to the chief, and insisted that "tigers don't talk" and that the hysteria was all for nothing. But the chief, not about to listen to an ignorant foreigner, responded, "You don't know anything about the jungle. You don't know how to hunt, you don't know what to eat. You can't keep up on the trail. What makes you think you know anything about tigers?"

After consulting alone with the tiger, the chief returned to report to the people that, "The tiger says that the spirits will come out of the rocks tonight. They will attack this home. Lives will be snuffed out. Languages will cease. There will be death."

"It was obvious that something really terrifying was happening," writes Bruce. "These people were not normally superstitious, and I had never seen them really frightened before. They routinely faced poisonous snakes and dangerous animals, and never showed a trace of fear. If they were afraid now, there must be something worth being afraid of. But what was it? How could they fight it?"

Even Bobby was afraid. Bobby was the only Christian convert in the tribal group, but he too feared the consequences of this terrifying night to come. "Can Jesus be taken out of my mouth?" he asked Bruce. "Can the devil kill me now that I walk in Jesus' path?" Bruce wanted to say that it was all superstitious nonsense, but he told Bobby to deal with the Lord about it himself, while he himself went alone in the jungle to pray.

When he arrived home just before dark, Bruce found Bobby lying in his hammock singing this song over and over again in monotonous repetition: "Jesus is in my mouth; I have a new speech. Jesus is in my mouth; no one can take Him from me." Bruce joined him, and they sang it all night. When the morning dawn appeared, the people could not believe they were safe. "It was the first time in anyone's memory that the spirits had walked and no one had died." After that both Bruce and Bobby could say more assuredly, "The one who is in me is greater than the one who is in the world."[22]

But every spirit that does not acknowledge Jesus is not from God. This is the spirit of the antichrist, which you have heard is coming and even now is already in the world.

You, dear children, are from God and have overcome them, because the one who is in you is greater than the one who is in the world. They are from the world and therefore speak from the viewpoint of the world, and the world listens to them. We are from God, and whoever knows God listens to us; but whoever is not from God does not listen to us. This is how we recognize the Spirit of truth and the spirit of falsehood.

*1 John 4:3–6.*

## "WILL A MAN ROB GOD?"

Robbing God is not an outdated charge applicable only to the people of Israel. Indeed, the indictment and curse on "the whole nation" could be aptly given to America in the twentieth century. Are the people of this rich land robbing God? God spoke of tithes, but he also spoke of offerings—that which was freely given above and beyond the requirements of the law.

Funds for the modern missionary movement, and especially for those early missionaries sent out from American shores, primarily came from offerings. At a Boston dinner party in 1800, hosted by Mehitable Simpkins, those attending discussed the need for missionary support. Out of that discussion the germ was planted in the minds of the women present to fund missions by setting aside a penny a week out of household budgets. The word spread quickly, and within months the Massachusetts Missionary Society was deluged with pennies, and soon the concept of "mite" societies spread down the eastern seaboard. This could not be considered sacrificial giving because no household went hungry as a result. The idea was simple and easily fulfilled, and it changed the course of world evangelization.

The "mite" society may seem outdated today, but there are newer versions that could revolutionize world missions. These are versions like that of 1800 which depend on offerings above and beyond what a family regularly supports. One of these ideas has been developed by K. P. Yohannan who serves as president of Gospel for Asia—an organization that supports native evangelists who are reaching out with the gospel in their homelands.

For many years Yohannan has been deeply burdened for the lost souls in the countries of Asia where he believes Western missionaries are not the best solution to the problem. Their partnership in ministry is crucial, but in some countries they are banned and in all instances their support is far more costly financially than the support of native missionaries and evangelists. It was this concern that sparked a modern "mite" society idea in his mind with its goal for members "to lay aside $1 a day for a native evangelist." It is a plan that has been growing slowly, and "soon," he writes, "we expect to be sponsoring over 10,000 missionaries each month." That, like that early "mite" concept, may spur another revolution in world missions and continue to give donors opportunities to give to, rather than rob from, God.[23]

"I the Lord do not change. So you, O descendants of Jacob, are not destroyed. Ever since the time of your forefathers you have turned away from my decrees and have not kept them. Return to me, and I will return to you," says the Lord Almighty.

"But you ask, 'How are we to return?'

"Will a man rob God? Yet you rob me.

"But you ask, 'How do we rob you?'

"In tithes and offerings. You are under a curse—the whole nation of you—because you are robbing me. Bring the whole tithe into the storehouse, that there may be food in my house. Test me in this," says the Lord Almighty, "and see if I will not throw open the floodgates of heaven and pour out so much blessing that you will not have room enough for it."

*Malachi 3:6–10.*

# "A SPRING OF WATER WELLING UP TO ETERNAL LIFE"

"I may, I suppose, regard myself or pass for being a relatively successful man. . . . Yet I say to you—and I beg you to believe me—multiply these tiny triumphs by a million, add them all together, and they are nothing—less than nothing, a positive impediment—measured against one draught of the living water Christ offers to the spiritually thirsty, irrespective of who or what they are."

These are the words of a man once known as "one of England's great skeptics and agnostics." Indeed, "the country's once great agnostic is now the country's great believer"—Malcolm Muggeridge.

Malcolm was born on March 24, 1903, near London, "where under the upbringing of a communist father he learned to despise capitalism." After college, he accepted a teaching position in India. There he became acquainted with Mahatma Gandhi and wrote of his findings in his first book, *Young India*. Writing quickly became a tool for advancing his leftist ideology, and after he returned to England he sought to right the wrongs of society as a journalist. Indeed, so disillusioned had he become that he and his wife moved to Moscow to live in the "utopian world . . . blossoming under Stalin's control.'" He burned their passports, convinced they had found the perfect society.

Malcolm's utopian fantasy was quickly shattered under Stalin's repressive regime, and he returned to England to write and later to serve as a spy in France during World War II. Following the war, his writing career soared when he became the editor of *Punch*. This position opened the door to television, and he was soon known by millions of viewers for his insight, wit and humor. He went on to make television documentaries and write bestselling books.

How did this supremely successful man of the world find Christ? Not through a "Damascus Road" experience. "Despite an agnostic upbringing," he writes, "I can't recall a time when the notion of Christ or Christianity was not enormously appealing to me. . . . I knew from an early age, how I cannot tell, that the New Testament contained the keys to how to live. I somehow knew it to be our light in a dark world. I believed, not in my father's sense that Jesus was a good man. He was God or he was nothing." Since his conversion, Malcolm has devoted his life to sharing the Good News.[24]

"Sir," the woman said, "you have nothing to draw with and the well is deep. Where can you get this living water? Are you greater than our father Jacob, who gave us the well and drank from it himself, as did also his sons and his flocks and herds?"

Jesus answered, "Everyone who drinks this water will be thirsty again, but whoever drinks the water I give him will never thirst. Indeed, the water I give him will become in him a spring of water welling up to eternal life."

*John 4:11–14.*

# "THE PRIDE OF YOUR HEART HAS DECEIVED YOU"

God's message to Edom through the prophet, Jeremiah, is a message that prominent Christian leaders and evangelists today would do well to heed. The easy access to publicity and media attention and the rapid rise to fame that some preachers attain can be a grave danger. This is not a new concern, however. Dwight L. Moody also had the opportunity to let the pride of his heart deceive him.

Moody had good reason to boast. His sermons, published both in newspapers and books, and the biographies about him "penetrated the length and breadth of the nation." His name was known everywhere. "In log cabins of the Appalachians, in frontier wagons . . . in Texan ranches where men and women lived hard and lusty and a clergyman might be seen twice a year; in the soot and grime of Detroit or Pittsburgh or Cleveland shadowed by unemployment; in Atlantic fishing villages, southern plantations, in skid rows and millionaire avenues, Moody and Sankey were read and sung."

Without the benefit of the mass media of today, there were, not surprisingly, many imitators. "The would-be Moodys abide and abound," lamented a Methodist preacher. "Moody and Sankey Meetings are advertised, at which Moody's sermons will be read, Moody and Sankey hymnbook used, etc., then somebody dashes out like Bro. Moody, or tries to sing a solo like Bro. Sankey—perfect copyist, and always more or less a failure."

If that was not enough, some profiteers sought to hawk their wares at the very doors of Moody-Sankey meetings. "Perhaps you noticed," Moody complained to his listeners, "that there is someone at the door selling photographs of Mr. Sankey and myself. I want to say that this is one of the thorns we have in the flesh. Those are no more photographs of Mr. Sankey and myself than they are of you or anyone else. . . . And now we ask you, if you have any regard for us, not to patronize them. . . . I hope I will never have to refer to it again, for I always feel like a fool when I have to talk about myself." In those days, Moody would have had to sit for a photograph, and he refused to do that simply for the sake of boosting his own image.

He did not want attention focused on himself. He regarded himself as "only the mouthpiece and expression of a deep and mysterious wave of religious feeling now passing over the nation." To reporters he insisted that he was "the most overestimated man in America."[25]

"Now I will make you small among the nations, despised among men. The terror you inspire and the pride of your heart have deceived you, you who live in the clefts of the rocks, who occupy the heights of the hill. Though you build your nest as high as the eagle's, from there I will bring you down," declares the Lord.

*Jeremiah 49:15–16.*

# "BY THIS GOSPEL YOU ARE SAVED"

Martin Luther was a successful reformer, and his story is told in hundreds of biographies in dozens of languages. But for every Martin Luther there are countless individuals who have sought to reform the church and have failed. Their stories also need to be told.

One such individual is Søren Kierkegaard, who is known today more for his philosophical contributions than for his commitment to reform his church—the Lutheran church in Denmark. But Kierkgard was first and foremost an outspoken reformer who sought to awaken a dead church to the principles of first-century Christianity.

In a newspaper article published on March 26, 1855, he described the religious condition in Denmark—"Christianity does not exist—as almost anyone must be able to see as well as I"—and called for a return of the New Testament faith.

"We have, if you will, a complete crew of bishops, deans, and priests; learned men, eminently learned, talented, gifted, humanly well-meaning, . . . but not one of them is in the character of the Christianity of the New Testament. . . .

"We have what one might call a complete inventory of churches, bells, organs, benches, alms-boxes, foot-warmers, tables, hearses, etc. But when Christianity does not exist, the existence of this inventory, so far from being, Christianly considered, an advantage, is far rather a peril, because it is so infinitely likely to give rise to a false impression and the false inference that when we have a complete Christian inventory we must of course have Christianity, too."

Kierkegaard dedicated his life to "the reintroduction of Christianity into Christendom." He viewed himself as a missionary, called by God to reach out to a "Christian" country. But his message went largely unheard. His talents were more as a brilliant scholar and writer than a spellbinding preacher, and though he wrote twenty books during his brief life, they were not widely circulated even in Denmark. "At the time of his death (at age forty-two) he was penniless, he had exhausted his family fortune and would have faced destitution if he had lived longer." He was "an intellectual's intellectual," and "he employed that genius to help people, intellectuals and nonintellectuals, regain a sense of what human life is all about, of what it means to exist as a Christian."[26]

Now, brothers, I want to remind you of the gospel I preached to you, which you received and on which you have taken your stand. By this gospel you are saved, if you hold firmly to the word I preached to you. Otherwise you have believed in vain. . . . Come back to your senses as you ought, and stop sinning, for there are some who are ignorant of God—I say this to your shame.

*1 Corinthians 15:1–2, 34.*

# "I WILL MAKE YOU FISHERS OF MEN"

The Christian and Missionary Alliance was founded by A. B. Simpson as an agency to sponsor missionaries. As it grew across America and became a denomination, more and more missionaries were sent into the farthest corners of the earth. The most "prolific spawning ground for missionaries, pastors and teachers in the entire Alliance" was western Pennsylvania, and the individual most responsible for that zeal was an obscure layman, Edward Drury Whiteside.

Whiteside had prepared for the ministry and for a short time served in a Methodist church on Prince Edward Island, but resigned due to poor health. He went from job to job until he finally settled in Pittsburgh, where he sold insurance. "Within a few months, however, his insurance work was taking a back seat to his volunteer activities with the Sunday school and city missionary work.... His diary for 1888 reveals that in one year he made personal visits in more than 5,000 homes. That amounts to more than thirteen calls a day in addition to his gainful employment."

As he met people in his visitation ministry, Whiteside was always thinking of possible recruits for foreign missionary service who could become fishers of men. Soon he had five young men enrolled in the missions course at Simpson's New York Missionary Training Institute. As Whiteside worked with laymen, he increasingly gave them more responsibilities "until the only alternatives were to enter the ministry full-time or go back into business."

In 1894, Simpson traveled to Pittsburgh to officially establish a branch of the Alliance, at which time Whiteside was elected superintendent of the branch. "Knowing my unfitness for such a responsibility," he recalled, "I nervously exclaimed, 'Don't make me superintendent; elect some other man and I will run his errands for him.' ... I was downright in earnest and turned to God and honestly and urgently said, 'O Lord, I appoint You as Superintendent of the Pittsburgh branch of the Alliance, and I will run errands for you.' I had wonderful relief in my soul that moment and have had ever since."

Pittsburgh became his mission field for the next forty years. "But not for one moment did Whiteside forget that he was to evangelize 'Judea.' Long before suburbs became the concern of city planners, Whiteside was busy setting up cottage prayer meetings and evangelistic campaigns in the towns and villages within a 50-mile radius of Pittsburgh." His goal was always to win lost souls for Christ and turn them into fishers of men—to reach out worldwide with the gospel.[27]

As Jesus was walking beside the Sea of Galilee, he saw two brothers, Simon called Peter and his brother Andrew. They were casting a net into the lake, for they were fishermen. "Come, follow me," Jesus said, "and I will make you fishers of men." At once they left their nets and followed him.

*Matthew 4:18–20.*

# "AS YOU HELP US BY YOUR PRAYERS"

Missionaries from the time of the apostle Paul have endured hardships—hardships that sometimes caused them to despair of their very lives. In these circumstances they have depended on the prayers of others to carry them through. This was remarkably true in the life of J. Hudson Taylor.

Prayer encompassed Taylor throughout his entire life. Indeed, his parents dedicated him to China before he was born, and it was while his mother was spending an afternoon on her knees in prayer for him, while out of town, that he committed his life to Christ. His own call to China was influenced by his father's oft-repeated prayers for the people of that vast nation. Before sailing to China as a young man, he made a solemn pledge: "When I get to China, I shall have no claim on anyone for anything; my only claim will be on God. How important, therefore, to learn before leaving England to move man, through God, by prayer alone."

But Taylor did not depend only on his own prayers. Two decades after he arrived in China he wrote to his mother of his spiritual struggles: "I have often asked you to remember me in prayer. . . . That need has never been greater than at the present. . . . I cannot tell you how much I am buffeted sometimes by temptations. . . . Often I am tempted to think that one so full of sin cannot be a child of God at all. . . . Do pray for me. Pray that the Lord will keep me from sin, will sanctify me wholly, will use me more largely in his service."

Taylor's evangelistic success was due to prayer—his own prayers and the prayers of his loved ones back home. On one occasion, while passing through Taiping, he was deeply burdened for the masses of people who filled the streets on that market day. "We did little preaching," he wrote, "but I was constrained to retire to the city wall and cry to God to have mercy on the people, to open their hearts and give us an entrance among them." God answered that prayer immediately: "Without any seeking on our part, we were brought into touch with at least four anxious souls."

But there were times when even Taylor was unable to pray. He confessed this when he heard the shocking news of the Boxer Rebellion—a uprising that brutally claimed the lives of scores of missionaries. The news was almost more than he could bear. "I cannot read," he wrote, "I cannot pray, I can scarcely even think— but I can trust." Even when this man of prayer was at his lowest point, he could still trust in God's faithfulness.[28]

We do not want you to be uninformed, brothers, about the hardships we suffered in the province of Asia. We were under great pressure, far beyond our ability to endure, so that we despaired even of life. Indeed, in our hearts we felt the sentence of death. But this happened that we might not rely on ourselves but on God, who raises the dead. He has delivered us from such a deadly peril, and he will deliver us. On him we have set our hope that he will continue to deliver us, as you help us by your prayers. Then many will give thanks on our behalf for the gracious favor granted us in answer to the prayers of many.

*2 Corinthians 1:8–11.*

# "MARY HAS CHOSEN WHAT IS BETTER"

The priorities we set in our daily lives indicate a great deal about what we hold most dear. Unfortunately, we frequently make decisions based on what is most pressing at the moment. Jesus made it very clear to Martha that meal preparation, which seemed very important to her at the moment, did not offer eternal values in comparison to Mary's choice to learn at his feet. Mary had made a conscious choice for the better use of her time, and it was something that could not be taken away from her.

Charles Haddon Spurgeon, the great nineteenth-century Baptist preacher from England, was a child prodigy in the eyes of many people. He was only eighteen years old when he received an invitation to be a pastoral candidate at the New Park Street Chapel in London, a large prestigious church that had tired of the philosophical and dry sermons of the other candidates who had been rejected.

Spurgeon at first believed the letter of invitation had been sent to the wrong person, but when he was assured it was not, he agreed to come. "The effect was amazing," wrote an observer. "After the service people too excited to leave the building gathered in groups talking about securing him for pastor." He was called, and soon began his long and much publicized career in the gospel ministry.

As young as he was, however, it is important to note that Spurgeon spent many years in preparation for the thrust he made into pastoral ministry as a teenager. Very early in life he began making important choices. Instead of playing frivolously, he read books—life-changing books such as *Pilgrim's Progress* and *Foxe's Book of Martyrs*, and he chose eternal values over money-making opportunities. Later he related that when his grandmother offered him a penny apiece for every one of Isaac Watts' hymns he memorized, he responded so well that she "reduced the bonus to a half-penny, then to a farthing, to keep from being quite ruined in the deal." Despite the low reward, young Spurgeon continued his memorization and resisted the temptation to focus on other things, even after his grandfather offered him a shilling for every dozen rats he could kill around the house. "I found rat-catching paid me better than learning hymns," he later reflected, "but I know now which employment has been more permanently profitable."[29]

As Jesus and his disciples were on their way, he came to a village where a woman named Martha opened her home to him. She had a sister called Mary, who sat at the Lord's feet listening to what he said. But Martha was distracted by all the preparations that had to be made. She came to him and asked, "Lord, don't you care that my sister has left me to do the work by myself? Tell her to help me!"

"Martha, Martha," the Lord answered, "you are worried and upset about many things, but only one thing is needed. Mary has chosen what is better, and it will not be taken away from her."

*Luke 10:38–42.*

# "WORSHIP THE LORD YOUR GOD AND SERVE HIM ONLY"

The temptation Jesus endured for forty days in the desert was far beyond what humans can comprehend, but Christians today do face severe temptations at times that call for the same response that Jesus gave to the devil: "Worship the Lord your God and serve him only." Amy Carmichael, who gave her life to children's work in India, testified to this.

Amy's first missionary experience was in Japan, and it was there, in the midst of loneliness and distress, that she endured a very difficult time of testing as she thought about being single all of her life. It was a very personal and private episode in her life, one she later, reluctantly, shared with some of her close associates.

"On this day many years ago I went away alone to a cave in the mountain called Arima. I had feelings of fear about the future. That was why I went there—to be alone with God. The devil kept on whispering, 'It's all right now, but what about afterwards? You are going to be very lonely.' And he painted pictures of loneliness—I can see them still. And I turned to my God in a kind of desperation and said, 'Lord, what can I do? How can I go on to the end?' And He said, 'None of them that trust in Me shall be desolate.' That word has been with me ever since. It has been fulfilled to me. It will be fulfilled to you."

From that point on Amy realized that God could fully meet her needs, and it was that attitude that paved the way for her very fruitful ministry with hundreds of children whom she rescued from temple prostitution. The success of her work depended heavily on national women who would devote their lives to the children's ministry that became known as Dohnavur Fellowship.

Devoted, single-minded service is what Amy required of her associates. In fact, she formed a religious order of sorts to accommodate these women— Sisters of the Common Life. The women were not compelled to take vows, but should they marry they automatically revoked their status in the sisterhood. Amy herself had committed her life to celibacy by overcoming the temptation she confronted early in life, and she expected those who lived and worked with her to do the same.[30]

**The devil said to him, "If you are the Son of God, tell this stone to become bread."**

**Jesus answered, "It is written: 'Man does not live on bread alone.'"**

**The devil led him up to a high place and showed him in an instant all the kingdoms of the world. And he said to him, "I will give you all their authority and splendor, for it has been given to me, and I can give it to anyone I want to. So if you worship me, it will all be yours."**

**Jesus answered, "It is written: 'Worship the Lord your God and serve him only.'"**

*Luke 4:3–8.*

## "INHERIT A THRONE OF HONOR"

Lillian and Jim Dickson pioneered missionary work among the mountain people of Formosa (present-day Taiwan), but in their ministry they were heavily dependent upon national Christians. They were pleased with the enthusiasm of these uneducated and lowly people, but sometimes they were wary about God's ability to "raise the poor from the dust and lift the needy from the ash heap."

Nevertheless it was through the ministry of a humble native woman that the work among the tribal peoples was initiated. "One day," wrote Lillian, "my husband came back from the far East Coast and about twenty feet behind him trailed a barbaric-looking woman. She had heavy tattooing across her whole face—a wide band from ear to ear which gave her a fierce expression."

She was the first believer in the head-hunting Tyal tribe, and when Jim informed Lillian that he had brought her to be enrolled in the Bible School, she scoffed at the idea, insisting the woman was too old. "But he was right and I was wrong," Lillian confessed, "for this was Chi-oang, who later was to start an underground movement of Christianity among the people of the hills and lead a thousand souls to Christ."

Chi-oang's ministry had an amazing effect that was later referred to as "The Pentecost of the Hills." Lillian described the impact this had on their lives and ministry: "Up the wild mountain regions where 'foreigners' had not been allowed to go during the time Japan ruled Formosa, now the missionary went, filled with overwhelming gratitude and wonder at what God had wrought. He found whole villages converted, all the people Christians and often a little church built in the middle of the village as their place to worship God. He found more than a dozen such churches in the mountains. Always he would ask the people there, 'Who brought you the news of the Gospel?'"

Often they would say, " 'Chi-oang came bringing us the story of the one true God and the Saviour whom He sent.'. . . In 1946, right after the end of the war, there were four thousand believers among the Tyals. They came down the mountains by hundreds, knocking at the doors of the little Formosan Chinese churches scattered along the foot of the mountains, asking to be prepared for baptism."

By accepting Jesus, the poor and needy indeed had inherited "a throne of honor."[31]

"The Lord brings death and makes alive; he brings down to the grave and rises up. The Lord sends poverty and wealth; he humbles and he exalts. He raises the poor from the dust and lifts the needy from the ash heap; he seats them with princes and has them inherit a throne of honor. For the foundations of the earth are the Lord's; upon them he has set the world."

*1 Samuel 2:6–8.*

# "A WITNESS—NOT A DEFENSE LAWYER—FOR GOD"

E. Stanley Jones, the great Methodist missionary to India who wrote such classics as *The Christ of the Indian Road*, tells about an experience early in his ministry that changed the course of his life. It was then that he began to understand what his role was as a follower of Christ. The occasion was his first public sermon in a small church that was filled, mainly, with his relatives. They were naturally eager for him to shine.

It was a momentous occasion for him. "I had prepared for three weeks, for I was to be God's lawyer and argue His case well. I started on rather a high key and after a half dozen sentences used a word that I never used before and I have never used since: indifferentism. Whereupon a college girl smiled and put down her head." With that, the preacher lost his train of thought. "My mind was an absolute blank. I stood there clutching for something to say. Finally I blurted out: 'I'm very sorry, but I have forgotten my sermon,' and I started for my seat in shame and confusion."

For a moment, Jones's plans for ministry seemed to fade, but then something happened. "As I was about to sit down, the Inner Voice said: 'Haven't I done anything for you? If so, couldn't you tell that?' I responded to this suggestion and stepped down in front of the pulpit—I felt I didn't belong behind it—and said, 'Friends, I see I can't preach, but you know what Christ has done for my life, how He has changed me, and though I cannot preach I shall be his witness the rest of my days.'"

It was through his failure that Jones learned a profound lesson and realized he could be effectively used by God. "At the close a youth came up to me and said he wanted what I had found. It was a mystery to me then, and it is a mystery to me now that, amid my failure that night, he still saw something he wanted. As he and I knelt together he found it. It marked a profound change in his life, and today he is a pastor, and a daughter is a missionary in Africa."

Jones later summed up the lesson God had taught him. "As God's lawyer I was a dead failure; as God's witness I was a success. That night marked a change in my conception of the work of the Christian minister—he is to be, not God's lawyer to argue well for God; but he is to be God's witness, to tell what Grace has done for an unworthy life."[1]

We accept man's testimony, but God's testimony is greater because it is the testimony of God, which he has given about his Son. Anyone who believes in the Son of God has this testimony in his heart. Anyone who does not believe God has made him out to be a liar, because he has not believed the testimony God has given about his Son. And this is the testimony: God has given us eternal life, and this life is in his Son. He who has the Son has life; he who does not have the Son of God does not have life.

*1 John 5:9–12.*

# "REMEMBER YOUR CREATOR IN THE DAYS OF YOUTH"

This passage that speaks of the time "when the keepers of the house tremble," and "when men rise up at the sound of birds, but all their songs grow faint" illustrates well the conversion of Adoniram Judson. He would become one of most revered missionaries in the Christian church, remembered for his sacrificial pioneer work in Burma. But had he not remembered his Creator in the days of his youth, he might have pursued a secular career and been altogether lost in history.

Judson was born in Massachusetts in 1788, the son of a Congregational minister. He was a brilliant child who entered Brown University at the age of sixteen and graduated three years later as valedictorian. One of his best friends in college was Jacob Eames, a deist who scoffed at the idea of a personal God. Judson was deeply influenced by him, and when he returned home after graduation, turned his back on his childhood faith.

Dissatisfied with life in small town New England, Judson soon set off for New York where he hoped to become a playwright. Here he roamed the streets, living "a reckless, vagabond life, finding lodgings where he could," and "bilking the landlord." He quickly found that New York was no place for a stranger without professional contacts.

Discouraged, he headed toward home, thinking he would stay with an uncle for a time. On his way, he stopped one evening at a small village inn. He was discouraged and tired. But as weary as he was he could not sleep. In a room down the hall, he could hear the moaning of a sick man, and voices of people going in and out of his room.

"What disturbed him," his biographer writes, "was the thought that the man in the next room might not be prepared for death. Was he, himself? A confusing coil of speculation unwound itself as he lay half dreaming, half waking, while the autumn chill stole down from the mountains and crept through every crack and cranny of the house. He wondered how he himself would face death. . .

"When Adoniram woke the sun was streaming in the window. His apprehensions had vanished with the darkness. He could hardly believe he had given in to such weakness." He was not prepared for the news he was about to hear. On his way out of the inn, he inquired about the sick man. He was shocked to learn that the man died, but even more stunned when he found that man was Jacob Eames, his unbelieving college friend. It was a powerful incident—one that changed the course of his life.[2]

Remember your Creator in the days of your youth, before the days of trouble come and the years approach when you will say, "I find no pleasure in them"—before the sun and the light and the moon and the stars grow dark, and the clouds return after the rain; when the keepers of the house tremble, and the strong men stoop, when the grinders cease because they are few, and those looking through the windows grow dim; when the doors to the street are closed and the sound of grinding fades; when men rise up at the sound of birds, but all their songs grow faint.

*Ecclesiastes 12:1–4.*

# "GO AND MAKE DISCIPLES OF ALL NATIONS"

One of the greatest missionary hymns of all times was first written as a poem to be incorporated into a sermon. Reginald Heber was visiting his father-in-law, who was to preach a sermon the next day to help promote the Church Missionary Society, an Anglican mission agency that had been formed some years earlier. The older man asked his son-in-law to write something appropriate, knowing of his gift for writing poetry.

After spending some time alone, Heber wrote these words that express so deeply the message of the great commission:

> From Greenland's icy mountains,
> From India's coral strand,
> Where Afric's sunny fountains
> Roll down their golden sand,
> From many an ancient river,
> From many a palmy plain,
> They call us to deliver
> Their land from error's chain.

As he penned those lines, Heber could not have imagined that one day he himself would become the missionary Bishop of Calcutta, serving in India and Ceylon—both of which are mentioned in the four verses of the poem. As Bishop of Calcutta he served tirelessly for three years. Among his accomplishments was the ordination of the first native Anglican minister. But the exhausting pace and the inhospitable climate took a toll on his health, he died on April 3, 1829, only days before his forty-fourth birthday. He was buried in St. John's Church at Trichinopoly, where a vast crowd of Christians joined in singing another poem that he had written: "Holy! Holy! Holy! Lord God Almighty!"

The hymn "From Greenland's Icy Mountains" might have been lost to history had not another minister later discovered it among some waste papers of a blacksmith near his hometown. The minister made copies and distributed them. Later a copy fell into the hands of a woman from Georgia. She passed it along to Lowell Mason, America's great hymn composer, who put the words to music.

Heber's commitment to missions is concisely summed up in the third verse: "Salvation! O salvation! The joyful sound proclaim, Till earth's remotest nation Has learned Messiah's name."[3]

**Then Jesus came to them and said, "All authority in heaven and on earth has been given to me. Therefore go and make disciples of all nations, baptizing them in the name of the Father and of the Son and of the Holy Spirit, and teaching them to obey everything I have commanded you. And surely I am with you always, to the very end of the age."**

*Matthew 28:18–20.*

# "THEY FORCED HIM TO CARRY THE CROSS"

The Wesleyan revival that changed the face of England in the eighteenth century was followed by a revival in the Anglican church. An extraordinary leader of this revival was Charles Simeon, who, according to one observer, was "more powerful in the English Church than any primate and his sway extended to the remotest corner of England."

Simeon was converted during Easter week of 1779, while he was a student at Cambridge University. He was reading Scripture and suddenly was stirred by the certainty that Jesus died for his sins so that he would have to bear them no more. "Accordingly," he wrote, "I sought to lay my sins upon the sacred head of Jesus and on Wednesday began to have a hope of mercy; on the Thursday that hope increased; on the Friday and Saturday it became more strong; and on Sunday morning, Easter day, April 4, I awoke with the words upon my heart and lips: 'Jesus Christ is risen today. Hallelujah!' From that hour peace flowed in rich abundance in my soul."

Simeon immediately confronted opposition and ridicule. He had been assigned to served as rector of the Church of the Holy Trinity in Cambridge, and was immediately scorned by most of the parishioners—so much so that they "refused to go to hear him and locked the pew doors to keep out other worshipers." Students at the university scoffed at him, and his faithful followers were called the "Sims."

On one occasion, he later recalled, "I strolled forth one day, buffeted and afflicted, with my little Testament in my hand. I prayed earnestly to my God that He would comfort me . . . from His Word and that, on opening the Book, I should find some text which should sustain me. The first which caught my eye was this 'They found a man of Cyrene, Simon by name; him they compelled to bear the cross' (KJV). You know Simon is the same name as Simeon. What a word of instruction was here, a blessed hint for my encouragement! To have the cross laid upon me that I might bear it after Jesus. What a privilege!"

In the twenty-five years that followed, Simeon traveled around preaching the gospel in Anglican parishes; he was sometimes banned from areas because of the revival that followed his ministry. His influence was felt worldwide, especially the help he gave in founding the Church Missionary Society, which was a major force in world evangelization during the nineteenth century.[4]

As they were going out, they met a man from Cyrene, named Simon, and they forced him to carry the cross. They came to a place called Golgotha (which means The Place of the Skull). There they offered Jesus wine to drink, mixed with gall; but after tasting it, he refused to drink it. When they had crucified him, they divided up his clothes by casting lots.

*Matthew 27:32–35.*

## "WHAT IS THAT IN YOUR HAND?"

Jake DeShazer was a military pilot during World War II. He took part in an operation known as the "Doolittle Raid" that was designed both as a retaliatory measure following Pearl Harbor and as an offensive against Japanese forces in the Pacific. Even though the mission was highly classified, it could not proceed as planned. The aircraft carrier was sighted by the Japanese before it reached the location from which the pilots were to take off. Jake and the other pilots immediately were ordered to carry out their bombing missions, even though they did not have enough fuel to return to safety. Soon after he completed his bombing mission, in the black of night, with the fuel gone, Jake was forced to abandon the bomber and parachute to the unknown expanse below. He was in China, in Japanese-controlled territory, and for the next three years he was kept in isolation in a Japanese internment camp.

It was in that camp that Jake acquired a Bible, and with nothing else to do, read it intently. With little hope of being rescued or saved from his captors, he read in Romans 10 that he would be saved for eternity if he confessed Christ and believed in his heart that God had raised him from the dead. Jake's life was transformed in that rat-infested prison.

Prior to his release in 1945, he became very ill. "Boils, big ugly boils, broke out all over my body . . . even on the bottoms of my feet." In despair, he writes, "One day I raised up my hands and said, 'Lord, I'm ready to go. I want to be up there where there are pleasures for evermore and no boils or sickness." But Jake sensed God looking at his hands. "It was so clear to me. My hands were up in the air and he was looking at my hands, and I didn't have anything in them. I wondered, 'Why are my hands so empty? Why is he looking at my hands?' Then it hit me. I was 33 years old and not one single soul had ever been influenced for Christ by me."

The realization that he had nothing in his hands prompted Jake to return to Japan as a missionary after his release and Bible college training. He spent thirty years reaching out with the gospel to the people he had once bombed, helping to plant more than twenty churches and speaking to crowds of thousands who wanted to hear the message of this unusual man. When his work was finished, Jake had something in his hands for God, but like Moses generations before him, he knew that his speaking depended on God. He said, "You present the Gospel the best way you know how and then you thank the Lord for each one who comes."[5]

Moses answered, "What if they do not believe me or listen to me and say, 'The Lord did not appear to you'?"

Then the Lord said to him, "What is that in your hand?"

"A staff," he replied.

The Lord said, "Throw it on the ground."

Moses threw it on the ground and it became a snake, and he ran from it. Then the Lord said to him, "Reach out your hand and take it by the tail." So Moses reached out and took hold of the snake and it turned back into a staff in his hand. "This," said the Lord, "is so that they may believe that the Lord, the God of their fathers—the God of Abraham, the God of Isaac and the God of Jacob—has appeared to you."

*Exodus 4:1–5.*

# "DO YOU TRULY LOVE ME MORE THAN THESE?"

Jesus' question, "Do you truly love me more than these?" is a question that faces all Christians, especially as they think of the sacrifice that often is required when one follows Jesus Christ. This was a question that Irene Webster-Smith had to face as she considered ministry in Japan. Indeed, the question came to her as a young child growing up in Dublin, before her conversion. She was lingering after an evangelistic meeting as she later related. "I felt conspicuous, because I had a feather on my hat. A lady said to me, 'Are you saved?' and before I could answer, she looked at the feather and added, 'I can see that you're not.'"

Despite such inconsiderate treatment, Irene was forced to determine what it was she really loved. She was converted that night—through the counsel of a more compassionate woman. As a young woman, she felt called to Japan to reach out with the gospel to geisha girls, but again she had to consider her love for God and her other priorities. Her sickly mother pleaded with her to stay home. It was a difficult decision, but Irene stayed with her until she died of cancer some time later.

Once in Japan, Irene again struggled with where her love would be focused. God had given her an effective ministry, but back home was Al, a young minister whom she had promised to marry. She did visit home for a time, but returned to Japan knowing that was where God wanted her. Once again she bade farewell to her fiancé . She returned the engagement ring, but he gave her another with the engraving, "The Lord watch between me and thee while we are absent one from the other." It was a difficult departure.

Again Irene served faithfully by caring for abandoned babies and girls. She continued to correspond with Al, and when she was forced to evacuate Japan in 1940, she believed this was God's indication that she could now become Al's wife. He was then living in New Jersey, and she came to America to join him. Before they were reunited, however, she was called to work among the Japanese Americans who had been forced into internment camps. Soon after, word came that Al had died of pneumonia.

Following the war Irene ("Sensei," as she was called) returned to Japan—destined to be the first missionary General Douglas MacArthur called back to that devastated land because of her extraordinary work there.[6]

When they had finished eating, Jesus said to Simon Peter, "Simon son of John, do you truly love me more than these?"

"Yes, Lord," he said, "you know that I love you."

Jesus said, "Feed my lambs."

Again Jesus said, "Simon son of John, do you truly love me?"

He answered, "Yes, Lord, you know that I love you."

Jesus said, "Take care of my sheep."

The third time he said to him, "Simon son of John do you love me?"

Peter was hurt because Jesus asked him the third time, "Do you love me?" He said, "Lord, you know all things; you know that I love you."

Jesus said, "Feed my sheep."

*John 21:15–17.*

## "PREACHING THE WORD WHEREVER THEY WENT"

The response to Acts 1:8 was Acts 8:1. In Acts 1:8 we read, "But you will receive power when the Holy Spirit comes on you; and you will be my witnesses in Jerusalem, and in all Judea and Samaria, and to the ends of the earth." But it was not until the martyrdom of Stephen and the persecution that followed that the early Christians spread out with the message. It was then that the growing church spilled out into the cities and towns and countryside beyond Jerusalem.

Today in the North Indian state of Rajasthan, a similar situation is developing. In the past there has been terrible persecution of Christians, and some have been martyred for the faith. But despite this persecution—and indeed because of it—there is a renewed commitment to spread out to reach others with the gospel.

"Typical of the many native missionary movements that have sprung up overnight is the work in the Punjab of P. G. Vargis and his wife, Lilly. A former military officer who gave up a commission and army career to help start a gospel team, he now leads 349 full-time missionaries." The work involves both evangelism and church planting. During one missionary journey to Maharashtra State, forty-two new churches were planted in twelve days.

"Vargis and his wife set an apostolic pattern for their workers similar to that of the apostle Paul. On one evangelistic tour that lasted 53 days, he and his family traveled by bullock cart and foot into some of the most backward areas of the tribal districts of Orissa State. There, working in the intense heat among people whose lifestyle is so primitive that it can be described only as 'animalistic,' he saw hundreds converted. Throughout the journey, demons were cast out and miraculous physical healings took place daily. . . .

"In just one month, he formed 15 groups of converts into new churches and assigned native missionaries to stay behind and build them up in the faith."[7]

On that day a great persecution broke out against the church at Jerusalem, and all except the apostles were scattered throughout Judea and Samaria. Godly men buried Stephen and mourned deeply for him. But Saul began to destroy the church. Going from house to house, he dragged off men and women and put them in prison.

Those who had been scattered preached the word wherever they went. Philip went down to a city in Samaria and proclaimed the Christ there. When the crowds heard Philip and saw the miraculous signs he did, they all paid close attention to what he said. With shrieks, evil spirits came out of many, and many paralytics and cripples were healed. So there was great joy in that city.

*Acts 8:1b–8.*

# "PARTICIPATE IN THE SUFFERINGS OF CHRIST"

As the pastor of the largest Baptist church in Romania, Josef Tson was regarded a nuisance and a threat to the repressive Communist regime in that country. In 1973, he published a document that delineated point by point how, in light of the constitution, Romanian authorities were illegally obstructing religious freedom. So angered were government officials by the audacity of this Christian minister that they began a prolonged attempt to break him through persecution and harassment.

The government's campaign began in October of 1974, when six senior officers officially indicted Tson for "propaganda that endangers the security of the state." After that initial meeting, when they realized that he was not about to recant what he had written, they took further steps to silence him. Later he testified: "They immediately consigned me to six months of interrogation, five days a week, sometimes up to 10 hours a day. . . . The interrogator has his special tools: arrogance, mockery, threats, guile, lies and force. I went into my questioning believing those were Satan's tools, and I should not use the weapons of my adversary. Instead, I had my Master's tools: trust in God, love, joy, truth, and self-sacrifice."

On one occasion when Tson was being beaten, he began screaming—mainly for effect, because he knew that his rights were being violated, and he wanted others to witness what was happening to him. The next time he met with the interrogator he apologized and explained to the puzzled official that the beating had occurred during holy week, and why therefore he felt an apology was in order: "Well, sir, for a Christian, nothing is more beautiful than to suffer during the time his Savior and Lord suffered. When you beat me, you did me a great honor. I am sorry for shouting at you. I should have thanked you for the most beautiful gift you could ever have given me. Since Tuesday I have been praying for you and your family."

Later, when threatened with torture and death, Tson had a ready response for his adversaries: "Your supreme weapon is killing. My supreme weapon is dying. Here is how it works. You know that my sermons on tape have spread all over the country. If you kill me, these sermons will be sprinkled with my blood. Everyone will know I died for my preaching. . . . So, sir, my sermons will speak 10 times louder than before. I will actually rejoice in this supreme victory if you kill me."

In 1981, Ison was exiled from Romania. He has since served the Romanian church from the outside through the Romanian Missionary Society.[8]

Dear friends, do not be surprised at the painful trial you are suffering, as though something strange were happening to you. But rejoice that you participate in the sufferings of Christ, so that you may be overjoyed when his glory is revealed. If you are insulted because of the name of Christ, you are blessed, for the Spirit of glory and of God rests on you.

*1 Peter 4:12–14.*

# "THE JUST SHALL LIVE BY FAITH"

This passage from the book of Romans transformed Martin Luther's life. As a monk living an ascetic life in an Augustinian monastery, he was determined to live an utterly holy and self-denying life. "He fasted, sometimes three days on end without a crumb. . . . He laid upon himself vigils and prayers in excess of those stipulated by the rule. He cast off the blankets permitted him and well-nigh froze himself to death."

He went to confession daily, sometimes spending as much as six hours wearying his confessor with every possible sin he might ever have committed. When visiting Rome, Luther climbed "Pilate's stairs on hands and knees repeating a *Pater Noster* for each one and kissing each step for good measure in the hope of delivering a soul from purgatory." In everything he did or thought, he was seeking to work his way out of purgatory and into heaven.

He later reflected on this early religious commitment: "I was a good monk, and I kept the rule of my order so strictly that I may say that if ever a monk got to heaven by his monkery it was I."

It was not until he began reading and lecturing on books of the Bible Luther began to see that his works were not pleasing to God. His study of Paul's epistle to the Romans—in the Greek—challenged him in areas of his thinking that were utterly new to him, as he himself later related.

"I greatly longed to understand Paul's Epistle to the Romans and nothing stood in the way but that one expression, 'the justice of God,' because I took it to mean that justice whereby God is just and deals justly in punishing the unjust. My situation was that, although an impeccable monk, I stood before God as a sinner troubled in conscience, and I had no confidence that my merit would assuage him. Therefore I did not love a just and angry God, but rather hated and murmured against him. Yet I clung to the dear Paul and had a great yearning to know what he meant.

"Night and day I pondered until I saw the connection between the justice of God and the statement that 'the just shall live by his faith.' Then I grasped that the justice of God is that righteousness by which through grace and sheer mercy God justifies us through faith. Thereupon I felt myself to be reborn and to have gone through open doors into paradise. The whole Scripture took on a new meaning, and whereas before the 'justice of God' had filled me with hate, now it became to me inexpressibly sweet in greater love. This passage of Paul became to me a gate to heaven."[9]

I am not ashamed of the gospel, because it is the power of God for the salvation of everyone who believes: first for the Jew, then for the Gentile. For in the gospel a righteousness from God is revealed, a righteousness that is by faith from first to last, just as it is written: "The righteous will live by faith."

*Romans 1:16–17.*

## "WHEN I CALL, ANSWER ME QUICKLY"

Spending time in prayer each day is a discipline that is often difficult to maintain, and missionaries sometimes struggle more with time pressures than do Christians who are not involved in full-time ministry. Carie Sydenstricker found this to be true during her years in China. She was a busy mother who prayed swiftly, and could have identified with the prayer of the psalmist, "When I call, answer me quickly."

Carie would have been lost in obscurity as so many other missionary women have been had it not been for her biographer—her illustrious daughter, the Nobel and Pulitzer Prize winning novelist Pearl S. Buck. From the beginning, Carie had mixed emotions about spending her life and raising her children in China. She had lost three little ones and feared for her other children.

Although she faithfully ministered among the Chinese women, Carrie struggled in her own spiritual life. "Deep down under all the fullness of her life, Carie felt at times still the inadequacy of her relation to God. She planned sometimes for a period when she would withdraw and really seek to find what she needed. She planned to read her Bible more and pray more and try to be 'good.'"

Her prayer life is graphically contrasted to her husband's in a story from Pearl Buck's own experience. She asked her mother one morning after breakfast, "What makes the red marks on Father's forehead?"

"They are marks from his fingers where he leans his head on his hand to pray," Carie answered soberly. "Your father prays for a whole hour every morning when he gets up."

Such holiness was awe-inspiring. The children looked for like marks of it on their mother's forehead, and one asked, 'why don't you pray, too, Mother?'

"Carie answered—was it with a trifle of sharpness?—'If I did, who would dress you all and get breakfast and clean house and teach you your lessons? Some have to work, I suppose, while some pray.'

"Andrew came out of his habitual abstraction long enough to overhear this, and to remark gently, 'if you took a little more time for prayer, Carie, perhaps the work would go better.'

"To which Carie replied with considerable obstinacy, 'There isn't but so much time and the Lord will just have to understand that a mother with little children has to condense her prayers.'

"The truth of it was that Carie was not very good at long prayers. She prayed hard and swiftly at times, but she prayed as she worked, and she was always perhaps a little conscious against her will that her voice seemed to go up and come back to her without surety of reply."[10]

**Hear my prayer, O Lord; let my cry for help come to you. Do not hide your face from me when I am in distress. Turn your ear to me; when I call, answer me quickly.**

*Psalm 102:1–2.*

# "SOWING IN TEARS AND REAPING WITH SONGS OF JOY"

The ministry of an evangelist is not only to be God's conduit to convert unbelievers to faith in Christ but also to reclaim believers who have backslidden in the faith. Indeed, the latter is often the most difficult and rewarding task: one of utter dependence on God, as the psalmist expressed, to restore our fortunes like streams in the desert, so that they who sow in tears will reap with songs of joy.

When Noriko Suzuki, a young Japanese woman, began her missionary work with the Eskimos in Northern Canada in 1977, she discovered that the ministry of evangelism was often a discouraging one. Indeed, many times she felt her efforts were fruitless and that she was wasting her time. People were converted, but they often reverted back to their old ways. This was true of Arik Sapa, a young man whom she met when she was making a trip to ten villages in the Ungava Peninsula to distribute Eskimo New Testaments.

Arik had a wife and children whom he had abandoned in a village three hundred miles further north, where he had been employed as a social worker. He had been expelled from that village when it was learned that he was using drugs, and so he returned to his home village to live with his parents. It was there, while staying in his parent's home, that Noriko first met him. She spent time with him, counseling him and seeking to dissuade him from going through with his planned divorce. When she left, she promised she would pray for him every day, but once again it seemed as though she was only sowing with tears.

Six months later, however, she received her "song of joy" in the form of a letter from Arik: "Dear Noriko, Praise the Lord! I came back to Lucy and my children this month. Thank you very much for your prayer every day. The books you have given are very helpful and encourage us. Lucy and I are reading them every day. Please come see us someday. People here will buy Eskimo New Testaments. . . . People in this village have received me like their friend again. So we are praising God. Thank you for being a true friend to me and for your understanding. . . . You are a special woman and a special friend to us. God has really chosen you to help people."

Noriko wrote to her supporting churches back home in Japan, and told them about Arik's letter and the effect it had on her: "I felt that the hardship in ten years seemed to fly away. 'Those who sow in tears will reap with songs of joy.' "[11]

**The Lord has done great things for us, and we are filled with joy.**

**Restore our fortunes, O Lord, like streams in the Negev. Those who sow in tears will reap with songs of joy. He who goes out weeping, carrying seed to sow, will return with songs of joy, carrying sheaves with him.**

*Psalm 126:3–6.*

# "FROM NOW ON YOU WILL CATCH MEN"

Cicero, Illinois was never the same after William McCarrell accepted a call in 1913 to a tiny Congregational church of thirty-five people—for a salary of five dollars a week. "Located in tough, gangland Cicero, he began to win souls both by personal work and pulpit evangelism." The church became known as the Cicero Bible Church, and in the decades that followed it became a landmark for outreach into the surrounding communities.

Under McCarrel's leadership, the church spawned more than a dozen other churches, sent missionaries around the world, was a pioneer in gospel radio, and operated a bookstore and press. It was also "the home of the famed Cicero Fishermen's Club, founded and nurtured by Dr. McCarrell."

The club was organized in 1923, and after three decades of outreach it reported 129,422 professions of faith through the outreach of its members. Membership in the club depended on meeting seven requirements: soundness of faith, absence of any "hobby," good common sense, a personal testimony, a consistent life, a passion for souls, and First Corinthians 13 (love).

At the weekly club meeting, members gave testimonies of conversions, and each member was expected to report on his witnessing involvement for the previous week—such as tract distribution. "When McCarrell calls for a report of tracts passed out in the past week," an observer reported, "answers of '40,' '60,' '20,' and '500,' may come from various parts of the room. Throw in an extra 500 for myself. Some of you fellows must be slipping. Are you going to let an old man like me best you?' he rejoins."

In addition to individual witnessing, the club conducted meetings in such facilities as hospitals, schools, prisons, nursing homes, and military bases—sometimes traveling hundreds of miles to take part in a particular ministry. Behind all these activities was the five-foot-four-inch, one-hundred-sixty pound, energetic Irishman, known as the "Big Fisherman," whose pockets were "always bulging with so many tracts and Gospels that he could hardly keep his clothes in press."

"Jesus said, 'Follow me, and I will make you fishers of men' (Matt 4:19). How can we keep on following unless we keep on fishing?"[12]

When Simon Peter saw this, he fell at Jesus' knees and said, "Go away from me, Lord; I am a sinful man!" For he and all his companions were astonished at the catch of fish they had taken, and so were James and John, the sons of Zebedee, Simon's partners.

Then Jesus said to Simon, "Don't be afraid; from now on you will catch men." So they pulled their boats up on the shore, left everything and followed him.

*Luke 5:8–11.*

# "LOVE IS AS STRONG AS DEATH"

Donald McClure, a great twentieth-century pioneer [to unreached] peoples in Africa, tells the [story of a boy] named Omot whom he had come to [love in his m]inistry among the Anuaks of Sudan. [Omot was one] of the boys who attended Don's mission school. He was faithful in his attendance and enjoyed the fellowship of the other children, but was simply unable to learn. Finally, Don broke the news to him one day that he would have to give his place to another child and he would have to leave the school. It was a difficult decision, but there were other children pleading for a chance to learn.

[Omot loved] Don, and a few days later he approached him asking if he could accompany him in his village work and have the privilege of carrying "God's book,"—a request that touched Don, as he related to his supporters back home. "I was delighted to have him go with me and Omot was serving his Lord in the only way he knew how. He was always faithful in his task and proud of his part in it."

This teamwork continued for some time, until tragedy struck. Don wrote to his friends of the incident:

"Yesterday, a group of small boys were playing near the river and a crocodile grabbed one of them. The other boys ran away screaming, but Omot jumped into the water to fight the crocodile. He succeeded in freeing the boy who had been taken, but the crocodile killed Omot instead. Greater love has no boy than to lay down his life for a friend.

"Of little Omot, Christian, we recovered for burial only one arm. Omot never owned a pair of shoes, he never finished the first grade, but when the roll is called up yonder—he will be there."

How appropriate are the verses from the Song of Songs: "Love is as strong as death, its jealousy unyielding as the grave. . . . Many waters cannot quench love; rivers cannot wash it away."[13]

Place me like a seal over your heart, like a seal on your arm; for love is as strong as death, its jealousy unyielding as the grave. It burns like blazing fire, like a mighty flame. Many waters cannot quench love; rivers cannot wash it away. If one were to give all the wealth of his house for love, it would be utterly scorned.

*Song of Songs 8:6–7.*

# "THERE WILL BE FALSE TEACHERS AMONG YOU"

During the late eighteenth and early nineteenth centuries, "a great apostasy prevailed in the Lutheran churches of Scandinavia as elsewhere." German Rationalism, according to Bishop Bang, was "preached from most pulpits, smuggled into the common schools and the villages," and "it moved as a plague over the spiritual life of the nation. Under its supposed 'enlightenment' the darkness was so great that the daylight seemed gone forever."

Enter Hans Nielsen Hauge. He felt called into the ministry on a spring day in 1796, while he was plowing his father's field. "I heard the Lord's voice," he testified, "saying 'Whom shall I send to invite to my great communion feast, calling them from east and west, from north and south?' I replied, 'Send me,' for my heart was burdened with love for all men." From that time on Hauge felt "driven" to preach, whether it be to families in farm houses, crowds in the open air or individuals he met as he traveled. It was a difficult life. He "was treated with such scorn that he longed even to die if he could but escape the burden of his mission."

Despite the ridicule that confronted him as he preached, he found hungry hearts wherever he went. He challenged a group of lay preachers who then joined him and went out into the countryside "on fire for souls." There they found people totally ignorant of the gospel—this was the fruit of the teachings of false prophets. Many to whom they spoke "did not know how many gods there are, not to speak of who had saved them, or how to be saved." In response to questioning, "some said there were three gods, others five, and others did not know."

So popular did he become with the people that "great companies would attach themselves to him when he was on the way to hold services and follow him thither, talking with him the while. . . . Between 1798 and 1804 Hauge traveled on foot about seven thousand miles. The resonance of his preaching filled the whole land." In the winter he traveled through the mountains on skis, reaching out to people in the most remote areas.

As his popularity grew, so did opposition. "Meetings were broken up. People were arrested merely for reading Hauge's writings in their own homes." Hauge was imprisoned for three years without a trial and was finally charged with violating an ordinance against preaching, but not before he had made a deep spiritual impact on his country.[14]

But there were also false prophets among the people, just as there will be false teachers among you. They will secretly introduce destructive heresies, even denying the sovereign Lord who bought them— bringing swift destruction on themselves. Many will follow their shameful ways and will bring the way of truth into disrepute. In their greed these teachers will exploit you with stories they have made up. Their condemnation has long been hanging over them, and their destruction has not been sleeping.

*2 Peter 2:1–3.*

# "WHAT I FEARED HAS COME UPON ME"

Leprosy is a disease that, if not treated properly, can make death seem appealing. Even with treatment, the victim often feels utterly alone and forsaken by society. As one of the world's leading leprosy specialists, Dr. Paul Brand, a medical missionary to India, was well aware of this stigma and the ostracism his patients felt even from friends and family. But his sympathy was not transformed into identification with them until he experienced the fear that accompanies the discovery that one has that dread disease. Most people are immune to leprosy; some are not. Those who work in close contact with lepers are always mindful that they themselves might become victims. Paul Brand was no different. He did not allow his fears to curtail his ministry, but he was never entirely free from feelings of apprehension.

On one occasion, after a grueling four months traveling and doing research in America under a Rockefeller Foundation grant, Paul returned to England in ill health. His wife Margaret was visiting her parents in South Africa, so he would not receive her warm welcome. "The train trip to London seemed interminable. When he arrived in his room in Nethania, he sank gratefully into a chair and pulled off his shoes. Then suddenly it came, without warning, perhaps the blackest moment of his whole life. For as he leaned over and pulled off his sock, he made a discovery. *There was no feeling in his heel.*

"He rose mechanically, found a pin, sat down again, and pricked the small area below his ankle. He felt no pain. He thrust the pin deeper, until a speck of blood showed. Still he felt nothing. For a few moments, which seemed an eternity, he remained seated, dabbing at the prick. . . . Then he got up and flung himself on the bed."

His sleep was agonizing and fitful that night. His future loomed grimly before him, and in his half-conscious sleep, he wrestled with what he should do with the rest of his life and how he could fulfill his obligation to never "live intimately with his family again." When the grey dawn woke him in the morning, he once again reached for the pin and jabbed it through his skin. This time there was a sudden and unexpected surge of pain. It was only then that he realized that the numbness from the train ride and the depression he was feeling had combined to delude him. Yet, after that, he was a changed man more conscious than ever of the horrors of leprosy.[15]

"Why is light
to those in m
and life to the
of soul, to tho
long for death
does not come,
search for it m
than for hidden
treasure, who a
filled with gladi
and rejoice whe
they reach the g
Why is life give
a man whose wa
hidden, whom G
has hedged in? For
sighing comes to me
instead of food; my
groans pour out like
water. What I feared
has come upon me;
what I dreaded has
happened to me. I
have no peace, no
quietness; I have no
rest, but only
turmoil."

*Job 3:20–26.*

## "WHEN THE ROLL IS CALLED UP YONDER"

Eunice Pike worked with Wycliffe Bible Translators among the Mazatec Indians of Mexico. While there, she discovered that the people were often consumed by their fears of evil spirits, and that the gospel brought comfort in ways that sometimes were unexpected. This kind of comfort was part of the testimony of her Christian language helper Juana. Eunice was surprised to learn that Juana's favorite hymn was "When the Roll Is Called Up Yonder."

"I had thought of a roll call as something outside the experience of people who had never been to school," writes Eunice, "and I had always been surprised at how popular that hymn was, not only with Juana but with others as well. Then one day I understood why.

"Anna was telling me about what people did when they built with stone. She told me, 'Forty-eight people were killed when Jose built his house.' I didn't believe it and I demanded names of the people and the dates when they were murdered. So she gave me a few more details.

"Because the walls were heavy when people built a stone bridge or stone house, they had to dig down and lay a foundation deep into the ground. That, according to them, disturbed the spirits who lived there. The spirits retaliated by killing the workmen or the owner of the house. In order to appease the spirits, and to protect himself, the owner would write names of other people on turkey eggs and bury the eggs in the foundation. Then there was a roll call of the names written on the eggs and the spirits 'ate' the people whose names were called. Supposedly the people then wasted away, or died of fever or diarrhea.

"So a roll call was *not* strange to these people. It delighted those who believed in Christ to remember that their names were on a list in heaven, and that they were included among those who would live forever."[16]

The seventy-two returned with joy and said, "Lord, even the demons submit to us in your name." He replied, "I saw Satan fall like lightning from heaven. I have given you authority to trample on snakes and scorpions, and to overcome all the power of the enemy; nothing will harm you. However, do not rejoice that the spirits submit to you, but rejoice that your names are written in heaven."

*Luke 10:17–20.*

# "A FAMINE OF HEARING THE WORDS OF THE LORD"

Christians who live in the West cannot identify with those who live in repressive regimes where Bibles often are not easily accessible. In such countries there is "a famine of hearing the words of the Lord," with people "searching for the word of the Lord." Robert Evans, the founder and director of the Greater European Mission, discovered this when he was visiting the ravaged, war-torn towns of Poland soon after World War II. He had gone to Poland to preach the gospel, not knowing how he would be received.

"Word spread like wildfire that a foreigner would speak in the Town Hall very soon," he later wrote. "That night while we preached the saving power of the Lord Jesus Christ, hundreds of decisions were made for Him. It was apparent that most of these simple country folk had never before heard a clear Gospel message. Time after time the building was emptied and a new capacity crowd admitted. The hours flew by until we were exhausted. My interpreters and I had preached for six and one-half hours, and still the people came.

"Finally we could take no more, and ended the meeting. Out in the dark waited a last great crowd of people who had been unable to get in. Their faces were not visible, but their presence could be felt. The rustle of their clothes and the murmur of their voices told of hundreds who had not yet heard about the Saviour.

"An old man plucked persistently at my sleeve. He was wrinkled, shriveled, and bowed down with age. He hung on to me through the jostling crowd, talking excitedly all the while. I asked my Russian interpreter what he was saying. 'He wants you to tell him if his piece of paper is really from the Bible,' the interpreter said. Then slowly and with solemn care the old man took some cloth wrappings from a folded paper he had drawn from his inside coat pocket. The page, yellow with age, its edges ragged, showed signs of much handling."

When the interpreter immediately recognized it as a page from the book of Exodus, the old man shook with excitement. "I have read this page again and again all my life," he told them. "I thought it was from the Bible, but I was never sure. There is something different about it—this I know. But I have always wondered *what comes on the next page*." It was a touching moment as this man began weeping for joy when Robert let him hold and page through his own Bible. "Past 80 years of age, almost ready to die, he had a copy of the Word of God in his hands for the first time in his life."[17]

"The days are coming," declares the Sovereign Lord, "when I will send a famine through the land—not a famine of food or a thirst for water, but a famine of hearing the words of the Lord. Men will stagger from sea to sea and wander from north to east, searching for the word of the Lord, but they will not find it."

*Amos 8:11–12.*

# "A PRUDENT WIFE IS FROM THE LORD"

It is often through the "plans in a man's heart" that courtship begins and romance blossoms, but the most lasting relationships often develop entirely apart from any conniving or scheming. Indeed, a prudent wife (or husband) is from the Lord.

What attracted George Boardman, a nineteen-year-old college student, to Sarah Hall, a seventeen-year-old girl, was not her beauty (though she was described as a woman with faultless features), but her commitment to missions and to God. They were brought together by their common sorrow and common concern for the evangelization of Burma.

They had much in common. They were both avid readers—especially of missionary literature. After reading a biography of the great missionary Samuel Mills, Sarah wrote, "Never shall I forget the emotions of my heart, while following thus in the footsteps of this devoted missionary. I have caught his spirit. . . . Oh, that I, too could suffer privations, hardships and discouragements, and even find a watery grave (as did he) for the sake of bearing the news of salvation to the poor heathen."

Sarah longed to be a missionary—as did George—but, unlike him, she faced a powerful barrier; during the early decades of the nineteenth century, single women were not accepted as missionaries.

It was the death of James Colman in 1820 that brought Sarah and George together. James was a young American Baptist missionary to Burma who died before he became fully established in the work. On hearing the news, George vowed that he would take the place of Colman. Sarah could make no such commitment, but as a poet, she expressed her grief in a poem that was published in the *American Baptist Magazine*. "The flower of our churches is withered is dead," she penned, "The gem that shone brightly will sparkle no more. . . . For Colman is gone!" The lines also spoke of his commitment "to bear to the nations all wrapp'd in thick gloom, the lamp of the gospel— the message of love."

It was this poem that caught George's eye, and he was determined that he would seek out the poet. He did find her and discovered she was all he could ask for in a "prudent wife." They served in Burma as missionaries until 1831, when George died. Sarah stayed on in Burma and later married the widowed Adoniram Judson, before she herself died in 1845. She had fulfilled her dream of suffering "privations, hardships and discouragements," as had Samuel Mills, "for the sake of bearing the news of salvation to the poor heathen."[18]

Houses and wealth are inherited from parents, but a prudent wife is from the Lord.

Many are the plans in a man's heart, but it is the Lord's purpose that prevails.

A good name is more desirable than great riches; to be esteemed is better than silver or gold.

*Proverbs 19:14, 21– 22a.*

# "THEN THE END WILL COME"

The future missionary statesmanship of A. J. Gordon seemed almost to be foreordained by his parents on April 19, 1836, when they named him after America's most famous missionary, Adoniram Judson. The missionary was then serving in Burma and only months before had baptized his one hundredth member of the Burmese church and completed his translation of the Burmese Bible.

Unlike his namesake, young Gordon did not prepare for missionary service, but rather the pastoral ministry. But it was from his pulpit at the Clarendon Street Baptist Church in Boston, where he served for twenty-five years, that he made his impact on missions—both home and foreign. During his first years at that fashionable church, he faced opposition from members when he emphasized missions and preached against such "ecclesiastical extravagances" such as Easter flowers and paid choirs. That began to change in 1877, when Dwight L. Moody came to Boston.

Moody erected his tent near the church, and through the pastor's encouragement, members joined in the outreach ministry of the crusade. As poor families and indigents were converted, they were brought into the church, and "nearly thirty reformed alcoholics had joined the church by the end of the crusade." People also became involved in "missions to Jews and Chinese in Boston, outdoor preaching, rescue work among women, and an industrial home for men."

But Gordon's concern for missionary outreach extended far beyond the boundaries of Boston. He had an overwhelming burden to reach Africa—in part to rectify the crime of slavery and the slave trade. He set forth this argument in a tract entitled "The Ship *Jesus*," a story of a ship *Jesus* that had brought Africans to this country, and how that same ship should return with the gospel. He led his own church in support of the Congo Mission.

Gordon's most significant influence on the evangelical world was his insistence that a belief in the soon return of Christ did not lessen the church's missionary responsibility, as some claimed. Rather, he argued for increased responsibility. He was the featured speaker at mission conferences in America and abroad, where he presented his premillennial interpretation of the end times with his concern for missions, insisting that the gospel must be preached to every nation before the Lord would return. To hasten the return of Christ, he established a missionary training school to thrust young people onto the mission field. That school has since become Gordon College and Gordon-Conwell Theological Seminary.[19]

At that time many will turn away from the faith and will betray and hate each other, and many false prophets will appear and deceive many people. Because of the increase of wickedness, the love of most will grow cold, but he who stands firm to the end will be saved. And this gospel of the kingdom will be preached in the whole world as a testimony to all nations, and then the end will come.

*Matthew 24:10–14.*

## "COME OVER AND HELP US"

Ruth Hitchcock, a missionary to China, was called to be a foreign missionary when she was only ten years old. It was not a visionary call like the one Paul had of the man from Macedonia, but it was very similar in many respects. It was the call of people in China that was transmitted through Horace Houlding, a missionary from that region. He was staying in her home and he brought a powerful message from China that changed her life.

He told how a man came to his home in China one winter day, having traveled two days in an open cart in the freezing temperatures. He had made the trip to plead for a missionary to come to his village. He explained that he lived in a village on the great plains near the Yellow River, and that during the winter the people had plenty of time to learn about God. Their wheat crop was sown in the fall, and during the cold months of winter they had nothing to do but to stay in their houses and busy themselves with sedentary activities. It was a perfect time, he reasoned, to learn about the God of the missionaries and the great book they had heard about.

Houlding and his fellow missionaries realized that this was an extraordinary opportunity to reach out with the gospel. Here was a whole village with their hearts and minds open to the Word of God. But he was too busy with other commitments to go—as were his colleagues. No one could go. The man pleaded with them, but to no avail.

"He finally had to return alone with his cart to that village where they wanted to hear the Gospel. At the beginning of the next winter he appeared again—and again the bleak decision was reached. No one could go. The cart crept slowly back across the miles."

After hearing that moving story, Ruth Hitchcock was deeply touched: "In my heart the resolve grew: 'Lord, when I grow up, I'll go.'"

She did go to China and served faithfully for many years.[20]

**When they came to the border of Mysia, they tried to enter Bithynia, but the Spirit of Jesus would not allow them to. So they passed by Mysia and went down to Troas. During the night Paul had a vision of a man of Macedonia standing and begging him, "Come over to Macedonia and help us." After Paul had seen the vision, we got ready at once to leave for Macedonia, concluding that God had called us to preach the gospel to them.**

*Acts 16:7–10.*

# "NOW IS THE DAY OF SALVATION"

The urgency of sharing the gospel is emphasized in this passage in 2 Corinthians and is powerfully illustrated by the conversion story of Dwight L. Moody. Had Edward Kimball on Saturday morning, April 21, 1855, not determined that "now is the day of salvation," the course of history might have been significantly altered. Dwight L. Moody might never have become one of this nation's greatest preachers and revivalists.

Kimball was Moody's Sunday school teacher, and it was early that morning that he vowed "to speak to Moody about Christ." Moody was a young shoe salesman living in Boston at the time, and Kimball determined there would be no stumbling block in his path.

"I started down town to Holton's shoe store. When I was nearly there I began to wonder whether I ought to go just then during business hours. And I thought maybe my mission might embarrass the boy, that when I went away the other clerks might ask who I was, and when they learned might taunt Moody and ask if I were trying to make a good boy out of him. While I was pondering over it all I passed the store without noticing it. Then, when I found I had gone by the door I determined to make a dash for it and have it over at once."

Kimball found Moody in a back storeroom wrapping and stacking shoes. "I went up to him and put my hand on his shoulder, and as I leaned over I placed my foot upon a shoe box." There in those few moments of privacy, he challenged Moody to turn his life over to God. "I asked him to come to Christ, who loved him and who wanted his love and should have it."

"It seemed," Kimball later recalled, "that the young man was just ready for the light that broke upon him, for there, at once, in the back of that shoe store in Boston," he "gave himself and his life to Christ."

From that day on Moody's life was different. When he got up the following morning—Sunday morning—he had a new perspective on the world: "I thought the old sun shone a good deal brighter than it ever had before—I thought that it was just smiling upon me; and as I walked out upon Boston Common and heard the birds singing in the trees, I thought they were all singing a song to me. Do you know, I fell in love with the birds. I had never cared for them before. It seemed to me that I was in love with all creation. I had not a bitter feeling against any man, and I was ready to take all men to my heart."[21]

As God's fellow workers we urge you not to receive God's grace in vain. For he says, "In the time of my favor I heard you, and in the day of salvation I helped you." I tell you, now is the time of God's favor, now is the day of salvation.

We put no stumbling block in anyone's path, so that our ministry will not be discredited. Rather, as servants of God we commend ourselves in every way. . . .

*2 Corinthians 6:1–4a.*

# "HEAP BURNING COALS ON HIS HEAD"

It was a stormy night in April, 1923, that was suddenly interrupted by the barking of dogs. The setting was a military outpost on the northern frontier of India, where raids by Afghan warring tribes were not uncommon. Only three years earlier a British Colonel and his wife had been murdered by an Afridi tribal gang, and tensions were still high. The officer on duty who investigated the commotion found his worst fears confirmed. The wife of Major Ellis (who was away on duty) had been brutally murdered, and his seventeen-year-old daughter Molly was missing.

Sir John Maffey, the Chief Commissioner, summoned help for this "delicate and dangerous" operation. He knew that one wrong move might not only endanger the life of Molly, but stir up inter-tribal military conflict in the whole region.

"Instead of the military force he summoned one woman. . . to penetrate . . . where no white face had ever before been." That woman was Lilian Starr, a missionary nurse who served at the mission hospital in Peshawar, a town "lying at the foot of the Khyber Pass, which many consider the very gate to India, and from which the road leads out into Afghanistan."

Lilian was known throughout the entire region for her compassion for people, regardless of their nationality or tribe. Her parents had been missionaries in Peshawar, and, after nurse's training in England, she returned to serve as a nursing sister at the mission hospital. There she married a missionary doctor, only to be widowed two years later when "he was stabbed to death by Afridis who were incensed, it is imagined, at the conversion to Christianity of a boy relative."

After a time in England following her husband's death Lilian returned to Peshawar, seeking to demonstrate the Christian ideal of forgiveness in contrast to the tribal commitment to "revenge and of blood-feuds that were carried on from generation to generation." This ideal prompted her to accept the challenge to rescue Molly—to enter the dangerous area as a nurse and as a woman who had forgiven even the murder of her husband.

"With the charm of her fair face and a woman's courage," Sir John Maffey later wrote, "she carried our standard for us behind those iron hills where no Englishman may pass. She had the great joy of bringing back to us the English girl unscathed and uninjured, and she made a British mark on the heart of Tirah better than all the drums and tramplings of an army corps."[22]

Do not repay anyone evil for evil. Be careful to do what is right in the eyes of everybody. If it is possible, as far as it depends on you, live at peace with everyone. Do not take revenge, my friends, but leave room for God's wrath, for it is written: "It is mine to avenge, I will repay," says the Lord. On the contrary: "If your enemy is hungry, feed him, if he is thirsty, give him something to drink. In doing this, you will heap burning coals on his head."

*Romans 12:17–20.*

# "THE PRAYER OF A RIGHTEOUS MAN IS POWERFUL"

It is often difficult for people in Third World countries to realize that Western missionaries, with all their apparent wealth, sometimes come upon hard times. That situation occurred in 1929 for Earl Lewis and his wife who were serving in Ethiopia. The stock market crash dried up their support, and so tight were their finances that they were hardly able to finance their monthly expenses.

Realizing that they would no longer be able to meet the salaries of their Ethiopian laborers at the mission station, they called a meeting and explained that they would have to let them go after their next pay period. The workmen were shocked, thinking it not possible that missionaries could ever run out of money. They were puzzled, too, because they knew Lewis was a man of prayer. After thinking it over, all the workmen but one decided to stay on without their pay and trust God to supply what was necessary.

"This action of the workmen seemed to be a turning point and the beginning of their interest in the message," writes Raymond Davis. "Every morning at prayer-time they would pray that God would supply the needs. The days of the month passed, and finally the mail came. . . . This mail contained a letter from a friend of Mrs. Lewis, a woman who had taught her in primary school. In the letter was a $5 bill. Exchanged into Ethiopian money . . . there was sufficient to pay the wages of all who worked—with some left over."

Soon after this there was another urgent need for prayer. A little boy named Asala was brought to the Lewis family. He was so ill and weak with parasites that he was not expected to live. They were warned by their Ethiopian cook not to take him in because they would then be blamed for his death. "When he dies the witch doctor will say that you have killed him," the cook insisted. "Then the people will all believe him when he says that it is your purpose in coming here to steal our little children, to eat them, and to send their blood and their spirits to your country. You cannot take him."

But Asala was so ill that there was no choice but to care for him. They prayed fervently that God would spare him, and slowly his frail little body began to gain strength and vitality—as did the power of the gospel with the local Ethiopians.[23]

And the prayer offered in faith will make the sick person well; the Lord will raise him up. If he has sinned, he will be forgiven. Therefore confess your sins to each other and pray for each other so that you may be healed. The prayer of a righteous man is powerful and effective.

Elijah was a man just like us. He prayed earnestly that it would not rain, and it did not rain on the land for three and a half years. Again he prayed, and the heavens gave rain, and the earth produced its crops.

*James 5:15–18.*

# "MAKE THE TEACHING ATTRACTIVE"

The apostle Paul was well aware of the tremendous opening slaves or workers of any sort had for making the gospel of Christ attractive enough to win the hearts of others. This opportunity has been available to Christians of all ages, and it has often been through Christians' work-a-day contacts that they have had the greatest occasion for witness.

This was true for John Warr, a young man of eighteenth-century England who was apprenticed to Clarke Nichols, a shoemaker. Although John had a rich evangelical heritage, he was unwilling to accept the restrictions that true discipleship would require. He was preparing for a trade, and that was his chief concern. But the more he worked the more he realized that manual labor alone would never make him happy. He committed his life to God and determined that he would live a sincere life of discipleship by reaching out with the gospel to others who came his way.

Not long after he came to grips with his own eternal destiny, his master, Clarke Nichols, accepted a new apprentice. The two young men worked side by side long hours in the shop, and John had many opportunities to share his newfound commitment to Christ. He prayed for his coworker and encouraged him to read the Bible and other literature that would awaken his soul. But the new apprentice wanted nothing to do with this evangelical fanaticism.

Then one day the new apprentice was caught exchanging a counterfeit shilling for one of his master's shillings. He felt shamed and guilty and was so burdened by a sense of remorse that he began to fear for his own soul. Whom else could he go to but his friend and fellow apprentice, John Warr? John prayed with him, and this young shoemaker's apprentice—named William Carey—committed his life to God.

Without the witness of a faithful worker, the course of modern missions might have been unalterably changed, because it was William Carey, more than anyone else, who inspired a generation to reach out across the seas to a lost world.[24]

Teach slaves to be subject to their masters in everything, to try to please them, not to talk back to them, and not to steal from them, but to show that they can be fully trusted, so that in every way they will make the teaching about God our Savior attractive.

For the grace of God that brings salvation has appeared to all men. It teaches us to say "No" to ungodliness and worldly passions, and to live self-controlled, upright and godly lives in this present age, while we wait for the blessed hope—the glorious appearing of our great God and Savior, Jesus Christ, who gave himself for us to redeem us from all wickedness and to purify for himself a people that are his very own, eager to do what is good.

*Titus 2:9–14.*

# "THE LORD WILL PROVIDE"

George Mueller is known for his sacrificial work in founding orphanages in England during the nineteenth century. Others in previous generations have been recognized for similar service, but G. Mueller is remembered for his dependence on God alone for the needs of his orphans. He had lived by faith before he began his orphan ministry, and it seemed natural that he would continue on in this manner.

But feeding and housing dozens, and eventually hundreds, of orphans was a far greater task than simply feeding and housing his family. Yet, he was convinced that God would provide, though through the years he had to remind himself of this fact constantly especially when he had utterly run out of provisions. On one occasion, as he stood looking out a window during a severe time of testing, he etched on the windowpane, "Jehovah-jireh," from Genesis 22:14 (KJV), meaning "the Lord will provide." It would stand as a reminder to him that God was indeed faithful.

There were many reminders of God's faithfulness from Mueller's past experiences. "One morning, the tables were all set for breakfast but the cupboard like that of the proverbial Mother Hubbard was bare, and so was the cash box. The children were standing waiting for their breakfast and Mr. Mueller said, 'Children, you know we must be in time for school.' Then lifting his head he prayed very simply, 'Dear Father, we thank Thee for what Thou art going to give us to eat.' There was a knock at the door. It was a local baker who said, 'Mr. Mueller, I could not sleep last night. Somehow I felt you didn't have any bread for breakfast, and the Lord wanted me to send you some. So I got up at 2:00 a.m. and baked some fresh bread and here it is.' Mr. Mueller thanked the baker and praised God for His care. Then there was a second knock at the door. It was a milkman whose cart had broken down right outside the orphanage. He had come to unload his milk onto the orphans so that he could get his wagon repaired!"

Depending on God to provide became almost routine for the Muellers. "In the two years between August 1838 and August 1840 there were fifty occasions when they were reduced to being penniless, or without sufficient funds for the day, but God always undertook and either money or food came in time."[25]

Some time later God tested Abraham. He said to him, "Abraham!"

"Here I am," he replied.

Then God said, "Take your son, your only son, Isaac, whom you love, and go to the region of Moriah. Sacrifice him there as a burnt offering on one of the mountains I will tell you about." . . .

Abraham looked up and there in a thicket he saw a ram caught by its horns. He went over and took the ram and sacrificed it as a burnt offering instead of his son. So Abraham called that place The Lord Will Provide. And to this day it is said, "On the mountain of the Lord it will be provided."

*Genesis 22:1–2, 13–14.*

# "YOU WILL SEEK ME AND FIND ME"

Missionaries who are stationed in Muslim countries know the discouragement of serving for years and years without having the joy of assisting even one convert. Rarely do they find someone who is ready and waiting to hear the gospel. Yet, the burden to reach Muslims for Christ is compelling. Such was the case with one young couple (whose names must remain anonymous) who went to Turkey to serve in the same region of the world that the apostle Paul had traveled as a missionary many centuries before. They could not witness openly, but they began language study, all the while hoping that one day they would be able to share Christ in their private contacts with Muslims.

There were many days when they were prone to question if any positive result would ever come from their sacrifice. Their Muslim neighbors were very committed to their religion and looked upon Christianity as a decadent religion of the West.

Not long after they had relocated to another city, however, they welcomed a visitor to their home, and his story quickly convinced them that God had a purpose for their residence among the Muslims of Turkey. The young man told them how he had been raised in a traditional Muslim home and that he had grown up studying the Koran and praying to Allah and fasting regularly. Yet, he was unhappy. Through all his religious practice, he had not found God.

In his search for God he traveled to Germany, hoping that he would find someone there who could tell him about the Bible and the God of the Christians. Language barriers, however, hindered his search and most people there cared very little about the Bible anyway. As he traveled around, he visited cathedrals, and one day, while praying in a cathedral, he sensed a deep peace sweep over him. God, he was convinced, was leading him in the right direction.

When he returned home, he continued his search for God by enrolling in a Bible correspondence course, but still he had many unanswered questions. He needed someone to talk to and someone who could encourage him in his search for true faith.

What a joy it was then for the missionary couple when this young Muslim arrived at their door. They were exhilarated by his eagerness to learn, and soon his commitment to Christ was sealed. He had searched with his whole heart and found the one true God.[26]

"For I know the plans I have for you," declares the Lord, "plans to prosper you and not to harm you, plans to give you hope and a future. Then you will call upon me and come and pray to me, and I will listen to you. You will seek me and find me when you seek me with all your heart."

*Jeremiah 29:11–13.*

# "A TIME FOR WAR AND A TIME FOR PEACE"

When Paul Kuo applied for admission to the Hong Kong Evangel Theological College, administrators were puzzled as to how they should respond. Paul was sixty years old, and by the time he could graduate he would be almost at retirement age. It would be virtually impossible to place him in a pastorate. No church would want to call a pastor ready to retire. It was not the proper time to be entering a new career.

Yet Kuo did have promise. Rarely did the school have applicants who were so eager to acquire a biblical education, and never before had anyone with his credentials applied for admission. He had been an officer in the Chinese army, and later served as a high-ranking spy for his government. He was in excellent health; he was a practitioner and teacher of the martial art of Kung-Fu. But more compelling than any other factor was his certainty that God had called him into the ministry.

Kuo was accepted as a student, and it was his certainty that he had a call that prodded him on through difficult years of study. He was unable to complete the requirements for a degree, but he obtained the training he needed for effective ministry. In 1975, after he finished his studies, he went to Northern Thailand where he began missionary work among a population of approximately sixty thousand Chinese refugees. These were Chinese soldiers and their families who had fled the Chinese communist regime in 1949, with the hope of one day returning and regaining control of their country. But after more than a generation had passed, hope had waned and many of the men had become mercenaries, bandits or opium farmers. The region was known as the "Golden Triangle," where there was no government or law.

It was in this difficult field of service that Kuo began his ministry. He immediately won the respect of the people because his military service and his age made him a celebrity. He conducted itinerant evangelism meetings and established training centers, soon finding himself overburdened with the work. He sent out a call for young missionaries to join him, and soon he was heading up a large missionary venture.

When Kuo retired from full time ministry, the work was well established in the "Golden Triangle." He returned home to seek more recruits and periodically visited the area as he oversaw the work.[27]

There is a time for everything, and a season for every activity under heaven: a time to be born and a time to die, a time to plant and a time to uproot, a time to kill and a time to heal, a time to tear down and a time to build, a time to weep and a time to laugh, a time to mourn and a time to dance, a time to scatter stones and a time to gather them, a time to embrace and a time to refrain, a time to search and a time to give up, a time to keep and a time to throw away, a time to tear and a time to mend, a time to be silent and a time to speak, a time to love and a time to hate, a time for war and a time for peace.

*Ecclesiastes 3:1–8.*

# "GO IN THE STRENGTH YOU HAVE"

Many missionaries have gone abroad utterly insecure about their own abilities to effectively work in a new culture. This is especially true of missionaries who have not had the benefit of a Bible college or seminary education and was the case with Denny and Jeanne Grindall when they first went to Kenya to work with the Maasai tribe.

The Grindalls had vacationed in Kenya in 1968, and went away with a heavy burden for the Maasai and their need for better health care. They felt God calling them to give their lives for the spiritual and physical well-being of these people, but common sense seemed to be telling them they were foolish. They had been florists in Seattle for more than thirty years, and had no formal training in the Bible or in missions.

Soon after they began their ministry with the Maasai, they realized that many of the health problems were due to contaminated drinking water. Drinking water came from the pond where the people bathed and where the cattle drank. The solution to this problem, the Grindalls determined, was to build a dam on a mountain stream and create a clean reservoir.

With no engineering skills and very little money, they summoned the tribespeople to help them and soon they had a dam nearly eighty-feet tall and a clean water reservoir. Then came the job of laying nearly three miles of pipe to bring the clean water from the mountain to the plains below.

With this fresh clean water, most of the health problems of the Maasai began to disappear. The people were impressed with what the Grindalls had done and they were ready to listen to their stories about God.

After fifteen years of ministry among the proud cattle-herding Maasai tribe, the Grindalls had established twenty churches and had the privilege of seeing hundreds of these people place their faith in Christ. What began as a vacation for two middle-aged florists turned into a powerful ministry that has eased the suffering in this life for many and has offered hope for all eternity. The Grindalls went out in the strength they had, and God was with them.[28]

The Lord turned to him and said, "Go in the strength you have and save Israel out of Midian's hand. Am I not sending you?"

"But Lord," Gideon asked, "how can I save Israel? My clan is the weakest in Manasseh, and I am the least in my family."

The Lord answered, "I will be with you, and you will strike down all the Midianites together."

*Judges 6:14–16.*

# "I DID NOT COME TO BRING PEACE"

James O. Fraser was a great pioneer missionary with the China Inland Mission, who worked among the Lisu tribe of northwest China and was instrumental in bringing thousands of Lisu people to faith in Christ. Among those was a pastry cook, Moh Ting-Chang, who was already on his way to saving faith when Fraser first met him. Fraser had been preaching in an open air meeting, amid jeering and opposition from people in the back of the crowd, but when he gave the invitation, Moh stepped forward without hesitation. "He wanted to follow Jesus Christ," he said. He already believed He was the Son of God.

Fraser accompanied Moh to his home, "and to his surprise Moh produced a small, well-read copy of Mark's gospel. Moh explained that his son had brought it back five years before after a visit to the Mangshi market, where a foreigner had given booklets out. Moh had read and reread this little book many times. He was strangely stirred by the story. He had longed to learn more all these years." Fraser spent the night explaining the gospel to Moh, but left early the next morning for another appointment, promising to return in a few days.

When he returned, Fraser spent two more days explaining biblical doctrine and answering questions. He was convinced that Moh's faith was genuine, but he was concerned that even after all the discussions they had had, Moh had not disposed of a large incense-burning idol. When Fraser finally questioned him, Moh explained that it was for the sake of his family that he kept it—that he feared for their lives if he destroyed it. Fraser suggested that he pray to God about this situation. Moh cried out to God, pleading for strength, and when he was through he got up from his knees, convinced he must destroy it. But still he hesitated. So, they prayed again, and then they burned the idol.

Neighbors and family members quickly heard about what happened to the idol and about Moh's new faith. There was an immediate backlash, but Moh held firm—even in the face of the most anguishing of the threats. These threats came from his own mother. She was an opium addict, and she so strongly objected to his faith in Christ that she vowed she would drown herself because of her son's disgrace to the family. It would have been easier for Moh to endure a threat on his own life than his mother's threat of suicide, but he lived with the anguish and held strong in the faith.[29]

"Do not suppose that I have come to bring peace to the earth. I did not come to bring peace, but a sword. For I have come to turn 'a man against his father, a daughter against her mother, a daughter-in-law against her mother-in-law—a man's enemies will be the members of his own household.' Anyone who loves his father or mother more than me is not worthy of me; anyone who loves his son or daughter more than me is not worthy of me; and anyone who does not take his cross and follow me is not worthy of me.

*Matthew 10:34–38.*

# "ALL NATIONS WILL COME"

In many ways this prophecy to Haggai applies to the expansion of the gospel worldwide, as all nations come to Christ and as he fills his house with glory and brings peace where there was no peace. The missionary work of James Calvert powerfully illustrates this change in just one tiny nation of the world.

Calvert and his wife were appointed by the Wesleyan Missionary Society to serve as missionaries in Fiji. They arrived on that island in the South Seas in 1838. After six months of intensive language study, James, in the tradition of the Methodist circuit rider, began a preaching circuit to villages on Fiji and on surrounding islands—some of which were more than one hundred miles from his home. His wife conducted women's work, but despite all their efforts, they saw little response to their ministry.

"At last there came the day for which Mr. Calvert had worked, longed and prayed. On April 30, 1854, the chief ordered that the death-drums be now used to call the people together to worship the true God. What was their joy to see more than three hundred wending their way to the large 'Stranger's House,' and among them was the great chief with his many wives and children. It was a memorable sight, as they now knelt in adoration of the Christian's God."

Three years later came another milestone. "In 1857, Thakombau, the king, after dismissing his many wives with all their wealth and influence, was baptized. Before his court, his ambassadors, his people, he stood up and humbly confessed his former sins and embraced the Christian faith. One thousand hearts throbbed in excitement as they listened in awe and astonishment to this king who had slain their husbands, strangled their relatives, murdered their friends and eaten their children; and now what was he saying? 'I have been a bad man! . . . God has singularly preserved my life. I desire to acknowledge him as the only and the true God.'"

Following his retirement, Calvert returned to his beloved Fiji in 1885 to celebrate the Jubilee of Christianity. "Where there was not a single Christian in 1835, there was not an avowed heathen now in 1885. He found over thirteen hundred churches," the vast majority of them led by native pastors and evangelists. Most amazing of all was that out of a population of 116,000, more than 104,000 regularly attended church.[30]

"This is what the Lord Almighty says: 'In a little while I will once more shake the heavens and the earth, the sea and the dry land. I will shake all nations, and the desired of all nations will come, and I will fill this house with glory,' says the Lord Almighty. 'The silver is mine and the gold is mine,' declares the Lord Almighty. 'The glory of this present house will be greater than the glory of the former house,' says the Lord Almighty. 'And in this place I will grant peace,' declares the Lord Almighty.

*Haggai 2:6–9.*

# "LORD, I HAVE HEARD OF YOUR FAME"

As the Taiping Rebellion was coming to a close in China in 1860, Yu Yuh-shan, a military officer in charge of Imperial forces in the city of Ningpo, came upon a missionary who was preaching the gospel. Yu was deeply interested, but other concerns were more pressing at the time, and the seed that was planted in his heart lay dormant.

Following the Rebellion, the Imperial army was disbanded, and Yu returned to civilian life. It was during this time that he joined a Buddhist sect that was committed to reforming Buddhism. With missionary zeal he began traveling around the countryside preaching against idols. In place of the sin of idolatry, he offered the people a belief in an impersonal and unknown Supreme Ruler of the heavens. Thousands of people in the provinces of Cheking and Kiangsi turned away from their idols as a result.

During these years of Buddhist evangelism, Yu never forgot the preaching of the missionary and often wondered about the meaning of the message. Then in 1875, fifteen years after hearing the missionary, he heard news of a foreigner living in Kinhwafu who had a similar message. The foreigner was Dr. Douthwaite, a missionary with the China Inland Mission. Yu visited him, and began to study the Bible. After a year of earnest study and discussion, he asked to be baptized, convinced that he had found the truth about God.

Several months later, after further study, Yu requested that he be allowed to travel as an evangelist: "I have led hundreds on the wrong road," he confessed, "and now I want to lead them to the way of Truth. Let me go; I ask no wages, nor do I want any of your money; I only want to serve Jesus."

Yu was commissioned by a small band of Christians to go out and preach. He went alone and took with him only those necessities that he could carry. After crossing the provincial border into Kiangsi, he began visiting his Buddhist friends. Here he shared the gospel of Christ with many of the very same people whom he had previously led away from idols only to worship an unknown god. Now he offered them the message of the living God, and many believed.[1]

"Of what value is an idol, since a man has carved it? Or an image that teaches lies? For he who makes it trusts in his own creation; he makes idols that cannot speak. Woe to him who says to wood, 'Come to life!' Or to lifeless stone, 'wake up!' Can it give guidance? It is covered with gold and silver; there is no breath in it. But the Lord is in his holy temple; let all the earth be silent before him.". . .

Lord, I have heard of your fame; I stand in awe of your deeds, O Lord. Renew them in our day, in our time make them known; in wrath remember mercy.

*Habakkuk 2:18–20; 3:2.*

## "WHOEVER LOSES HIS LIFE FOR ME WILL FIND IT"

The life of a missionary pilot is a dangerous one. Frequently pilots are called upon to risk their own lives while saving others. This was true of Nate Saint, who had put his life on the line on many occasions before his final flight into the jungles of Ecuador in an effort to reach the Auca Indians. This was also true of his missionary colleague Roger Youderian, who worked among the unreached Jivaro Indians, and who also died at the hands of the Auca Indians in 1956.

As a missionary living in a remote jungle Indian tribe, Roger often depended on Nate for flight service, and it was no different one day when he radioed his friend requesting an emergency medical flight for a Jivaro Indian who had been injured while preparing an airstrip. Roger had returned to his base eighteen miles away in order to radio Nate. At that time he promised Nate that he would make the arduous return hike through the dense jungle by late afternoon before the sun set to build smudges to warn Nate of any serious downdrafts that would prevent him from landing safely. True to his word, Roger made it on time, and Nate was able to land safely.

As he flew to a medical station, Nate began to question the entire ordeal. "Lying beside me on the floor of the plane was a stinking, repulsive, mangled Jivaro Indian," he wrote in his journal. "The sight of the rotten wounds on the disfigured face turned my stomach. . . . Here was an immortal soul hanging over the brink of hell by a tattered thread. Here was one of the hopelessly lost ones that the Lord Jesus had come to seek and to save. . . . I kept one reassuring hand on the trembling frame at my side and reflected on Roger's race thru the jungle:

"Suppose he had given up. Suppose he had strained a little less. . . . What is the drive behind that sort of performance? What is it? What can take a happy-go-lucky prewar lad and forge him into a man capable of that marathon? . . . He was convinced that the cause was worth dying for and therefore put no price or value on his own life. He was trained and disciplined. He knew the importance of unswerving conformity to the will of his Captain. Obedience is not a momentary option . . . it is a die-cast decision made beforehand.

"I need to draw some conclusions so that I won't lose the blessing of the experience in the whirl of activities at the base. The answer is surely discipline—guess that's where real disciples come from. How about me now? . . . lots of room for improvement . . . lots of battles ahead. Discipline-devotion-decision . . . Christ the Captain."[2]

Then Jesus said to his disciples, "If anyone would come after me, he must deny himself and take up his cross and follow me. For whoever wants to save his life will lose it, but whoever loses his life for me will find it. What good will it be for a man if he gains the whole world, yet forfeits his soul? Or what can a man give in exchange for his soul?

*Matthew 16:24–26.*

# "DO THIS IN REMEMBRANCE OF ME"

The observance of the Lord's Supper that the apostle Paul passed on to the believers in Corinth is one that has been repeated countless times since then in every generation and every culture. It is one that has been fashioned by church councils and by local traditions, but whatever its particular form is, it has the potential for deep meaning if hearts are right with God. This truth was brought home to Charles Ernest Scott while he was serving as a missionary in China during the early decades of the twentieth century.

Scott traveled some distance one afternoon to officiate at a communion service for a group of believers that evening. It would be a service without the atmosphere his supporters back home considered necessary: "soft cushions, a comfortable temperature, carpeted floors, noiselessly moving ministrants, a holy hush, exquisitely beautiful music." No. This service was very different.

"On the table, covered by a dirty towel, was a foreign beer bottle containing native wine, plates with whole Chinese biscuits upon them, and several dirty and cracked bowls. . . . Here was not the time or place to remove the bottle or to rebuke the elders. So with a prayer for grace the minister began his sermon. In the midst of it some naked boys, standing just in front of the communion table called the preacher's attention to a big-lettered poster in English and Chinese which hung across the paper panes of the window sash— 'Pabst Beer Is Always Pure!' Extraordinary accompaniments of a communion service!

"Another episode broke in upon the sermon when a patriarch in years and in the faith, who had come a long way and walked laboriously, but who wanted to be there to meet the Lord, tottered in. All—boys and girls, men and women—arose to receive him, and the preacher stopped preaching till he had seated the old man directly in front of him."

Despite the surroundings, "it was a blessed communion," according to Scott. Several people, prompted by the testimony of a young boy, made professions of faith and received communion for the first time. Others committed themselves for the first time to the support of the local ministry. It was a humble service that truly reflected Jesus' words: "In remembrance of me."[3]

For I received from the Lord what I also passed on to you: The Lord Jesus, on the night he was betrayed, took bread, and when he had given thanks, he broke it and said, "This is my body, which is for you; do this in remembrance of me." In the same way, after supper he took the cup, saying, "This cup is the new covenant in my blood; do this whenever you drink it, in remembrance of me." For whenever you eat this bread and drink this cup, you proclaim the Lord's death until he comes.

*1 Corinthians 11:23– 26.*

## "HE REVEALS HIS THOUGHTS TO MAN"

Until his untimely death in 1977 at the hands of terrorists, Don McClure was a missionary to Africa who had an effective ministry among various unreached peoples in Sudan and Ethiopia. He recognized the need for missionaries to reach out to people who had never before heard the gospel, but he also recognized God's power to influence lives where men and women had never preached the gospel. He wrote of such an incident when he was working in Akobo among the Anuaks of Sudan.

"It is obvious that the Holy Spirit is working even in places a missionary has never been. Recently, an Anuak boy, a slave in the Murle country, was startled by a strange glow in his hut, and an unmistakable summons to find someone who could tell him about God. Lado had never seen a missionary, nor had he heard anything of the gospel story, but he felt compelled to travel a hundred miles through enemy country to find, as it turned out, the only white man who could speak his language. This man, Richard Lyth, a devout Christian government official, telling me about it later said, 'Lado had never heard the name of Jesus Christ before I talked to him but he was already a believer before he came to me.'

"Lado is now here in Akabo," McClure continues. "Daily and constantly his life testifies that he has been born again. Perhaps he is a brand plucked from the burning for some special task. His great desire is to read and write and learn something of the Bible and then go back to teach the people who had enslaved him. Since there is no translation of any part of the Bible in the Murle language, Lado will have to memorize the Bible in the Anuak language (he speaks it with difficulty, since he was a very small boy when he was stolen) and then make his own translation for his former masters."

It is amazing that those who have God's Word often struggle to find or follow God's direction, and sometimes others, who do not have God's Word, see his direction very clearly. God does indeed reveal his thoughts to those who will listen.[4]

**He who forms the mountains, creates the wind, and reveals his thoughts to man, he who turns dawn to darkness, and treads the high places of the earth—the Lord God Almighty is his name.**

*Amos 4:13.*

## "I CANNOT HOLD IT IN"

Robert Evans, the founder and director of the Greater European Mission, has made it a practice to witness to people wherever he is whether he is on or off the job. On one occasion while he was enjoying a vacation as a guest on the French Riviera, he discovered that most of the people employed at the hotel where he was staying had an understanding of what it meant to be a true Christian. This took him aback because his previous discussions with French people indicated to him that they had very little knowledge of the gospel. At that time, only a small percentage of French people regularly attended church, and the vast majority of them were only nominally Christian. And, as he had found through experience, "most of the minority who *are* saved fail to talk about the Lord regularly."

The situation presented itself as a mystery—"a hotel whodunit"—and he was determined to solve it. "Witnessing for Christ is done by so few that the chances of a whole hotel's personnel hearing the Word of God from a French source are mathematically almost zero," he reasoned. "You can understand then why we were mystified."

In his investigation, he found that the maintenance men seemed to be the most knowledgeable about the Bible, and by questioning various sources and narrowing the suspects through a process of elimination, he finally found the source. "The mystery witness turned out to be a house painter who worked under contract to the hotel, but not as a regular member of the staff." Evans found him high on a ladder and asked him to come down.

He seemed like a very ordinary individual, and was perplexed that Evans would be surprised to learn that he had so readily shared his faith. For him it seemed routine: "It's like this. Almost everything here gets constant painting, because this kind of hotel is kept in top condition. We redecorate often too. I paint my way everywhere. My work gets me into every department of the building—dining room, kitchens, offices, and all the guest rooms. I know everybody and everybody knows me. Of course I tell them about my Lord."

For him, it was not a matter of duty. Indeed, he could have said with the Prophet Jeremiah, "I cannot hold it in." Witnessing was a part of his lifestyle. He enjoyed it. "That's the only hobby I have," he confessed.[5]

To whom can I speak and give warning? Who will listen to me? Their ears are closed so they cannot hear. The word of the Lord is offensive to them; they find no pleasure in it. But I am full of the wrath of the Lord, and I cannot hold it in.

*Jeremiah 6:10–11.*

# "A PROMISE FROM SCRIPTURE"

It was this short passage from the Old Testament that carried Mabel Francis and her sister Anne Dievendorf through the difficult days following World War II. They had been missionaries to Japan with the Christian and Missionary Alliance for many years. Mabel arrived in 1909 and was joined by her widowed sister in 1922. Their ministry was very effective and they were committed to the task of working with the Japanese despite many obstacles.

The first major obstacle confronted them during the Depression of the 1930s, when the Alliance recalled its missionaries to Japan due to insufficient funding. Despite the hardship of receiving no regular support, Mabel and Anne determined they would stay on, convinced that God would uphold them if they were faithful to their calling. They continued their work in relative freedom until the bombing of Pearl Harbor. They then confronted another major obstacle—internment. But even during their house arrest, they were able to reach out with the gospel in a limited way.

It was after the war that the real test of their strength came, and it was then that Mabel claimed the assurance that "The eyes of the Lord run to and fro throughout the whole earth, to show himself strong in the behalf of them whose heart is perfect toward him" (KJV). God would spot her, she was convinced, alone and far from home, and he would show his strength through her if her heart was right with him. But how could she and her sister do all that needed to be done by themselves? It was a time when they needed missionary personnel more than ever, but except for three other missionaries, their colleagues were gone.

"They didn't have to wonder very long. An American soldier in the occupation forces and his Christian buddies were on a crowded train in Tokyo. They saw the American lady—but it wasn't until she smiled that the light dawned. 'She's got to be an American missionary,' the leader of the GI group said. So when Mrs. Dievendorf pushed her way out of the train, the American soldiers were right with her."

Through the help of these soldiers, Mabel and Anne expanded their work. They introduced the servicemen to a Japanese pastor who offered the use of his church located on the main street of Tokyo, and from that center GIs spread out in street evangelism, bringing those interested back for an evening Bible study and music sung by a GI choir of as many as forty men.

This ministry grew and soon was organized as the Far Eastern Gospel Crusade (now SEND, International). Mabel and Anne headed the ministry until it was well established. God had been faithful and had given them strength through an unexpected source.[6]

Yet when you relied on the Lord, he delivered them into your hand.

For the eyes of the Lord range throughout the earth to strengthen those whose hearts are fully committed to him.

*2 Chronicles 16:8b–9*

## "SATAN ENTERED INTO HIM"

Bible translators often heave a sigh of relief when they come to narrative passages that simply tell stories. That was the case when Wycliffe Bible Translators Denis and Diana Masson were working on the passage on the Last Supper from the gospel of John. Unlike certain doctrinal passages filled with concept nouns, it was an action story that they assumed would be easier to convey to the Dida people of the Ivory Coast, West Africa.

They quickly realized, however, that this particular narrative contained a serious problem for the Dida people. The phrase "Satan entered into him"—even though the phrase referred to Judas, led the Dida people to conclude that Jesus was a witch.

"In the Dida world view, a 'witch' is a murderer who kills secretly through an evil force which inhabits him. If anyone eats food that a witch has purposely contaminated, then he also becomes a witch. That's why any Dida person who heard this translation would immediately believe that Jesus was a witch, and that Judas became a witch because he took food from Jesus.

"How could they possibly be expected to put their faith in someone they believed was a witch out to kill people? No amount of explanation, no amount of teaching could make them think differently."

When they realized that this little phrase had entirely distorted the gospel for the Dida people, Denis and Diana immediately corrected their translation. Through conversations with the people they learned that "the Dida expression, 'the devil spoiled his head,' conveys the true meaning and is also close to the word-for-word original."

The problem was solved, and they broke down this barrier to understanding the gospel. Judas was seen as an ordinary man under the control of Satan, and Jesus could now be perceived as the Son of God, not a witch who destroys others through his evil powers.[7]

After he had said this, Jesus was troubled in spirit and testified, "I tell you the truth, one of you is going to betray me."

His disciples stared at one another, at a loss to know which of them he meant. One of them, the disciple whom Jesus loved, was reclining next to him. Simon Peter motioned to this disciple and said, "Ask him which one he means."

Leaning back against Jesus, he asked him, "Lord, who is it?"

Jesus answered, "It is the one to whom I will give this piece of bread when I have dipped it in the dish." Then, dipping the piece of bread, he gave it to Judas Iscariot, son of Simon. As soon as Judas took the bread, Satan entered into him.

*John 13:21–27a.*

# "HOW BEAUTIFUL ON THE MOUNTAINS ARE THE FEET"

In 1949, four years after the end of World War II, Toshiko Tanaka, a deeply depressed Japanese school teacher, was on the brink of suicide. Her husband had been killed in the war and she was struggling to keep her household together and care for her young daughter. Suicide seemed like a logical solution to her despair. She had utterly lost hope for any happiness in her future. Then her life suddenly changed. She had heard about a missionary family living in a village over the mountains. They had a message—a message that offered hope for even the most hopeless situations.

After trekking over the mountains, Toshiko found the missionaries and found the hope they offered through faith in Christ. Her life was transformed. She had peace and hope that she had never experienced before and she was ready to return home and face the future with optimism.

So exuberant was she in her newfound faith that she wanted to share it with others when she returned to her village, but she was apprehensive, since she was young in her faith. What a surprise it was then for the missionary family when the following week they saw Toshiko walking through their gate. It was an arduous mountain walk—and here she was again, the second time in the space of a week. And more astounding than that was the fact that she had not come alone. With her was her class of twenty-six primary school students.

The children listened attentively to the story of Jesus before they began the hike of several hours back over the mountains. But it was not enough for just the children to hear. Toshiko pleaded with the missionaries to come and share the good news with her entire village.

"Shortly after Mrs. Tanaka's visit Robert Reese with an interpreter and some Christian helpers made a trip to Doshi village and the home of this school teacher. When they saw the deeply rutted, narrow, winding road which was barely passable even with an army jeep, they almost gave up. But after laboriously crossing the mountain, they saw this beautiful long valley with clusters of thatched roof houses. Soon they came upon the school house, where over two hundred adults and children were waiting to hear the gospel story. These country folks listened intently for several hours, and begged to hear more. As the missionary team prepared to leave, again and again they heard, 'Please come back and be our friend!' "

They had traveled through the mountains and were received warmly as they brought good news and good tidings, and proclaimed peace and salvation.[8]

"And all day long my name is constantly blasphemed. Therefore my people will know my name; therefore in that day they will know that it is I who foretold it. Yes, it is I."

How beautiful on the mountains are the feet of those who bring good news, who proclaim peace, who bring good tidings, who proclaim salvation, who say to Zion, "Your God reigns!"

*Isaiah 52:5b–7.*

# "CHOOSE THIS DAY WHOM YOU WILL SERVE"

Joshua's choice for the people was very plain. There was no opportunity to waffle on the issue. The alternatives were clear—they could choose the gods of their forefathers or the Lord—and there was no middle ground. It is the lukewarm, middle-of-the-road course, however, that often has the most appeal to people, as Charles G. Finney witnessed in his ministry.

Finney became the best-known revivalist of the Second Great Awakening that swept America in the early decades of the nineteenth century. He was not a likely candidate, however, for this role. During his earliest years of ministry he was insecure and ambivalent about his ability to preach. "Having had no regular training for the ministry," he wrote, "I did not expect or desire to labor in large towns or cities or minister to cultivated congregations. I intended to go into the new settlements and preach in schoolhouses and barns and groves as best I could."

He was commissioned by the Western New York Female Missionary Society, and his term of service was projected for three months. One of the little villages to which he was assigned was Evans Mills, New York. There he found people that were hardened to the gospel. "Rebellion against the blessed God, under almost every form and in every shocking degree stalked aboard with unblushing front. . . ."

People attended his services, but there was no visible response, except their "ruinous rejection of the gospel of God's dear Son." Why did they even come to the meetings? Simply to sit on the benches and sullenly reject God's message? In an effort to shake them from their middle-of-the-road course, Finney threw out this challenge one Sunday evening: "Now I must know your minds, and I want all of you who will give your pledge to make your peace with God immediately, to rise up; but all of you who are resolved not to become Christians and wish me to understand so and Christ to understand so, remain sitting."

The congregation was stunned. "They looked at one another and at me, and all sat still, just as I expected. Then you are committed. You have taken your stand. You have rejected Christ and His Gospel," he concluded. He had overstepped his bounds. The people walked out. The preacher's work in that town was over—or so he thought. During the days that followed he and a godly deacon were on their knees in prayer. When they arrived at the next scheduled service, they found the building packed and a great revival followed. What had the people chosen? "As for me and my house, we will serve the Lord."[9]

"Now fear the Lord and serve him with all faithfulness. Throw away the gods your forefathers worshiped beyond the River and in Egypt, and serve the Lord. But if serving the Lord seems undesirable to you, then choose for yourselves this day whom you will serve, whether the gods your forefathers served beyond the River, or the gods of the Amorites, in whose land you are living. But as for me and my household, we will serve the Lord."

*Joshua 24:14–15.*

## "THE WICKEDNESS OF NINEVEH"

It was a sermon from the book of Jonah that transformed the life of Andrew Dong-sup Chung. The preacher described the people of Nineveh as being among the most wicked and unworthy people of all time, and emphasized that if God could forgive them, he could forgive anyone. That was just the message that Andrew needed.

From the time he was a little boy Chung considered himself to be unwanted, unloved, and utterly worthless. He was born in the 1940s into a Korean farm family of eleven children. As the fourth son, he always felt that he was treated as the "left-over" child. That feeling was more than simply his imagination. Having been born on the same day as his older brother, he was always forgotten on his birthday, while great celebration was made over his brother. Then, beginning at the age of five, his parents and others in his family began to prod him to go and live with other relatives who had no children. To make matters worse, his next oldest brother was much better looking than he was, and instead of calling Chung by his name, he referred to him in derogatory terms.

It was not until Chung entered high school that he came in contact with Christianity. The only religion he had previously known was that of his grandmother, an animistic shaman, who worshiped such things as the stars, trees, and mountains. "Whenever any member of the family became ill, she became a shaman, chanted her charms, swung scissors to find out what angered the evil spirits and then performed some rituals to pacify the evil spirits." Chung gladly exchanged animism for Christianity, but he still did not have peace. During his college years, he joined a group known as the "Salvation Sect," a cultic group that claimed that they alone possessed the secret knowledge of the Bible. It was here that Chung found acceptance, and for eight years he totally surrendered himself to the authoritarian leadership of this cult.

It was not until he was traveling abroad that Chung realized there were other Christians outside the movement, and it was only then that he realized the power of prayer—a practice that was disavowed by his sect. Leaving this group, the only group that had ever accepted him, was a traumatic experience, and for the next three years he was spiritually confused, and was almost lured into Mormonism. Then one Sunday he was invited to a Christian church where he heard a message on Jonah and the people of Nineveh. His life was transformed that day. He had found Christ, the only one who could ever fully accept him as he was. He grew in the faith and became a professor at Baptist Theological Seminary in Taejon.[10]

**The word of the Lord came to Jonah son of Amittai: "Go to the great city of Nineveh and preach against it, because its wickedness has come up before me. . . ."**

**When God saw what they did and how they turned from their evil ways, he had compassion and did not bring upon them the destruction he had threatened.**

*Jonah 1:1; 3:10.*

# "DO YOU WANT TO GET WELL?"

Some Bible teachers have suggested that the man at the pool might not really have wanted to be healed. After thirty-eight years, he may have had a sense of complacency in his condition and might have been afraid of trying to make his own way in the real world. The gospel account does not record an affirmative answer to Jesus' question, "Do you want to get well?"; it only records an excuse. People in the medical profession have testified that such attitudes are not entirely uncommon. The fear of a radically changed lifestyle can be threatening. Indeed, healing can be a disservice in some instances, as Dr. Paul Brand, a medical missionary to lepers, discovered.

Two months after Dr. Brand completed extensive surgery on a leper's hands, the young man returned to the hospital, "woefully thin" and "with no laughter in his sad, hungry eyes." He held out his hands to the doctor and dejectedly told him that he had "bad begging hands." Dr. Brand was puzzled, until the leper disclosed his predicament. Before his surgery, he explained, people pitied him and were more willing to toss him a few coins, but now that his hands had been healed he looked almost normal, and people passed him by.

The doctor was distressed and he began to question his mission. "What was he doing? Repairing men's bodies only to make their spirits more disabled than before? . . . Was he merely creating beggars with less ability for begging?" He had suddenly come face-to-face with the reality that he had to be more than a missionary physician who healed bodies and helped to save souls. Soon after that experience, another patient returned complaining of the same predicament.

Determined to reverse this situation, Dr. Brand, with funding from an eighty-four-year-old retired missionary, built a training school where his patients would learn to become self-sufficient as skilled craftsmen. They would still face hostility as outcasts in society, but they would no longer lament their "bad begging hands."[11]

Some time later, Jesus went up to Jerusalem for a feast of the Jews. Now there is in Jerusalem near the Sheep Gate a pool, which in Aramaic is called Bethesda and which is surrounded by five covered colonnades. Here a great number of disabled people used to lie—the blind, the lame, the paralyzed. One who was there had been an invalid for thirty-eight years. When Jesus saw him lying there and learned that he had been in this condition for a long time, he asked him, "Do you want to get well?"

"Sir," the invalid replied, "I have no one to help me into the pool when the water is stirred. While I am trying to get in someone else goes down ahead of me."

*John 5:1–7.*

# "STRENGTHENED IN THE FAITH AS YOU WERE TAUGHT"

Abraham Kuyper, the great theologian of the Dutch Reformed Church, was the son of a minister, but, according to his testimony, "the inherited faith lost its root in my heart; it shrivelled under the withering heat of unbelief. Of the old treasures I retained nothing. . . . I was for long robbed of my childhood faith."

Despite this crisis of faith, he nevertheless followed in his father's footsteps and entered the ministry. After his training at the University of Leyden, he accepted a small parish in the country. Here he found a dedicated group of Christians who in many ways seemed far beneath their brilliant pastor, an "intellectual superman." Yet, he quickly recognized that they were in many ways his superior. "I could not measure my impoverished Bible knowledge, the fruit of university study," he wrote, "with that of these plain people."

As Kuyper met with them, his life began to change, as he later recalled: "What drew me most to them was that here the heart spoke—there was inner experience. . . . I found myself ever at the fork of the way. Either must I take sharp position against them or go with them without conditions, putting myself under sovereign grace."

His conversion came through the counsel of a young girl named Pietje Baltus. She had none of this world's luxuries, but she had a deep faith that amazed Abraham. "In his first visit to her parents' home the new Dominie sat for two hours listening to the statement of the hope that was in her. She warned him that he, too, must have this hope if he would not perish eternally." She confessed how she had prayed almost constantly for him. "I could not relax until the Lord Himself came and took him from my soul, and until I had the happiness of knowing that Christ had him in charge," she later said.

"What a contrast! This gifted, cultured son of the university, versed in all the philosophies, chatting in five languages with ease at his dinner-table . . . and the unschooled but Spirit-taught peasant girl. Kuyper throughout life retained a profound gratitude to this intercessor and her photograph stood in his study till the end."

In the years that followed, Kuyper led the fight against the theological liberalism that was gaining control of his church. For fifty years he edited a Christian daily paper, and he established the Free University that helped to bring about a revival of orthodoxy.[12]

So then, just as you received Christ Jesus as Lord, continue to live in him, rooted and built up in him, strengthened in the faith as you were taught, and overflowing with thankfulness.

See to it that no one takes you captive through hollow and deceptive philosophy, which depends on human traditions and the basic principles of this world rather than on Christ.

*Colossians 2:6−8.*

# "WHEN THE HOLY SPIRIT COMES ON YOU"

Down through history, revivals that were characterized by an outpouring of the Holy Spirit were followed by missionary outreach, even as the Lord prophesied to his disciples before his Ascension. A powerful example of this was the revival in 1886, that sparked the Student Volunteer Movement.

In 1885, Grace and Robert Wilder, who had grown up as missionary children in India, had begun praying for a new wave of missionary enthusiasm in the United States. It seemed that the churches were lethargic, and Grace and Robert began praying that God would raise up a thousand new missionaries. At first they prayed together alone, but then Robert shared his vision with some of his fellow students at Princeton Seminary, and after that every Sunday afternoon five of them joined him in prayer for missions.

The following summer, Robert attended a Bible Conference at Mt. Hermon, Massachusetts, where Dwight L. Moody was the featured speaker. Robert had not planned to attend, but his sister strongly urged him to go, convinced that he might have the opportunity there to see God answer their prayers. She was determined to trust God for one hundred missionary volunteers from that conference. Here he joined more than two hundred other college students from around the country, and immediately he began sharing with them his concern for missions and inviting them to join him each afternoon for prayer. Beginning with only four others, the group soon surpassed twenty.

Having stirred up the students, Robert then went to the featured speaker himself. Moody had not planned to focus on missions during the conference, but Robert persuaded him to devote two evening sessions to the subject, the second of which was led by students who presented the spiritual impoverishment of ten different countries.

At that time many students committed their lives to missions, including John R. Mott, who later became one of the nation's leading missionary statesmen. To his parents he wrote: "The Holy Spirit is working here with mighty power. He has brought about the greatest missionary revival the world has ever known. Up to this noon, over eighty of the students have consecrated themselves to foreign missionary work and I know by Sunday night they will number 100. It thrills me through and through to record this fact. Here I received a far richer anointing of the Spirit than I had dared to ask for before I came." One hundred young men did volunteer, and the Student Volunteer Movement was born.[13]

So when they met together, they asked him, "Lord, are you at this time going to restore the kingdom to Israel?"

He said to them: "It is not for you to know the times or dates the Father has set by his own authority. But you will receive power when the Holy Spirit comes on you; and you will be my witnesses in Jerusalem, and in all Judea and in Samaria, and to the ends of the earth."

*Acts 1:6–8.*

## "CONSIDER THE LILIES"

In 1886, during a spiritual-life conference in England, Amy Carmichael, who later became a great missionary to India, encountered God in a way that changed her entire outlook on life. Her expensive taste in food and clothing suddenly vanished. She first realized this when she was invited to a restaurant by a friend, only to be served very poorly prepared mutton chops. Such an incident would have previously upset the well-brought-up young woman, but she realized that she no longer cared about such trivial things in life.

"If mutton chops didn't matter anymore, neither did clothes," writes Elisabeth Elliot. "When Amy got back to Belfast, the long mourning period for her father was over and it was time, her mother said, to purchase a few pretty dresses—among them, of course, an evening dress for parties. They went to the shop. The shopman displayed his loveliest things. Suddenly Amy decided she could not have them. She was now, in the language of the apostle Paul . . . 'dead to the world.' To Amy, the world meant fashion, finery, luxury of any sort. She would follow Him who had no home, no earthly possessions beyond the bare minimum. She would be 'dead to the world and its applause, to all its customs, fashions, laws.' For a girl with her eye for beauty, it is the measure of her commitment that she did not hesitate to relinquish all that seemed to her inimical to the true life of discipleship."

Amy's commitment to following Christ who had no earthly possessions and challenged his disciples not to "worry about your life, what you will eat, or about your body, what you will wear" (Luke 12:22), was one of the most important decisions she made during her early life. It was a decision that prepared her for a long life in India. Here she would have many mouths to feed and bodies to clothe as she reached out in selfless ministry of caring for hundreds of children she rescued from Hindu temple prostitution. It was through those years that she could utterly rely on the God who clothes the lilies of the field.[14]

"Consider how the lilies grow. They do not labor or spin. Yet I tell you, not even Solomon in all his splendor was dressed like one of these. If that is how God clothes the grass of the field, which is here today, and tomorrow is thrown into the fire, how much more will he clothe you, O you of little faith! And do not set your heart on what you will eat or drink; do not worry about it. For the pagan world runs after all such things, and your Father knows that you need them. But seek his kingdom, and these things will be given to you as well."

*Luke 12:27–31.*

# "FOR GOD SO LOVED THE WORLD"

Myron Bromley was a member of the first party of Christian and Missionary Alliance missionaries to enter the Baliem Valley of Irian Jaya in 1954. He was a brilliant linguist and a single man with no family responsibilities to tie him down. He hoped that he could quickly use his training and skills to break down the Dani language and reach out with the gospel to these "stone-age" people. His optimism, however, was swiftly shattered. "It was one of the most discouraging experiences I've ever had," he later wrote. "I used pictures from a Scripture calendar and tried my best to say all I could as simply and intelligently as possible. But the natives looked as if I were talking in Latin about the price of corn in Asia." In the summer of 1955, he wrote to his mother about his struggle in translating one of the most familiar Bible verses in the English language.

"I've tried to talk about John 3:16, but I'm sure I made a lot of blunders. . . . You can imagine how faulty my interpretation must have been, since we have no adequate terms for 'God,' 'believe,' or 'everlasting life.' I talk about 'Jesus' father' because we know as yet of no belief of these people that would furnish a good term for 'God.' . . .

"As for everlasting life, I can say that we will remain alive, but that is not Jesus' or John's idea. Or I can say our skin and bones and our meat and blood will die but our souls will live, but this is not the Biblical idea either. How to say that God creates in us a new kind of life that will be ours right now and forever is something I don't know yet.

"When I try to explain the whole concept of Jesus' dying for us I say that he died in our interest that we may remain alive . . . but the whole central concept of atonement is beyond the grasp of our language. Probably this is because we don't really know how to talk about sin. I usually use the expression 'bad acting,' but that's quite different from the true concept of sin."

Despite his discouragement, Bromley did make progress in language learning and communication, and by 1961, the Alliance could report some eight thousand believers in the more than twenty churches among the Danis.[15]

"For God so loved the world that he gave his one and only Son, that whoever believes in him shall not perish but have eternal life. For God did not send his Son into the world to condemn the world, but to save the world through him. Whoever believes in him is not condemned, but whoever does not believe stands condemned already because he has not believed in the name of God's one and only Son.

*John 3:16–18.*

# "SAVED THROUGH FAITH NOT BY WORKS"

"I never read a word of my Bible from the time I was seven to the time I was twenty-one." These were the words of a young man who had everything it seemed. John Charles Ryle was born into a wealthy family in England in 1816. His father was an heir to a vast fortune and a member of the House of Commons. "As for John, whatever he turned his hand to also prospered. Handsome of feature and striking of figure, he had captained the cricket teams at Eton and at Oxford, rowed with the Oxford crew, besides winning a name as an intellectual."

But despite his success and wealth, he knew something was missing in his life. In that frame of mind, he entered a church service at the time the Scripture was being read: "For by grace are ye saved by faith; and that not of yourselves: it is the gift of God." The words seemed to be spoken directly to him, and they prompted him to put his faith in Christ.

After his university graduation he had intended to follow the footsteps of his father into business and government service, but a sudden financial reversal plunged the family into near poverty. Although it was tempting to seek to regain the family fortune, Ryle took the setback as a sign from God that he should enter the ministry. His first appointment was to a small parish in southern England, which thrived under his ministry.

His second appointment in 1843 was to serve as rector of St. Thomas Church in Winchester. Here he gave his ministry a new focus. "Soon after he made the change, a horrible accident occurred near his parish. At Great Yarmouth a suspension bridge crowded with men and women broke down, plunging the multitude into the waters below. About one hundred of the victims drowned." The shock and distress prompted Ryle to use the incident to warn people about the uncertainties of life. "In reality it was the setting off of a movement, for out of it emerged the idea of a series known as the Ipswich Tracts. Before his death, Bishop Ryle was to write three hundred messages in pamphlet form. Their printings would pass the twelve-million mark and be read in a dozen different languages."

In addition to tracts he wrote some twenty books—books known for profound commentary on the gospel and for pithy sayings: "What we weave in time, we wear in eternity;" "Meddle with no man's person, but spare no man's sin;" and "Here is rock," speaking of the Word. "All else is sand."[16]

And God raised us up with Christ and seated us with him in the heavenly realms in Christ Jesus, in order that in the coming ages he might show the incomparable riches of his grace, expressed in his kindness to us in Christ Jesus. For it is by grace you have been saved, through faith—and this not from yourselves, it is the gift of God—not by works, so that no one can boast. For we are God's workmanship, created in Christ Jesus to do good works, which God prepared in advance for us to do.

*Ephesians 2:6–10.*

# "I STAND AT THE DOOR AND KNOCK"

The artist's conception of Jesus standing at the door and knocking is familiar. Jesus is alone in that picture, and that is the correct perception that one ought to receive from the biblical passage. But that is not the picture that is always perceived by those to whom the message has been given.

When the great missionary statesman E. Stanley Jones went to India, he discovered that Christ indeed had been offered to India, but not Christ alone. So often there were other issues or culturally bound institutions that obscured Christ, and he vowed that in his own preaching he would focus on Christ alone—that he would not become sidetracked with the non-essentials and with extraneous points of interest.

"I would not mention the non-Christian religions. I would not speak to Hindus or Muslims, but to persons—persons in spiritual need. Jesus Christ had met my need, and he could meet theirs. It would be a head-on presentation of Christ, combined with a witness that he had met my need so he could meet theirs. . . . The Christ I presented would be the disentangled Christ—disentangled from being bound up with Western culture and Western forms of Christianity. He would stand in his own right, speaking directly to the needs of persons as persons without any cancelling entanglements."

Following one of the evangelist's messages, a Hindu principal of a college stood to make the closing remarks—remarks that indicated he had understood and received the message Jones was seeking to convey: "Jesus has stood four times in history before the door of India and has knocked. The first time he appeared in the early days he stood in company with a trader. He knocked. We looked out and saw him and liked him, but we didn't like his company, so we shut the door. Later he appeared, with a diplomat on one side and a soldier on the other, and knocked. We looked out and said: 'We like you, but we don't like your company.' Again we shut the door. The third time was when he appeared as the uplifter of the outcastes. We liked him better in this role, but we weren't sure of what was behind it. Was this the religious side of imperialism? Are they conquering us through religion? Again we shut the door. And now he appears before our doors, as tonight, as the disentangled Christ. To this disentangled Christ we say: 'Come in. Our doors are open to you.'"[17]

Those whom I love I rebuke and discipline. So be earnest, and repent. Here I am! I stand at the door and knock. If anyone hears my voice and opens the door, I will go in and eat with him, and he with me.

*Revelation 3:19–20.*

## "INSIDE THEY ARE FULL OF GREED AND SELF-INDULGENCE"

Motlalepula Chabaku is a black South African woman who travels widely speaking forcefully about the evils of apartheid. She was raised in a Christian home, but became disillusioned with Christianity because of the racism evident among the white people who professed to be Christians. She could simply not reconcile the two ideologies.

"I began to ask, 'How can brothers and sisters in Christ deny me a vote in my own motherland? How can they pay me less wages than a white worker—even if I know how to read and write and the white worker doesn't? How can I say we are all God's people and belong to the same family of God—while a white alcoholic sitting in a position of authority, claiming to be a Christian, insists on determining my destiny?' I began to realize that whites were misusing the church—just to keep blacks in subservience."

Chabaku experimented with Transcendental Meditation and the Hare Krishnas and other religions, but found no peace. Then one night she walked by a small black church and heard a woman singing an old-time hymn. She returned home and dug out her hymnbook, and took it to the outhouse where no one would see her. The first hymn she turned to was "Take My Life and Let It Be Consecrated, Lord, to Thee."

"I began to look at myself, almost as if a movie of my life was flashing in front of me. I discovered I was as selfish as the whites. I was as racist as the whites. I was as bitter as the whites. I had made the same mistakes as those whites whose hypocrisy made me leave the church.

"Then it was as if a voice said, 'Kneel down.' So I knelt down on that cold, concrete, outhouse floor. And as the cold, biting wind came through, I confessed to God who I was and what I was going through. There in the outhouse, I accepted Jesus Christ as my Savior and liberator."

As she travels around the United States speaking out for justice, Chabaku sees herself as a screwdriver, "thrown into the drawer with other tools, where it waits until it is needed for another job. . . . I am here to do that for God—to be a tool, a catalyst for peace, justice, and reconciliation."[18]

"Woe to you, teachers of the law and Pharisees, you hypocrites! You clean the outside of the cup and dish, but inside they are full of greed and self-indulgence. Blind Pharisee! First clean the inside of the cup and dish, and then the outside also will be clean.

Woe to you, teachers of the law and Pharisees, you hypocrites! You are like whitewashed tombs, which look beautiful on the outside but on the inside are full of dead men's bones and everything unclean. In the same way, on the outside you appear to people as righteous but on the inside you are full of hypocrisy and wickedness.

*Matthew 23:25–28.*

## "A TOUCH OF HEALING"

The healing ministry that characterized Jesus' mission is a model for medical missionaries today as they seek to reach out in love to those who are physically suffering. Medical missionary work in the Third World is a ministry that is hampered by a lack of supplies and equipment; it is a ministry that is utterly dependent on the healing hand of the Lord. Donald McClure found this true as he worked among various tribal peoples in Sudan and Ethiopia. Sometimes when he failed, God worked through his mistakes and blunders. This was the case one day when he was about to collapse from fatigue after seeing more than a hundred patients and he was about to head home. He later related the story:

"Then after dark I started for the house to clean up a bit for supper, but I was called to the river bank. Another canoe had come in through the rain and this time a young girl was lying in bloody water. As two women lifted her out of the canoe, her big brown eyes looked piteously at me. Then I saw her trouble was caused by an umbilical cord which had not been removed and trailed behind her as they dragged her out of the boat and laid her on the wet ground naked, except for a loin cloth.

"I was told that she had given birth to a stillborn baby yesterday and the placenta would not detach itself. The poor little girl did not look to be more than thirteen and she was frightened nearly to death and had lost so much blood that her eyes were glaring white and she was too weak to stand. I stooped over to pick her up in my arms and bring her into the house where I could treat her. As I lifted her and straightened up, she suddenly clutched my neck and screamed in pain, and I heard one of the women cry, 'It is out.'

"And so it was. In the dark the great Dr. McClure had stepped on the trailing cord when he stooped to pick her up and in lifting her with his foot still firmly planted on the umbilical cord the whole placenta had pulled free. I dare say this is the only case on record where a placenta was removed in this manner. I think I will write it up for a medical journal. . . . I do not know what I would have done if God in His Grace had not taken care of that poor young girl. She is now sleeping quietly in my study and already feels much better."[19]

Just then a woman who had been subject to bleeding for twelve years came up behind him [Jesus] and touched the edge of his cloak. She said to herself, "If I only touch his cloak, I will be healed."

Jesus turned and saw her. "Take heart, daughter," he said, "your faith has healed you." And the woman was healed from that moment.

*Matthew 9:20–22.*

# "I HAVE HIDDEN YOUR WORD IN MY HEART"

Henry Moorhouse was known as one of the great preachers of the nineteenth century. He was a man who had a profound influence on Dwight L. Moody and the founding of Moody Bible Institute. He was a brilliant lecturer and under his ministry "Princeton was moved like the tides of the sea." Indeed, many Princeton graduates who went on into the ministry testified that "it was Moorhouse who set my heart on fire when I was a student."

Moorhouse was an unlikely individual for renown, especially within academic circles. His early life was fashioned on the streets of Lancastershire and he was "a detention home candidate before his teens." His best quality was his voice, and while still in his teens became an auctioneer; it was an ignoble occupation associated with charlatans, and it brought him little contentment. It was during a time of suicidal despondency that he talked with a Christian friend and was converted.

Soon after his conversion, while he was on the auction block one day, a man in the crowd called out, "Thou ought to have the Bible in thy hand . . . and not that hammer of the Devil!" With that "call" to ministry prodding him on, he contacted John Hambleton, a converted vaudeville actor turned revivalist, and requested that he serve as his spiritual mentor. Hambleton agreed, and became his teacher "at the side of a haystack, or in a private room, or in a corner in a railway carriage—wherever the man and boy could find a quiet spot for Bible study."

Moorhouse's trademark as a preacher was his emphasis on the Bible. His sermons were commentaries on verses, and because he had hidden God's Word in his heart, he was able to quote verses freely by memory. He brought the Bible alive through his "smooth auction block delivery," and often the comment was made, "He made the Bible a new book to me." He was outspoken in his insistence that the Bible ought to be the focus of preaching, and when he heard Dwight L. Moody on his first visit to the British Isles, he bluntly advised him: "God will make a great preacher of you if you will preach His word instead of *your* word." Moody was offended, but later when Moorhouse preached from his pulpit in Chicago, he said "I just couldn't keep the tears back. Moorhouse made me see just how much *God loved me!*"

When a heart problem prevented Moorhouse from continued preaching, he began selling the Bible he so loved on the streets from his carriage. He sold approximately seventy thousand in 1880 alone.[20]

How can a young man keep his way pure? By living according to your word. I seek you with all my heart; do not let me stray from your commands. I have hidden your word in my heart that I might not sin against you. Praise be to you, O Lord; teach me your decrees. With my lips I recount all the laws that come from your mouth. I rejoice in following your statutes as one rejoices in great riches. I meditate on your precepts and consider your ways. I delight in your decrees; I will not neglect your word.

*Psalm 119:9–16.*

# "A LONG SERMON"

Paul's all-night sermon has often been compared in jest to long-winded preachers of today, but Paul ws not droning on simply to hear himself preach. He was on a missionary journey, and he was leaving town the next morning. There was much teaching to be done and so little time to do it. This same situation has confronted missionaries in the generations since the apostle Paul—John Sung of China being an example.

When Sung visited the island of Java on his third missionary journey to Indonesia in 1939, he startled the congregation in Surabaja with this announcement: "I have 22 messages to give to you this week. This means that I must hold three meetings every day at which you must all be present, otherwise you will fail to discover what God's message is for you."

How could they come to three meetings a day? The demand seemed outrageous. There was work to be done and children had to attend school. But, as Sung began preaching, the congregation's doubts vanished. The next day, shopkeepers closed their doors with signs that read, "Closed for the week—Missionary Campaign." Children stayed home from school, and virtually the whole community became involved in day-long meetings as the revival spread.

But attending meetings would not be enough. "Do not think that following Jesus is only a matter of being uplifted inside," the evangelist implored. "There are millions who do not know the Lord Jesus. Go out and take the gospel to them." With that encouragement, young people organized themselves into evangelistic teams. When they were not in meetings, they were busy preaching the gospel to passersby in the streets, to patrons of the bars—wherever they could find a listening ear.

When the week was over, Sung went on for a week of meetings in another town, praying that the revival in Surabaja would carry on because of the people's commitment to Christ, and that his teaching—packed into twenty-two messages—would not be forgotten.[21]

On the first day of the week we came together to break bread. Paul spoke to the people and, because he intended to leave the next day, kept on talking until midnight. There were many lamps in the upstairs room where we were meeting. Seated in a window was a young man named Eutychus, who was sinking into a deep sleep as Paul talked on and on. When he was sound asleep, he fell to the ground from the third story and was picked up dead. Paul went down, threw himself on the young man and put his arms around him. "Don't be alarmed," he said. "He's alive!" Then he went upstairs again and broke bread and ate. After talking until daylight, he left. The people took the young man home alive and were greatly comforted.

*Acts 20:7–12.*

## "NEEDLESS BRUISES? AND BLOODSHOT EYES?"

It is amazing how a biblical passage written many generations ago can reflect a contemporary situation almost word-for-word. That was true with Proverbs 23 in its description of Gregory's life. Gregory grew up in a Roman Catholic family in Rwanda and attended Catholic schools and went on to train for the priesthood. He struggled, however, with beliefs he could not accept. In the process, he was having a negative influence on other students.

"While attending school," he writes, "I studied the Bible and other religious literature on my own. Because of this I asked a lot of probing questions which showed opposition to the beliefs being taught. Soon, they refused to let me continue my studies."

Rejected by the religious establishment, Gregory joined the Army for a time and then worked on a government project. He was promoted to an accounting position, and the work paid well, but he was not fulfilled. "On my free time," he writes, "I did a lot of hard drinking, and fought in many drunken barroom brawls. My hands were often broken from hitting people so hard. Not eating properly reduced me physically to just skin and bones. My face was dull, and my life was a mess." Gregory lost his job when he refused to relocate in Kibungo, a "horrible place" that was beneath his dignity. He was sinking deeper into debauchery when his life suddenly changed.

One Sunday, on his way to visit some relatives—to invite them to go out drinking with him—he passed by a little outdoor Baptist church that was meeting on a hillside. Here he heard the pastor preach from Proverbs 23. "It was as if the pastor was preaching directly at me," he later recalled. "Those verses were the exact story of my life. The message had a tremendous impact on me, and I went home without going drinking. That night I committed my life to the Lord, and spent the next three days reading the Bible and praying. The following Sunday found me back at the new church making a public profession of my faith."

Soon after that Gregory heard a message of challenge for full-time ministry, and he responded by vowing to become a pastor. Despite strong opposition from his family, and language and financial hardships, he enrolled in a Bible institute. After completing the course, he accepted an assignment to a tiny church in Kibungo—that same "horrible place" he had vowed he would never go.[22]

Who has woe? Who has sorrow? Who has strife? Who has complaints? Who has needless bruises? Who has bloodshot eyes? Those who linger over wine. . . . You will be like one sleeping on the high seas, lying on top of the rigging. "They hit me," you will say, "but I'm not hurt! They beat me, but I don't feel it! When will I wake up so I can find another drink?"

*Proverbs 23:29–30a, 34–35.*

# "UNDERSTANDING TO THE SIMPLE"

The Auca tragedy that cost the lives of five American missionaries in Ecuador in 1956 made headlines, but very little was publicized about the efforts in the years that followed by Elisabeth Elliot and Rachel Saint to reach these people with the gospel. They entered the territory in the company of Dayuma, an Auca woman who had fled her tribe as a young woman. She was welcomed back as were the two women accompanying her. Both Elisabeth and Rachel immediately began working on the language, while Dayuma became reacquainted with her people.

Dayuma was a Christian, and even though she was uneducated, she was eager to share her faith. Indeed, she enthusiastically accepted her role as a "teacher, preacher, and evangelist." Her simple style was one the Aucas could understand, even though it was marred in some ways by the American culture she had learned on a publicity trip with Rachel.

"Not surprisingly, Dayuma patterned her Sunday services after what she remembered from worship with missionaries and American Christians. 'I'm going to speak to God,' she would announce to the informal congregation that lounged in hammocks and sat on logs, squinting against the morning sun that was rising above the trees. 'Stop talking. Close your eyes as if you're going to sleep.'

"Her morning prayers would run on and on, naming every missionary she knew . . . and every person she could recall meeting in the United States, including Dr. Edman and Billy Graham. She asked God to protect her people from devils, jaguars, snakes, and enemy spears. She besought Him to help the Aucas believe in Jesus and follow 'God's Carving' so they would live well and stop spearing. When a member of the congregation interrupted, as often happened, she would say, 'Shut up,' then go on with her petition.

"She led them in one-line hymns, chanted over and over in the familiar, nasal, singsong minor key used in singing about hunts and spear fights. She strung Bible stories together on a theme, embellishing as she went along, supplying understandable illustrations from daily life, keeping a sharp eye on her audience to make sure that everyone was paying attention. . . ."

Dayuma's preaching style was far removed from what is taught in homiletics classes, but there's no doubt that she was more effective in her simplistic efforts than a missionary would have been.[23]

Your statutes are wonderful; therefore I obey them. The unfolding of your words gives light; it gives understanding to the simple. I open my mouth and pant, longing for your commands. Turn to me and have mercy on me, as you always do to those who love your name.

*Psalm 119:129–133.*

## "SAVED FROM THE LAW OF SIN AND DEATH"

He was thirty-eight and single and would have rather stayed home from the church meeting that spring evening of May 24, 1738, but he attended, not knowing that what would transpire there would change the course of history. "I went very unwillingly to a society in Aldersgate Street," he confessed, "where one was reading Luther's preface to the Romans. About a quarter before nine, while he was describing the change God works in the heart through faith in Christ, I felt my heart strangely warmed. I felt I did trust in Christ alone, for salvation; and an assurance was given me, that He had taken away my sins, even *mine*, and saved *me* from the law of sin and death."

John Wesley had been raised in a Christian environment, and had been exhorted by both parents—especially his mother—to live a holy life. He took their advice seriously and when he was a student and later a tutor at Oxford University he shunned the worldliness that was prevalent on campus. Rather, he sought the company of likeminded individuals—including his brother Charles and George Whitefield—a little group that was soon dubbed the "Holy Club."

John and Charles left the University in 1735 and sailed to America to serve as missionaries to the Indians. Although their work there was unsuccessful, the entire experience had a profound influence in their lives. On the sea voyage they met with Moravian missionaries, who demonstrated a faith that astounded them—especially during a turbulent storm that nearly capsized the vessel. The Moravians calmly prayed and sang hymns, while most of the other passengers cried out in terror. "Conversations with these godly people during the voyage, and in Georgia, led the Wesleys to doubt their own conversion to Christ."

So it was that when they returned to England, they had less peace of heart than when they had departed. On his voyage home, John wrote, "I went to America to convert the Indians; but oh! who shall convert me!" He contemplated what he had learned from the Moravians, and was convinced that he had his theology turned around—especially in his effort to save himself through good works. So it was that his heart was prepared that evening to hear the words of Martin Luther on the subject of salvation by faith alone. The truth finally penetrated. There was no condemnation in Christ Jesus. John was free from the law of sin and death.[24]

Therefore, there is now no condemnation for those who are in Christ Jesus, because through Christ Jesus the law of the Spirit of life set me free from the law of sin and death. For what the law was powerless to do in that it was weakened by the sinful nature, God did by sending his own Son in the likeness of sinful man to be a sin offering. And so he condemned sin in sinful man, in order that the righteous requirements of the law might be fully met in us, who do not live according to the sinful nature but according to the Spirit.

*Romans 8:1–4.*

# "HE WILL NOT FORGET YOUR WORK"

It is a comfort to know that God does not forget the faithfulness of his children. Church history books "forget" all but a small minority, remembering only those who were recognized as leaders—mainly white males. But there have been countless others who have served valiantly without recognition, many who are lost forever in obscurity, or nearly so. Lucy Thurston, the "Mother" of American missions in Hawaii, is an example.

Lucy grew up a farm girl in Massachusetts, and at the age of twenty-five sailed for Hawaii with fifteen other people who had formed a "missionary church" to be transplanted on those islands. They arrived after five months at sea, totally unprepared for the cultural shock that would quickly engulf them. Yet, they endured the hardships and were successful in evangelizing the natives. Lucy was very active in the work with women in addition to the task of supervising her own household and six children.

She often worried about her children growing up in an environment where "heathen" wickedness "enthroned every hut and stalked every village." She questioned her own good judgment as a parent: "Are missionaries with their eyes open to the dangers of their situation to . . . give over their own children to Satan?"

In addition to her worries, illness took its toll. She suffered from breast cancer and was operated on without an anesthetic. "The pain was intense and unremitting," one writer has described. "She was so weak for days afterward that she had to be fed with a spoon." Yet, four weeks later she wrote to her daughter: "Here is again your mother, engaged in life's duties and life's warfare." She worked closely with her husband in evangelistic work. "She shared his trials, made long missionary tours with him on foot and equaled him in heroism."

Lucy continued the work after her husband died, and in 1870, after fifty years of service, she "made a stirring address of an hour and a half in the first Street Church in Honolulu, the first woman to speak in a pulpit there." Unlike so many of her married missionary sisters, she lived far beyond her childbearing years. She died in 1876, just before her eighty-first birthday.[25]

Even though we speak like this, dear friends, we are confident of better things in your case—things that accompany salvation. God is not unjust; he will not forget your work and the love you have shown him as you have helped his people and continue to help them. We want each of you to show this same diligence to the very end, in order to make your hope sure. We do not want you to become lazy, but to imitate those who through faith and patience inherit what has been promised.

*Hebrews 6:9–12.*

# "FALSE CHRISTS AND FALSE PROPHETS WILL APPEAR"

Salim Sulamane was raised a strict Muslim of the Shiite sect. As a young man he voluntarily joined a group of Muslim extremists living in Saudi Arabia who took their orders from Iran and were heavily involved in terrorist activities. He himself offered to be part of an assignment to blow up an embassy, knowing full well that it would cost him his life. "I knew I would die in the explosion," he writes, "but I believed that my death would reserve a place for me in heaven!"

The bombing mission was postponed, and in the meantime Salim became acquainted with another employee at the restaurant where he worked. "I had a lot of trouble getting along with the other workers, but he did not," Salim confessed. "One day I asked him why his life was so different. He told me that Jesus was living in his heart. . . . When he told me that Jesus was God, all my body began to shake because of these words which are blasphemous to a Muslim. . . . That evening I could not sleep. All night long I kept hearing the words, 'Jesus is God. God is Jesus.'"

So enraged was Salim with this young man that the next day he conspired with some fellow workers to arrange for soldiers to arrest him, but the young man, sensing the danger, had fled. Still, Salim could not forget him. "Night and day his life and his words were always on my mind."

Not long after this Salim took another job, and providentially, his new roommate turned out to be a former friend who had converted to Christianity. Still struggling with his inability to get along with coworkers, Salim was fired from his new position. Sensing his discouragement, his roommate shared some passages from the Bible with him. "It was the first time in my life I had ever seen a Bible," he later recalled. Yet he was angry, especially as he insisted that Muhammed was the prophet that the Bible declared would come after Jesus. No, his roommate insisted. Jesus said that "false Christs and false prophets will appear," and Muhammed was one of those.

"The Holy Spirit truly worked in my heart that night. . . . My friend called me by name and said, 'Jesus has been waiting for you for 20 years. He knows everything that is going on inside you.'. . . That night I prayed with my friend and gave my life to Jesus Christ. I also prayed that God would give me love for the people at work. When I said that prayer, I felt it was the first time I had ever really prayed."[26]

> "At that time if anyone says to you, 'Look, here is the Christ!' or, 'There he is!' do not believe it. For false Christs and false prophets will appear and perform great signs and miracles to deceive even the elect—if that were possible. See, I have told you ahead of time.
>
> "So if anyone tells you, 'There he is, out in the desert,' do not go out; or, 'Here he is, in the inner rooms,' do not believe it."
>
> *Matthew 24:23–26.*

# "JESUS IS LORD"

For the great missionary statesman E. Stanley Jones, the early Christian confession "Jesus is Lord" summed up Christianity. It was a motto that could be shared by all Christians from the earliest ones that Paul wrote to in Rome to contemporary Christians from every corner of the earth. To reinforce the confession, Jones encouraged people to make it a form of salute, as he later related.

"So we have put these three words, 'Jesus is Lord,' into three fingers, 'Jesus is Lord.' It began in Japan about twenty years ago. The Emperor had announced that he was not divine. The bottom dropped out of the inner life of Japan, for their philosophy of life was built around the Emperor as divine. This left a vacuum. So it occurred to me as I sat on the platform looking at their eager faces that into the emptiness we should place 'Jesus is Lord.'"

Elsewhere, as he shared the gospel throughout the world, Jones introduced his salute. "In the Congo," he wrote, "the churches end their services after the benediction, with the raised three fingers and say together, 'Yisu ni Bwana,' 'Jesus is Lord.' . . . When a crowd of Africans came toward a mission station in the Congo during the riots, the missionary hurriedly locked up the women and then went out tremblingly to meet them. When they got near, a big African stepped out in front with his three fingers raised: 'Jesus is Lord.' They were Christians come to protect them."

One of the reasons Jones emphasized this brief confession was because he was convinced that the only way to reach the unconverted was with a message that was clear. "The gospel begins with Jesus," he wrote, "not with God. . . . Jesus is the self-revelation of God: God meeting us in understandable form, human form, the Word became flesh. God is a Jesus-like God. A Hindu said to me: 'We can talk about God; you talk to us about Jesus.' He was right. For apart from Jesus your ideas of God become strange and uncertain. When you lose Jesus, you lose God."27

But the righteousness that is by faith says: "Do not say in your heart, 'Who will ascend into heaven?'" (that is, to bring Christ down) "or 'Who will descend into the deep?'" (that is, to bring Christ up from the dead). But what does it say? "The word is near you; it is in your mouth and in your heart," that is, the word of faith we are proclaiming: That if you confess with your mouth, "Jesus is Lord," and believe in your heart that God raised him from the dead, you will be saved. For it is with your heart that you believe and are justified, and it is with your mouth that you confess and are saved.

*Romans 10:6–10.*

# "A DREAM IN THE NIGHT"

After serving three years working as missionaries among the Gruague of Ethiopia, Howard Brandt and his family returned to the United States because of concern about their personal security. In May of 1977, Howard had been taken prisoner by a militant group, and was released only after intense negotiations. Many people would have been tempted to give up on tribal missionary work after such an experience, but not the Brandt family. In seeking further ministry, Howard prayed: "Lord, somewhere in Africa there are unreached people to whom You would have us take the gospel. We are willing to go. Please lead us to the place where they live."

In 1978, Brandt joined a team sponsored by the Sudan Interior Mission to make a survey of northern Ghana. There he first learned of the Koma people living in a remote area far removed from towns or roadways. Making contact with the people was difficult, but finally they encountered a man named Ali, who "seemed overjoyed at their coming and offered to lead them into the village."

The missionaries did the best they could to explain their purpose in coming. They told about the book they had brought, and when the chief showed that he already had a book—"one published by a North American cult"—they offered to exchange it for the Bible, to which the chief readily agreed. When the missionaries returned several months later to explain further what was in the book they had left, they were surprised to learn that a trader had since come to the village and that he had confirmed that the book was about Jesus.

After lengthy discussions, the chief and Ali and sixteen other elders, together with more than one hundred villagers, decided to burn their fetishes and follow Jesus. The elders subsequently traveled to another village for Bible training and a nurse later came to help the Koma people with severe medical problems. It was then that Ali explained his initial welcome to the missionaries. Many tribal children had been desperately ill with measles, and he prayed to Mung, the only god he knew, to spare them. That night he had a dream that three white men had come with the message of God and healing for the children. He knew his dream was prophetic when the missionaries appeared.

"God had answered Ali's prayer for someone to be sent to tell the Koma people the way back to God and how to keep their children from dying. God also had answered Howard Brandt's prayer to be sent to some unreached people in Africa to whom he and his family could take the gospel."[28]

**For God does speak—now one way, now another—though man may not perceive it. In a dream, in a vision of the night, when deep sleep falls on men as they slumber in their beds, he may speak in their ears and terrify them with warnings, to turn man from wrongdoing and keep him from pride, to preserve his soul from the pit, his life from perishing by the sword.**

*Job 33:14–18.*

# "SUCH A GREAT CLOUD OF WITNESSES"

This passage in Hebrews follows the "hall of faith" chapter that highlights many of the great saints of the Old Testament, who together comprise "such a great cloud of witnesses." They have since been joined by New Testament saints and by Christians from around the world. One of those witnesses that merits "hall of faith" recognition is Raquel Mairotta, an Argentine woman who overcame many obstacles in her Christian pilgrimage.

After completing studies at an Argentine Bible Institute, Raquel began a ministry in a church in the small city of General Alvear. She "took up residence in two dingy rooms behind an ugly, grey sanctuary, and began to serve the people under the leadership of two nearby pastors who came to the city to take charge of meetings that involved the sacraments, weddings or funerals." That a woman would assume the leadership of the *Evangelicos* was unusual in itself, but Raquel was not an ordinary woman. She was born a dwarf. She might have been handicapped or embarrassed by her condition, but the call of God on her life did not allow for such excuses.

"Raquel hit General Alvear on the run. Her small figure became familiar on the streets of the city as she raced around on her child's bicycle while visiting members of her congregation and doing personal work or attending to the needs of the sick. (As well as praying for her people, she learned how to give injections to those who required them, and used this skill among the townspeople in general!) Very soon every person in General Alvear had either seen or heard of Raquelita (Little Rachel), the new pastor of the *Evangelicos*.

"Raquelita, wise enough to recognize some of her own limitations, chose two young men, both of them over six feet tall, to do much of the preaching. She taught them homiletics and advised them about basic books to purchase with their meager salaries. Under this kind of leadership, the Alvear congregation blossomed like a rose." Later, after the young men moved on to other things, Raquel took over all the parish responsibilities, and was ordained as a pastor by the Christian and Missionary Alliance of Argentina. "She is believed to be the first female ever ordained in the Alliance worldwide."

In 1988, she marked her thirtieth anniversary in pastoral ministry, which at that time included gospel radio broadcasts heard six days a week. Like saints of old, she shines forth in "such a great cloud of witnesses."[29]

Therefore, since we are surrounded by such a great cloud of witnesses, let us throw off everything that hinders and the sin that so easily entangles, and let us run with perseverance the race marked out for us. Let us fix our eyes on Jesus, the author and perfecter of our faith, who for the joy set before him endured the cross, scorning its shame, and sat down at the right hand of the throne of God. Consider him who endured such opposition from sinful men, so that you will not grow weary and lose heart.

*Hebrews 12:1–3.*

## "UNLESS I SEE THE NAIL MARKS IN HIS HANDS"

Preaching a sermon on the subject of hands might seem like an unlikely topic for most preachers, but it was very natural for missionary doctor Paul Brand. He spoke about hands when he was asked to give an impromptu sermon while he was making one of his frequent visits to a home for lepers in India. Indeed, the message that he gave that day he later polished and gave many more times and, according to his biographer, it became "one of his best known and best loved sermons."

His inspiration for the sermon was his congregation that day—leprosy patients whom he had sought to heal, some with greater and others with lesser success. To all of these people he was a beloved physician, and it was always at their request that before he left he speak some words of encouragement and share the gospel. On this particular day, however, he was exhausted. He "felt empty of ideas. But he knew he must think of something. As he rose to his feet he became suddenly conscious of hands, dozens of them, many raised palm to palm in the familiar gesture of *namaste*, some arched in the shape of claws, some with all five fingers, some with no fingers, some with a few stumps, some half hidden to cover their disfigurement. *Hands.*"

Brand began simply by reminding them that he was a hand surgeon who was fascinated by people's hands. "So when I meet people I can't help looking at their hands. The palmist claims he can tell your future by looking at your hands. I can tell your past. For instance, I can tell what your trade has been by the position of the calluses and the condition of the nails. I can tell a lot about your character. I love hands."

But how could he talk about hands without talking about his Savior? "How I would love to have had the chance to meet Christ and study his hands," he told his eager listeners. "But knowing what he was like, I can almost picture them, feel them, see the changes that took place in them. Suppose—suppose we follow him through his life and look at his hands together." Beginning with his boyhood and continuing on through his years as a carpenter, as a teacher, as a healer, and finally as the crucified Lord, he movingly shared the life and ministry of Jesus—through his hands.[30]

Now Thomas (called Didymus), one of the Twelve, was not with the disciples when Jesus came. So the other disciples told him, "We have seen the Lord!"

But he said to them "Unless I see the nail marks in his hands and put my finger where the nails were, and put my hand into his side, I will not believe it."

A week later his disciples were in the house again, and Thomas was with them. Though the doors were locked, Jesus came and stood among them and said, "Peace be with you!" Then he said to Thomas, "Put your finger here; see my hands. Reach out your hand and put it into my side. Stop doubting and believe."

Thomas said to him, "My Lord and my God!"

*John 20:24–28.*

# "HE WHO BEGAN A GOOD WORK WILL CARRY IT ON"

Sometimes there are painful setbacks in missionary work—setbacks that can make a missionary question why God in his sovereignty allowed such circumstances. That was true for Frank and Marie Drown who served with the Gospel Missionary Union in the Amazon jungles of eastern Ecuador, a place were tribal warfare often flared up and revenge killings were commonplace. Frank had reached out with the gospel to different tribes in that region and many people were converted, but the old ways often lingered on.

One of those who was converted was Tsantiacu, a powerful chief who had been in the vanguard of jungle warfare. He and his people built an airstrip for the missionaries, and he often accompanied Frank on missionary journeys to other tribes. "The old chief fearlessly told how God had changed him from a scheming, revengeful killer to a lover of men."

Tsantiacu sometimes went alone on these evangelistic tours, and on one occasion decided to bring the gospel to his most feared enemies. The men listened to his testimony and forgave him. Then, to show his confidence in them, he slept in their house. But the forgiveness had been a sham, and as soon as he was asleep, Tsantiacu's enemies killed him. When his own tribal family heard the news they retaliated, and before the carnage was over more than thirty people had died.

Frank and Marie prayed that this tragedy would not destroy the work of the Lord in that region, but whenever Frank returned, he found the airstrip more overgrown with grass each time. Survivors of the enemy tribes had fled. All hope seemed to be gone.

Eight years later, however, when Frank and some companions were exploring a new area, they were suddenly startled by music in the distance—gospel hymns in the tribal language. "As they called loudly to announce their arrival, young men came out of the house and down the trail to meet them. Once inside, Frank heard his own voice coming from the radio. . . . Though they had never met each other, the men of the house all knew Frank by his voice." The people were eager to learn more of the gospel and they took Frank to visit more distant people who were also hungry for the Word of God—people from Tsantiacu's family who had fled years earlier. These remembered their chief and knew he was a real Christian because he had forgiven his enemies and proven it by sleeping in their house.

Frank's and Marie's prayers had been answered. The good work of the gospel that had begun in the tribe was carried on.[31]

I thank my God every time I remember you. In all my prayers for all of you, I always pray with joy because of your partnership in the gospel from the first day until now, being confident of this, that he who began a good work in you will carry it on to completion until the day of Christ Jesus.

*Philippians 1:3–6.*

## "THE WORD BECAME FLESH"

When Peter Kingston, a missionary to Brazil, was translating the Gospel of John for the Mamainde people, he left the first fourteen verses of the book to be done last. That passage was a crucial passage not only because of its placement in the book, but also because of its doctrinal content. It was late afternoon when he finally arrived at the very last verse, as he later recounted.

"With me was Timoteo, a young man with a highly astute mind, one who was seeking God, one of the best translation helpers. We began to grapple with the tremendous sentence: 'The Word became a human being and lived among us.' And it took time to get that verse right.

"The sun was not so hot now, though the air was heavy and humid; gnats circled in agitated clouds above us. The sun slipped further down; mosquitoes began to buzz and whine impatiently, anxious for an evening meal. . . . Soon it would be dark; but still we talked on, trying to understand together what that one verse was really saying; what it meant for the Word to become a human being—and how it came about; what grace was and glory was; how a man could be full—not of food or of anger, but of truth; how it should all be translated into Mamainde."

Finally after more struggling, Timoteo grasped the full meaning. Together they went over the verse and Peter carefully copied it down to complete his first draft. With a sigh of relief, he was finished. He could go back to his house, get something to eat, and sleep with the satisfaction of having jumped another hurdle in his ministry as a Wycliffe Bible Translator.

For Timoteo, there was a sense of release as well. Indeed there was a feeling of exhilaration as he ran across the village and shouted, "Hey everybody, come and listen to this! This person called Jesus Christ was not just a spiritual being, as we thought; he was a man at the same time! He was two and yet one!" The people gathered around and a lively discussion followed. Forgetting his hungry stomach, Peter stood and listened, "fascinated to hear a man expertly explain one of the very deepest of spiritual truths to his family and friends—even though he had just understood it himself."[1]

He was in the world, and though the world was made through him, the world did not recognize him. He came to that which was his own, but his own did not receive him. Yet to all who received him, to those who believed in his name, he gave the right to become children of God— children born not of natural descent, nor of human decision or a husband's will, but born of God.

The Word became flesh and made his dwelling among us. We have seen his glory, the glory of the One and Only, who came from the Father, full of grace and truth.

*John 1:10–14.*

# "REMEMBER ME WHEN YOU COME INTO YOUR KINGDOM"

The prisoners in the Montinlupa Prison who gathered for a large assembly were astonished to see a woman in her seventies make her way up the steps of the platform to address them. What would an old woman have to say to them, and how did she even obtain permission to get in? Mass assemblies were rare, and usually only armed men were brave enough to enter this maximum security prison that housed only the most hardened criminals.

As she began to speak, these defiant men—most of them in chains—had difficulty understanding her words through her thick Dutch accent, but slowly she captured their attention. She told how she and her family had hidden Jews from the Nazis during World War II and how German police, because of a tip from two of her fellow citizens, had pounded on their door one frigid February day in 1944 with warrants for their arrest. The speaker was Corrie ten Boom. She knew what life was like in a death-camp prison, and she could identify with these men in their misery. But there was more to her story than her own suffering.

After the war was over, the two Dutchmen who had betrayed her family were taken into custody and put on trial. That they were getting what they deserved would have been the natural response, but not so. "My sister Nollie," Corrie told her audience, "heard of the trial of these two men who told the Gestapo about us, and she wrote a letter to both of them. She told them that through their betrayal they had caused the death of our father, our brother and his son, and our sister. She said we had suffered much, although both of us had come out of prison alive. She told them that we had forgiven them and that we could do this because of Jesus, who is in our hearts."

Both men responded. One wrote: "I have received Jesus as my Savior. When you can give such ability to forgive to people like Corrie ten Boom and her sister, then there is hope for me. I brought my sins to Him." The other letter gave an opposite viewpoint: "I know what I have done to your family, that I have caused the death of several of you who have saved Jews, and above that I have helped to kill many hundreds of Jewish people. The only thing I regret is that I have not been able to kill more of your kind." Corrie went on to challenge the prisoners that every one of them— even as those criminals who had been on the cross— could accept or reject Christ and his forgiveness.[2]

One of the criminals who hung there hurled insults at him: "Aren't you the Christ? Save yourself and us!"

But the other criminal rebuked him. "Don't you fear God," he said, "since you are under the same sentence? We are punished justly, for we are getting what our deeds deserve. But this man has done nothing wrong."

Then he said, "Jesus, remember me when you come into your kingdom."

Jesus answered him, "I tell you the truth, today you will be with me in paradise."

*Luke 23:39–43.*

## "BRINGING A BROTHER TO JESUS"

When Jesus admonished his disciples to be fishers of men, he certainly was aware that such a commission might very well arouse anger, kindle persecution, and tear apart families. Yet it was a command that he did not give lightly, and he expected his followers—even as Andrew had done—to bring their brothers to him.

For Christiana Tsai, the daughter of a wealthy Chinese provincial governor, bringing her brother to Jesus was a dangerous proposition. She was raised in a Buddhist home, but attended a mission school to take advantage of the excellent education it offered. She vowed, however, that she would never convert to Christianity, and she deeply resented the religious services she was required to attend. "This only increased my resistance," she later wrote, "and I made up my mind that I was not going to 'eat' their Christianity, so I used to take a Chinese novel with me to chapel and read it as I knelt at the bench."

What Christiana wanted most from her education was to perfect her skills in the English language so that she could quench her insatiable thirst for knowledge. To do that she joined an optional English Bible class, and, by her own testimony, "God used my love for English to draw me to Himself." It was through reading Scripture that she was converted—an experience that created anger and despair among her family members. One of her brothers tore up her Bible and hymnbook, and her mother openly grieved that her daughter would care so little about her as to deny her future homage through ancestral worship.

Eventually, however, Christiana's testimony and changed life began to have an effect on her family, and one by one they converted to Christianity. "So the brother who tore up my Bible and persecuted me in the early days at last confessed my Lord," she wrote. "In all, fifty-five of my relatives, adults and children, have become God's children and expressed their faith in Jesus. I have never been to college, or theological seminary, and I am not a Bible teacher; I have only been God's 'hunting dog.' I simply followed at the heels of my Master, and brought to His feet the quarry He sent me after."[3]

Andrew, Simon Peter's brother, was one of the two who heard what John had said and who had followed Jesus. The first thing Andrew did was to find his brother Simon and tell him, "We have found the Messiah" (that is, the Christ). And he brought him to Jesus.

*John 1:40–42a.*

## "BEAUTY IS FLEETING"

Paul Brand, a physician known worldwide for his medical breakthroughs for leprosy patients, paid high tribute to his mother and the formative influence she had on him. Who was this uncommon woman known by the people she served as "Granny" Brand? "I say it kindly and in love," writes Paul, "but in old age my mother had little of physical beauty left in her. She had been a classic beauty as a young woman—I have photographs to prove it—but not in old age. The rugged conditions in India, combined with crippling falls and her battles with typhoid, dysentery, and malaria had made her a thin, hunched-over old woman. Years of exposure to wind and sun had toughened her facial skin into leather and furrowed it with wrinkles as deep and extensive as any I have seen on a human face. She knew better than anyone that her physical appearance had long since failed her—for this reason she adamantly refused to keep a mirror in her house."

When she was seventy-five, Granny fell and broke her hip. Workmen carried her on a stretcher down the mountain, after which she was taken over one hundred and fifty miles of bumpy roads by jeep to the nearest hospital. When Paul visited her some time later she was walking with two bamboo canes and managing to travel on horseback to outlying villages.

"I came with compelling arguments for her retirement," writes Paul. "It was not safe for her to go on living alone in such a remote place. . . . With her faulty sense of balance and paralyzed legs, she presented a constant medical hazard. . . .

"Granny threw off my arguments like so much nonsense and shot back a reprimand. Who would continue the work? There was no one else in the entire mountain range to preach, to bind up wounds, and to pull teeth. 'In any case,' she concluded, 'what is the use of preserving my old body if it is not going to be used where God needs me?'

"And so she stayed. Eighteen years later, at the age of ninety-three, she reluctantly gave up sitting on her pony because she was falling all too frequently. Devoted Indian villagers began bearing her on a hammock from town to town. After two more years of mission work, she finally died at age ninety-five. She was buried, at her request, in a simple, well-used sheet laid in the ground—no coffin. . . .

"One of my last and strongest visual memories of my mother is set in a village in the mountains she loved. . . She is sitting on a low stone wall that circles the village, with people pressing in from all sides. . . They are looking at an old wrinkled face. . . . To them she is beautiful."[4]

"Many women do noble things, but you surpass them all." Charm is deceptive, and beauty is fleeting; but a woman who fears the Lord is to be praised. Give her the reward she has earned, and let her works bring her praise at the city gate.

*Proverbs 31:29–31.*

# "FREELY YOU HAVE RECEIVED, FREELY GIVE"

Growing up the son of a prosperous textile retailer offered young Francesco di Pietro di Bernardone a privileged lifestyle with plenty of opportunity for leisure-time activities. He studied French and Latin in school, but was far more interested in spending money and socializing with his friends. His one fascination in life was the adventure of military conquests, and he looked forward to the day when he would become a soldier himself.

At the age of twenty, his dream came true. But the excitement of a military campaign quickly dissipated when he was taken a prisoner of war. He was released after two years, and he vowed that he would return to complete his mission. On his way to the battlefront, however, his mission suddenly changed. A voice in a dream commanded him to serve God and not man. His marching orders were very clear as he later related: "When I was yet in my sins it did not seem to me too bitter to look upon the lepers, but the Lord Himself did lead me among them, and I had compassion upon them. When I left them, that which had seemed to me bitter had become sweet and easy." His response to God was volunteer work at a leper hospital.

Soon after this he heard a voice from God charging him to repair the house of God, which he interpreted as being St. Damien's Cathedral. How could he take on such a momentous task? The most obvious means was to appropriate expensive cloth from his father's warehouse. His father was furious and the local bishop ordered him to return the goods. With that, he renounced his wealthy upbringing and his own fine clothing and donned a hair shirt and began living the life of a solitary hermit.

For two years he lived by himself spending his energies repairing the old church. Then in 1209, at the age of twenty-eight, he heard a sermon from Matthew 10 about Jesus sending out his disciples with no money or belongings. That was just the inspiration he needed. He would spend his life preaching the gospel and helping the poor.

As he traveled around, others joined him—many of them like him, sons of middle-class merchants. They took a vow of poverty, and used an old cow barn as their headquarters. It was the beginning of what became the Franciscan order headed by a man who would later be canonized in the Roman Catholic church—St. Francis of Assisi.[5]

These twelve Jesus sent out with the following instructions: "Do not go among the Gentiles or enter any town of the Samaritans. Go rather to the lost sheep of Israel. As you go, preach this message: 'The Kingdom of heaven is near.' Heal the sick, raise the dead, cleanse those who have leprosy, drive out demons. Freely you have received, freely give. Do not take along any gold or silver or copper in your belts; take no bag for the journey, or extra tunic, or sandals or a staff; for the worker is worth his keep.

*Matthew 10:5–10.*

# "WHY DO YOU PERSECUTE ME?"

Saul's conversion story is unique. Very few people testify to such an electrifying salvation experience. But there are those rare conversion stories that are similar. One of those is the story of Sundar Singh, a man who turned away from his heritage of wealth to travel, barefoot, the dusty paths of India and Tibet with the gospel of Christ.

Sundar Singh was raised in India in a Sikh family, but through his mother he had come to appreciate not only the Sikh scriptures, the Granth, but the Bhagavad Gita and the Koran. The Bible, however, was not on his reading list. He hated the Bible—not because he had read and studied it, but because he hated Christians. Their religion was not part of his heritage, and in an effort to express his outrage for their presence in his country, he joined with others in a Bible-burning ceremony in his village square. But burning the Bible was an act of outrage against God, as Sundar learned through a vision.

"Though I thought I had done a good deed in burning the Gospel, yet my unrest of heart increased. On the third day, when I felt I could bear it no longer, I got up at three in the morning and, after bathing, prayed that if there was a God at all He would reveal himself to me, and show me the way of salvation. I firmly made up my mind that if this prayer was not answered, I would before daylight go down to the railway, and place my head on the line before the incoming train.

"I remained till about half past four, praying and waiting and expecting to see Krishna or Buddha, or some other avatar of the Hindu religion; they appeared not, but a light was shining into the room. I opened the door to see where it came from, but all was dark outside. I returned inside, and the light increased in intensity and took the form of a globe of light above the ground, and in this light there appeared, not the form I had expected, but the living Christ whom I had counted as dead. To all eternity I shall never forget His glorious loving face, nor the few words which He spoke: 'Why do you persecute me? See, I have died on the cross for you and for the whole world.' These words burned into my heart as by lightning and I fell to the ground before Him. My heart was filled with inexpressible joy and peace, and my whole life was entirely changed."[6]

Meanwhile, Saul was still breathing out murderous threats against the Lord's disciples. He went to the high priest and asked him for letters to the synagogues in Damascus, so that if he found any there who belonged to the Way, whether men or women, he might take them as prisoners to Jerusalem. As he neared Damascus on his journey, suddenly a light from heaven flashed around him. He fell to the ground and heard a voice say to him, "Saul, Saul, why do you persecute me?"

"Who are you, Lord?" Saul asked.

"I am Jesus, whom you are persecuting," he replied.

*Acts 9:1–5.*

# "ALL WILL SHARE ALIKE"

It seemed logical for those followers of David who had finally been victorious in defeating the Amalekites, to divide the spoil themselves and not to share it with those who stayed behind—some of them "too exhausted" to continue on in the pursuit of the enemy. But David vehemently disagreed, insisting that "All will share alike" because all of them had contributed to the conquest. So it is with the work of the Lord. The unsung heroes of the church will also have their reward.

It was this passage from 1 Samuel that served as the text for one of Charles Haddon Spurgeon's most memorable sermons. "The very last time Spurgeon preached in Metropolitan Tabernacle was the Lord's Day morning of June 7, 1891. He appeared a broken man, 'utterly weary in the Lord's work, but not of it'; prematurely old, though but fifty-six; his hair white, anguish lines in his face, so enfeebled that he supported himself with his right hand on the back of a chair." That afternoon, he suddenly became ill and remained bedridden for most of the remaining eight months of his life.

His final sermon reflected his own situation: a man too exhausted to go on in the battle. But he was not speaking of himself as much as he was of his parishioners—many of whom had worked faithfully over the years without receiving public acclaim. One such individual was William Higgs, the contractor and builder of the Metropolitan Tabernacle. Two others were Joseph Passmore and James Alabaster, the printers who served Spurgeon and the ministries of the church over the years. Still another was Lavina Strickland Bartlett, who for sixteen years taught a Bible class for young women. "The class averaged six hundred in attendance, one thousand of whom had joined the church when she died in 1875." Of her Spurgeon said, "She aimed at soul-winning every time she met the class. Her talk never degenerated into story-telling, or quotations of poetry. She kept close to the cross, extolled her Saviour, pleaded with sinners to believe, and stirred up saints to holy living."

Spurgeon loved the people in his congregation individually and collectively, and knew well how dependent he was on them. "Truly I may say, without the slightest flattery, that I never met with any people on the face of the earth who lived more truly up to this doctrine—that chosen of God, and loved by him with special love, they should do extraordinary things for him—than those among whom I have been so long and so happily associated."[7]

David replied, "No, my brothers, you must not do that with what the Lord has given us. He has protected us and handed over to us the forces that came against us. Who will listen to what you say? The share of the man who stayed with the supplies is to be the same as that of him who went down to the battle. All will share alike." David made this a statute and ordinance for Israel from that day to this.

*1 Samuel 30:23–25.*

# "I WAS IN PRISON AND YOU CAME TO VISIT ME"

The king referred to in this passage is, of course, the Lord, and the verses go on to explain that reaching out to those most in need is reaching out in love to the king himself. Elizabeth Fry did this, and she was honored by kings. Indeed, when Frederick William IV, King of Prussia, visited England, he requested a meeting with her. She was an uncommon woman, and her deeds of kindness were known worldwide. After John Randolph, a Virginia legislator, had traveled to London and visited such places as Westminster Abbey, the British Museum, Parliament, the Tower, and Summerset House, he insisted that they "sink into utter insignificance in comparison to Elizabeth Fry" and the "miraculous effects of true Christianity" she had wrought at Newgate Prison. *

Elizabeth was born into a wealthy family in 1780, and in her late teens converted to Quakerism. At the age of twenty she married a wealthy Quaker merchant and dedicated the remainder of her life to Christian philanthropy. During the early years of her marriage, in addition to bearing eight children, she spent her days working in the London slums, helping needy families who needed food and medicine. But as hopeless as the conditions were in the streets, they were even worse, she discovered, in the prisons.

In 1813, Elizabeth approached the governor of the Newgate Prison with a simple request: "Sir, if thee kindly allows me to pray with the women, I will go inside." The request was granted; her life was irrevocably changed. There she found hundreds of women and their children crowded into four filthy rooms. They slept on the cold floor and begged food from people outside the window bars. They were foul-mouthed women hardened by their circumstances, but Elizabeth looked at them through eyes of love. And she knew that the task ahead of her would involve far more than prayer.

In the years that followed, she organized a movement to help female prisoners that instigated massive reform in the prison system. She was a regular visitor who brought her humanitarian outreach behind the prison gate. But she brought more than material goods. She shared the gospel with these women, preaching from her favorite passages in Isaiah and the Psalms or from the Sermon on the Mount. The result, according to one observer, was a miraculous transformation of these "most depraved . . . wretched outcasts" who "have been tamed and subdued by the Christian eloquence of Mrs. Fry."[8]

"Then the King will say to those on his right, 'Come, you who are blessed by my father; take your inheritance, the kingdom prepared for you since the creation of the world. For I was hungry and you gave me something to eat, I was thirsty and you gave me something to drink, I was a stranger and you invited me in, I needed clothes and you clothed me, I was sick and you looked after me, I was in prison and you came to visit me.' "

*Matthew 25:34–36.*

## "FORGIVE ALL OUR SINS"

"Take *words* with you and return to the Lord," Hosea admonished Israel, because "your sins have been your downfall!" What were the words? *"Forgive* all our sins." But how can people bring those *words* to God, if they have no *words* to bring?

This was true with the Bine people of Papua New Guinea, as Lillian Fleischmann and her partner discovered after they began breaking down the language as Wycliffe Bible Translators. It was frustrating for them. How could they explain the gospel without a word for "forgiveness"?

"At first we tried using phrases explaining how a forgiving person does not pay back when he is wronged, but just forgets the offense. That didn't work, however, because in the Bine culture, only a coward forgets an offense. We had to find some way of saying that God was a forgiving God without implying that He was a coward.

"Then one day we were invited to a funeral feast. After everyone had eaten, the headman in the clan of the one who had died took a coconut shell full of water. Dipping certain leaves in the water, he sprinkled the water into the air saying the name of each village that had people in attendance at the feast. He pronounced each village 'kalya'—released from blame concerning the death of the one who had died. There it was! A Bine word for forgiveness!

"We asked some questions, however, because we thought it might simply mean 'innocent.' We learned that a person doesn't need to be innocent to be pronounced 'kalya.' 'Kalya' simply means he will not be punished; he is released from blame. Does this describe God's forgiveness? Yes, God says we are kalya from our sins because Jesus has already paid for them."

The Bine people were no different from the people of Israel. Their sins had been their downfall. Now they had a word to use in their own language by which they could ask God to *forgive* their sins. What would forgiveness mean to them? Hosea went on to express God's response to Israel—the same response that he offers today to the Bine people: "I will heal their waywardness and love them freely, for my anger has turned away from them."[9]

Return, O Israel, to the Lord your God. Your sins have been your downfall! Take words with you and return to the Lord. Say to him: "Forgive all our sins and receive us graciously, that we may offer the fruit of our lips."

*Hosea 14:1–2.*

# "LIVE IN PEACE, PRAY CONTINUALLY"

The apostle Paul's admonition to "live at peace with each other," to "pray continually," and to "give thanks in all circumstances" is a high standard that is difficult to attain. Indeed, in a world with so much strife and so many distractions and disappointments, these exhortations often seem to be out of reach to the ordinary Christian. Yet, they are standards to seek and standards that we can sometimes attain more easily when we see them incorporated into the character of another. The life of Nicholas Herman—better known as Brother Lawrence—is one such example.

He has been all but forgotten in history, and not surprisingly so. He was an obscure lay brother in a seventeenth-century Paris monastery. For forty years he worked in the kitchen preparing food and washing pots and pans. He was "discovered" by M. de Beaufort, a church administrator, who was astonished by his consistent outward testimony of the love and peace of God. "His very countenance was edifying," wrote Beaufort, "such a sweet and calm devotion, appearing in it as could not but affect the beholder."

In one of Brother Lawrence's rare letters he wrote, "Were I a preacher, I should preach above all other things, the practice of the presence of God: Were I a teacher, I should advise all the world to it; so necessary do I think it, and so easy."

His testimony was well-known to those around him, according to Beaufort: "As he proceeded in his work he continued his familiar conversation with his Maker, imploring His grace, and offering to Him all his actions. When he had finished, he examined himself how he had discharged his duty; if he found well, he returned thanks to God: if otherwise, he asked pardon, and, without being discouraged, he set his mind right again, and continued his exercise of the presence of God as if he had never deviated from it."

But how could he "practice the presence of God" in the midst of chaos? "That time of business does not with me differ from the time of prayer," he told Beufort, "and in the noise and clatter of my kitchen, while several persons are at the same time calling for different things, I possess God in as great tranquility as if I were upon knees at the blessed sacrament."[10]

Now we ask you, brothers, to respect those who work hard among you, who are over you in the Lord and who admonish you. Hold them in the highest regard in love because of their work. Live in peace with each other. And we urge you, brothers, warn those who are idle, encourage the timid, help the weak, be patient with everyone. Make sure that nobody pays back wrong for wrong, but always try to be kind to each other and to everyone else.

Be joyful always; pray continually; give thanks in all circumstances, for this is God's will for you in Christ Jesus.

*1 Thessalonians 5:12–18.*

# "THAT THEY MAY SEE YOUR GOOD DEEDS"

The commotion outside her window interrupted Dr. Ruth Slifer, a Lutheran missionary to India, as she sat at her desk busily trying to finish some important paperwork. The noise was not coming from the street, but from the side of her house. Concerned, she called to Rajo Rao, her house helper. When there was no answer, she went herself to check, and there she found Rajo Rao filling containers of water for a long line of people from her own garden faucet.

When she inquired, she learned that the water had been cut off at the clapboard village across town. But why had they come so far, she questioned. The people knew they could get water there, because she had a "Christian pipe," she was told.

It was a strange adjective to use for a water pipe, but Ruth recalled that she had heard the same adjective used one time previously when she had given people a ride in the mission station wagon. "You have a Christian car," was the comment.

Another instance that she could recall was similar. "I noticed that the top shelf of the refrigerator was crammed with the contents of both shelves, while a bowl of something strange was on the lower one. I was away, Raja Rao had said, when Mrs. Subramaniam (my landlady, lived next door) had brought it over. She was expecting family from places distant. The next day when she came for her bowl, I was at home. She thanked me and added, 'You have a Christian refrigerator.'"

" 'There's a sermon here,' I mused, turning from the window to go back to my desk. 'A Christian pipe, car or refrigerator—person too!—looks like any other. It's how useful they are, whom they serve and why that makes the difference.'

"Let your light shine before men, that they may see your *good deeds* and praise your Father in heaven."[11]

"You are the salt of the earth. But if the salt loses its saltiness, how can it be made salty again? It is no longer good for anything, except to be thrown out and trampled by men.

"You are the light of the world. A city on a hill cannot be hidden. Neither do people light a lamp and put it under a bowl. Instead they put it on its stand, and it gives light to everyone in the house. In the same way, let your light shine before men, that they may see your good deeds and praise your Father in heaven."

*Matthew 5:13–16.*

# "IN THE HOLINESS AND SINCERITY THAT ARE FROM GOD"

In an effort to make the gospel appealing, many preachers and evangelists have sought to entertain and to water down the message. There is little market, it is often presumed, for serious, somber, uncompromising Bible teaching. This supposition was proven wrong by David Martyn Lloyd-Jones, one of the most acclaimed preachers of the twentieth century.

Lloyd-Jones was born in South Wales in 1900 and after graduating from medical school in 1921, he became an assistant to one of his former teachers. But he was not content in that profession, believing that God was calling him to preach the gospel. "By 'gospel' he meant the old-fashioned, Bible-based, life-transforming message of radical sin in every human heart and radical salvation through faith in Christ alone—a definite message quite distinct from the indefinite hints and euphoric vagueness that to his mind had usurped the gospel's place in most British pulpits."

In 1927, without seminary training, he became a lay pastor of a Presbyterian church in Wales, and from the first Sunday of his ministry had made it very clear to his parishioners what kind of a minister he would be. He preached "holiness and sincerity . . . not according to worldly wisdom."

"Young men and women, my one great attempt here at Aberavon, as long as God gives me strength to do so, will be to try to prove to you not merely that Christianity is reasonable, but that ultimately, faced as we all are at some time or other with the stupendous fact of life and death, nothing else is reasonable. . . . My request is this: that we all be honest with one another in our conversation and discussions. . . . Do let us be honest with one another and never profess to believe more than is actually true to our experience. Let us always, with the help of the Holy Spirit, testify to our belief, *in full*, but never a word more. . . . If the church of Christ on earth could get rid of the parasites who only believe that they ought to believe in Christ, she would, I am certain, count once more in the world as she did in her early days. . . ."

In 1938, Lloyd-Jones became the pastor of London's Congregational cathedral, Westminster Chapel, where he served for the next three decades. It was there that for the last twelve years of his ministry, he conducted Friday night lectures on Romans, drawing crowds upwards of two thousand.[12]

Now this is our boast: Our conscience testifies that we have conducted ourselves in the world, and especially in our relations with you, in the holiness and sincerity that are from God. We have done so not according to worldly wisdom but according to God's grace. For we do not write you anything you cannot read or understand. And I hope that, as you have understood us in part, you will come to understand fully that you can boast of us just as we will boast of you in the day of the Lord Jesus.

*2 Corinthians 1:12–14.*

## "HOW FLEETING IS MY LIFE"

Elizabeth Freeman embarked on her missionary adventure to India in 1851, after a short engagement and only five weeks of marriage to John Freeman, a twelve-year veteran missionary with the Presbyterian Board of Foreign Missions. She knew full well the risks that were ahead of her. Her husband's first wife, Mary Ann, had died on the mission field, leaving two little children behind.

Elizabeth found it difficult to acclimate herself to the rigors of life in India, but she was convinced of her call. To her niece who was yearning for missionary adventure, she wrote, "Let me tell you, my dear girl, unless you should come with your heart filled with love to God and these poor perishing heathens, you would be sadly disappointed." But she did not end her advice with that warning: "I hope you will be a missionary wherever your lot is cast, and as long as God spares your life; for it makes but little difference after all where we spend these few fleeting years, if they are only spent for the glory of God. Be assured there is nothing else worth living for!"

When she wrote those words she was fully aware of the fleeting nature of missionary life, but she could not know that her own days and the days of her loved ones would pass as quickly as they did. The missionaries were aware of Indian opposition to their presence, but were not prepared for the violence that erupted in 1858. Word reached them that four companies of a nearby military regiment mutinied and murdered many English citizens in the area.

The Freemans and their colleagues quickly realized they were stranded: "On Saturday," Elizabeth wrote, "we drove to the station, found all the ladies in tears, and their husbands pale and trembling. We all consulted together . . . but what could we do? Every place seemed as unsafe as this."

A week later, on June 2, 1858, Elizabeth wrote that she had gone to bed the previous night with "a violent, sick headache," after hearing "two regiments from Lucknow had mutinied, and were on their way here." It was her last letter, and her final words were poignant: "Can only say good-bye, pray for us, will write next mail if we live; if not you will hear from some other source. Your affectionate sister, E. Freeman."

There would be another week of terror before the ordeal ended: "On the 13th of June, at seven o'clock in the morning, they were released, marched to the parade-ground, and ruthlessly shot, according to one author. Their death was agonizing, but not long delayed." Elizabeth had spent fewer than seven fleeting years in India, but they were "spent for the glory of God."[13]

"Show me, O Lord, my life's end and the number of my days; let me know how fleeting is my life.

"You have made my days a mere handbreadth; the span of my years is as nothing before you. Each man's life is but a breath.

Man is a mere phantom as he goes to and fro: He bustles about, but only in vain; he heaps up wealth, not knowing who will get it.

But now, Lord, what do I look for? My hope is in you."

*Psalm 39:4–7.*

# "THERE IS NEITHER MALE NOR FEMALE"

The equality of women and men in the eyes of God is a liberating concept for women all over the world. This was true for Kana, a woman from Irian Jaya who was the featured speaker at a large retreat in 1980—the first one ever—for the women of the Pyramid-Tagi districts. As she stood before the vast audience seated on the grass for this historic occasion, she reflected on the effect of Christianity on women in her culture.

"When the gospel came to us Dani people, we were told that the gospel was for the men," she reminded them. "The men said we women did not have souls, so we did not need the gospel message. The men crowded around the speakers of the good news. We women were told to sit out on the edges of the crowd and to keep the children quiet so the men could get all of the profit from the message."

So convinced was she that she wasn't a full human and did not have a soul that she questioned her own reality. "Once I was in a group when a photo was taken by the missionary," she related. "I was so excited I could not wait until the picture had been developed and came back. When word came that the picture had arrived, I elbowed my way through the crowd to see if my face would show up or if, as the men insisted, I would not appear because I was only a spirit." She was ecstatic. "There I was! . . . I had shown up the same as the men had! I, too, was a real person."

The gospel had made Kana free. She was living proof of that, but it was not until the end of the retreat that she began to realize what this freedom entailed. A missionary gave the final address—one that challenged the women regarding their obligation to share the gospel with others. "The Great Commission is to every believer—men *and women*," the missionary said. "We all have a responsibility to spread the good news of the gospel message."

For Kana, the message was sobering. As the women departed from the retreat, Kana later recalled, "I lingered behind not wanting to join in their jubilant singing and chatter. I was battling with the Lord over this new thought that I was also responsible to carry the gospel to my unsaved neighbors." As a leader among the women she recognized her obligation and she did not want to face it. But she had no choice when a woman sought her out and announced the decision she and her friends had made. "We have decided that we will gather your firewood and dig and plant your gardens if you will just teach us how to witness to others." In the years since, Kana and her friends have been reaching out to new areas with the gospel.[14]

You are all sons of God through faith in Christ Jesus, for all of you who were baptized into Christ have clothed yourselves with Christ. There is neither Jew nor Greek, slave nor free, male nor female, for you are all one in Christ Jesus. If you belong to Christ, then you are Abraham's seed, and heirs according to the promise.

*Galatians 3:26–29.*

# "NOT IN SEXUAL IMMORALITY AND DEBAUCHERY"

It was Romans 13:13 that brought a young philosophy student to his knees and sparked his conversion to Christianity. He had turned away from the pious teachings of his mother and, as a teenager, spent much of his time with his friends enjoying the night life of the city. By the age of eighteen, he had a mistress and an illegitimate son, but he was not happy. For a time he joined a cult—the Manicheans—but still he found no satisfaction. He continued to be plagued by internal struggles and physical lust.

Confused and uncertain about his life and his future, he moved to Rome where he joined a group of skeptics. Still he had no peace. They freed him from the clutches of Manicheanism, but offered nothing to fill the vacuum. It was then that he heard about the preacher Bishop Ambrose, who had a reputation as a great orator. But more important than his style was his message. It was through listening to Ambrose that this young man was reintroduced to the Bible.

Still, he struggled with lust. He took another mistress, convinced that he was doomed to live a life of debauchery. But then one summer day while outside in a garden, as he later recalled, his life was changed.

"I heard from a neighboring house a voice, as of boy or girl, I know not, chanting and oft repeating, 'Take up and read; Take up and read.' . . . I arose; interpreting it to be no other than a command from God, to open the book, and read the first chapter I should find. . . . Eagerly then I returned to the place where . . . I laid the volume of the Apostle . . . I seized, opened and in silence read that section on which my eyes first fell: *not in rioting and drunkenness, not in chambering and wantonness, not in strife and envying: but put ye on the Lord Jesus Christ, and make not provision for the flesh.*"

There in the garden in the year 386, this man was converted. His life was gloriously transformed, and he would go on to become a bishop and one of the greatest writers and theologians the church has ever known. He is known today as Augustine of Hippo, or simply St. Augustine.[15]

And do this, understanding the present time. The hour has come for you to wake up from your slumber, because our salvation is nearer now than when we first believed. The night is nearly over; the day is almost here. So let us put aside the deeds of darkness and put on the armor of light. Let us behave decently, as in the daytime, not in orgies and drunkenness, not in sexual immorality and debauchery, not in dissension and jealousy. Rather, clothe yourselves with the Lord Jesus Christ, and do not think about how to gratify the desires of the sinful nature.

*Romans 13:11–14.*

# "A GRAIN OF MUSTARD SEED"

Nicolaus Ludwig von Zinzendorf was born into a wealthy German family in 1700 and was raised with every opportunity to carry on his family tradition and live the life of a nobleman. Through the influence of his grandmother and aunt, however, as a child he became deeply interested in spiritual things. This interest was further developed through the godly example of one of his teachers at a Lutheran school at Halle, where he was sent to study at the age of ten.

While at Halle, Zinzendorf organized a small prayer band with some of his fellow students, and upon their graduation they vowed that they would remain committed to their pledge of praying and trusting God for his care and protection. In a solemn trust, they joined together in what they called the Order of the Grain of Mustard Seed.

"Zinzendorf and friends took the name of their order from Jesus' parable of the Kingdom of God growing from small beginnings. They hoped their youthful enthusiasm, nourished by God, would become leaven in the world. No public organization was formed. Members individually pledged to work for the conversion and salvation of all people, including the 'heathens' across the seas, to improve human morals, to promote the unity of all Christians, and to protect persons persecuted for faith. In short, 'knights' of the mustard seed were to 'love the whole human family.'"

For his part, Zinzendorf's outreach was a model for what Jesus described as a tiny seed that would grow into a tree that spread its branches far. He founded a movement that became known as the Moravians. They were committed to overseas evangelism in an age when missions was not considered a vital aspect of the church.

Zinzendorf used his wealth to provide a community for religious refugees and then challenged them to take their faith abroad to those who had never heard the gospel. By 1760, more than two hundred of his followers had taken up that challenge, and in the years that followed their mission effort spread out across the globe. As a grain of mustard seed, he became one of the world's greatest missionary statesmen of all time and "sparked the Protestant missionary movement."[16]

He told them another parable: "The Kingdom of heaven is like a mustard seed, which a man took and planted in his field. Though it is the smallest of all your seeds, yet when it grows, it is the largest of garden plants and becomes a tree, so that the birds of the air come and perch in its branches. . . . I tell you the truth, if you have faith as small as a mustard seed, you can say to this mountain, 'Move from here to there' and it will move. Nothing will be impossible for you."

*Matthew 13:31–32; 17:20b.*

# "USING POLITICAL CONNECTIONS"

The apostle Paul knew full well the answer to his own question about the legality of beating a Roman citizen. Indeed, the question might be viewed as more of a threat than an inquiry. Paul was simply letting his persecutors know his rights. When facing aggression, sometimes the appropriate response is to turn the other cheek; sometimes it is to challenge the accusor.

Lillian Dickson, who served with her husband as a missionary to Formosa in the decades after 1927, made use of threats in her effort to protect Christians in the remote mountain regions where she worked. Standing at a height of five feet, she might not have appeared to be imposing, but, like Paul, she had political connections that worked to her advantage. She had initiated various humanitarian projects for the people in that country, and as a result had become acquainted with some of the national leaders who were eager to repay her kindness. These political connections gave her boldness in times of opposition.

Lillian had a reputation for toughness. "Once, while making a survey trip to seventy mountain churches to find out what kind of shape they were in, she heard of a chief who had been persecuting members of his tribe who had become Christians. A native policeman told her that this chief had been in the habit of going with a group in the middle of the night to a new Christian convert, sometimes a widow or an old person, and beating the victim or demanding protection money. Lil was in a village five miles away from the chief's when she heard this report. It was near midnight. 'Let's go and see the man,' she said."

The policeman protested, knowing the chief probably would be asleep and drunk, but Lillian insisted. They found him in his hut in precisely that condition. Lillian "shook him violently" and demanded to know why he had been beating Christians. "I can make big trouble for you," she threatened. "I don't want to do it, but I can. If I hear of just one more instance, I'll get after you." With that, she left as abruptly as she came, and the chief never persecuted Christians again.[17]

As they were shouting and throwing off their cloaks and flinging dust into the air, the commander ordered Paul to be taken into the barracks. He directed that he be flogged and questioned in order to find out why the people were shouting at him like this. As they stretched him out to flog him, Paul said to the centurion standing there, "Is it legal for you to flog a Roman citizen who hasn't even been found guilty?"

When the centurion heard this, he went to the commander and reported it. . . .

Those who were about to question him withdrew immediately. The commander himself was alarmed when he realized that he had put Paul, a Roman citizen, in chains.

*Acts 22:23–26a, 29.*

# "PREACHING FROM A BOAT"

A boat is not typically thought of as a likely base of evangelism. It was for Jesus because he had to escape from the crowds. For others, though, it has been a base for evangelism in order to reach the crowds. This was true of Ethel Groce and several other "boat ladies," who evangelized among China's boat people during the decades before China was closed to missionaries in the early 1950s.

Ethel grew up in Missouri and studied at Moody Bible Institute. She took nurses' training before going abroad to work with the Oriental Boat Mission, a small mission agency started by an Englishwoman, Miss Alexander, who had been burdened for the boat people in the Hong Kong harbor. Missionaries had previously tried to minister to the boat people by living on land and going out to preach to them, but the boat people did not identify with them. Miss Alexander and her "boat ladies" vowed to live on the boats and become one with the people.

For a time there were nine boats from which these women ministered to boat people in the Hong Kong harbor and other harbors. Sometimes the people were hostile, but often they were interested, as Ethel discovered when she initiated cooking classes and schooling for the children.

"Little by little, the boat ladies began attracting more followers, and over the years they worked out a regular routine of ports of call. It was a lonely life, for months would often go by in which they did not see another person who spoke English. They seldom heard from their relatives in the States, for they were able to get back to the points where they could receive mail only at rare intervals. Yet they had so much work to do that they did not mind. At one point, one of the boat ladies established a leper colony aboard her craft. It survived there for two years and later moved ashore."

By 1949, Ethel realized that she could no longer continue her work along the China coast. "The Communists were taking over everywhere; all the Christians were fleeing." She moved her boat to Hong Kong, where she continued her evangelistic outreach. She established another clinic and set up a school for approximately eighty children. She worked with Chinese volunteers in a visitation program and conducted church services on Sunday with the assistance of a Chinese pastor—all of this work on board a boat, which became her floating home.[18]

That same day Jesus went out of the house and sat by the lake. Such large crowds gathered around him that he got into a boat and sat in it, while all the people stood on the shore. Then he told them many things in parables. . .

*Matthew 13:1–3a.*

## "THEY WERE WEARING WHITE ROBES"

The setting was a women's neighborhood Bible study—not around the dining room table of a suburban ranch house, but on the dirt floor of a thatched house in Bolivia. Joyce Prettol, a Bible translator, was the leader and the passage under study was Revelation 7, the portion of Scripture she had been translating for the Ese Ejja people.

The women listened with interest, but the phrase that caught their attention more than any other was the reference to white robes. People from every tribe and nation would be wearing these white robes, and that meant them. They were excited at the thought. White was an uncommon color of clothing in their remote tribal region.

But would everyone be dressed in white? "As we continued to discuss the lesson," writes Joyce, "we mentioned that it was only those who had received Jesus as Savior who would go to heaven and receive a white robe." Would that include Asha? she asked the women. Asha had been crippled from polio as a young woman, and as a second wife with no children had always been outside the village women's clique. She was ridiculed and often the butt of jokes.

Now, however, the reality of heaven had suddenly been impressed upon these women. They previously had no interest in sharing the gospel with her, and Joyce herself had been unsuccessful in communicating with her. So it was, spurred on by the anticipation of being attired in white robes before the throne of God, the women decided that Asha should not be left out.

"We filed over to Asha's house, stooped and entered the low, dark room," writes Joyce. "Our eyes slowly became accustomed to the darkness and we could see Asha lying curled up on a thin woven mat. A tattered, stained blanket covered her thin body and her faded dress hadn't been washed in a long time. If anyone needs a new white robe, Asha does, I thought. Oh God, let this be the day of salvation for Asha. . . .

"As I watched the Ese Ejja women sitting there, holding hands, touching, caring and reaching out to God in prayer with Asha, my heart began to swell. I knew it was time to let go of them. God would show them how to share His Word in an infinitely better way than I ever could. . . .

"Asha died only a few weeks later. But her transformation was apparent." So, too, had the Christian women who reached out to her been transformed. Asha had exchanged her rags for a white robe, and they could identify with that.[19]

After this I looked and there before me was a great multitude that no one could count, from every nation, tribe, people and language, standing before the throne and in front of the Lamb. They were wearing white robes and were holding palm branches in their hands. And they cried out in a loud voice: "Salvation belongs to our God, who sits on the throne, and to the Lamb."

*Revelation 7:9–10.*

# "AFTER ME WILL COME ONE MORE POWERFUL THAN I"

John the Baptist paved the way for Jesus. He did not offer the complete message. He was only preparing hearts to be receptive to the message that would follow. William Wade Harris played a similar role in West Africa.

Propelled by a heavenly vision in 1910, this African Christian from Liberia began a preaching ministry that took him into the neighboring country of the Ivory Coast. Wearing a white robe and carrying a cross in one hand and a Bible in the other, he walked barefoot from village to village. He believed he was a prophet sent by God to warn the people of the holy commands. His message was simple: "Repent, burn your fetishes, believe in the One God, and be baptized."

In 1913, Harris reached the Dida region of the Ivory Coast. Thousands of people thronged around him to hear his message, and about one hundred thousand people were baptized and hundreds of churches were built. When people accepted his simple message in one village, he moved on to another, always exhorting them to wait for the white missionaries—"for people to open this book and you must obey its message."

When missionaries did come into this region, they were amazed at the churches and congregations of Christians who were waiting for them. When J. W. Platt, a Methodist missionary, visited the area in 1924, "he was received in village after village with overflowing joy. Everywhere there were flags, torchlight processions, crowded churches, and excited people who hailed the new messenger of the gospel, whose coming Harris had foretold. 'We have waited ten years for you,' they said."

While the missionary was reaping the harvest, Harris was back in his homeland. He had been deported from the Ivory Coast and imprisoned for a time. Like John the Baptist, he was "a man sent from God," who paved the way for the gospel message but did not have the joy of seeing it come to fruition. His death went virtually unnoticed a few years later, "but thousands of earnest Christians in the Ivory Coast remembered him as their spiritual father with deep gratitude and respect."[20]

And so John came, baptizing in the desert region and preaching a baptism of repentance for the forgiveness of sins. The whole Judean countryside and all the people of Jerusalem went out to him. Confessing their sins, they were baptized by him in the Jordan River. John wore clothing made of camel's hair, with a leather belt around his waist, and he ate locusts and wild honey. And this was his message: "After me will come one more powerful than I, the thongs of whose sandals I am not worthy to stoop down and untie. I baptize you with water, but he will baptize you with the Holy Spirit."

*Mark 1:4–8.*

# "THE LORD IS ABOUT TO DESTROY THE CITY"

Charles G. Finney was the most noted revivalist of the early nineteenth century, partly because he was very controversial. He parted company theologically from the staid Calvinistic Puritans of Colonial New England, and preached sermons that stirred up his listeners to the point of frenzy as they agonized their way to God. Finney's style was unconventional, to say the least, and he had a reputation for being "a half-crazed fanatic." Yet, many souls were saved through his preaching.

Early in his ministry he was invited by an old man to speak at a little town in Western New York. "Finney arrived and gave out a hymn, but the singing was so awful—they bawled very loudly and so out of tune—that Finney with his trained musical ear literally put his hands over his ears and got down on his knees and prayed until they had finished."

As he prayed, "the Lord gave him a text—he had deliberately not chosen his subject, feeling he should wait until he had assessed the congregation. He was not even sure just where the text was to be found which he felt impressed upon his heart, but he stood up and delivered it: 'Up, get you out of this place; for the Lord will destroy this city.' He knew that it came from the story of Abraham and Lot and the city of Sodom and so he expounded the story in his own way. The more he spoke the more he could see the people looking angry; he then applied the Word to them in a particular and pointed way."

Gradually a change came over the people. "As he pressed home the truth of God upon this rough crowd of backwoods people they suddenly began to fall from their seats all over the building, crying out for God to have mercy on them. . . He began to deal with some of them individually and as he pointed them to Christ, one after another found peace with God."

Finney later discovered why the people had initially been upset with his text. "The place was known as Sodom and the only good man in the place was the old man who had invited him and whom they nicknamed Lot! They had thought Finney had deliberately chosen his text because of this, but he was completely ignorant of it all and preached without inhibitions because he knew God had given him the text as he prayed."[21]

So Lot went out and spoke to his sons-in-law, who were pledged to marry his daughters. He said, "Hurry and get out of this place, because the Lord is about to destroy the city!" But his sons-in-law thought he was joking.

With the coming of dawn, the angels urged Lot, saying, "Hurry! Take your wife and your two daughters who are here, or you will be swept away when the city is punished."

When he hesitated, the men grasped his hand and the hands of his wife and of his two daughters and led them safely out of the city, for the Lord was merciful to them.

*Genesis 19:14–16.*

# "THE IMPORTANCE OF GENEALOGIES"

We often skip over the genealogy lists in the Bible. They are difficult to read, and they offer little for sermon material or devotional inspiration. For a missionary who is struggling to translate the Bible into a new language, the genealogy lists can be drudgery—a necessary chore in order to complete the job. Surely a genealogy list would be of no value for evangelism. Or would it?

When Jo Shetler began working as a Wycliffe Bible Translator among the remote Balangao people of the Philippines in 1962, she found them entirely puzzled as to why she would want to translate God's Word into their language. In fact, later when she was injured in a helicopter crash, one young woman feared Jo would die because her translation work had angered God. Many of the villagers believed that it was wrong to put God's Word into new words—especially into their own, such a lowly language.

These were discouraging times for Jo as she worked in the Balangao valley. During her first six years of missionary service, only two Balangaos became Christians. Most people simply were not interested in her concept of God. One such individual was Canao, who had become a father of sorts to her. "When Juami arrived, I was shocked," he later recalled. "Didn't she know it wasn't safe for girls in our area? Didn't she realize we were headhunters? So I had to become her 'father' and take care of her. I had to be sure people saw her eating at our house so they would know I was protecting her with my life, as is our custom here in Balangao."

But, Canao was not interested in her God. "Juami always talked about God, but I didn't like to always talk about Him," he confessed. "Juami kept telling me about God and how to believe. I already believed there was a god, so I just tried to be polite."

Then one day Jo showed him some of the translation work she had done and asked him to help her with it. Canao was amazed to find that God's Word could actually be written in a book and be read in a language he could understand. Most astonishing of all was that it was true. How did he know that? "It actually had a genealogy—absolute proof to a Balangao that it's true. This one went back to the beginning of time. Through the impact of the genealogy, I really began to understand and believe the truth about Jesus Christ."[22]

Now Jesus himself was about thirty years old when he began his ministry. He was the son, so it was thought, of Joseph, the son of Heli, the son of Matthat, the son of Levi, the son of Melki, the son of Jannai, the son of Joseph . . . the son of Methuselah, the son of Enoch, the son of Jared, the son of Mahalalel, the son of Kenan, the son of Enosh, the son of Seth, the son of Adam, the son of God.

*Luke 3:23–24, 37–38.*

# "GREET ONE ANOTHER WITH A HOLY KISS"

Greetings and expressions of love vary from culture to culture, and to someone unfamiliar with the customs these greetings and formalities often seem strange. Four of the New Testament epistles end with the exhortation to give others a holy kiss or a kiss of love. Precisely what this meant is uncertain, but it is not a custom widely practiced among Western Christians today. It is unfortunate that such greetings and expressions of love have been lost, and modern-day Christians, especially from the West, would do well to learn from biblical and non-Western customs.

Todd and Karla Poulter, missionaries to Ghana, learned from their African friends new ways to express love and warmth.

"While returning one afternoon to our home in rural Ghana, we came upon a disabled van. It looked familiar and as we slowed down, we recognized Atiteng, one of the local chief's sons, standing by the roadside. He'd run out of gas, an easy thing to do since fuel was scarce at the time."

Todd siphoned enough gas out of his own tank to get Atiteng to a gas station, and as they parted, he indicated that he would not be paying for the gasoline—at this time. "If I pay you today, I can't greet you tomorrow," was his rationale. Todd and Karla went on their way, not thinking about the strange comment.

"The following afternoon," writes Todd, "we returned from visiting one of our village neighbors to find Atiteng and two young men waiting at the house for us. We all sat down on the porch and went through the traditional Bulsa greetings, which may last up to a full minute. Only after such formalities could he come to the point of his visit."

Atiteng had brought the Poulters a rooster—worth far more than the gasoline—as an expression of thanks. It was a moving experience for Todd and Karla, as they later recalled. "Our inclination would have been to settle everything right there on the road that afternoon. But to Atiteng his relationship with us meant far more than the gasoline or the money. He saw it as an opportunity not only to express gratefulness, but also to cement our friendship."[23]

Finally, brothers, good-by. Aim for perfection, listen to my appeal, be of one mind, live in peace. And the God of love and peace will be with you.

Greet one another with a holy kiss. All the saints send their greetings.

May the grace of the Lord Jesus Christ, and the love of God, and the fellowship of the Holy Spirit be with you all.

*2 Corinthians 13:11–14.*

# "YOU CANNOT SERVE BOTH GOD AND MONEY"

One day in 1861, Sarah Dunn, a young school teacher who lived in Waterloo, Iowa, was sitting in her home finishing an elaborate piece of handwork for her home, when she sensed a voice speaking to her, asking, "What are you doing to decorate your heavenly home?"

This question haunted her in the weeks and months that followed. She had professed faith in Christ several years earlier, but she had not been faithful in reaching out to others with the gospel. Now the salvation of lost souls became her life's goal.

When she moved to Chicago some years later, she saw all around masses of needy people, and she dedicated herself to meeting their physical and spiritual needs. She recruited friends to help in her outreach efforts, and in 1869 organized a mission Sunday school. She was convinced that she had found God's will in his service. But, four years later, at the age of thirty eight, her life changed dramatically. She married Colonel George R. Clarke, a wealthy Chicago realtor. She struggled through "four merry years in the fashionable circle to which Colonel Clarke clung despite his Christianity." Her "conscience was troubling her" because of what she perceived to be "a misuse of God's time in social functions."

Sarah was convinced that God wanted them to reach out to the poor and establish a mission, but her husband was bent on pursuing his business career and amassing wealth. In his quest for this dream, he traveled to the Rocky Mountains on a lucrative business venture that Sarah feared would ruin any possibility of their mission work together. While he was gone, she "agonized many hours in prayer. It was no surprise then that while the colonel laid his plans for riches, the Spirit of God spoke to him with sharp conviction. Alone with God a thousand miles from home, he fell to his knees and consecrated himself to divine service for mission work. He telegraphed his wife of his change of life purposes and added that he was returning to Chicago at once to join her in founding a mission."

In 1877 they founded a mission on South Clark street in Chicago—"the first rescue mission in the Northwest"—the forerunner of the Pacific Garden Mission. Although Colonel Clarke was known as "the poorest preacher that ever tried to expound God's Word," he was sustained by his devoted wife. She had a remarkable personal manner with needy people, and together they became instruments in the transformation of countless lives.[24]

"No one can serve two masters. Either he will hate the one and love the other, or he will be devoted to the one and despise the other. You cannot serve both God and Money.

"Therefore I tell you, do not worry about your life, what you will eat or drink; or about your body, what you will wear. Is not life more important than food, and the body more important than clothes?"

*Matthew 6:24–25.*

## "DESIRES THAT PLUNGE MEN INTO RUIN"

Although Hipolito Alvarez had made a profession of faith and wanted to be identified with the Christian community in Pelechuco, Bolivia, he also wanted to continue his life as a prosperous merchant who traveled from town to town selling various products. He was a capitalistic workaholic, and it was his money that brought him satisfaction.

"I saved every peso I could and my savings grew," he later recalled. "That made me feel good. I lived right by the church, but Sunday was the best day for my work. So instead of going to meetings, I would sneak around the back and carry on my business."

In order to earn even more money, Hipolito rented six mules. He calculated that he could pay the rental fee from his earnings from one mule, and the earnings from the other five would be his to keep. He was convinced that he would soon become a wealthy man. "I was happy," he recalls, "expecting to make lots of money."

The market town where Hipolito could sell his produce for the highest profit was on the other side of a deep canyon with a river below. The only means of crossing the raging river was a narrow swinging bridge. It was treacherous, but he was convinced that he could cross safely if he led one mule at a time, leaving the remaining mules back with his young helper.

"Just past the middle of the bridge the sound of galloping hoofs tore my heart with fear. The bridge began to sway and I looked back. One mule had pushed past my helper and was galloping to catch up with us. I hurried to get across before the bridge gave way. No such luck. Another mule broke loose and came running across. The bridge couldn't handle the load. Just before we reached the end, the cables broke and we plummeted to the river below."

Miraculously, Hipolito, who could not swim, survived the ordeal. The mules and all his produce were lost, but he recovered from his near-fatal injuries. Some of his friends thought he would be safer if he turned his back on God, but he disagreed: " 'No,' I answered. 'Money deceived me. Because of my greed for money I almost lost my life.' And I told God, 'I'm not interested in money anymore. I no longer want to get rich. I just want enough to live on each day, and that's all.' "[25]

But godliness with contentment is great gain. For we brought nothing into the world, and we can take nothing out of it. But if we have food and clothing, we will be content with that. People who want to get rich fall into temptation and a trap and into many foolish and harmful desires that plunge men into ruin and destruction. For the love of money is a root of all kinds of evil. Some people, eager for money, have wandered from the faith and pierced themselves with many griefs.

*1 Timothy 6:6–10.*

# "WORTHY OF GREATER HONOR"

The problem of who should be in authority and who should receive honor is an age-old struggle. As this passage indicates, the one who comes after—Jesus, in this case—receives more honor than the one who was faithful in the foundational work—as was Moses. But "Moses was faithful as a servant in all God's house, testifying to what would be said in the future." In many ways missionaries represent the task that belonged to Moses, that of a servant, testifying to what will come in the future. Missionaries who do foundational evangelistic work must expect that the future will not belong to them, but rather to the leaders of the local churches they establish.

This was true in Nigeria where W. Harold Fuller served as a missionary with the Sudan Interior Mission. He illustrates this from his own observation of the partnership between missionaries and Africans.

"A while ago I was riding in the back seat of the ECWA (Evangelical Churches of West Africa) General Secretary Simon Ibrahim's car. He was at the wheel. Sudan Interior Mission missionary Gordon Beacham sat beside him.

"I thought about the fathers of those two men. Gordon's father had been a pioneer SIM missionary among the Tangale people of Nigeria. Simon's father had been one of the first Tangale preachers. They often traveled together in the missionary's car. Gordon's father sat at the wheel; Simon's father sat beside him.

"That's the way it was in the work, too. Of necessity at that time, Gordon's father was the driver. Today, their sons have changed places. The church is in the driver's seat, and the mission sits alongside.

"That's what has happened in the transfer of responsibility. The team members are still the same; they're still traveling together to the same destination, but ECWA is now behind the wheel. . . . Taking over responsibility means taking over leadership. It doesn't mean suddenly being able to finish the task all by oneself. It's a change of leadership, of authority, of responsibility, but it's not the completion of the work."[26]

Therefore, holy brothers, who share in the heavenly calling, fix your thoughts on Jesus, the apostle and high priest whom we confess. He was faithful to the one who appointed him, just as Moses was faithful in all God's house. Jesus has been found worthy of greater honor than Moses, just as the builder of a house has greater honor than the house itself. For every house is built by someone, but God is the builder of everything. Moses was faithful as a servant in all God's house, testifying to what would be said in the future. But Christ is faithful as a son over God's house. And we are his house, if we hold on to our courage and the hope of which we boast.

*Hebrews 3:1–6.*

## "MULTIPLYING THE BREAD OF LIFE"

Ken Taylor, who has become famous for his best-selling paraphrased version of Scripture, *The Living Bible*, confronted one rejection after another when he initially sought to have his paraphrase of Paul's epistles published. Finally he and his wife decided that they would finance the project themselves and hire a friend to do the printing. He had been prompted to simplify the Bible at the urging of his ten children as they were growing up and struggling with the meaning of the King James Version. Thus the project had deep personal meaning.

Taylor was in Jerusalem when he received the galley proofs for final checking, and he walked to the Mount of Olives where he read them through. "When I came to the end, I lingered for a time of prayer and reflection," he writes. "I sat fewer than 100 miles from where Jesus had fed more than 5,000 people with five loaves of bread and two fish. I held in my hands what would become 2,000 copies of *Living Letters*, and I thought of these copies as 2,000 loaves for feeding God's people."

How many people could his "loaves" feed? "I pondered a simple mathematical equation: If five loaves fed 5,000 people, how many would 2,000 feed? I pulled out a pencil and found the answer: 2 million. An incredible number. Nevertheless, I bowed my head and prayed that someday 2 million copies of *Living Letters* would be in print."

The sales were initially very slow. For one four-month period there were no new orders. Soon, however, word spread, and before long the sales were in the hundreds of thousands, and appeals were being made to Taylor to complete the Bible. In 1972 and 1973 *The Living Bible* was the nation's best-seller, and by 1988 it had sold more than 33 million copies. The entire volume has been translated into ten languages and *The Living New Testament* has been translated into fifty.

This had been a dream fulfilled for Taylor who read *Borden of Yale* while studying at Wheaton. It is the story of a wealthy young man who gave up his inheritance to follow God's call to Egypt, where he served only a short time before his untimely death. Taylor, at that time, prayed that God would use him in a similar way—never realizing how greatly God would multiply his humble offering of 2,000 loaves.[27]

Then Jesus directed them to have all the people sit down in groups on the green grass. So they sat down in groups of hundreds and fifties. Taking the five loaves and the two fish and looking up to heaven, he gave thanks and broke the loaves. Then he gave them to his disciples to set before the people. He also divided the two fish among them all. They all ate and were satisfied, and the disciples picked up twelve basketfuls of broken pieces of bread and fish. The number of the men who had eaten was five thousand.

*Mark 6:39–44.*

# "HE WHO HAS BEEN STEALING MUST STEAL NO LONGER"

In some societies and under certain circumstances, the negative command not to steal and the positive exhortation to work with one's hands are mutually exclusive—that is, if the hands have already been cut off as punishment for stealing. Stealing is a grave offense in African societies, and thieves are sometimes punished almost as severely as murderers. Mika Banzako of Zaire, was one of those who experienced the harsh penalty of being branded a thief.

Mika was a compulsive thief who had been apprehended and imprisoned for his crimes, but in prison he stole from other prisoners and the guards. Local authorities did not know how to stop him. The only solution, the local magistrate insisted, was to cut off his arm, a punishment more severe than the old, now outlawed, practice of cutting off the hand. Chloroform was used to deaden the pain, and male nurses were ordered to perform the mutilation of amputating Mika's left arm at the shoulder.

The loss of an arm did not deter Mika. His old ways continued until he was caught breaking into the home of a government official. Again he was imprisoned, and this time warned that if he was caught stealing, his right arm would also be cut off. Fear gripped Mika, and for a time he controlled his urge to steal, but soon he was back to his old ways. The threatened punishment became reality, and Mika was forced to endure the agony of having his remaining arm amputated.

Amazingly, Mika adapted. He learned to eat and dress himself, using wires held in his mouth. He also learned to steal with his mouth. One night he was in a chicken house stealing eggs when the householder discovered him. He outran his pursuers, but a sense of failure overwhelmed him. What was the use of living? He contemplated suicide.

As he approached a nearby town, he heard singing and saw great crowds of people surrounding a platform. Curiosity brought him closer until he could hear the voice of John Makanza, the country's most well-known evangelist. At the close of his message, John made an appeal to those who wanted to turn their lives around—to make a completely fresh start—and commit their lives to Christ. It was the message Mika needed. He was ready for a drastic change, but how could he make that known? The evangelist was asking people to raise their hands. But suddenly he looked Mika in the eye, and asked him directly, if he wanted to receive Christ as his Savior. Mika nodded, and he went on to live a changed life.[28]

**Therefore each of you must put off falsehood and speak truthfully to his neighbor, for we are all members of one body. "In your anger do not sin": Do not let the sun go down while you are still angry, and do not give the devil a foothold. He who has been stealing must steal no longer, but must work, doing something useful with his own hands, that he may have something to share with those in need.**

*Ephesians 4:25–28.*

## "A WOMAN'S LOVE"

This passage in Isaiah has been a source of comfort to women, married and single, who have not experienced the joy of having children. Though written for the nation of Israel and not expressly for a woman, the verses nevertheless offer consolation to barren women who can joyfully lengthen their tent cords and strengthen their stakes and serve the Lord faithfully.

Kathryn Kuhlman was a well-known healing evangelist who captured the hearts of millions of followers from the 1940s to the 1970s. She was a woman of deep emotion. Her healing ministry was not one that focused on herself but on others as she compassionately bent over them, seeking to alleviate their pain. It was this ministry that allowed her "to spread out to the right and to the left" and to have "descendants" in all nations.

Her biographer, Jamie Buckingham, poignantly describes the love that was evident in her ministry: "I saw her, on dozens of occasions, take a child that was lame, maybe paralyzed from birth, and hug that child to her breast with the love of a mother. I am convinced she would have, at any moment required of her, given her life in exchange for that child's healing. She would hug bleary-eyed alcoholics and mix her tears with theirs. And the prostitutes who came to her meetings, with tears smearing their mascara, knew that if they could but touch her they would have touched the love of God. And those little old women, hobbling along on canes and crutches, some of whom couldn't even speak the English language but were drawn by the universal language of love."

The love she demonstrated was God's love, but it was also a woman's love. "No man could have ever loved like that," writes Buckingham. "It took a woman, bereft of the love of a man, her womb barren, to love as she loved. Out of her emptiness—she gave. To be replenished by the only lover she was allowed to have—the Holy Spirit."[29]

"Sing, O barren woman, you who never bore a child; burst into song, shout for joy, you who were never in labor; because more are the children of the desolate woman than of her who has a husband," says the Lord.

"Enlarge the place of your tent, stretch your tent curtains wide, do not hold back; lengthen your cords, strengthen your stakes. For you will spread out to the right and to the left; your descendants will dispossess nations and settle in their desolate cities.

*Isaiah 54:1–3.*

# "TORMENTED BY THE GUILT OF MURDER"

Described as a modern Joan of Arc, Eunice Morago led warring braves from her Pima Indian tribe on an attack against the Apaches. When she was sixteen years old, her father had been killed by the Apaches, and she vowed that she would avenge that murder one day. "She called the Pima braves together and organized them for battle. She asked them to follow her into the Apache country, where they would kill the first Apache they could lay hands on. Astride a buckskin pony, she led her tribesmen, armed with Indian war clubs, bows and arrows.

"Many miles from home, they caught an Apache on the open desert. Two Pima braves held him; Eunice put spurs to her horse, rode full tilt, smashed him with her war club and killed him. At home again, she went through the traditional purification rites. But they brought her no peace. Sleep abandoned her. Her mind was in turmoil."

It was during this period of turmoil that Eunice visited the little adobe church started by Charles Cook. He was a missionary who supported himself by teaching and operating a store, with partial support from the Presbyterian Mission Board. The response to his ministry had been slow. Indeed, after his arrival in 1870, he spent fifteen years in evangelistic work before he had one convert. His faithfulness paid off, however, and by the end of his forty year ministry, he had baptized more than one thousand Indians.

One of those converts was Eunice. The sermon she heard on the day she stood in the doorway of that little church was on forgiveness. It was a message of hope, and she sought out the elderly missionary-pastor to find out if what he said could apply to her. She explained that she had killed a man, and that she was convinced that God could not truly forgive her. Charles Cook explained otherwise.

"It was a wonderful moment, peace came back to her. Eunice was baptized and taken into the church, becoming a faithful member of the Missionary Society. Last time I talked to her," writes George Walker, another missionary to the Pima, "she was well past 80, and did not have long to live. She repeated to me that the greatest thing that had ever happened to her in her long life was the forgiveness of God." Her torment over the guilt was removed, and she no longer was doomed to be "a fugitive till death."[30]

He who conceals his sins does not prosper, but whoever confesses and renounces them finds mercy.

Blessed is the man who always fears the Lord, but he who hardens his heart falls into trouble.

Like a roaring lion or a charging bear is a wicked man ruling over a helpless people.

A tyrannical ruler lacks judgment, but he who hates ill-gotten gain will enjoy a long life.

A man tormented by the guilt of murder will be a fugitive till death; let no one support him.

*Proverbs 28:13–17.*

# "UNLESS THEY ARE SENT"

The apostle Paul's list of four rhetorical questions in this passage has been a powerful basis for the world-wide missionary movement. Without faith in Christ, there is no hope of eternal life, and the only way to faith is to hear the gospel that is conveyed by a "sent one"—a missionary.

Helen Roseveare, a missionary medical doctor to Zaire with the Worldwide Evangelization Crusade, tells a story that powerfully illustrates this message. She briefly left her medical post to transport another missionary on emergency leave to Uganda. She made the three hundred mile drive in one day and was exhausted when she arrived late that night. Before daybreak the next morning she began the long trip home and was enjoying the flat, well-paved road, which was a luxury not known in Zaire. But as she sped along the empty highway, she began to nod and knew she must stop to stretch and drink some coffee.

There was no sign of life—no villages for miles around—as she pulled off the road near a bush. But then, out of nowhere, appeared an African man. From where he came she could not imagine, but he was the last person she wanted to see at that hour and at that place. She was savoring her moments alone and she was not in the mood for conversation. Besides, she knew she must be on her way. She had medical work piling up for her back at the mission station. She could not ignore him, however, and she knew it was her duty to go through the usual African greetings. With that accomplished, he stood silently until she asked him what he wanted. "Are you a sent one?" he asked. She was taken aback. Of course she was, that is what a missionary is, but she asked him what he meant. "Are you a sent one by a great God to tell me about something called Jesus?"

Here she was, out in the middle of nowhere, and an illiterate herdsman had appeared from behind a bush and asked if she was a sent one? Though he spoke East African Swahili and she West African Swahili, she explained the gospel to him through simple terms, and he accepted it by faith.

Then he explained that some days earlier his brother, a teacher, had come home from school early because classes had been dismissed to let a man speak. The brother was not interested. All he knew was that this man claimed to be sent by a great God to tell about something called Jesus. He had gone out drinking rather than hear the message, but this herdsman could not forget what had been said. The words kept ringing over and over in his mind, and he knew he could not be at peace until he found a "sent one" to tell him about the great God and Jesus.[1]

How, then, can they call on the one they have not believed in? And how can they believe in the one of whom they have not heard? And how can they hear without someone preaching to them? And how can they preach unless they are sent? As it is written, "How beautiful are the feet of those who bring good news!"

*Romans 10:14–15.*

# "IN MY DISTRESS I CALLED TO THE LORD"

Jonah's story is not uncommon; his experience has been replayed in many situations and many cultures throughout the world. After hearing God's call, he ran away, thinking he could escape the obligation he knew was his. That obligation was to reach out to others with the gospel.

Roy Ahmaogak ran away from the call of God in 1936. Roy's story begins when he was born in Barrow, Alaska in 1898. His mother was an unmarried Inupiat Eskimo and his father a Portuguese whaler, a man Roy never knew. His mother gave birth, as was the custom, in very trying circumstances: "When I was born," he later reflected, "our people thought a woman was unclean when she gave birth. So when the time came for my mother to deliver me, she was taken out of her warm sod house and put inside a small snow igloo." During the next four days, food and water were handed in through a tiny opening. It was a precarious way to enter the world. Roy's nine older brothers and sisters had all died very young, so, in his mother's eyes, Roy was very special.

Presbyterian missionaries had come to Barrow when Roy was a young child and his mother and adoptive father were among the first believers. His mother was a sincere Christian and was certain that God was calling her young son into ministry. Roy recognized this call, but he was far more interested in going on exciting hunts with his dogs.

When an invitation came from a missionary medical doctor for Roy to accompany him and preach the gospel on his distant rounds, Roy shrunk from what he knew to be the voice of the Lord. He "fled to an isolated fish camp on the Beaufort Sea." Here he could hide from God and enjoy the excitement of an Alaskan seal hunt with his friend. Their dogs carried them far out on the ice, and they were successful in their hunt.

As evening approached, they headed home, and suddenly they realized that the wind had changed directions. They were headed into a blinding blizzard, facing the most dreaded terror of all: being caught on an island of ice. Late the next day, "they reached the landward edge of the ice island and found what Roy had feared—open sea." For the next three days their lives hung in the balance. Would they drift at sea and freeze to death, or would the wind change direction and bring them to land? It was there on the ice that Roy committed his life to God. The wind changed direction and their lives were spared. Roy went on to be a great preacher among his people and a translator of the Inupiat New Testament. [2]

From inside the fish Jonah prayed to the Lord his God. He said: "In my distress I called to the Lord, and he answered me. From the depths of the grave I called for help, and you listened to my cry. You hurled me into the deep, into the very heart of the seas, and the currents swirled about me; all your waves and breakers swept over me. I said, 'I have been banished from your sight; yet I will look again toward your holy temple.'"

*Jonah 2:1–4.*

## "TAKING UP THE CROSS OF CHRIST"

A life centered around religion can be a frustrating one for a young person, especially if it involves lengthy daily rituals that become boring and meaningless. That was the attitude of A. Stephen as he grew up in a devout Hindu home in Tirunelveli, Tamil Nadu State, India. Religious faith was everything to his family—so much so that his father built his own temple in the village where they lived. But young Stephen began to have doubts. "My parents taught me how to do 'pujas' and offer sacrifices to the idol gods," he later recalled. "We made many pilgrimages and performed many good works, but still my life was empty."

At fifteen, Stephen rebelled. He stole money from the temple and ran away from home. For three months he visited temples and talked with gurus, but still he had no peace. Finally he returned home and there attempted suicide, convinced that there were no answers and that life was not worth living. As he "sat in his room with a rope tied around his neck," he began to call out for God. "Just then," he writes, "I heard a voice saying, 'My son, there is a peace for you . . . my son, there is a peace for you.'

"I went out and started walking along the street. A happy-looking young man came out of the night. He stopped and asked me why I was so sad. He said, 'I want to help you." In the minutes that followed, Stephen heard the gospel for the first time and professed faith in Christ.

The news of his conversion was upsetting to his family. "His brothers rejected him. His sister was so overwhelmed by shame at his new faith that she killed herself. And his father finally disavowed him and sent him away." For the next years Stephen wandered without a home with the Bible as his only real friend. He had taken up his cross to follow Christ and willingly suffered the consequences.

But as he wandered, he began sharing his faith, and in 1971, at the age of twenty, he founded Cornerstone World Challenge. In the years that followed he established more than fifteen churches, and recruited other workers to join with him in an itinerant ministry of distributing tracts and showing Christian films. Through it all he shares his own testimony of how through losing his life he saved it.[3]

Then he called the crowd to him along with his disciples and said: "If anyone would come after me, he must deny himself and take up his cross and follow me. For whoever wants to save his life will lose it, but whoever loses his life for me and for the gospel will save it. What good is it for a man to gain the whole world, yet forfeit his soul? Or what can a man give in exchange for his soul? If anyone is ashamed of me and my words in this adulterous and sinful generation, the Son of Man will be ashamed of him when he comes in his Father's glory with the holy angels."

*Mark 8:34–38.*

# "THE CORDS OF THE GRAVE COILED AROUND ME"

Life often takes on new meaning after near-death encounters. There is a sense of urgency to live life to the fullest. For believers, it is often a time of recommitment to God and a time for reassessment and redirection of ministry. This was true in the life of Dr. V. Raymond Edman, who is remembered most for his twenty-five years as president of Wheaton College.

In 1923, Edman began what he thought would be lifelong missionary service with the Christian and Missionary Alliance to work among Ecuador's Quechua Indians. His fiancée joined him the following year, and after their wedding they set out on a two-day ride on horseback to their mission outpost. Their ministry, however, was suddenly interrupted the following summer. Edman was stricken with typhoid fever. "He eventually sank into a coma and was deemed to be dead. A coffin draped in black was ordered, and the funeral service announced for Saturday afternoon, July 4, 1925. Mrs. Edman had her wedding dress dyed black for the service.

"At that very time, far away in Attleboro, Massachusetts, the people attending the Alliance's Camp Hebron, without any knowledge of the situation, felt a compelling urge to go to prayer for Edman. After two hours of burdened praying, the day's schedule of services was resumed." Edman recovered from that near-death encounter, and after a time of recuperation back in the United States, returned to Ecuador to serve as the director of a training school which is today Guayaquil Seminary of the Alliance. His missionary service, however, came to an end in 1928, when he was faced with a second near-fatal illness.

Back home in Massachusetts, Edman served as the pastor of an Alliance church while he took graduate studies culminating in a doctoral degree in American History. He lived a disciplined life. "He never rose later than 5:00 a.m. . . . for reading the Bible and prayer." He was a scholar and a writer, and "a man who could converse, teach and preach in Swedish, German, Spanish, French, and Quechua." His mind was "saturated with reams of memorized Scripture" and with names of students.

After three more close encounters with death, Edman died following a Wheaton chapel message in 1967, entitled "In the Presence of the King."[4]

"The Lord is my rock, my fortress and my deliverer; my God is my rock, in whom I take refuge, my shield and the horn of my salvation. He is my stronghold, my refuge and my savior—from violent men you save me. I call to the Lord, who is worthy of praise, and I am saved from my enemies.

The waves of death swirled about me; the torrents of destruction overwhelmed me. The cords of the grave coiled around me; the snares of death confronted me. In my distress I called to the Lord; I called out to my God. From his temple he heard my voice; my cry came to his ears.

*2 Samuel 22:2–7.*

# "SHE OPENS HER ARMS TO THE POOR"

For Rosalind Goforth and her husband Jonathan, Presbyterian missionaries to China during the early decades of the twentieth century, reaching out to the poor was an everyday matter. Much of their time was spent in itinerant evangelistic work, and everywhere they went they saw poverty. But during the famine of 1920–1921, they suddenly confronted poverty on a massive scale like they had never seen before. Rosalind later described the situation.

"I was unable, because of illness, to accompany my husband as he left our home on Kikungshan Mountain in the late summer of 1920. The news of the great famine reached me there in a letter from a coworker in Changte. The letter described vividly some of the awful conditions prevailing throughout our whole field, which was in the center of a vast area affecting, it was said, from thirty to forty millions of people. . . .

"Crushed at the thought of what hundreds of those who looked upon us as mother and father were passing through, I cried aloud in agony of soul, 'O God, is there not something I can do? Oh, show me!' " The answer to her plea was direct and simple: "Use your pen!"

She hastened to her desk and began to write, praying as she wrote, "Lord use my pen!" In a letter describing the anguish of these famine-stricken people, she poured out her heart. Then she went around the compound to other missionaries from various countries, and had her letter translated into their languages. "Within twenty-four hours of the writing of the appeal it was translated into several languages and on its way throughout the world!"

Her next step was to obtain permission from authorities to collect famine relief, and in the months that followed she collected more than one hundred and twenty thousand dollars and distributed it where it was most needed. "I kept close touch with several relief centers, and to these I sent checks as needed. Many were the thrills that came that winter as appeals reached me, and I was able to write checks off the Famine Relief Fund for amounts of $5,000 or even $10,000."

The following year Rosalind was able to leave the compound and accompany her husband on his revival tour to the famine-stricken area. "The experience was wonderful," she later recalled. "Everywhere hearts were opened to the Gospel message as a result of the splendidly organized famine relief carried on all through the previous winter by the band of faithful missionaries in Changte, often at the risk of their lives."[5]

She sets about her work vigorously; her arms are strong for her tasks. She sees that her trading is profitable, and her lamp does not go out at night. In her hand she holds the distaff and grasps the spindle with her fingers. She opens her arms to the poor and extends her hands to the needy.

*Proverbs 31:17–20.*

# "STORIES THAT DON'T TIRE THE HEAD"

The story of Joseph and his brothers is a simple story to follow. It is simple, that is, if it is told in one's own language, but very difficult, like other Bible stories, if it is told in a language that is not well-known. This was true for the Quechua people in Peru. Heidi and David Coombs worked closely with Cruz Landa, their language helper, in translating Bible stories for the people, so that they can understand and enjoy them.

Reading Bible stories in the Quechua language was a delight for Cruz because it allowed him to better understand how he ought to live the Christian life. But most of the Quechua believers did not benefit from God's Word in their own language.

On one occasion when he was attending a baptismal service in a nearby town, he became acutely aware that the people were not fully understanding the meaning of what was being spoken and read in Spanish. He was troubled by the persistence of the churches to continue the use of a "foreign" language. As usual, he had brought along his Quechua Bible story books, and he offered to read from them. He began reading the story of Joseph and his brothers, which was one of the more lengthy Bible stories.

Halfway through, Cruz hesitated, wondering aloud if he should continue on, promising that he would complete the story later. But the people insisted he go on. " 'Our heads aren't tired! We want to hear to the end.'

"So Cruz went on. Soon he arrived at the part where Joseph's brothers, not recognizing him as the ruler of Egypt said to him, 'Our brother died many years ago.' The crowd burst into laughter. They loved the irony. And when Cruz finished, no one wanted him to leave. He stayed until the next day, teaching Quechua choruses to the people and reading more Scripture."

For them it was a pleasure not to have to strain to understand, and to be able to catch the more subtle aspects of the stories that had been lost when read in a language that was not their own.[6]

Now Joseph was the governor of the land, the one who sold grain to all its people. So when Joseph's brothers arrived, they bowed down to him with their faces to the ground. . . . Although Joseph recognized his brothers, they did not recognize him. Then he remembered his dreams about them and said to them, "You are spies! You have come to see where our land is unprotected."

"No, my lord," they answered. "Your servants have come to buy food. We are all the sons of one man. Your servants are honest men, not spies."

"No!" he said to them. "You have come to see where our land is unprotected."

But they replied, "Your servants were twelve brothers, the sons of one man, who lives in the land of Canaan. The youngest is now with our father, and one is no more."

*Genesis 42:6, 8–13.*

# "THE SPIRIT OF THE LORD CAME UPON GIDEON"

Samuel Chadwick was one of England's great Methodist preachers. His success, he was convinced, was due to his dependence on the Holy Spirit. Early in his ministry, when he was serving as a lay evangelist, he preached fifteen sermons with no spiritual response from the people. They were unmoved by what he said. Was it them, or was it him? Samuel concluded that the problem lay with him. "He realized that God must be in control of everything. Then came surrender which brought him a realization of Christ's full salvation, a fresh vision of the Almighty, and a heart-felt yearning to see people saved. By the next day God had given him the joy of leading seven people to Christ. Peace, joy, and power were now his through the Spirit."

This prompted Chadwick to seek the Spirit's power even more. He was persuaded that the Holy Spirit was the key to any spiritual victories—a conviction that was reinforced one day when he was reading from the book of Judges about Gideon's power from above. It was the Spirit of the Lord that came upon him, and on further examination of the marginal notes, Chadwick learned that, "The Spirit of the Lord clothed itself with Gideon." It was a pivotal discovery in Chadwick's life. "My eyes were opened," he later wrote. "With great daring I crossed out Gideon's name and put in my own."

When he accepted a pastorate in Leeds, this Spirit power became evident immediately: "What a time we had!" he wrote. "The revival began on the first Sunday and by the end of September the chapel was full half an hour before the time to begin, and police regulated the crowd." He filled the coliseum with three thousand people during the two or three winters he preached there. Conversions took place almost every Sunday in or out of the chapel. Chadwick claimed there was hardly a room in his house in which someone had not accepted Christ.

He organized converts into classes, and before he left Leeds, about two thousand people were meeting in those groups. "Whole classes were organized for converted alcoholics. Street urchins were saved; some were to become preachers. . . . The great secret of his ministry was the Holy Spirit."[7]

But Joash replied to the hostile crowd around him, "Are you going to plead Baal's cause? Are you trying to save him? Whoever fights for him shall be put to death by morning! If Baal really is a god, he can defend himself when someone breaks down his altar." So that day they called Gideon "Jerub-Baal," saying, "Let Baal contend with him," because he broke down Baal's altar.

Now all the Midianites, Amalekites and other eastern peoples joined forces and crossed over the Jordan and camped in the Valley of Jezreel. Then the Spirit of the Lord came upon Gideon, and he blew a trumpet, summoning the Abiezrites to follow him.

*Judges 6:31–34.*

## "I BRING YOU DOWN, DECLARES THE LORD"

It was the peak of the hippie era in the 1960s when Tom Mahairas was soaring high in New York City as the leader of a rock band. "By the time I was eighteen," he recalls, "I had cut some records and was ready to sign a recording contract. Some people would say I had everything, but deep down I was not happy." Like so many around him, he was deep into the drug scene. "If I wasn't high, I wasn't happy"— but his highs only brought more lows, and his friends became his enemies. He lived with his girlfriend, Vicky, but his thinking had become so distorted that he became convinced she was the devil trying to trick him. Finally, he realized how low he actually was as he pondered his situation one summer day in Central Park.

"I was sitting by Bethesda Fountain high on LSD. In front of me were a group of Hare Krishnas chanting. To the left some hippies were tossing a Frisbee, and on my right an Indian guru sat surrounded by his followers. I looked at the scene like I was in the future; I disassociated myself from it. I watched and thought, 'Man, I'm not going to do this for the rest of my life!' So I walked over to the West Side Highway and hitched a ride upstate to Lake George. By this time, I thought I was the reincarnation of Christ, and I wanted to be in touch with something higher."

After Tom arrived at Lake George, he met a young man on an evangelism outing from Word of Life Island in nearby Schroon Lake, who invited him to visit that youth retreat and to meet with its founder Jack Wyrtzen. That memorable day in July of 1966 was the beginning of a new life for him. He committed his life to Christ and immediately called Vicky to share the news with her. She was initially skeptical "because under the influence of LSD he had already seen Krishna, Buddha and Allah," but as soon as he poured out his testimony she knew he was sincere and she too believed.

In 1971, he and Vicky were married, and in the years since they have pioneered a far-reaching ministry in New York City. Their ministry is associated with the church they founded, the Manhattan Bible Church, which began in their living room and has since grown to over seven hundred people. Reaching out into the largely Hispanic neighborhoods, the ministry sponsors a Christian Academy, a Gospel Outreach program, a Love Kitchen offering meals to the homeless five days a week, and a Transformation Life Center, a drug-rehabilitation program that ministers to young men, many of whom, like Tom, go on to lead productive Christian lives.[8]

"The pride of your heart has deceived you, you who live in the clefts of the rocks and make your home on the heights, you who say to yourself, 'Who can bring me down to the ground?' Though you soar like the eagle and make your nest among the stars, from there I will bring you down," declares the Lord. . . "All your allies will force you to the border; your friends will deceive and overpower you; those who eat your bread will set a trap for you, but you will not detect it."

*Obadiah 3–4, 7.*

# "IF YOU SEEK HIM, HE WILL BE FOUND"

Gipsy Smith, the well-known evangelist of a generation ago, was fortunate to be reared by a father who was determined to search for God, fearing that if he forsook God, he would be rejected forever. Gypsy tradition confirmed this because they believe they are descended from Judas Iscariot and are thus cursed.

For Cornelius Smith, that search began just before his wife died, leaving him with four little children to raise. He had one time asked his wife if she ever thought about God and if she ever prayed. "I try," she responded. "But a black hand comes before me and reminds me of all the wrongs I have done, and something says that there is no mercy for me." Just before she died, however, he heard her singing in the tent where they lived. It was an old chorus she had learned as a child: "I have a father in the promised land, and I must go to meet him in the promised land." That song reminded him of a gospel message he had heard while he had been imprisoned, and after she died, he vowed he would find God.

He did not forget that vow despite the sorrow and turmoil surrounding her death. "The authorities would permit the funeral to be held only at night. Cornelius was the sole mourner. . . . Earlier that day their tent had caught fire. . . . It was a dark day, indeed."

Cornelius inquired of various people about God, and finally was told that there was a meeting that would be held that very night at a city mission. "I will not come home again," he warned his children as he left for the meeting, "until I am converted." The children were fearful, not knowing what he meant nor whether they would ever see him again. There at the meeting, while a hymn was being sung, Cornelius fell to the floor in agony before God. Little Rodney, who later became known as "Gipsy," feared his father was dying. He had followed his father to the meeting and was distressed by what he saw.

Up from the floor, Cornelius jumped and shouted, "I am converted." His brother was also converted at that meeting, and later that night his brother's wife also professed her faith in Christ. The following morning the two brothers began sharing their witness to the other gypsies at the camp, and fourteen of them were converted. They also witnessed to their other brother, and he too was converted. "They became evangelists," writes David Lazell, "and you always had to take all three—as long as they were all alive. . . . Many were brought to Christ through that ministry." Cornelius had searched for God, found him, and served him with wholehearted devotion.[9]

"And you, my son Solomon, acknowledge the God of your father, and serve him with wholehearted devotion and with a willing mind, for the Lord searches every heart and understands every motive behind the thoughts. If you seek him, he will be found by you; but if you forsake him, he will reject you forever."

*1 Chronicles 28:9.*

# "BECAUSE HE TRUSTED IN HIS GOD"

"These people have been praying to Shang-ti Je-ho-hua (Jehovah God) and we could do nothing against their prayers." This was the reason given by five guards who were holding prisoner three missionaries and two young children.

Miraculous deliverance from the enemy can be a striking testimony to the power of God over natural circumstances. There was no rational explanation for Daniel's survival in a lion's den, nor was there any rational explanation for the survival of Rev. A. E. Glover, his wife and two children and Miss Gates, all serving with the China Inland Mission, during the Boxer Rebellion in the Shan-si Province of China in 1900. "For sixty-seven days they traveled through the heart of the most anti-foreign section of China, one thousand miles, to the seacoast."

At one point, the missionaries were imprisoned in a wayside inn, with no way of escape except by God's miraculous deliverance. "We prayed that He would not permit the officials, or our captors, in the room, to touch a hair of our heads, and that no power might be given them against us," Glover later wrote. "There was dead silence as the prayer went up. Five men were lying about the room. Presently the silence was broken, and out of the semi-darkness came the words: 'They have been praying to their God to deliver them. . . . Too late for that now! What is the use of praying when everything is fixed?' "

Soon after midnight, the guards at the inn got their orders to "Kill them at once." With that directive, "one of the men lit a vessel. At once the fumes of some narcotic began to fill the room to suffocation. In spite of his efforts, Mr. Glover was overcome. The watcher brought his lamp to see if his work was done. All were insensible but Miss Gates. When he saw her condition he waited. She continued to pray throughout the night. The fumes had no effect on her, and the men seemed afraid to do anything while she was conscious."

So the fearful guards set the missionaries free, and the reason given was that they "could do nothing against their prayers."[10]

At the first light of dawn, the king got up and hurried to the lion's den. When he came near the den, he called to Daniel in an anguished voice, "Daniel, servant of the living God, has your God, whom you serve continually, been able to rescue you from the lions?"

Daniel answered, "O king, live forever! My God sent his angel, and he shut the mouths of the lions. They have not hurt me, because I was found innocent in his sight. Nor have I ever done any wrong before you, O king."

The king was overjoyed and gave orders to lift Daniel out of the den. And when Daniel was lifted from the den, no wound was found on him, because he had trusted in his God.

*Daniel 6:19–23.*

# "YOU HAVE BEEN FAITHFUL WITH A FEW THINGS"

Those who are faithful in small tasks within the body of Christ are the ones who are rewarded with greater opportunities for ministry. Operating a YMCA canteen for servicemen in France during World War I certainly could be considered an inauspicious position in the kingdom of God. Yet, it served as an opportunity for a young man to bear witness in a small way. That man would become known as one of the twentieth-century's most powerful defenders of the faith.

When he volunteered for service overseas in 1917, J. Gresham Machen was a New Testament professor at Princeton University. He was thirty-four years old and had just completed his eleventh year of teaching. He knew well that this was no opportunity to advance his scholarly pursuits, but he was eager to serve his countrymen who had gone to war and he was hopeful that he would have great opportunities for ministry.

The opportunities for ministry, however, were disappointing. There were few worship services, and those that were scheduled were poorly attended. When he did preach, Machen felt compelled to set aside polished sermons and simply tell Bible stories that could be applied to everyday circumstances. It was a humbling job for a brilliant seminary professor. But even more humbling was his daily routine of work.

"Machen first ran a canteen in the town of St. Mard, which though still inhabited had been desolated by German artillery. In a damp and rat-infested house whose roof had been almost entirely blown off but which still possessed the ceiling of the first floor, Machen set up the canteen in his own living quarters. He distributed hot chocolate to soldiers and village residents and also tried to organize games. Preparing hot chocolate was almost a two-hour process—large bars of sweet chocolate had to be shaved up—which began early in the morning to open the canteen by 7:30. Even more difficult was securing supplies which often required walking four to eight miles to nearby villages just to place an order."

Distributing hot chocolate to soldiers might seem like a waste of Machen's talents, but seeing the anguish and devastation of war gave him a kind of compassion he could not have learned in the ivy halls of Princeton. He would go on to play a leading role as a conservative intellectual in the Fundamentalist-Modernist controversy of the 1920s, with few people realizing that he had taken a detour for lowly service in France.[11]

"After a long time the master of those servants returned and settled accounts with them. The man who had received the five talents brought the other five. 'Master,' he said, 'you entrusted me with five talents. See, I have gained five more.'

"His master replied, 'Well done, good and faithful servant! You have been faithful with a few things; I will put you in charge of many things. Come and share your master's happiness!'"

*Matthew 25:19–21.*

# "HUMBLY ACCEPT THE WORD PLANTED IN YOU"

In China many years ago, a father brought his baby boy to a missionary for baptism, and asked that the baby be given a Christian name: Moo Dee. The missionary was puzzled by the choice and when he inquired, he learned that the man had been so deeply moved by the stories he had heard about an evangelist way off in America that he wanted to name his little boy after him. Besides, in his dialect, *moo* meant love, and *dee* meant God.

Dwight L. Moody, that American evangelist, was known the world over for his love for God, and this little Chinese boy was certainly not the only youngster named after him. But Moody was also known—by those who knew him well—for his temper. Turning the other cheek was not a reaction that came naturally to him.

The story is told of one occasion when his temper got the better of him: "One evening, after a very earnest meeting, Mr. Moody was standing at the door of the room where the inquiry meeting was to be held, urging the men to come in. The door to this room was on the lower landing of the stairway, at the head of a short flight, and as Moody stood there a man came up to him and deliberately insulted him. Mr. Moody would never repeat the insult, but it was such as to make him thrust the man from him so violently as to send him reeling down the stairway."

Moody's associates were shocked. "This meeting is killed," one friend remarked. "The large number who have seen the whole thing will hardly be in a condition to be influenced by anything more Mr. Moody may say to-night."

But Moody went ahead with the meeting. These were people who had indicated further interest in the gospel and he could not let his temper stand in the way of their coming to Christ. He opened the meeting with a trembling and humble apology.

"Friends," he said, "before beginning to-night I want to confess that I yielded just now to my temper, out in the hall, and have done wrong. . . . I lost my temper with a man, and I want to confess my wrong before you all, and if that man is present here whom I thrust away from me in anger, I want to ask his forgiveness and God's. Let us pray."

He made no attempt to excuse himself or to blame the other man. He knew he was wrong and he humbly accepted the Word of God planted in him, and went on with the inquiry meeting.[12]

My dear brothers, take note of this: Everyone should be quick to listen, slow to speak and slow to become angry, for man's anger does not bring about the righteous life that God desires. Therefore, get rid of all moral filth and the evil that is so prevalent and humbly accept the word planted in you, which can save you.

*James 1:19–21.*

# "ZEALOUS FOR THE TRADITIONS OF MY FATHERS"

For many people who become Christians there is little outward change in their lives, but for others, like the apostle Paul, there is a radical change. He made an about-face. What had been an all-consuming and "extremely zealous" commitment to Judaism became a powerful and uncompromising zeal for Christ. The very movement he had been persecuting he began promoting. So it was with Shudir, a zealous Hindu.

Shudir's zealous opposition to Christianity was aroused by Jeannie Lockerbie, a missionary to Bangladesh with the Association of Baptists for World Evangelization. She had traveled to a village where she provided medical treatment to a poor woman named Shoba, who was Shudir's distant relative.

"Shudir feared we were out to destroy his family's faith," writes Jeannie. "To prevent that, he was prepared to have the local rowdies throw us out of the village.

"Then he discovered the Gospels and the Christian booklets we had left for Shoba to read. Angrily, he flung them out of the house and forbade her to read them." But having done that, his sense of curiosity and intellectual honesty prompted him to retrieve them, and check out for himself what was being written in the name of the Christian God.

As he read, Shudir became so engrossed in the new doctrine that he visited a Christian church to learn more. Here he was befriended by an elderly Christian who "loved him as a son, and through that love won him to a saving faith in Christ. Shudir was baptized in 1977, two years after he threw out the Christian publications—and almost threw out the missionaries as well!

"Since then Shoba has gone to be with the Lord, but Shudir continues to live out his faith. His job? He is the head printer at our Bible Literature Center! He now prints tracts and booklets to lead others to Christ, including the very same pieces that introduced him to the Lord"—that despicable literature he had once thrown out in anger.[13]

For you have heard of my previous way of life in Judaism, how intensely I persecuted the church of God and tried to destroy it. I was advancing in Judaism beyond many Jews of my own age and was extremely zealous for the traditions of my fathers. But when God, who set me apart from birth and called me by his grace, was pleased to reveal his Son in me so that I might preach him among the Gentiles, I did not consult any man, nor did I go up to Jerusalem to see those who were apostles before I was, but I went immediately into Arabia and later returned to Damascus.

*Galatians 1:13–17.*

## "A FATHER TO THE FATHERLESS"

This psalm that speaks of God being a father to the fatherless, touched the heart of a young man in England who himself had grown up rebellious in a sun-scorched land. George Mueller was born in Germany in 1805, the son of a government worker who indulged George and his brother. He was a rebellious trouble-maker, and before he "reached the age of ten, he had become an expert thief, cheater and liar. By the time he was 14, he was spending much time playing cards and drinking. George was even drunk the night his mother died."

By the time he was sixteen he had been imprisoned. His future seemed less than promising until he attended a prayer meeting and there was remarkably converted. In 1830, at the age of twenty-five, he moved to England where he became the pastor of a tiny chapel in Tiegnmouth. While there he read Psalm 68, and learned that God is the "father of the fatherless." If this is true, he reasoned, God will provide for the fatherless; all he would have to do is be an agent for God. With that promise launching him out, he and his young wife rented a home and within a month they had twenty-six orphans under their care.

Within months they opened a second orphan home that housed thirty more children, and after the end of the first year they opened still another home. They committed the care of the children to God in faith, and miraculously their needs were met. In the years that followed, they acquired larger and bigger homes, some of them housing as many as three hundred children.

At the age of seventy, Mueller retired, leaving his son-in-law in charge of the work. For the next seventeen years, he traveled throughout the world conducting missionary work.

"On Mr. Mueller's 90th birthday he preached to the congregation where he had been the pastor for sixty-nine years. His last sermon, preached on the Sunday evening before his death, was on the verse: "For we know that if our earthly house of this tabernacle were dissolved, we have a building of God, an house not made with hands, eternal in the heavens" (2 Cor. 5:1). Such a message must have been chosen by the Holy Spirit to close Mr. Mueller's life. He died during that night.[14]

Sing to God, sing praise to his name, extol him who rides on the clouds—his name is the Lord—and rejoice before him. A father to the fatherless, a defender of widows, is God in his holy dwelling. God sets the lonely in families, he leads forth the prisoners with singing; but the rebellious live in a sun-scorched land.

*Psalm 68:4–6.*

# "STANDING BEFORE THE AREOPAGUS"

Paul was not the only missionary to be brought before a meeting of the Areopagus. Eighteen centuries later, Jonas King, an American missionary to Greece, had a similar experience. It is assumed by some that Europe has been perceived as a mission field only in recent decades, but Jonas felt called to that needy continent in the 1820s.

King was a brilliant scholar—a graduate of Williams College and Andover Theological Seminary—who turned down teaching offers at both Amherst and Yale to pursue his calling as a missionary. He arrived at the time when Greece was struggling for its independence from Turkey, and he brought humanitarian aid from supporters in America. Along with this aid, he established schools that required study of the Bible and offered theological education to those who desired advanced training. So successful was he that Greek Orthodox leaders became alarmed.

"At the instigation of the Greek Synod Dr. King, like St. Paul, was brought before the Areopagus in Athens. There he was condemned to be tried before the felons' court in Syria. As in the case of St. Paul, again there was a conspiracy of fifty men against his life. Finally, in 1847, there was such popular excitement against him in view of false charges and of seditionary pamphlets against him that the king advised him, for his own safety, to leave the country for a time."

In 1851, King returned as a consular agent of the United States in Athens, a position that offered very little security. "The next year he was again brought to trial on a charge of blaspheming God and the religion of the Greek Church. He was found guilty and was incarcerated in a loathsome prison." When he was released he was expelled from the country.

Despite his unfortunate expulsion, King left behind a legacy that lived on: "Perhaps no man ever stirred a nation more intensely than Dr. King did Greece by his writings. It is owing to him that 'the Word of God is not bound' in that kingdom. His power lay in his Luther-like courage, his pure doctrine, consistent life, and steadfastness under oppression."[15]

While Paul was waiting for them in Athens, he was greatly distressed to see that the city was full of idols. So he reasoned in the synagogue with the Jews and the God-fearing Greeks, as well as in the marketplace day by day with those who happened to be there. A group of Epicurean and Stoic philosophers began to dispute with him. Some of them asked, "What is this babbler trying to say?" Others remarked, "He seems to be advocating foreign gods." They said this because Paul was preaching the good news about Jesus and the resurrection. Then they took him and brought him to a meeting of the Areopagus, where they said to him, "May we know what this new teaching is that you are presenting? You are bringing some strange ideas to our ears, and we want to know what they mean." Acts 17:16–20.

# "COME OUT FROM THEM AND BE SEPARATE"

The Lord's call "to come out from them and be separate" and his promise to be a Father is powerfully illustrated in the life of Victor Landero. Victor had the undeserved reputation in his village and in the surrounding Colombian countryside for being an evangelical—a term equivalent to being referred to as a cult member. All he had done to merit the label was his purchase of a Bible. At the time he bought it, he could not even read it, and in the years that followed he kept it in an old suitcase most of the time.

When asked if he were an evangelical, Victor denied it, but the rumor persisted, especially after he began meeting with a lay evangelist who frequently visited his town. It must be true, neighbors reasoned. Why else would he be struggling to learn to read that Bible? But others were not so sure. He was the proprietor of the local cantina—a bar, a dance hall, and a brothel. It was well-known that he was living with three different women—one who took care of his farm, one who lived in another village, and one who worked in his brothel as a prostitute, and everybody knew that he smoked and drank. Evangelicals did not do those things.

The disparity between his different interests suddenly emerged one day after he had been out of town on business. "Returning with my burro heavily laden with rum, God spoke to me through two women," he later recalled. "They took note of my cargo of liquor. 'You still sell rum in your store?' It was more a statement than a question. . . . They looked at each other, then at me. 'But, Don Victor, you're an Evangelical. . . and Evangelicals don't buy rum, or use it, or even *sell* it.' Their words cut deeply into my heart, and I plodded on in misery."

It was in his misery that Victor heard the voice of God calling him. "I nudged my burro off the trail into the grass and fell to my knees," he testified. "I had never prayed before. Not till that moment on the road. And never had I experienced such peace, such joy, and such release as I felt now." In the weeks and months that followed, his lifestyle changed. He turned his cantina into a general store, and terminated his illicit sexual relationships. Now there was no doubt among his neighbors that he truly was an evangelical—an evangelical whose life supported his testimony. In the years that followed, hundreds of people in his village and nearby communities came to Christ through his witness.[16]

"Therefore come out from them and be separate, says the Lord. Touch no unclean thing, and I will receive you." "I will be a Father to you, and you will be my sons and daughters, says the Lord Almighty."

Since we have these promises, dear friends, let us purify ourselves from everything that contaminates body and spirit, perfecting holiness out of reverence for God.

*2 Corinthians 6:17–18; 7:1.*

# "HE CHOSE US BEFORE THE CREATION OF THE WORLD"

It is impossible to explain, apart from God's providence, how certain individuals have found Christ and gone on to serve him. One individual chosen by God was Toshihiro "Tom" Takami, the founder and director of the Asian Rural Institute: "I became convinced that I could never find God, grasp God by my own strength. . . .Why I became a Christian is very plain. It is because God exists, and God found and caught me. God sought me."

Takami was born into a poor Japanese family who could not afford to send him to school beyond the elementary level. When he was offered a scholarship for high school, he considered himself fortunate. The one stipulation, however, was that he would have to leave his hometown and family and enter a Zen monastery and live as a monk. For the next five years, he lived a strict monastic existence, spending "many hours in meditation, sitting still for hours every day."

World War II interrupted Takami's monastic life, and he returned to live near his family and seek work. The countryside was impoverished, and so there were few opportunities for employment. Then one day he spotted an advertisement for a cook—a private cook for an English missionary, Albert Farout, at Kobe College. He arranged for an interview and told him he could cook, though his only experience was cooking rice at the Zen monastery. He was hired and immediately bought a copy of *The Fanny Farmer Cookbook*. With the help of a dictionary he translated recipes into Japanese, and cooked a different meal every day for the unsuspecting missionary.

Farout entrusted Nakami with money and important tasks, which utterly amazed the new employee: "I never met this kind of person before. I was ready to cheat and I knew how. But when I experienced such trust, this really began to change my own life." Takami, in return, trusted Farout so much that he inquired about his religion and asked if he could attend church. He began reading the Bible. "Often when I was reading the Bible," he testified, "I had to close it because it was so powerful that I could not keep reading, but this same experience urged me to read on. . . . Finally I asked the pastor of the church to let me join and receive baptism."

Because of his own painful memories of poverty, Takami was determined to devote his life to helping others in poverty. He went on to found the Asian Rural Institute, which offers people from third world nations modern agricultural skills and techniques along with Christian instruction.[17]

Praise be to the God and Father of our Lord Jesus Christ, who has blessed us in the heavenly realms with every spiritual blessing in Christ. For he chose us in him before the creation of the world to be holy and blameless in his sight. In love he predestined us to be adopted as his sons through Jesus Christ, in accordance with his pleasure and will—to the praise of his glorious grace, which he has freely given us in the One he loves.

*Ephesians 1:3–6.*

# "DO IT ALL FOR THE GLORY OF GOD"

Peter Cartwright was one of the great nineteenth-century frontier evangelists who fired up crowds at camp-meeting revivals. He was converted in a small-town revival that was spawned by the celebrated Cane Ridge camp meeting. The year after his conversion he was issued an exhorter's license, and at the age of eighteen he became a Methodist circuit preacher.

Although he was convinced he was called by God, nevertheless Cartwright was consumed by fear the first time he was called upon to preach. He was convinced he could not go through with the ordeal. "At length I asked God, if He had called me to preach, to give me aid that night, and give me one soul, that is, convert one soul under my preaching, as evidence that I was called to this work." God answered his prayer, and a "professed infidel" was "soundly converted." From that point on Cartwright was sure of his calling, and many fascinating experiences were to follow.

On one occasion when he was traveling through the Cumberland mountains Cartwright was offered lodging at a place where a dance was being held. With nothing else to do, he stationed himself in an out-of-the-way corner. Without warning, he tells, "a beautiful ruddy young lady walked very gracefully up to me, dropped a handsome courtesy, and pleasantly, with winning smiles, invited me out to take a dance with her. I can hardly describe my thoughts or feelings on that occasion. However, in a moment I resolved on a desperate experiment. I rose as gracefully as I could. . . . The young lady moved to my right side; I grasped her right hand with my right hand, while she leaned her left arm on mine. In this position we walked on the floor. The whole company seemed pleased at this act of politeness in the young lady, shown to a stranger. . . . I then spoke to the fiddler to hold a moment, and added that for several years I had not undertaken any matter of importance without first asking the blessing of God upon it. . . .

"Here I grasped the young lady's hand tightly, and said 'Let us all kneel down and pray,' and then instantly dropped on my knees, and commenced praying with all the power of soul and body that I could command. The young lady tried to get loose from me, but I held her tight. Presently she fell on her knees. Some of the company kneeled, some stood, some fled, some sat still, all looked curious. . . . About fifteen of that company professed religion, and our meeting lasted next day and next night, and as many more were powerfully converted. I organized a society, took thirty-two into the church, and sent them a preacher."[18]

So whether you eat or drink or whatever you do, do it all for the glory of God. Do not cause anyone to stumble, whether Jews, Greeks or the church of God—even as I try to please everybody in every way. For I am not seeking my own good but the good of many, so that they may be saved.

*1 Corinthians 10:31–33.*

## "HONOR GOD WITH YOUR BODY"

When Bill Cutts was about to be born, the doctor was in a quandary as to whether he should try to save him or his mother. Both were saved, but not without severe deformity of baby Bill's spine. He was unable to walk until he was four, and throughout his life he needed a cane or assistance from others. He wanted to serve his country in World War II, but was found to be unsuitable for military service.

At the age of twenty-seven, Cutts's life was suddenly transformed. He was passing by the Gospel Tabernacle in Philadelphia one day, and felt an inner prompting to go inside. He was converted that day, and two weeks later, after hearing a missionary for the first time, felt God calling him to serve overseas. He immediately applied to the Christian and Missionary Alliance for an appointment, but was categorically rejected. This denial, however, was not like a military rejection. His call had come from God, and he refused to accept the decision. His persistence paid off, and he and his wife Grace were later commissioned to go to Irian Jaya, to make contact with the unreached Moni tribe.

"Murder, revenge killings, hatred, war and ambush were the normal patterns for the men of the area to which we were assigned," writes Grace. "Life was cheap. To kill a widow or a woman for witchcraft, to throw an adulteress into the churning river, to step on the neck of a newborn twin baby were honorable ways to pay tribute to the evil spirits that haunted and ruled the lives of the men of Irian's hinterland."

The work with the people was slow until a revival swept across the valley in 1958. " 'Hazi ndona. We are hungry for eternal life,' they cried as they danced about our yard and milled about the station. 'Teach me a Bible story. Tell it again. Listen to see if I have understood it correctly.' We heard this over and over again.

"People stopped us on the trail. They woke us up in the night. They tugged at our sleeve while we were working. They came by the hundreds. They came from many miles away, from different tribes. They all said the same thing, 'We are hungry—hungry for God'. . . . The man who had been considered too frail to be a missionary stood with national church elders for hours, shivering in the cold river, baptizing up to a hundred persons in one day."

Bill was forced to return for medical treatment for a severe eye problem in 1964, but returned to the field with a wooden eye for two more decades of service. His motto was, "God glorify Yourself through my body."[19]

Do you not know that your body is a temple of the Holy Spirit, who is in you, whom you have received from God? You are not your own; you were bought at a price. Therefore honor God with your body.

*1 Corinthians 6:19–20.*

# "YOU DO NOT DELIGHT IN SACRIFICE"

Life held few options for a Hindu widow in nineteenth-century India. Although Chundra Lela was born into a wealthy Brahman family, she nevertheless became one of "the most despised of all creatures in India," at the age of nine, when her two-year marriage ended due to the death of her husband. Hinduism taught that "the death of a husband is caused by some sin which his wife has committed, perhaps in some previous existence and as long as she lives she is an outcast, scorned and ill treated by everyone."

To avoid ill-treatment, Chundra became a religious pilgrim in the years that followed. She studied the Hindu holy books and wandered through the countryside and towns visiting one sacred shrine after another. As she walked she counted her sacred beads, and repeated incantations she had learned from the scriptures. But there was no peace, and her search for God became more intense. She observed holymen offering penance: "Some were lying on beds of spikes; others buried in the sand; still others lying over smoking wood." Maybe self-denial would help her find God, she reasoned.

"Chundra Lela vowed that all during the six most scorchingly hot months of India's hot year, she would sit all day and every day in the burning sun, with five fires built close around her. From midnight until daylight each night she stood in front of an idol, standing on one foot, with the other drawn up against it, imploring the god to reveal himself to her. . . . But no sense of peace came, and at the end of three years of this self-inflicted suffering she felt that she had done all that she possibly could." Disillusioned, she renounced her search for God.

During this time of doubt she encountered a friend with a Bible. Chundra began reading it—not only in private but to her women friends. She was threatened by their husbands, but she would not be deterred. She insisted that she had found the peace she had been looking for.

"I have worshiped every idol I know," she confessed. "I have gone on all pilgrimages and done all the Hindu religion has taught; but I know nothing about pardon, and have no peace. . . . I have now read about Jesus, and learn that he is the Savior and can save and pardon me. Believing this, I wish to become a Christian." Chundra went on to have a powerful ministry of reaching out with the gospel to Hindus who visit shrines and practice the self-inflicting torture that she knew so well.[20]

Then I will teach transgressors your ways, and sinners will turn back to you. Save me from bloodguilt, O God, the God who saves me, and my tongue will sing of your righteousness. O Lord, open my lips, and my mouth will declare your praise. You do not delight in sacrifice, or I would bring it; you do not take pleasure in burnt offerings. The sacrifices of God are a broken spirit; a broken and contrite heart, O God, you will not despise.

*Psalm 51:13–17.*

# "THE FRAGRANCE OF LIFE"

Miron Winslow was one of the first foreign missionaries to sail from the shores of America. He served faithfully in Ceylon and India for forty-four years, but has been overshadowed by the famous Adoniram Judson, who went abroad seven years earlier. By his side in the ministry for more than four decades was his wife Harriet. She, too, has been overshadowed by a Judson, Adoniram's wife Ann, though Harriet served abroad more than three times as long.

Harriet was well-prepared for Christian ministry. She could well be characterized as one who "spreads everywhere the fragrance of the knowledge of him"— one who radiated "the aroma of Christ among those who are being saved and those who are perishing." This was evident in her life before she sailed to foreign shores.

She was a pioneer in the American Sunday school movement—the movement that was very controversial in the early days. "Hearing of what was then new in America, the Sunday-school, she gathered a little Sunday-school in the galleries of her home church. The church authorities deemed this a desecration of the house and day, and they drove her and her charge out from the church. Then she gathered the little ones in a neighboring schoolhouse. But public sentiment would not tolerate this there, and again she and her charge were expelled. Nothing daunted, she taught the little ones on the church steps in the open air, until public sentiment was changed and the gallery was again opened to her."

In her efforts she was, as the apostle Paul affirms, "to the one . . . the smell of death; to the other, the fragrance of life." In one instance, when an "old pastor, in his knee breeches and cocked hat, passed the schoolhouse where this young and devoted teacher had her Sunday-school class for a season, he shook his ivory-headed cane towards the building, and said in honest indignation, 'You imps of Satan doing the Devil's work!'"

She was the first one in her family to make a profession of faith in Christ. "But her father and mother followed her into the church, and so did every other member of the . . . family. When she became a foreign missionary three of her sisters followed her in that step. One of her brothers died just before he entered the ministry. Another brother . . . went West as a home missionary. A daughter of hers labored as a missionary's wife in India." She indeed was "the fragrance of life."[21]

But thanks be to God, who always leads us in triumphal procession in Christ and through us spreads everywhere the fragrance of the knowledge of him. For we are to God the aroma of Christ among those who are being saved and those who are perishing. To the one we are the smell of death; to the other, the fragrance of life. And who is equal to such a task? Unlike so many, we do not peddle the word of God for profit. On the contrary, in Christ we speak before God with sincerity, like men sent from God.

*2 Corinthians 2:14–17.*

# "GOD CREDITS RIGHTEOUSNESS APART FROM WORKS"

Life consisted of rules and regulations for Jesse Irvin Overholtzer, whose pioneering family had moved West with others of like faith during the Civil War. They were known as Dunkards, adherents of the tiny Church of the Brethren denomination. Baptism was by *trine* immersion (three times forward into the water), and they believed that "salvation of the soul depended on the proper baptism of the body." Women were required to wear bonnets, and only bonnets—no hats. And men wore untrimmed beards, as prescribed in Leviticus. "Almost without exception, the ministers in that conference preached and practiced 'salvation by works.'"

Jesse embraced this tradition wholeheartedly and became a minister. "I accepted it fully," he later recalled, "right down to the beards and the bonnets. I believed that the Bible was the very Word of God, that Jesus was God the Son, that Christ died on the cross for my sin and rose again from the grave. But I had added something to the *finished* work of Christ on the cross. Salvation was not a free gift—salvation was not by grace."

It was easier to preach a "works salvation," Jesse discovered, than to live it. He struggled in his spiritual life, never sure that he was good enough and always fearing death. Yet, he abhorred what he considered to be the "cheap grace" of revivalist preachers. That was evident one day when he bought a box of books at an auction for twenty-five cents. In the box was *The Life of Moody*. "That deluded evangelist!" he muttered when he sorted through the books. "I'll not waste time reading that." But the book haunted him, and sometime later, after a lengthy struggle, he reluctantly read the book. There he found that Dwight L. Moody had what he longed for.

The evangelist's testimony alone did not turn Jesse's life around. In the months that followed, he studied the Bible, especially passages in Romans and other epistles of Paul that challenged his belief in salvation by works. Slowly the message penetrated his heart, until one day when he was on a ladder pruning his fruit trees, he cried out, "It must be so! I accept it for myself!" He got down from the ladder and rushed into the house to his wife shouting "I'm saved, I'm saved." Jesse shared his newfound faith with others, and was required to face a trial before church leaders. The leaders were divided, and a second trial was called, after which he resigned from his church—a resolution that was crucial to his later decision to found and direct Child Evangelism Fellowship.[22]

Now when a man works, his wages are not credited to him as a gift, but as an obligation. However, to the man who does not work but trusts God who justifies the wicked, his faith is credited as righteousness. David says the same thing when he speaks of the blessedness of the man to whom God credits righteousness apart from works: "Blessed are they whose transgressions are forgiven, whose sins are covered. Blessed is the man whose sin the Lord will never count against him."

*Romans 4:4–8.*

# "DO NOT GET DRUNK, BE FILLED WITH THE SPIRIT"

Nobody ever doubted the genuineness of Billy Bray's conversion. He was a miner in Cornwall, England, who, after a long day of work, spent his nights in the beer shops of the mining district. Night after night, his wife had to go out and find him and help her drunken husband home. But he was not without a conscience. "I never got drunk without feeling condemned for it," Billy recalled. But, he was convinced that the Devil had a hold on his life.

Then one night in 1823, after he had attended a meeting of the Bible Christians, he came home and cried out to God for mercy and was converted. "In an instant," he testified, "the Lord made me so happy that I cannot express what I felt. I shouted for joy."

A year after his conversion Billy became a lay preacher for the Bible Christian Church, and he was often called upon to preach when no one more qualified was available. His most effective ministry, however, was in the mines. "He would pray for his fellow miners before they went to work in the mornings. 'Lord,' he would say, 'if any of us must be killed, or die to-day, let it be *me*; let not one of these men die, for they are not happy and I am, and if I die today I shall go to heaven.'"

He was an eccentric character, often dancing and singing in the streets, and professing to be joyful no matter what the circumstances. "I can't help praising God," he said. "As I go along the street I lift up one foot, and it seems to say 'glory!' and I lift up the other, and it seems to say, 'Amen'; and so they keep on like that all the time I am walking." Even at the time of his wife's death, he shouted for joy: "Bless the Lord! My dear Joey is gone up with the bright ones! My dear Joey is gone up with the shining angels! Glory! Glory! Glory!"

His preaching always had a homespun quality about it. He exhorted sinners to get saved and to forsake their sinful habits. "He frequently said that if the Lord had intended people to snuff he would have turned their noses upside down, and that if he had intended them to smoke He would have put a chimney in the back of their heads. He said that an architect who would build a house so that the smoke had to come out at the front door was in his opinion a very poor architect, and surely the Lord could not be a worse architect than man."[23]

Be very careful, then, how you live—not as unwise but as wise, making the most of every opportunity, because the days are evil. Therefore do not be foolish, but understand what the Lord's will is. Do not get drunk on wine, which leads to debauchery. Instead, be filled with the Spirit. Speak to one another with psalms, hymns and spiritual songs. Sing and make music in your heart to the Lord, always giving thanks to God the Father for everything, in the name of our Lord Jesus Christ.

*Ephesians 5:15–20.*

# "YOU WILL TREAD OUR SINS UNDERFOOT"

He was raised in Harlem, the son of a preacher, and he grew up learning how to behave as a preacher's kid. But while he outwardly conformed, he inwardly rebelled. By his own testimony, he was an extraordinary success: "I was president of the student body at school. I was a member of the Arista Society, made up of the cream of the intellectual crop. I was president of the Shakespearean Club. And I was a member of the baseball team. I was also president of the young people's department in my own church. By the time I was fourteen years of age, I'd acted out full length plays of Shakespeare, Hamlet and Macbeth, playing the title roles."

Such was the young man who was confronted one night by a street gang member and asked facetiously if he wanted to be a member of the Harlem Lords. The gang member was taken aback when the preacher's kid said yes. "In order to be a member of the Harlem Lords you gotta pass the initiation test," he warned. "We'll see if you're tough enough to be in the gang!"

He was tough enough, as he later recalled. "After six weeks of fighting with the Harlem Lords, getting involved in several rumbles, breaking into a few stores and doing some other stealing, I sized up the leader of our gang. I decided, 'Why should I be just a member of the gang when I can be the *leader?*'" He challenged the leader to a fight and won. For the next two years he "would reign as undisputed leader of the gang" and would earn twenty-two notches on the handle of his knife—one for each time he used his knife on someone. And all the while he continued his active involvement in church and school activities—his parents not realizing he was a gang leader.

One night while he was listening to his radio and planning his strategy for a massive attack by a coalition of gangs against gangs on the other side of the city, an unscheduled gospel program came on. He was annoyed—especially by the preacher's obvious lack of education and his emotional, uncouth manner. But somehow he could not force himself to get up and change the station. The more he listened, the more he was convicted, and by the end of the program he turned his life over to God.

That was the turning point in Tom Skinner's life. After that decision, he boldly began sharing the gospel and led many members of his own gang and rival gangs to the Lord. He later went on to become America's leading black evangelist.[24]

They will lick dust like a snake, like creatures that crawl on the ground. They will come trembling out of their dens; they will turn in fear to the Lord our God and will be afraid of you. Who is a God like you, who pardons sin and forgives the transgression of the remnant of his inheritance? You do not stay angry forever but delight to show mercy. You will again have compassion on us; you will tread our sins underfoot and hurl all our iniquities into the depths of the sea.

*Micah 7:17–19.*

## "CHRIST WILL REIGN FOREVER"

This verse from the book of Revelation has become famous the world over through the singing of Handel's *Messiah* and its most familiar stanzas of the "Hallelujah Chorus." The words are sometimes sung glibly and without meaning, as singers are caught up in the overpowering music. But Kurumada Akiji did not speak these words glibly. He was one of the two hundred Christians in Japan who were imprisoned during World War II for their religion.

To the Japanese authorities, Kurumada's crime was serious. He was guilty of treason. Divinity, according to Japanese belief, rested in the Emperor, and he alone would rule the world. Kurumada was asked to attest to that fact, but he could not. His response was to quote Revelation 11:15, stating that Christ is the one who will reign for ever and ever.

Kurumada first heard the gospel message in 1903 when he was working as a telegraph operator. He heard that an American telegraph operator had come to his city and was offering English classes. He was eager to improve his English, and was willing to overlook the fact that the American was Ernest A. Kilbourne, the cofounder of the Oriental Missionary Society, and that he was using the Bible as his text. Also in the class was Yamazaki Teigi, another telegraph operator and an arch rival of Kurumada. The competition between them was strong, and the more they perfected their English the more biblical knowledge they acquired. Both men soon professed faith in Christ and attended Bible school, and Kurumada became the director of the Oriental Missionary Society churches that eventually comprised some two hundred groups of believers in Tokyo alone.

Considering the vast population of Japan, the growth of Christianity was slow, but there was, nevertheless, a spirit of optimism. That optimism was shattered with the outbreak of the war in the Pacific in 1941. Christianity was perceived as the religion of the enemy, and all Christians were viewed with suspicion. Small churches were closed, and guards were posted at the larger churches to make sure that all who attended offered proper obeisance to a symbolic vestige of the Emperor. Kurumada and Yamazaki both refused to bow down, believing it to be a sign of worship, and were thus imprisoned for their treason.

During their imprisonment they were often confined in tiny cells. They were required to endure long hours of interrogation, but they used every such opportunity to give their testimonies of faith in Christ. "I preached my best sermon to the police," recalled Kurumada.[25]

The seventh angel sounded his trumpet, and there were loud voices in heaven, which said: "The kingdom of the world has become the kingdom of our Lord and of his Christ, and he will reign for ever and ever."

*Revelation 11:15.*

# "ABOUT THREE THOUSAND WERE ADDED TO THEIR NUMBER"

The revival meetings and evangelistic campaigns that have become a standard part of modern Christianity were not readily accepted in earlier generations. The outreach of Charles G. Finney and Dwight L. Moody was denounced as work of the Devil, and old-line Calvinists argued it detracted from the sovereignty of God. Yet, though these campaigns were new on the scene, they were not unlike what occurred under Peter's ministry on the day of Pentecost.

One of the most successful early evangelists in America was Jacob Knapp, who left the pastorate in the 1830s and devoted the remainder of his life to itinerant evangelism. He faced considerable opposition from fellow ministers, but he was convinced that God was calling him. The response to his preaching quickly confirmed that call. "So many people professed conversion in his meetings that he finally lost count of them, and he gave up the effort after he passed the hundred thousand mark."

Often the revival fervor would become so great that businesses would shut down in towns and people would attend meetings all day and into the night. In one town, the local doctor sold his property and left for Canada, because, as the story is told, "he could not go to his barn, but some one was praying in the hay-mow; he could not go to the woods, but some one was praying behind every bush-heap; that the women pestered the life out of him, tormenting him with their religion, so that he would rather live in purgatory."

In Auburn, New York, some young hoodlums tried to disrupt the ministry, but "on the same night some of them came into the meeting, were smitten down by the power of God's truth, and had to be carried to their homes." In Lowell, Massachusetts, a large cotton mill was shut down because so many people were carried away by the enthusiasm of the revival, and when Knapp left the town, according to a contemporary witness, "the air resounded with the songs of the rejoicing and weeping multitudes." In Baltimore, Maryland, some ten thousand people professed faith in Christ as a result of Knapp's first series of meetings there.

Was this mass hysteria or the work of God? Many critics claimed the former, but Knapp viewed it as the routine work of the Holy Spirit—even as was Pentecost.[26]

Peter replied, "Repent and be baptized, every one of you, in the name of Jesus Christ for the forgiveness of your sins. And you will receive the gift of the Holy Spirit. The promise is for you and your children and for all who are far off—for all whom the Lord our God will call."

With many other words he warned them; and he pleaded with them, "Save yourselves from this corrupt generation." Those who accepted his message were baptized, and about three thousand were added to their number that day.

*Acts 2:38–41.*

# "WE WILL NOT SERVE YOUR GODS"

God is able to save, these three young Hebrew men affirmed, "but even if he does not" they would not even entertain the thought of denying him and worshiping false gods. This has been the testimony of Christians down through the ages. In some instances, even after the ultimatum is decreed, God intervenes and spares his servants—even as he did Shadrach, Meshach, and Abednego; but in other instances he does not—as in the case of Blind Chang Shen of China.

Before he became a Christian, Chang Shen was referred to as a *Wu so pu wei te* ("one without a particle of good in him"). He was dishonest in his business dealings and abusive to his family, and when he lost his eyesight, people insisted it was punishment from the gods for his wickedness.

It was in 1886, after traveling hundreds of miles, that Chang arrived at a mission hospital. He desperately hoped for a cure for his physical blindness. What he found was a cure for his spiritual blindness. "Never had we a patient who received the gospel with such joy," his doctor testified. Although his eyesight was not fully restored, he was completely content in his newfound faith.

"When Chang asked for baptism, missionary James Webster replied, 'Go home and tell your neighbors that you have changed. I will visit you later and if you are still following Jesus, then I will baptize you.' When Webster returned some months later, there were hundreds of people who were eagerly waiting to hear the gospel message.

"A clumsy native doctor robbed Chang of the little eyesight the missionaries had restored. No matter— Chang continued his travels from village to village, winning hundreds more, praising God when cursed and spit upon, even when ferocious dogs were turned loose to drive him away. He learned practically the whole New Testament by memory and could quote entire chapters from the Old Testament. Missionaries followed after him, baptizing converts and organizing churches."

When the Boxer Rebellion unleashed its fury in 1900, Chang was an obvious target because he was spreading a "foreign religion." He hid, but when word came that fifty Christians would be killed if he did not come before the Boxers, he readily appeared. When he refused to worship the god of war or Buddha, he was taken to a cemetery and beheaded.[27]

Shadrach, Meshach and Abednego replied to the king, "O Nebuchadnezzar, we do not need to defend ourselves before you in this matter. If we are thrown into the blazing furnace, the God we serve is able to save us from it, and he will rescue us from your hand, O king. But even if he does not, we want you to know, O king, that we will not serve your gods or worship the image of gold you have set up."

*Daniel 3:16–18.*

# "A PROVIDENTIAL ENCOUNTER"

It is indeed providential that Paul, in prison in Rome, would have encountered Onesimus, a runaway slave who had belonged to a friend of his—a slave who was then converted through Paul's ministry. The details of how they met are not known, but perhaps he was in prison as well. The well-known preacher Harry A. Ironside told a story that offers, in his words, "a wonderful illustration of this very thing: the divine ability to bring the needy sinner and the messenger of Christ together."

Evangelist Sam Hadley, at the invitation of J. Wilbur Chapman, was conducting a midnight meeting at the Metropolitan Theater in Oakland, California. The meeting began with a procession through town led by the Salvation Army, and ended at the theater, where every seat was quickly filled.

Observing this procession was a man who had run away from his home in Detroit. Jim had turned away from his Christian upbringing and had gotten in trouble with the law one night when he was drinking with his friends. Fearing he would ruin his parents' reputation, he decided to flee to California and become lost in the crowds of transients. His parents were heartbroken, but their hopes were revived when they received a letter from a former friend of his saying he thought he had spotted Jim on a streetcar in San Francisco.

Jim's parents met Sam Hadley in Detroit when he was conducting meetings there, and they called upon him for help. They knew he would be going to California, and they asked him to pray that God would bring him together with their son. It seemed like a preposterous request—that he would encounter their son among the millions of people in California, but he agreed to pray daily at an appointed time when the parents would also be praying.

Despite his commitment to prayer, it must have astonished Hadley to discover that the young man who had taken his seat when he arose to speak (because there were no other empty seats in the crowded auditorium) was the young man for whom he had been praying. Jim was touched by the stirring message, and he was converted that night.[28]

"I then, as Paul—an old man and now also a prisoner of Christ Jesus—I appeal to you for my son Onesimus, who became my son while I was in chains. Formerly he was useless to you, but now he has become useful both to you and to me.

I am sending him—who is my very heart—back to you. I would have liked to keep him with me so that he could take your place in helping me while I am in chains for the gospel. But I did not want to do anything without your consent, so that any favor you do will be spontaneous and not forced. Perhaps the reason he was separated from you for a little while was that you might have him back for good— no longer as a slave, but better than a slave, as a dear brother."

*Philemon 9b–16a.*

## "MEMORIES OF A MOTHER'S FAITH"

"Come down to the mission tonight . . . if you've wandered far away from God and your mother's religion." With these words Harry Monroe admonished a group of young men sitting along a Chicago curbstone one Sunday afternoon in 1886. The words "mother's religion" pierced the heart of one of the young men. The man noticed that with Harry were "some men and women in a horse-drawn wagon . . . playing horns, flutes and slide trombones, and . . . singing hymns he had heard in Sunday school and which his mother used to sing in the Iowa log cabin."

The memories that flooded him though, were not all happy ones. His mother and grandmother had been the ones most dear to him. When his grandmother died when he was a young boy, he was heartbroken. "The second day after the funeral he vanished; no searching party could locate him. Finally his pet dog picked the scent through the snow, and, leading to the cemetery, stopped where the lad lay thrown across the grave, chill-bitten by a cold November wind, and sobbing so that friends despaired of his ever stopping." Soon after this, his impoverished widowed mother relinquished her sons to a nearby orphanage. It was a sorrowful farewell.

The love for his mother and grandmother had not faded, but his childhood faith had dimmed over the years. Now the reminder of this old-time religion so moved him that he vowed he would go to the mission meeting that night. He knew he would be ridiculed. He and his buddies were baseball players with the Chicago White Stockings, and "getting religion" was not the manly thing to do.

That night at the Pacific Garden Mission, Harry Monroe gave the message, and Billy Sunday, "the speediest base-runner and most daring base-stealer in baseball" was converted. Though he dreaded the ridicule he feared he would face from his teammates, it was a decision he knew he had to make. To his amazement, though, his buddies respected him, and the first game after his conversion was one of the best in his life. After catching a long fly ball far out of his range, "the crowd went almost insane" and carried him off the field on its shoulders. Five years after his conversion, Billy turned down a $3,500 baseball contract in order to enter Christian ministry for less than $1,000 per year. He went on to become one of the nation's most widely acclaimed evangelists.[29]

I thank God, whom I serve, as my forefathers did, with a clear conscience, as night and day I constantly remember you in my prayers. Recalling your tears, I long to see you, so that I may be filled with joy. I have been reminded of your sincere faith, which first lived in your grandmother Lois and in your mother Eunice and, I am persuaded, now lives in you also. For this reason I remind you to fan into flame the gift of God, which is in you through the laying on of my hands. For God did not give us a spirit of timidity, but a spirit of power, of love and of self-discipline.

*2 Timothy 1:3–7.*

# "I WAS OVERCOME BY TROUBLE AND SORROW"

The pain and sorrow that missionaries sometimes face is often magnified by their isolation. Because they are far away from loved ones, they often have few with whom to share their sorrows. This was true for Geraldine Guinness during her first term in China with the China Inland Mission. She had been faithful in her work, and was committed to Hudson Taylor's plan to reach all of China before the end of the century. As such, she traveled in remote areas and often faced outbursts of anti-foreign hostility. Her Chinese helpers advised her, after one particularly difficult situation, to return to the mission compound, but she refused. She was certain that God had called her to a pioneering ministry. She was willing to sacrifice her life for that ideal.

But in the midst of this sacrifice came a wrenching sorrow and a sense of overwhelming failure. Mrs. Herbert Taylor, the daughter-in-law of Hudson Taylor, had given birth to a healthy baby girl at the mission compound, but Mrs. Taylor was slow in regaining her strength. Geraldine was called upon to assist in the care of the baby. "After a time the baby sickened with dysentery, and it was then that Geraldine made a terrible mistake. She had prepared a dose of medicine for the baby, which Nurse Crewdson administered, but had taken the wrong bottle, and very soon the little one lost consciousness and died.

"The shock had been overwhelming. After months of expectation and the last days of tension, there had been the joy of the little one's coming, and then—by *her* mistake—the newly given life had fled. They could have no funeral there among the heathen, where a dead baby girl counted for less than nothing. The sorrowing father carried his little daughter's tiny human frame out at night, and buried her somewhere in Honan.

"Geraldine was stricken in heart. She wept for days and nights." She wrote to Hudson Taylor, then in England, and confessed to what had happened. He asked his son, Howard, to respond, knowing he cared deeply for her, even though she had previously turned down his marriage proposal. "That led to correspondence between Howard and Geraldine and an altogether new intimacy. The fact that no other knew of her sorrow over this thing strengthened the bond between them." It was sorrow that brought them together, but on their wedding day in 1894, she wrote in the margin of Psalm 35:27, "The Lord be magnified, which hath pleasure in the prosperity of his servant." As Mrs. Howard Taylor she served for more than fifty years as a missionary, author, and "first lady" of the China Inland Mission.[30]

I love the Lord, for he heard my voice; he heard my cry for mercy. Because he turned his ear to me, I will call on him as long as I live. The cords of death entangled me, the anguish of the grave came upon me; I was overcome by trouble and sorrow. Then I called on the name of the Lord: "O Lord, save me!" The Lord is gracious and righteous; our God is full of compassion. The Lord protects the simplehearted; when I was in great need, he saved me.

*Psalm 116:1–6.*

## "IF THEY PERSECUTED ME, THEY WILL PERSECUTE YOU"

Persecution is often associated with foreign countries and non-Christian religious fanaticism, but there is another kind of persecution that comes because the world hates Christians, as Jesus warned his followers. It is a persecution that comes not because someone has converted to a new religion or because someone is seeking to share a new religion, but rather because someone is standing strong for the faith and making others uncomfortable in the process.

This kind of persecution often confronted frontier evangelists as they traveled from town to town preaching the gospel. It required courage to face the hostility that often confronted them, as an episode in the ministry of Amanda Gustafson and Christina Matson illustrates. The setting was Orrock, Minnesota, in the early years of the twentieth century.

A contemporary observer told the story: "While Miss Matson was speaking and the schoolhouse was full of people one evening, we heard a breaking of glass, and the lower part of the window nearest the platform was smashed in, then the same thing happened at the next window on the same side, and a great shower of eggs, some rotten, was hurled in through these two windows over the audience. Our neighbor, Gustafson, had also come along; sitting next to the window he tried to peer out into the darkness to see who these were who threw the eggs but they plastered his face so full it was impossible for him to see. He did not know until getting up to walk around later, that an embryo chick was securely lodged in his flowing whiskers. I sat near the platform and my head of thick hair was smeared full of 'egg-shampoo,' and parts of my guitar were varnished with the vile stuff. Women screamed and crawled under the benches, but the 'bombardment' did not last very long, which indicated that enemy forces were numerous, and order was soon restored.

"The first egg smashed on Miss Matson's head, as she was on the platform and made a good target. She was preaching with the Lord's prayer as her subject, and significantly had come to the very sentence 'forgive us our trespasses as we forgive those who trespass against us,' when the enemy struck! . . . It was during and after such visits of preachers and missionaries that the yearning awakened in my heart to some day and in some way become one of God's messengers in the Gospel work."[31]

"If the world hates you, keep in mind that it hated me first. If you belonged to the world, it would love you as its own. As it is, you do not belong to the world, but I have chosen you out of the world. That is why the world hates you. Remember the words I spoke to you: 'No servant is greater than his master.' If they persecuted me, they will persecute you also. If they obeyed my teaching, they will obey yours also. They will treat you this way because of my name, for they do not know the One who sent me."

*John 15:18–21.*

# "RETURN TO YOUR FORTRESS, O PRISONERS OF HOPE"

Some of the earliest recollections of Timothy Kituo were those of going to witch doctors in the hope of finding a cure for his illness. His family was part of the Kamba tribe in southeast Kenya, and he was the only child of seven children who was frail and sickly. His parents loved him and they desperately hoped the witch doctors could save him, but each time they were disappointed. But what other alternative did they have? Suddenly, however, their outlook changed. Missionaries came to their district of Kitui, and his parents were among those who believed.

During this same period of time, Timothy began growing stronger and soon he was well enough to begin school in 1964 at the age of ten. It was a struggle for him to catch up, but finally at the age of eighteen he was ready to begin high school—ready academically and spiritually. Although his parents had been Christians for several years, he himself did not commit his life to Christ until a team of Bible college students visited his school and shared their faith.

Their ministry had a powerful impact on him, and when he entered high school he soon became known as "a student-pastor" because he readily shared his faith with others—both at school and at local churches—and many were converted through his ministry.

Following high school, it seemed natural for Timothy to go on and study for the ministry, but there was one big obstacle. Money. The salaries of Kenyan pastors are very low, and Timothy was being irresistibly drawn into secular work where the pay would be much higher. He studied accounting for a time, and in 1978 joined the Kenyan Air Force, where he performed so well that he soon was promoted to the rank of corporal. He felt gratified in this leadership role and was convinced that he could serve God in the military.

His complacency was suddenly disrupted, however, on August 1, 1982. That was the day of the Kenyan coup instigated by the Air Force. Though Timothy himself knew nothing of this conspiracy, he was imprisoned, but was among the fortunate ones who were not killed or maimed. For six months he was confined in three different maximum security prisons; for three of those months he was in a dark, dank cell with no sunlight, and he lived off the scraps of food provided by other prisoners. Yet it was a rewarding time, as many prisoners came to Christ through Timothy's testimony. Finally after six months as he was languishing at the point of death, he made a covenant with God that if he were released he would spend the rest of his life preaching. The very next day he was miraculously released. He was freed from the pit. Today, after graduating from Moffat College of Bible, Timothy is a pastor.[1]

As for you, because of the blood of my covenant with you, I will free your prisoners from the waterless pit. Return to your fortress, O prisoners of hope; even now I announce that I will restore twice as much to you.

*Zechariah 9:11–12.*

## "AND BOOKS WERE OPENED"

These verses from Revelation were the text for the funeral sermon of Susannah Wesley given by her son John. Many people had gathered that late Sunday afternoon in August of 1742, and John wrote that, "It was one of the most solemn assemblies I ever saw or expect to see on this side of eternity." It was solemn because a great woman of faith was no longer with them. John had written of her passing two days before:

"About three in the afternoon I went to my mother and found her change was near. I sat down on the bedside. She was in her last conflict, unable to speak but I believe quite sensible. Her look was calm and serene, and her eyes fixed upward while we commended her soul to God. From three to four the silver cord was loosing, and the wheel breaking at the cistern; and then without any struggle, or sigh, or groan, the soul was set at liberty. We stood round the bed and fulfilled her last request, uttered a little before she lost her speech: 'Children, as soon as I am released, sing a psalm of praise to God.' "

The psalm of praise was certainly not a hollow one. Her children knew she would have nothing to fear before the white throne judgment at the opening of the Book of Life. The record of her life would stand forever in that book, and in the lives of countless people touched by her living faith. John spoke of her as a "preacher of righteousness," and that, in a simple way, summed up her life. In a letter to her husband thirty years before her death, she had written of her desire to please God:

"But soon after you went to London last, I lit on the account of the Danish missionaries. I was, I think, never more affected with anything; I could not forbear spending good part of that evening in praising and adoring the divine goodness for inspiring with such ardent zeal for His glory. For several days I could think or speak of little else. At last it came into my mind, though I am not a man nor a minister, yet if my heart were sincerely devoted to God and I was inspired with a true zeal for his glory, I might do somewhat more than I do. I thought I might pray more for them and might speak to those with whom I converse with more warmth and affection."

In the months that followed, Susannah began reaching out to her neighbors with the gospel, and she held church services in her husband's absence. They came to her home in the evenings, and one Sunday, she wrote, "we had above two hundred. And yet many went away for want of room to stand." Will the Book of Life simply say, "she was a 'preacher of righteousness'?"[2]

Then I saw a great white throne and him who was seated on it. Earth and sky fled from his presence, and there was no place for them. And I saw the dead, great and small, standing before the throne, and books were opened. Another book was opened, which is the book of life. The dead were judged according to what they had done as recorded in the books.

*Revelation 20:11–12.*

# "GOOD NEWS TO THE POOR"

The story of Rufina is a heartrending saga of poverty—a saga that began when she was in her mother's womb and one that continues in a seemingly unending cycle with her own pregnancies. Like millions of other victims of war, Rufina and her family have been displaced, in their case, by civil strife in the Philippines. No longer able to eke out a subsistence living from a tiny rice paddy, she and her family fled to a squalid refugee camp when soldiers took control of the countryside. She grieves for her little ones who have died, while harboring mixed emotions about the baby she is carrying in her womb. Her immediate concern, however, is for her child who is writhing in pain from fever. Will starvation and malnutrition once again brutally snatch away what she holds most dear?

Most Western Christians would be very uncomfortable with Rufina. She is emaciated and her eyes tell the story of years of pain. Her hair is unwashed and her clothes are ragged and dirty. She does not get up in the morning and shower or brush her teeth or put on deodorant. She is uneducated and some would say she has a one-track mind—feeding her family. Yet, she is a part of the family of God. She is as precious in God's sight as the stylish operatic singer enthusiastically applauded at the elegant Tuesday luncheon of the Christian Women's Club.

Only in very recent years has Rufina realized that God values her. The poverty that ravaged her physical life in the here and now also affected her spiritual life—her eternal life. Or so she thought. Like others who had grown up in the shadow of the Catholic church, Rufina's parents were too poor to baptize their children and Rufina faced the same situation with her own children. "We just didn't have money for the baptismal fees and nice clothes to wear for the occasion."

Through the persistent and challenging message of a local evangelist, however, Rufina discovered that salvation is a free gift. She committed her life to God and became part of a community of believers. The poverty is still very real and death is always lurking in the shadows, but she also has a sense of hope—hope that is generated by those close by who share her pain and by those far away who share their riches so that food and medicine can be made available to Rufina and those she loves.[3]

The Spirit of the Sovereign Lord is on me, because the Lord has anointed me to preach good news to the poor. He has sent me to bind up the brokenhearted, to proclaim freedom for the captives and release from darkness for the prisoners, to proclaim the year of the Lord's favor and the day of vengeance of our God, to comfort all who mourn, and provide for those who grieve in Zion—to bestow on them a crown of beauty instead of ashes, the oil of gladness instead of mourning, and a garment of praise instead of a spirit of despair.

*Isaiah 61:1–3a.*

# "THE YEARS OF YOUR LIFE WILL BE MANY"

In 1989, more than a century after he had been dedicated to the Lord by his godly mother, Archie Harrison is still active in evangelistic ministry. When he was born in Milwaukee in 1887, Grover Cleveland was President of the United States.

What is the secret of his longevity and vitality in Christian ministry? His answers in many ways reflect the message of the Psalmist. "Obedience. Look to Jesus. Do what He tells you to do, whatever it is. . . . Surrender your all to the Lord Jesus Christ. That is the great secret. He must be Lord, then you are out of the picture. . . . Get on the shouting side and praise the Lord."

Archie has never feared being on "the shouting side." Indeed, years ago a pastor's young daughter succinctly described him to a friend: "He hollers!" And at one hundred and one, he "continues to 'holler' for Jesus with his strong, flexible voice and agile body. He may walk with a slower step, but when he speaks about Jesus Christ his body becomes a visual sermon. His voice rises with enthusiasm and becomes so high it nearly breaks."

Before he became an evangelist, Archie was employed as a meat cutter. Then a revival came to his home town of Glendale, California, and at 9:14 P.M. on August 4, 1914, "he walked the old sawdust trail" and was converted. He immediately began preparing for ministry—a "self-taught education" in the desert at "Cactus Bible College," as he referred to it. "I went there because everyone in the Bible seemed to go out in the desert."

For a time he settled into the pastorate, but later felt God calling him to be an evangelist. His former employer rallied other businessmen to his support, and together they bought him an automobile, a tent, and some chairs. That ministry was still continuing— though at a slower pace at the time of his one hundred and first birthday.

Although he has so many years to look back and reflect on, Archie focuses on the future—especially as he contemplates the Lord's return. "As we started to walk out of his room, a deeply revealing incident happened," writes a friend. "Without any sense of show or awkwardness, in a perfectly natural tone of voice, he turned to the photograph of his wife on the cluttered, wooden bureau and spoke softly, 'Honey, I'm going out to dinner now. I'll see you soon in the rapture.'"[4]

Listen, my son, accept what I say, and the years of your life will be many. I guide you in the way of wisdom and lead you along straight paths. When you walk, your steps will not be hampered; when you run, you will not stumble. Hold on to instruction, do not let it go, guard it well, for it is your life.

*Proverbs 4:10–13.*

# "AS THE FATHER HAS SENT ME, I AM SENDING YOU"

A mission field does not have to be a country chosen by a mission board as a designated place of ministry. It can be any place where people are in need of the gospel. E. Margaret Clarkson, who was raised in Ontario, found this to be true in her life.

"In 1935," she writes, "teaching jobs were so scarce that I had to take my first job as a teacher in a lumber camp some 1400 miles from home, out in the Rainy River District of northwestern Ontario. From there I moved to the gold mining camp of Kirkland Lake, 450 miles north of Toronto. In all, I spent seven years in the north. I experienced loneliness of every kind—mental, cultural, but particularly spiritual, for in all of those seven years I never found real Christian fellowship—churches were modern and born-again Christians almost non-existent."

"I was studying the Word one night and meditating on the loneliness of my situation and came in my reading to John 20, and the words, 'so send I you.' Because of a physical disability I knew that I could never go to the mission field, but God seemed to tell me that night that this was my mission field, and this was where He had sent me. I was then twenty-three, in my third year of teaching. I had written and published verse all of my life, so it was natural for me to put my thoughts into verse."

The lines she penned that night have since become one of the most familiar of all the missionary hymns, "So Send I You." The words reflected her sad and lonely spirit that night: "So send I you to labor unrewarded, to serve unpaid, unloved, unsought, unknown." The third and fourth verses continue this lament: "So send I you to loneliness and longing," and "so send I you to leave your life's ambition."

To many missionaries this hymn reflected true feelings of sacrifice, but others felt it told only part of the story or none of it at all. Margaret later regretted the emphasis it placed on sacrifice: "I began to realize that this poem was really very one-sided; it told only the sorrows and privations of the missionary call and none of its triumphs." In 1963 she added two more verses that were more positive.

But even in the original, this powerful hymn had a deep impact on missions. In one instance it challenged an actress who was struggling with the decision to fully dedicate her life to Christian ministry.[5]

On the evening of the first day of the week, when the disciples were together, with the doors locked for fear of the Jews, Jesus came and stood among them and said, "Peace be with you!" After he said this, he showed them his hands and side. The disciples were overjoyed when they saw the Lord.

Again Jesus said, "Peace be with you! As the Father has sent me, I am sending you."

*John 20:19–21.*

# "GOD IS OUR REFUGE"

Yoshikosan Taguchi was one of the "living dead" who survived the infamous atomic bombing of Hiroshima on August 6, 1945. Some seventy thousand people died from the bombing, and approximately that same number were severely injured like Yoshikosan. She was a fifteen year-old and a student at a Christian school who deeply resented the teachings about Jesus, since she thought him to be a god of the Americans who were the enemy of her people.

On that August morning, Yoshikosan was sitting at her desk when she heard a thunderous blast as the walls began to fall down around her. In her half-conscious state she heard shouts of anguish, and then realized someone was helping to pull her out of the rubble. Though she did not realize it at the time, that day more than three hundred students and teachers were killed in that very school, which was only a short distance from the center of the blast.

Those who died instantly were the lucky ones, or so it seemed to Yoshikosan as she sought shelter with the crowds of dying people. She spent the first night in terror, and the day brought no comfort. "The morning, beautiful and hot, revealed the horror of all that had happened, the sickening condition of the half-alive, the city in waste, and all the backwashes of debilitating fear."

Days of suffering followed. "Radiation sickness is a horrible thing," writes Gladys Hunt. "Yoshikosan was hemorrhaging internally and knew she was dying. When it seemed unbearable, she would vacillate between wishing she could die and terror that she might." It was in this mindset that the words of a Psalm—a hymn she had learned at school came to mind.

> God is our refuge,
> Our refuge, and our strength
> In trouble, in trouble, a very present help.

It was that song that prompted her to reflect on Jesus and what she had heard about him and his ministry of healing. She began to pray "in the name of Jesus." "A peace came over her instantaneously; the fear was gone. She knew He had heard and that He cared about her." Gradually she grew stronger as the hemorrhaging and vomiting ceased.

So convinced was Yoshikosan that God indeed had become her refuge in the time of trouble that she began sharing her faith with her family, who had witnessed her remarkable healing. "Her older sister believed first. . . and one by one others in her family came to trust Christ. Yoshikosan herself went on to reach out to students through a campus Christian ministry."[6]

**God is our refuge and strength, an ever-present help in trouble. Therefore we will not fear, though the earth give way and the mountains fall into the heart of the sea, though its waters roar and foam and the mountains quake with their surging.**

*Psalm 46:1–3.*

# "I HAVE FOUND NO GROUNDS FOR THE DEATH PENALTY"

Pontius Pilate is a figure who receives mixed reviews by Bible scholars. He was convinced that Jesus had committed no crime that warranted the death penalty and he sought to convince the crowd, but in the end, he gave in to their demands. In the centuries since the trial of Jesus, Christians on many occasions have stood before their accusers not knowing what the outcome would be. Would a Pilate allow them to be unjustly sentenced, or would justice be served? This was the very predicament that Annie Shau Bernsten encountered while serving in China as a missionary with the Overseas Missionary Fellowship before she was forced to evacuate in 1951.

Annie was a nurse, and during her years in China she became a messenger of goodwill to many of the people in the remote villages of the Shansi Province. She was a traveling preacher with tiny churches in several poor villages, and everywhere she went she offered her services to the sick. She faced opposition but none so powerful as that of the Communists during the 1940s, as Mao Tse Tung was rising to power. On one occasion, Communist officials in the region where she lived ordered a public meeting to determine the guilt of this foreign woman. Each family in the area was required to send a representative, and a local village leader was chosen by the Communists to conduct the meeting.

As she was brought before the six thousand in attendance, Annie's eyes met those of the man who was conducting the meeting. She had nursed his daughter back to life, and now he was being forced to preside over her public trial. His words were halting as he asked for accusations against this woman. There was no response. For nine minutes there was silence. The Communists ordered the people to accuse her, but no one spoke.

Finally, the man forced to chair the meeting spoke, with tears in his eyes: "None of us wants to attack our missionary. Did she do anything wrong to anyone of us? No! She saved many lives among us! She always helps everyone in our villages." With that the meeting broke up. The Communists had sought to discredit Annie and terminate her work. Instead, she was honored by the minutes of silence and by a man, who unlike Pilate, was courageous enough to risk his life for justice.[7]

Wanting to release Jesus, Pilate appealed to them again. But they kept shouting, "Crucify him! Crucify him!"

For the third time he spoke to them: "Why? What crime has this man committed? I have found in him no grounds for the death penalty. Therefore I will have him punished and then release him."

But with loud shouts they insistently demanded that he be crucified, and their shouts prevailed. So Pilate decided to grant their demand. He released the man who had been thrown into prison for insurrection and murder, the one they asked for, and surrendered Jesus to their will.

*Luke 23:20–25.*

# "DO NOT BE YOKED TOGETHER WITH UNBELIEVERS"

This passage in 2 Corinthians is frequently applied to marriage relationships in which a believer would be "unequally yoked" to an unbeliever. The admonition is as valid today as it was in the New Testament church, and it is valid for all cultures, even in situations where the chance of finding a believing mate is very slim. This was true for Rose whose Muslim father became a believer when she was eight years old. His faith had an impact on her, and soon she also committed her life to Christ.

Initially her father's conversion created trauma for the family. He lost his job, and family members turned against him. Life was difficult for Rose as well. When she was eleven she was forced to leave school and care for her sickly grandmother, and after her grandmother died, she cared for her younger brothers and sisters.

As she grew up, her greatest joy in life was reading her Bible and teaching Sunday school in her tiny church. Her family was close and she longed for the day when she would have a family of her own. But marriage was not a foregone conclusion for her. She lived in a Muslim society and there were almost no eligible Christian men.

"In her country, where most marriages are arranged by families and where there are only a handful of believers, the chance of finding a Christian husband was slim." Rose was determined, however, that she would remain unmarried rather than marry an unbeliever. Also she was determined that she would not marry a man simply because he professed to be a believer, as was the case when a very persistent young man sought her hand in marriage. Finally her patience was rewarded when she received a photo in the mail from a Christian man who was looking for a Christian wife.

"Joseph was from the same ethnic group and seemed to fit into the family. . . . He had been a Christian for several years and shared Rose's view on Christians marrying only Christians." Their friendship grew into love and then into marriage—a ceremony performed in a church, "something common in the United States, but unheard of in their country.

"Two young people, both from Muslim backgrounds, both who love Jesus, had fallen in love and now are married. Here is the beginning of a new generation of Christians, and a new hope for their country."[8]

Do not be yoked together with unbelievers. For what do righteousness and wickedness have in common? Or what fellowship can light have with darkness? What harmony is there between Christ and Belial? What does a believer have in common with an unbeliever? What agreement is there between the temple of God and idols? For we are the temple of the living God. As God has said: "I will live with them and walk among them, and I will be their God, and they will be my people."

*2 Corinthians 6:14–16.*

# "FORGIVE AND COMFORT HIM"

Martin Luther is remembered mainly for his rigorous discipline as a monk and his courageous leadership as a Protestant reformer, but he was also an outstanding teacher. This was evident by his popularity among the students when he was teaching at the university in Wittenberg, in the years before he nailed his ninety-five theses to the church door. "They flocked to his lectures until other professors complained. Luther was keen on new methods of teaching. When he lectured on the Scriptures he tried to apply Paul directly to the lives of the students who sat before him."

He also sought to apply Paul's teachings in his own ministry, and this was especially evident in his pastoral duties. He had a deep compassion for the souls of others—especially for the lost sheep who had wandered from the fold. This compassion is illustrated in a letter that he wrote to the prior at the monastery in Mainz. At the time, Luther was serving in a similar capacity—supervising eleven monasteries—in Wittenberg.

"The sad news has reached me that one of my brothers from the monastery at Dresden has gone far astray and fled to you for refuge. I regret that the whole affair was so disgraceful. Nevertheless I am happy that you were honourable and helpful in taking him in and have made it possible to end his shame.

"He is a lost sheep and belongs in the fold. It is my duty to seek him out and turn him from the error of his ways, if the Lord Jesus be willing. I therefore beg you, most reverend Father and Prior, by our common faith in Christ and common oath to St. Augustine, if it is in any way possible for you to help, to send him back to Dresden or Wittenberg.

"Persuade him to come yourself; treat him so kindly he will come of his own wish. I shall welcome him with open arms. He has nothing to fear. I am aware that great sins happen; it is nothing unusual when a man goes wrong. The miracle occurs when he comes to his senses again. An angel once sinned even in heaven. So did Adam in paradise. Peter fell. Every day a cedar of Lebanon topples to the ground. So there is nothing unusual if a reed is blown here and there by the wind."[9]

If anyone has caused grief, he has not so much grieved me as he has grieved all of you, to some extent—not to put it too severely. The punishment inflicted on him by the majority is sufficient for him. Now instead, you ought to forgive and comfort him, so that he will not be overwhelmed by excessive sorrow. I urge you, therefore, to reaffirm your love for him. The reason I wrote you was to see if you would stand the test and be obedient in everything. If you forgive anyone, I also forgive him. And what I have forgiven—if there was anything to forgive—I have forgiven in the sight of Christ for your sake, in order that Satan might not outwit us. For we are not unaware of his schemes.

*2 Corinthians 2:5–11.*

## "REMEMBER THOSE EARLIER DAYS"

The summons to "remember those earlier days" is one that has a profound significance to Christians who have kept the faith in spite of fierce persecution. In some instances the oppression has been so merciless that the very survival of Christianity was in jeopardy. This was the case in Japan during the sixteenth century.

The Jesuits were the first missionaries to enter Japan, and by 1575 there were more than fifty thousand professing Christians in one region. "Of the depth and sincerity of these conversions," writes Stephen Neill, "it is hard to judge. As in the case of other mass movements there were no doubt many weaknesses and shadows; but unquestionably there was in Japan an elite of convinced and devoted Christians." By the end of the century, there were approximately three hundred thousand Christians, but there were storm clouds on the horizon for this rapidly growing infant church. As more foreigners entered the country, Japanese officials became alarmed.

Initially, missionaries faced only an expulsion order, but by the second decade of the seventeenth century the country was safe neither for missionaries or Japanese Christians. Nearly two thousand Christians—sixty-two of those missionaries—were executed during a quarter of a century of tyranny.

"Every kind of cruelty was practiced on the pitiable victims of the persecution. Crucifixion was the method usually employed in the cases of Japanese Christians; on one occasion seventy Japanese at Yedo were crucified upside down at low water, and were drowned as the tide came in. For Europeans the penalty was generally burning alive."

By 1630, "the Christianity of Japan had been destroyed"—or so it was thought. In the generations that followed, missionaries urgently sought to reenter Japan, but their efforts were frustrated until 1859. Only when missionaries reentered Japan did they discover that Christianity had not been entirely destroyed. "Some women approached the missionary Father (later Bishop) Petitjean, at first very cautiously and later with more confidence, and put to him questions that seemed to relate to the Virgin Mary and to the great 'king of the doctrine,' the Pope. Questioning by the missionaries soon made it clear that these were indeed descendants of the ancient Church. Living in Nagasaki and Okuma and on the Goto islands, they had maintained the faith in secrecy through all the years of persecution."[10]

**Remember those earlier days after you had received the light, when you stood your ground in a great contest in the face of suffering. Sometimes you were publicly exposed to insult and persecution; at other times you stood side by side with those who were so treated. You sympathized with those in prison and joyfully accepted the confiscation of your property, because you knew that you yourselves had better and lasting possessions.**

*Hebrews 10:32–34.*

# "BE SHEPHERDS OF GOD'S FLOCK"

Stories abound of Chinese and foreign Christians who suffered the atrocities of the Boxer Rebellion of 1900. Far less common are stories of Christians who profited by the uprising—or who thought they could profit by it. One of those stories is about Leng Shu Kien, a convert who was described as one of the "brightest and ablest graduates of Tung Chow College."

During the summer of 1900, Leng Shu Kien volunteered to serve as an evangelist and relief worker for the mission station at Tsingtao. It was a time of crisis, and the missionaries at the station were overwhelmed with the task of caring for refugees who had flooded across the provincial border to safety. Leng's service was desperately needed. In the midst of the turmoil, a message came from a German military general requesting the aid of "an alert, able, foreign-speaking Chinese who could accompany him as translator to the seat of the disturbance." Leng offered his services and was chosen for the prestigious assignment of serving the general.

Leng quickly forgot his ministry of Christian service and became deeply caught up in a new life of wealth and power and self-indulgence that he had never known before. After the Rebellion was crushed, the spoils of war were at his disposal, and self-gratification became his only ambition. "The frenzy to loot . . . took possession of him; to loot before it was too late; to loot while fortunes in silver ingots could . . . be had by the mere carrying them away." Leng took all that he could haul on a cart and headed for his village. "To salve his conscience . . . he sent to a missionary friend one of his 'souvenirs.'

"Settled in his native village, the devil speedily drove him from one excess to another, until he was quite crazy in his colossal egotism, lordly pride, contemptuous disdain, and pseudomilitary imperiousness, tyrannizing over his humble neighbors. To drown memory, he drank hard and lived fast." But such a lifestyle could not last forever. He was arrested and sent to a prison with dirt floors and no sanitation facilities and where daily torture awaited him.

Local Christians became concerned and asked a missionary to intervene with local authorities. She refused, insisting rather that they pray first for his repentance and let God take care of his release. God answered that prayer but in the reverse order. He was released and only then repented of his sins, warning others about the dangers involved in greed for money.[11]

**Be shepherds of God's flock that is under your care, serving as overseers—not because you must, but because you are willing, as God wants you to be; not greedy for money, but eager to serve; not lording it over those entrusted to you, but being examples to the flock. And when the Chief Shepherd appears, you will received the crown of glory that will never fade away.**

*1 Peter 5:2–4.*

# "IF THE SON SETS YOU FREE, YOU WILL BE FREE INDEED"

During the heat of a New England August summer day in 1740, a sixteen-year-old farm boy suddenly became conscious of his need to commit his life to Christ. George Whitefield, the great revivalist from England, had begun a religious awakening in the region, warning people to turn to the Lord before it was too late. That message had haunted the youth, and he realized he could not put off the decision any longer. He dropped to his knees and poured out his soul to God.

The young man was Isaac Backus, one of America's pioneer Baptists. Later he described the experience: "My soul yielded all into his hands, fell at his feet, and was silent and calm before him. . . . The Word of God and the promise of his grace appeared firmer than a rock, and I was astonished at my previous unbelief. My heavy burden was gone, tormenting fears were fled, and my joy was unspeakable." Backus was free.

He was free, yet he was not free. Indeed, Christ had set him free, but he was living in colonial New England, where religious freedom was severely curtailed by the Puritan ruling elite. His own mother, Elizabeth Backus, had been imprisoned for refusing to support the established Congregational church. And he had encountered this same lack of religious freedom when he refused to support the church and was imprisoned, some years later. Prior to this, he had served for a short time as a Congregational minister, but had separated from that denomination after he had become convinced that believers' baptism by immersion was the only water baptism taught in the Scriptures.

He "led six members of the church into the water to be baptized, and they formed the Middleborough Baptist Church." Elsewhere Baptists were threatened by mobs during baptismal services. In more than one instance their services were disrupted by rowdies who "baptized" dogs in an effort to bring shame on the believers.

In an effort to counter the persecution, representatives from Baptist congregations met together and formed the Warren Association. They chose Backus as their leader to fight on behalf of religious liberty. He was rebuffed—even by the first Continental Congress in Philadelphia—and his life was threatened, but his cause was too great to abandon. Backus traveled on horseback for most of sixty years, fighting for religious toleration so that he and his fellow Baptists and others might be free, indeed.[12]

To the Jews who had believed him, Jesus said, "If you hold to my teachings you are really my disciples. Then you will know the truth, and the truth will set you free."

They answered him, "We are Abraham's descendants and we have never been slaves of anyone. How can you say that we shall be set free?"

Jesus replied, "I tell you the truth, everyone who sins is a slave to sin. Now a slave has no permanent place in the family, but a son belongs to it forever. So if the Son sets you free, you will be free indeed."

*John 8:31–36.*

# "BLESSED IS HE WHOSE HOPE IS IN THE LORD"

The motto over the door has symbolized for more than a century the spirit inside: "Hope For All Who Enter." Through this door entered the oppressed and hungry—all of whom were offered hope—and many were the testimonies of how the Lord frustrated the ways of the wicked. The Pacific Garden Mission, whose name was taken from the previous tenant, the Pacific Beer Garden, provided food, clothing, shelter, and a warm welcome to needy street people of Chicago. But more than anything else it offered hope through salvation in Christ.

It was the search for hope that brought many hopeless men and women to this place of refuge. Sarah Clarke, who, with her husband, founded the mission, would often walk the streets of Chicago passing out small cards that summed up the ministry:

H O P E   F O R   A L L   W H O   E N T E R

### PACIFIC GARDEN MISSION
67 West Van Buren Street
W O N D E R F U L   T E S T I M O N I E S
*Strangers and the Poor Always Welcome*
Special Song Service 7:30 Every Night

Many cards were thrown away or lost, but others were treasured because they offered an immediate source of relief for someone who had nowhere else to turn. Sometimes a card would be crumpled into a worn coat pocket and forgotten for days or weeks until, eventually, it brought some forgotten, homeless, desperate person through the door of hope. Many of those who came rejected the hope that was offered, but others did not.

"There was John Troy, . . . son of a famous European physician and law-maker. But here he was, adrift in Chicago, far from family and friends, penniless, and unable to speak English. It was a sorry state for one who had enjoyed so many privileges. One night in the winter of 1907–1908 he walked into the Pacific Garden Mission. It was the first Protestant service he had ever attended. Unable to understand the language, he nevertheless sensed the radiance and joy that welled from the hearts of the speakers." He was converted, and after graduating from Moody Bible Institute in 1915, he traveled throughout the United State and Europe as an evangelist.[13]

Blessed is he whose help is the God of Jacob, whose hope is in the Lord his God, the Maker of heaven and earth, the sea, and everything in them—the Lord, who remains faithful forever. He upholds the cause of the oppressed and gives food to the hungry. The Lord sets prisoners free, the Lord gives sight to the blind, the Lord lifts up those who are bowed down, the Lord loves the righteous. The Lord watches over the alien and sustains the fatherless and the widow, but he frustrates the ways of the wicked.

*Psalm 146:5–9.*

# "THE FIELDS ARE RIPE FOR HARVEST"

This passage from the gospel of John is most commonly applied in the context of foreign missions, but it is a passage that is also appropriate in the context of the local church. There must be a harvest time in the church, so said Solomon Stoddard, or the church will die.

Solomon Stoddard is often remembered as the grandfather of the great American theologian and preacher, Jonathan Edwards. But he was a great preacher in his own right who served for nearly sixty years as the pastor in Northampton, Massachusetts. As a pastor, one of his chief ambitions was to reap "harvests" of souls. "In response to the strong preaching and pastoral methods of Stoddard, five awakenings (or 'harvests' as he called them) in 1679, 1683, 1696, 1712, and 1718, converted souls in numbers probably unequaled anywhere else in New England before the Great Awakening."

Stoddard was heavily criticized by the more "conservative" ministers because of his departure from tradition regarding the communion service. He refused to deny communion to those who could not claim a definite conversion experience. Rather, he insisted that only God knows the hearts of true believers, and thus all "visible saints" who were "not scandalous" in their behavior should be welcomed in church and permitted, according to their own conscience, to partake in communion. His purpose was to bring as many people into the church as possible, and to seek to influence them toward conversion while he had them under his sway. Despite the harsh criticism of his contemporaries, he was, according to historian Perry Miller, one of the most successful soul-winners in Colonial New England:

"He appears to our eyes as the herald of a new century and a new land, the eighteenth against the seventeenth, the West against the East. He was the first great 'revivalist' in New England. . . . His sermons were outstanding in his day for the decision with which he swept away the paraphernalia of theology and logic, to arouse men to becoming partakers of the divine nature, and he was the first minister in New England openly to advocate the preaching of Hell-fire and brimstone in order to frighten men into conversion."[14]

"My food," said Jesus, "is to do the will of him who sent me and to finish his work. Do you not say, 'Four months more and then the harvest'? I tell you, open your eyes and look at the fields! They are ripe for harvest. Even now the reaper draws his wages, even now he harvests the crop for eternal life, so that the sower and the reaper may be glad together. Thus the saying 'One sows and another reaps' is true. I sent you to reap what you have not worked for. Others have done the hard work, and you have reaped the benefits of their labor."

*John 4:34–38.*

## "WITNESSING BEHIND BARS"

The story about Paul and Silas in prison does not end with their praying and singing hymns at midnight. An earthquake shakes the prison so violently that the doors fly open and their chains are loosened. But instead of making their escape, they stay around to witness to the jailor who is converted, along with his family. This remarkable ending to the story sometimes overshadows the earlier prayer and praise meeting inside the jail that could be considered nothing less than audacious. To be praying and singing, after being beaten and chained, was, in effect, a spiritual means of taunting their accusers.

A little-known Salvation Army officer of generations back may well have taken his cue from Paul and Silas. "Joe the Turk was jailed in East Portland, Oregon, for tooting his cornet despite an ordinance against 'blowing horns.' Several other Salvationists were sentenced to ten days but Joe got 15 extra for shouting, 'Praise the Lord!' when the sentence was pronounced. One night he got a new cell-mate, a drunken painter named Jake, who had brought his paraphernalia with him."

During the night, when the painter complained of the hard board he had to sleep on, Joe encouraged him to ask the Lord to help. The next morning, the painter inquired about Joe's faith. "The two had a long and earnest conversation and Jake got converted. Elated, Joe considered Jake and his paints and brushes, then shouted, 'Let's paint the walls for God.'

Freshly white-washed walls made a fine canvas and soon a rainbow of letters a foot high proclaimed: PREPARE TO MEET YOUR GOD, WHERE WILL YOU SPEND ETERNITY? JESUS IS THE DRUNKARD'S FRIEND, REMEMBER MOTHER'S PRAYERS, and other startling reminders. The stunned jailer wailed, 'What does this mean?' "

The judge who had sentenced Joe to the additional fifteen days was called in. What followed was as remarkable as the earthquake recorded in the book of Acts. A contemporary account gave the story: "The judge lost his dignity, was gloriously saved and in church and everywhere he goes testifies to the saving power of Jesus." More than that, "he often carried the Army flag in the open-air march and for many years protected Joe's cell signs, which were viewed by people from all parts of the country. At one time the local railroad company allowed stop-over tickets for this purpose."[15]

The crowd joined in the attack against Paul and Silas, and the magistrates ordered them to be stripped and beaten. After they had been severely flogged, they were thrown into prison, and the jailer was commanded to guard them carefully. Upon receiving such orders, he put them in the inner cell and fastened their feet in the stocks.

About midnight Paul and Silas were praying and singing hymns to God, and the other prisoners were listening to them.

*Acts 16:22–25.*

# "SAVE THE SON OF YOUR MAIDSERVANT"

Mrs. Wang was a Chinese Bible woman during the terrifying days of the Boxer Rebellion in 1900. She served with missionaries at the Wei Hsien Station in the Shantung Province. When Boxers moved into the region, she had sufficient time to evacuate, but she chose instead to wait at the station for two single women missionaries who had been doing evangelistic work out in the villages. They were unaware of the sudden turn of events, and would need help in their escape once they reached the station.

Her sacrifice paid off. The Boxers set fire to the mission house, and with the help of Mrs. Wang, the women escaped to safety at Tsingtau. Here they were given refuge by the wife of the German Admiral, Oscar von Truppel, who immediately noticed Mrs. Wang's fine needlework. "So Mrs. Wang, child of poverty and squalor, by a strange turn of fortune, became a sewing woman at twenty dollars a month, a fabulous sum for her, in the big, comfortable mansion."

When the uprising was over, Mrs. Wang was encouraged to continue her work for the admiral's wife, but she chose instead to go back to her ministry as a Bible woman for one quarter of the earnings. She served as an evangelist and church planter, and according to a missionary leader, "She became no inconsiderable factor in building up the church in one center of our country field."

Her success in ministering to others may have been due, in part, to the great trial she was enduring in her own life and the understanding it gave her for others who were suffering. When her unbelieving husband had learned that she had left her high-paying position to resume her work as a lowly Bible woman, he "roundly cursed and beat" her. This she might have expected, but when her adult son joined in his father's outrage, she was too distressed to be consoled. He ridiculed her and turned away from her teachings. As she traveled reaching out to others, she never failed to fervently pray for her son, convinced God would somehow grant her desire.

God did answer her prayer—in a way she never could have expected. Out of work and penniless, her son went to a coal mine for temporary employment. He had hardly begun when an explosion occurred, trapping him and more than one hundred other miners "to face a slow and horrible death." It offered the young man time to think and to reconsider his errant ways, and there in the coal mine, he turned his life over to God. After his miraculous rescue, he was baptized to the joy of his faithful mother.[16]

But you, O Lord, are a compassionate and gracious God, slow to anger, abounding in love and faithfulness. Turn to me and have mercy on me; grant your strength to your servant and save the son of your maidservant. Give me a sign of your goodness, that my enemies may see it and be put to shame, for you, O Lord, have helped me and comforted me.

*Psalm 86:15–17.*

# "NONE OF HIS SINS WILL BE REMEMBERED"

The gospel offers a message of hope—hope for even the worst criminals—that "none of the sins he has committed will be remembered against him." It was this message that Evangeline Booth, the Salvation Army Commander in Canada, brought to Skagway, Alaska, in 1898. She was the daughter of William and Catherine Booth, who had pioneered a worldwide ministry that reached out to those who were often considered the most hopeless elements in society.

Skagway, Alaska, was a gold-mining site, "a rip-roaring camp of tents and shacks," consisting mainly of "gambling halls, saloons and brothels"—known as the "devil's headquarters of the northwest." Why would the hardened men who lived there listen to a "lady preacher"?

Evangeline's decision to conduct an evangelistic campaign at that outpost raised opposition. Even though Salvation Army officers were working in the area, it was considered a dangerous assignment for a young single woman. But William Booth, the Salvation Army General and her father, had the final word: "Let her go."

Accompanied by Canadian mounties she journeyed to this arctic sin city, and found exactly what she had expected to find: "Sinners—the old and hardened—the young tenderfeet just from home and plunging into degradation—the once well-to-do but now debased, the once poor but now rich. . . ." But they were all spellbound by the lady preacher.

"They clapped wildly for her and knelt en masse to sing, 'Home, Sweet Home' as a benediction. At one meeting, 25,000 miners sat on a mountainside and sang, as she directed, 'Nearer My God to Thee.'"

Many were converted through her ministry—the most celebrated of the sinners who was converted was the notorious Soapy Smith, who with his gang "terrorized the town." After two members of his gang were converted, he decided to investigate for himself. "As he approached with a five-man bodyguard, his group was confronted by Evangeline's Northwest Mounties, guns drawn on both sides. . . . Then Evangeline drew him aside and talked with him for three hours. At the end of that time they knelt together. Tearfully, Smith promised he would stop killing people and give himself up.

A witness testified that he heard Smith promise to "live the life of a Christian," but that promise had little time to be carried out. "Shortly afterward, a citizens' meeting decided it was time to rid Skagway of Smith. A gun battle resulted, and both Frank Reid, leader of the Citizens' Committee, and Smith were killed."[17]

"Therefore, son of man, say to your countrymen, 'The righteousness of the righteous man will not save him when he disobeys, and the wickedness of the wicked man will not cause him to fall when he turns from it. The righteous man, if he sins, will not be allowed to live because of his former righteousness.' If I tell the righteous man that he will surely live, but then he trusts in his righteousness and does evil, none of the righteous things he has done will be remembered; he will die for the evil he has done. And if I say to the wicked man, 'You will surely die,' but he then turns away from his sin and does what is just and right—if he gives back what he took in pledge for a loan, returns what he has stolen, follows the decrees that give life, and does no evil, he will surely live; he will not die. None of the sins he has committed will be remembered against him. He has done what is just and right; he will surely live.

*Ezekiel 33:12–16.*

# "NO LONGER A SLAVE, BUT A SON"

The assurance that we are no longer slaves but sons is a comfort to all believers, but more so to ones who know personally the oppression of slavery and who have lost their own fathers in that oppressive system. For those, the privilege of being a son and of having the Spirit that calls out *"Abba*, Father" is particularly meaningful.

The year was 1821. The setting was the town of Oshogun in Yorubaland, a region in what is today the country of Nigeria. It was nine o'clock in the morning. Women were preparing breakfast. Little children played nearby. Suddenly the tranquility was broken. The news had come that the enemy was approaching. The fighting men grabbed their weapons, but their efforts were futile. The women fled with their children, but they were quickly captured and secured with ropes tied around their necks. "I was thus caught with my mother, two sisters, one infant about ten weeks old, and a cousin," wrote one of the young prisoners. "The last time I saw my father was when he came from the fight to give us the signal to flee. I learned some time afterwards that he was killed in another battle."

The young boy's captors were Muslim slave traders, who traded him for a horse before he was bought and sold three more times in the space of twenty-four hours. He was then chained to other captives and marched to a market town, where he was sold to Portuguese traders. From there he was taken to a coastal town where "men and boys were chained together with a chain about six fathoms in length, drawn through an iron fetter on the neck of each individual, and fastened at both ends with padlocks." After four months of this torturous confinement, he was taken one night to the slave ship *Esperanza Felix*, where he began his journey across the ocean.

The journey had hardly begun when there were gunshots. Fear gripped the young boy. He had dreaded all along that he would be killed so that the white man could "make medicine out of us—medicine to help them in their witchcraft." But the guns were those of cannons from a rescue ship. The young boy was taken with the rest of the slaves to Liberia where he was educated by British missionaries. Through their influence he became a Christian and went on to serve in the ministry, eventually becoming the first African Bishop of the Anglican Church— Bishop Samuel Adjai Crowther. One of the most touching moments of his life was his reunion with his mother and sisters. He had been absent from his village for twenty-five years, and, providentially, he visited just in time to rescue his brother and sisters from slavers.[18]

So also, when we were children, we were in slavery under the basic principles of the world. But when the time had fully come, God sent his Son, born of a woman, born under law, to redeem those under law, that we might receive the full rights of sons. Because you are sons, God sent the Spirit of his Son into our hearts, the Spirit who calls out *"Abba*, Father." So you are no longer a slave, but a son; and since you are a son, God has made you also an heir.

*Galatians 4:3–7.*

# "THIS VERY NIGHT YOUR LIFE WILL BE DEMANDED"

Sometimes just one verse of Scripture is enough to motivate a person to seek God, and sometimes that one verse is taken out of context. Yet it is true that even when there is very little biblical and theological understanding, the Holy Spirit convicts men and women of sin. Such a conviction occurred in the life of "Sunshine" Harris, who was converted at the age of seventy-one after spending most of his life wandering shiftlessly without a home.

While living on the streets of Chicago, he often came to the Pacific Garden Mission for a meal or shelter, but went back out on the streets to drink or pick up cigarette butts along the curbs. His visits to the mission, however, were not for nought. It was there that he acquired a New Testament—it was a little book that would change his life.

Flipping through it one day, his eyes fell on the phrase, "Thou fool, this night thy soul shall be required of thee." His initial response was one of anger and he read no further. "Later, he wanted to reread the passage but could not find the verse. That made him more furious. In vexation he began with Matthew's genealogy and kept reading until the words were located." Again he read the verse. It did not matter that the passage was speaking of a "rich man" with "plenty of good things laid up for many years," and that he was a penniless derelict. The words were for him, and they prompted him to return to the mission to escape the peril of which this verse spoke.

"When the invitation was given," he later recalled, "I looked at one hand and it was so black and sinful, and then at the other and that was just as bad, so I raised both hands and was assisted by a Christian lady to the altar." He was transformed that night in 1899, and spent the remaining eight years of his life telling others of God's glorious salvation.

Those who had known him from earlier days were dumbfounded. He was a changed man, and "he served God with such spiritual fervor and delight that the mission workers called him 'Sunshine' Harris. He loved everybody and everybody loved him. . . . Night after night he continued to testify at the mission, eager to tell how the Lord had cleaned his life. When he died . . . all the hoboes on the levee knew his soul had gone to God."[19]

And he [Jesus] told them this parable: "The ground of a certain rich man produced a good crop. He thought to himself, 'What shall I do? I have no place to store my crops.'

"Then he said, 'This is what I'll do. I will tear down my barns and build bigger ones, and there I will store all my grain and my goods. And I'll say to myself, 'You have plenty of good things laid up for many years. Take life easy; eat, drink and be merry.' "

"But God said to him, 'You fool! This very night your life will be demanded from you. Then who will get what you have prepared for yourself?' "

*Luke 12:16–20.*

## "THE SERVANT OF ALL"

Working with young children is often considered "women's work," and it is not considered to be the route to career advancement. But Jesus emphasized that those who would be first, must be "the servant of all"; that included being a servant to little children. This philosophy was dear to the heart of Dwight L. Moody.

As a young man, Moody moved to Chicago to pursue his dream of escaping poverty through a career as a shoe salesman. Soon after, he became actively involved in reaching out to Chicago's youth. He inquired one day at the North Wells Street Mission if there was a need for Sunday school teachers, but was informed that they already had almost as many teachers as they had children enrolled. "Moody persisted. At last he heard the proposition that was music to his ears. He could teach as many scholars as he could bring. Next Sunday there were eighteen—bareheaded, barefooted, ragged and dirty—more than doubling the school's sixteen. 'That,' recalled Moody, 'was the happiest Sunday I have ever known. I had found out what my mission was.'"

The class grew to a size that the mission could no longer accommodate, and Moody had to seek another location. He chose "an abandoned saloon, dilapidated, with dingy brick surrounding a huge grimy hall. . . . Squeezed in among shacks and over two hundred 'gambling and drinking dens,' it sucked in quantities of bold, restless, inquisitive riffraff disgorged from their teeming lairs."

But not all who attended Moody's classes were "sucked in" on a voluntary basis. One day he spotted a little girl who had been skipping Sunday school and avoiding him. "There, coming down the sidewalk, was the absentee. Suddenly she stopped, reversed her direction, and took off like a rabbit before a hound dog. Moody, convention to the winds, raced after her. Down the side walk, across the street, though an alley, down another sidewalk—the chase was on! Suddenly the fugitive disappeared through the swinging doors of a saloon, dashed the length of the room, out the back door, up the steps into her tenement, across the kitchen into the bedroom, and dove beneath the bed—the Sunday-school teacher breathing down her neck every inch of the way. Hardly had he retrieved his quarry and asked her whereabouts on Sunday, than he found himself face-to-face with an irate mother with some explaining of his own to do. Between huffs he . . . explained the purpose of his 'call,' inquired as to the size of the good woman's family, and within weeks had everyone of the tribe in his mission school."[20]

Sitting down, Jesus called the Twelve and said, "If anyone wants to be first, he must be the very last, and the servant of all."

He took a little child and had him stand among them. Taking him in his arms, he said to them, "Whoever welcomes one of these little children in my name welcomes me; and whoever welcomes me does not welcome me but the one who sent me."

*Mark 9:35–37.*

# "THE GOD WHO ANSWERS BY FIRE—HE IS GOD"

One of the most celebrated instances of a power encounter since the time of Elijah and the prophets of Baal was the dramatic episode involving Kapiolani and the priests of Pele. Kapiolani was a Hawaiian chieftainess who was married, as was the custom of such important women, to many husbands and given to much drinking. Then through the tireless efforts of missionaries "she had become a Christian, giving up her drinking and sending away all her husbands save one. She had thrown away her idols and now taught the people in their huts the story of Christ."

This turn of events outraged the priests. "Pele the all-terrible, the fire goddess, will hurl her thunder and her stones, and will slay you," they threatened the people. "You no longer pay your sacrifices to her. Once you gave her hundreds of hogs, but now you give nothing."

The people were frightened. "They were Christians; but they had only been Christians for a short time, and they still trembled at the name of the goddess Pele, who lived up in the mountains in the boiling crater of the fiery volcano, and ruled their island." The people looked to Kapiolani for direction.

"Pele is nought," Kapiolani declared. "I will go to Kilawea, the mountain of the fires where the smoke and stones go up, and Pele shall not touch me. My God, Jehovah, made the mountain and the fires within it too, as He made us all."

Despite threats from the priests, Kapiolani ascended the mountain with an entourage of her followers. "Up she climbed until the full terrors of the boiling crater of Kilawea burst on her sight. . . . Then she stood on a ledge of rock, and, offering up prayer and praise to the God of all, Who made the volcano and Who made her, she cast the Pele berries into the lake, and sent stone after stone down into the flaming lava. It was the most awful insult that could be offered to Pele!" She and the people then began singing songs of praise. "The power of the priests was gone."[21]

Then Elijah said to them, "I am the only one of the Lord's prophets left, but Baal has four hundred and fifty prophets. Get two bulls for us. Let them choose one for themselves, and let them cut it into pieces and put it on the wood but not set fire to it. I will prepare the other bull and put it on the wood but not set fire to it. Then you call on the name of your god, and I will call on the name of the Lord. The god who answers by fire—he is God."

Then all the people said, "What you say is good." . . .

Then the fire of the Lord fell and burned up the sacrifice, the wood, the stones and the soil, and also licked up the water in the trench.

When all the people saw this, they fell prostrate and cried, "The Lord, he is God! The Lord—he is God!"

*1 Kings 18:22–24, 38–39.*

# "PREACH THE GOSPEL WHERE CHRIST IS NOT KNOWN"

Ministry focused on reaching unreached peoples is not new. The apostle Paul spoke of that ministry as his *ambition*, and countless missionaries in the generations since have focused their efforts on those who have never heard the gospel before. Western missionaries have not been the only ones with that priority. Many of those who have carried the Good News to the unevangelized have been dedicated Christians from the non-Western world. And some of the most inhospitable regions have been penetrated by these courageous missionaries. The island of Rarotonga is one such place.

So remote is the island of Rarotonga that missionary John Williams and his sailing party had trouble finding it. At last, they "discovered" Rarotonga. Williams was accompanied by some of the native Christians from the island of Raiatea—Christians who had volunteered to be the first to enter this land. "They had burned their idols, and now they too were missionaries of Jesus Christ. Their leader was a fearless young man, Papeiha. He was so daring that once, when everybody else was afraid to go from the ship to a cannibal island, he bound his Bible in his loin cloth, tied the bundle to the top of his head, and swam ashore, defying the sharks, and unafraid of the still more cruel islanders."

Papeiha and another native Christian volunteered to go ashore first and investigate the situation on Rarotonga. After they determined the people were friendly, they called on their fellow teachers to join them. The chief assured them they would not be harmed, but that night he came with his warriors to the place where they were sleeping and demanded that the wife of one of the teachers be given to him to become his twentieth wife. The battle lines were drawn, and the Christians would have been surely defeated, "had not Tapairu, a brave Rarotongan woman . . . fought with her hands to save the teacher's wife. At last the fierce chief gave in, and Papeiha and his friends, before the sun had risen, hurried to the beach, leapt into their canoe and paddled swiftly to the ship."

But Papeiha was not about to give up. He insisted that he return and preach the gospel no matter what the cost. He did, and his sacrifice was rewarded. One day a local priest brought his son to Papeiha for safekeeping because the priest had decided to defy his idol and turn to God. He carried the idol on his back to the missionaries, who chopped it up and burned it before the awe-struck crowd. Within a year hundreds of idols had been burned as Rarotongans turned to Christ.[22]

It has always been my ambition to preach the gospel where Christ was not known, so that I would not be building on someone else's foundation. Rather, as it is written: "Those who were not told about him will see, and those who have not heard will understand."

*Romans 15:20–21.*

# "A WISE SON HEEDS HIS FATHER'S INSTRUCTION"

We do not usually think of the book of Proverbs as a book with great evangelistic potential, but for Africans who are used to teaching through the proverbial method, that book can be a powerful tool of conviction. This was true in the life of Dongo Pewee, who grew up as an "army brat" in Liberia. It was a difficult life for Dongo—he moved from one army base to another, and his life reflected the turmoil that sometimes accompanies the military life. His father was a heavy drinker, who, in one day, would spend half of his paycheck on liquor. When he was drunk, he terrorized his family. He often beat Dongo's mother, who was weak and in ill health.

When Dongo's father was assigned to military bases in remote areas, Dongo and his brothers and sisters took advantage of whatever schooling and learning opportunities were available. For a time they were taught by a Jehovah's Witness who had come to the village, and after he left they learned from the Seventh-day Adventist teacher who had come. In order to attend his school the children were required to go to Sabbath school, which infuriated Dongo; he much preferred to go fishing. Initially he complied, knowing the alternative was a beating. He was missing one day, however, and the other children were sent to bring him back. When Dongo threatened the children with his machete, Dongo's father fetched the boy personally, and his wrath was fierce. He tied up Dongo and beat him. Although Dongo attended Sunday school from then on, he hated it.

Dongo did not realize when he was given a small copy of the book of Proverbs that he had been given a portion of the Bible. If he had, he probably would not have read it. But as he began reading it, he discovered wise sayings that were even more true to life than the proverbs he was accustomed to hearing from his own people. Those verses launched him on his pilgrimage toward faith in Christ. He faced many setbacks and struggles, but through the perseverance of dedicated Christians, he eventually made a commitment to Christ and went on to organize Bible clubs in all the schools in his city of Buchanan. It was his vision to bring the Bible—the book of Proverbs, especially—to others for whom its message would generate new life.[23]

A wise son heeds his father's instruction, but a mocker does not listen to rebuke. From the fruit of his lips a man enjoys good things, but the unfaithful have a craving for violence. He who guards his lips guards his life, but he who speaks rashly will come to ruin.

The sluggard craves and gets nothing, but the desires of the diligent are fully satisfied. The righteous hate what is false, but the wicked bring shame and disgrace. Righteousness guards the man of integrity, but wickedness overthrows the sinner.[23]

*Proverbs: 13:1–6.*

## "PROCLAIM THE POWER OF GOD"

According to his biographer, "No living preacher ever possessed such a combination of . . . pure doctrine, simple and lucid style, boldness and directness, earnestness and fervor, descriptiveness and picture-drawing, pathos and feeling—united with a perfect voice, perfect delivery, and perfect command of words."

Benjamin Franklin was less extravagant in his praise, but moved by his preaching just the same. This American founding father had been perturbed by the decision of this preacher not to locate his proposed orphanage in Philadelphia, where he thought it ought to be. So he swore he would not contribute even a penny to support it, as he later confessed.

"I happened soon afterwards to attend one of his sermons, in the course of which I perceived he intended to finish with a collection, and I silently resolved he should get nothing from me. I had in my pocket a handful of copper money, three or four silver dollars, and five in gold. As he proceeded I began to soften and concluded to give the copper. Another stroke of his oratory made me ashamed of that and determined me to give the silver, and he finished so admirably that I emptied my pocket into the collection dish, gold and all."

This great preacher was George Whitefield, who, with John Wesley, fanned the revival fires of the great Evangelical Awakening in England during the eighteenth century. Because of his fiery preaching, Whitefield was often denied pulpits in his own church, the Church of England. But such opposition did not silence him. When he was barred from the churches, he preached outdoors. Indeed, he utilized the natural setting of the outdoors to enhance his own preaching to "proclaim the power of God"—the God "who rides the ancient skies above, who thunders with mighty voice."

One day a storm approached while he was preaching in an open field, and he did not let the occasion pass unnoticed. "And where will you be, my hearers, when your lives have passed away like that dark cloud! . . . Let not the wrath of God be awakened! Let not the fires of eternity be kindled against you! See there!" he exclaimed, as lightning flashed across the sky, "it is a glance from the angry eye of Jehovah! Hark!" he cried out, as a crack of thunder roared over his words, "it was the voice of the Almighty as He passed by in His anger!" When asked for permission to publish that sermon, the preacher said yes, with the condition that the printer, in addition to the words, include the thunder and lightning.[24]

**Sing to God, O kingdoms of the earth, sing praise to the Lord, to him who rides the ancient skies above, who thunders with mighty voice. Proclaim the power of God, whose majesty is over Israel, whose power is in the skies. You are awesome, O God, in your sanctuary; the God of Israel gives power and strength to his people. Praise be to God!**

*Psalm 68:32–35.*

# "TURN TO ME AND BE SAVED"

The setting was a tiny Methodist chapel in England. It was a stormy night and only eight people were present. One was a visitor who had been on his way to a church social, but due to the weather had stopped at the chapel instead. In the absence of the minister, a layman—"a swarthy faced and grimy handed blacksmith"—arose to speak. He read from Isaiah 45 (KJV), "Look unto me and be ye saved."

His pointed and personalized commentary on the passage was very simple, and is equally appropriate if the opening imperative is translated *turn* rather than *look*: "Well, a man needn't go to college to learn to look. Anyone can look. You may be a fool and yet you can look. You will never find comfort in yourself. Look to Christ. Young man, you look very miserable. You always will be miserable if you don't obey the text; but if you obey now, this moment you may be saved."

The young man who was visiting was Charles Haddon Spurgeon, and he was converted that night. "I could dance all the way home," he testified. "I understand what Bunyan meant when he declared that he wanted to tell the crows on the plowed land all about his conversion."

That night marked a mighty change in Spurgeon's life. At the age of seventeen he began his preaching ministry, and during the nearly forty years that he was a pastor in London he had brought some twenty thousand people into his church. He was convinced "that there was not a seat in the Tabernacle but someone had been saved in it."

In addition to his pastoral ministry, "he conducted a pastor's college for the training of preachers; opened through his workers 36 chapels in London; conducted an orphanage with as many as 500 children in it at one time, and wrote scores of volumes."

Spurgeon will always be remembered as one of England's greatest preachers. The nameless blacksmith, who was willing to stand in for the pastor and was courageous enough to challenge him about his lost condition, has been forgotten. Forgotten by man, but not by God.[25]

"Turn to me and be saved, all you ends of the earth; for I am God, and there is no other. By myself I have sworn, my mouth has uttered in all integrity a word that will not be revoked: Before me every knee will bow; by me every tongue will swear. They will say of me, 'In the Lord alone are righteousness and strength.'" All who have raged against him will come to him and be put to shame. But in the Lord all the descendants of Israel will be found righteous and will exult.

*Isaiah 45:22–25.*

# "THE BATTLE IS NOT YOURS, BUT GOD'S"

It was this passage from the Old Testament that James O. Fraser claimed when he was most discouraged in his missionary outreach among some Lisu villages near the China-Burma border. His work was often frustrated by loneliness, and it was easy for him to become depressed when he saw no response to his preaching.

So it was after reaching out to a little village of thirteen families. "He had spent hours alone on the mountainside in prayer for this village. His expectation was high when he met with the heads of the families who came to discuss the message of Jesus with him." This was no ordinary group of people. "It was a strategic village. Fraser knew that the whole group of hamlets in the area would be opened up for the gospel if this leading village began by accepting the message." Thus, "His discouragement was bitter when they rejected it."

In his despondency, Fraser turned to 2 Chronicles 20, and committed himself to abiding by that passage—to turning the responsibility of reaching these people entirely over to God.

The next morning, after having spent much of the night in "fighting prayer," Fraser returned to the village. After explaining the gospel to them again, eleven of the families indicated they desired to become disciples of Jesus. The following day, twelve more families from other villages sought him out to tell him they wanted to become Christians. That night he was on his knees in prayer for yet another village, convinced that God had truly opened the way for the gospel in this region.

When he arrived at this other village, he was accompanied by one of his new converts, and he eagerly challenged the villagers to commit their lives to Christ even as the other villagers had.

"The people were cold and hostile. They did not want him there and they did not believe his message. So strong was their reaction against him that his companion turned against him too, renouncing his so-called faith and denouncing him as an impostor." Fraser "retreated to his little empty room. It seemed a total defeat and his spirits reached a new low. But here God showed His loving kindness. . . . He had begun to assume victory would be automatic; village after village would turn to Christ if he prayed the fighting prayer. He saw again that there was no room for cavalier faith in the work of God; it had the wrong kind of confidence."[26]

"This is what the Lord says to you: 'Do not be afraid or discouraged because of this vast army. For the battle is not yours, but God's. . . . You will not have to fight this battle. Take up your positions; stand firm and see the deliverance the Lord will give you. . . . Do not be afraid; do not be discouraged. Go out to face them tomorrow, and the Lord will be with you.'"

*2 Chronicles 20:15b, 17.*

# "CHANGED HEART AND CHANGED NAME"

When the German Lutheran Leipzig Mission sent its first two missionaries to Tanzania, officials from that country granted permission for them to establish their work in a suitable area. The officials promised to send someone out to introduce them to the local tribespeople once they had their camp set up.

When the tribespeople discovered them, however, they were apprehensive about having strangers in their midst. "Concealed in the bushes, the people watched. They watched that strange tent erected. They watched boxes opened and strange utensils taken out. Fears grew as they listened to strange speech none could understand. All day long they watched and listened. When night fell and all was still, they crept into the tent and killed both missionaries."

Government officials sought to apprehend the guilty, but no one would admit they knew who the murderers were. In the years that followed, more missionaries came—despite this incident—and established a church on Mt. Meru, near these two graves. And an African evangelist held Bible classes under a large tree only a short distance away.

One day when the evangelist was teaching his group of young boys, an old man stopped by. He listened with interest and returned the following days as well. On the final day, "the evangelist explained the custom of choosing a new Christian name at Baptism. The evangelist questioned the old man, and when assured of his faith, told him that he, too, could be baptized and receive a new Christian name. . . ." The idea of a new name was not initially appealing to the old man, and the evangelist assured him he could keep his old name if he liked.

"Sunday morning the old man arrived dressed (as is customary) in a new white garment. He hurried to the evangelist; with face shining he said, 'A new name I shall have. Call me Paulo!' Then he confessed, 'I was one of those who entered the tent and killed our first missionaries. You taught us of how God forgave Paulo and made him anew. I want to be forgiven, baptized, cleansed and made anew. Call me Paulo.'"

The old man identified his old life with Saul who had persecuted and killed Christians, but he wanted his new life to reflect that of Paul, a man who was transformed by the love of Jesus.[27]

Saul spent several days with the disciples in Damascus. At once he began to preach in the synagogues that Jesus is the Son of God. All those who heard him were astonished and asked, "Isn't he the man who raised havoc in Jerusalem among those who call on this name? And hasn't he come here to take them as prisoners to the chief priests?" Yet Saul grew more and more powerful and baffled the Jews living in Damascus by proving that Jesus is the Christ.

*Acts 9:19b–22.*

# "I WANT THOSE YOU HAVE GIVEN ME TO BE WITH ME"

One of the most familiar testimonies of adult males who have been converted—especially down-and-outers who have heard the gospel from street preachers or at rescue missions—is that their salvation was sparked by something that reminded them of their mother's prayers. Time and again this testimony has been repeated. It is the testimony of mothers who have prayed the prayer that Jesus prayed: "I pray also for those who will believe" and "Father, I want those you have given me to be with me where I am."

In the early years of the Pacific Garden Mission in Chicago, Harry Monroe would often sing the plaintive old hymn about a mother's prayers that often brought tears to the eyes of those listening:

Tell mother I'll be there
In answer to her prayer;
This message, blessed Savior, to her bear!
Tell mother I'll be there,
Heav'n's joys with her to share;
Yes, tell my darling mother I'll be there!

Harry's own testimony was common to those who frequented the mission. "He was no stranger to Whiskey Row, where he lost what money he had in the gambling dens, and where he saw many of his friends go to drunkard's graves." The night he was converted, he wrote a letter to his mother who had not heard from him for twelve years and believed him dead. Billy Sunday, also converted at the mission, likewise spoke of the influence of his mother's faith.

Another such testimony was that of George Preston, "the prayers of whose mother reached from north Ireland across the sea." George heard Harry Monroe preach in an open-air meeting one day, saying "I am impressed that there is a man here who has been thinking that years ago he promised his mother he would meet her in heaven." Hardly able to contain himself, George shouted out, "I am that man!" Still another man opened a New Testament that had been given to him, with the inscription, "From one who is praying for you." This reminded him of his mother, who had put him on the top of her prayer list. He returned to the mission and was converted.[28]

"My prayer is not for them alone. I pray also for those who will believe in me through their message, that all of them may be one, Father, just as you are in me and I am in you. May they also be in us so that the world may believe that you have sent me. I have given them the glory that you gave me, that they may be one as we are one: I in them and you in me. May they be brought to complete unity to let the world know that you sent me and have loved them even as you have loved me.

"Father, I want those you have given me to be with me where I am, and to see my glory, the glory you have given me because you loved me before the creation of the world."

*John 17:20–24.*

# "HE WILL RULE FROM SEA TO SEA"

Psalm 72 is one of the great missionary passages in the Old Testament, and it has inspired one of the greatest missionary hymns ever written. The first verse is familiar throughout Protestantism:

Jesus shall reign where'er the sun
Does his successive journeys run,
His kingdom spread from shore to shore
Till moons shall wax and wane no more.

Those words were penned by the great English hymnologist Isaac Watts, who thought of himself as a pastor and theologian far more than a hymn writer. He wrote a number of textbooks that were still used in major universities and seminaries more than a century after he died in 1748. A lifelong bachelor, Watts served for twenty-two years as a Puritan pastor of the Mark Land Independent Chapel in London. He wrote poetry as a sideline, and more than six hundred of these have been sung as hymns, including "When I Survey the Wondrous Cross," "O God, Our Help in Ages Past," and "Joy to the World."

What is so remarkable about his great missionary hymn, "Jesus Shall Reign," is that it predated the onset of the modern missionary movement by more than a half century. It was derived not so much from Watts's personal commitment to foreign missions, but from his commitment to expressing Scripture—particularly the Psalms—in modern poetic verse. "Watts was a poet because he loved the biblical psalter. His fascination with the Psalms was part of his birthright as a Reformed Christian belonging to the Congregationalist tradition."

"Grasping the messianic and missiological import of Psalm 72, Watts transformed it into a compelling vision of how the Great Commission of Christ will be realized (Matt. 28:19–20). As a result of the preaching of the gospel of Christ,

To him shall endless prayer be made,
And praises throng to crown his head;
His name, like sweet perfume, shall rise
With every morning sacrifice.[29]

He will rule from sea to sea and from the River to the ends of the earth. The desert tribes will bow before him and his enemies will lick the dust. The kings of Tarshish and of distant shores will bring tribute to him, the kings of Sheba and Seba will present him gifts.

All kings will bow down to him and all nations will serve him. . . .

May his name endure forever, may it continue as long as the sun. All nations will be blessed through him, and they will call him blessed.

*Psalm 72:8–11, 17.*

## "I WILL COME WITH YOU"

Sometimes the follower or the "attendant" becomes as great as the leader himself, as in the case of Elijah and Elisha. This has often been true of missionaries who have been attended by native believers. Starting out in a lowly servant position, the national sometimes surpasses the missionary in evangelistic outreach. So it was with Shomolekae, who worked for missionary John Mackenzie at Kuruman, the mission station in South Africa founded many years earlier by the great missionary pioneers Robert and Mary Moffat. Shomolekae's was a lowly job; he was a human scarecrow who saved the crops from the birds. But he was faithful in that position, and when he discovered another worker stealing fruit, he reported the theft.

Recognizing Shomolekae's dependability, Mackenzie invited him to accompany him on an extended evangelistic tour and serve as his wagon driver and personal attendant. For years he served faithfully in this capacity. Later when Mackenzie returned to Kuruman to establish a Bible school, Shomolekae came with him and became a student.

With this as his preparation, he set out as an evangelist, working initially with another missionary, and then on his own. He followed in the footsteps of David Livingstone and did evangelistic work in regions where the explorer had traveled years earlier. Shomolekae had the same instinct for exploration as did his predecessor, and he penetrated farther and farther into the unknown, always reaching out with the gospel and establishing groups of believers.

Along with the Scripture he taught music. The children particularly enjoyed the hymns. Indeed, "they learned them so well that sometimes when the mothers were out hoeing in the fields, or the little boys were paddling in their canoes and fishing in the marshy waters, they would hear them singing the hymns that they had learned in Shomolekae's little school hut."

Though he had served most of his life as an attendant, Shomolekae eagerly took up the mantle of his mentor and served with equal distinction—forgotten by most historians, but not by God.[30]

So Elijah went from there and found Elisha son of Shaphat. He was plowing with twelve yoke of oxen, and he himself was driving the twelfth pair. Elijah went up to him and threw his cloak around him. Elisha then left his oxen and ran after Elijah. "Let me kiss my father and mother good-by," he said, "and then I will come with you."

"Go back," Elijah replied. "What have I done to you?"

So Elisha left him and went back. He took his yoke of oxen and slaughtered them. He burned the plowing equipment to cook the meat and gave it to the people, and they ate. Then he set out to follow Elijah and became his attendant.

*1 Kings 19:19–21.*

# "AS I MEDITATED, THE FIRE BURNED"

Alexander Maclaren is known as one of the great expository preachers of nineteenth-century England, though he never sensed a definite call to be a preacher. "I cannot recall ever having had any hesitation as to being a minister," he wrote to a college friend. "It seems to me it must have been simply taken for granted by my father and my mother and myself; it just had to be."

McClaren began his preaching as a pulpit supply pastor for the Portland Chapel in Southampton, a church without a pastor. After his first two sermons, the church asked him to continue on for three months, which he did with certain misgivings. The church was utterly barren. "If the worst comes to worst I shall at all events not have to reflect that I killed a flourishing plant," he wrote, "but only assisted at the funeral of a withered one." At the end of three months the church called him to serve full-time, and he accepted.

After thirteen years, he accepted his second pastoral call to the Union Chapel in Manchester, where he served for the following fifty years. Here, as in Southampton, he preached simple expository sermons. "I have abjured forever all the rubbish of intellectual preaching," he said. "The sole purpose lies in the true, simple, sincere setting forth of the living Christ." He rarely spoke from notes, and when lecturing to a group of Presbyterian ministers, he admonished them: "Burn your manuscripts."

In spite of his great success as a preacher, he was insecure about his own abilities. "Always before a sermon or lecture in public, he would be overcome with nervous agitation. It vanished as soon as he launched into his message. And frequently after the service, waves of depression would engulf him, and he wanted to be alone."

McLaren was very shy, and avoided social contacts whenever possible. He was convinced that the primary task of the pastor was prayer and preaching the Word. This was the secret of his effective ministry, as he himself reflected: "I sometimes think that a verse in the Psalms carries the whole path of homiletics: 'While I was musing the fire burned: then spake I with my tongue.' Patient meditation, resulting in kindled emotions and the flashing-up of truth with warmth and light—and not till then—the rush of speech 'moved by the Holy Ghost'—there are the processes which will make sermons live things with hands and feet, as Luther's words were said to be."[31]

I said, "I will watch my ways and keep my tongue from sin; I will put a muzzle on my mouth as long as the wicked are in my presence." But when I was silent and still not even saying anything good, my anguish increased. My heart grew hot within me, and as I meditated, the fire burned; then I spoke with my tongue."

*Psalm 39:1–3.*

# "CHRIST JESUS CAME INTO THE WORLD TO SAVE SINNERS"

Hugh Latimer was a well-known sixteenth-century English churchman who was initially a strong opponent of the Reformation. After he graduated from Cambridge, he became an Anglican priest and was much loved by his parishioners. "All who heard him fell under the spell of his transparent honesty and rugged eloquence."

One of those who recognized that he was a gifted and sincere minister was Thomas Bilney, who heard him preach in Cambridge. Ten years Hugh's junior, Thomas, who had also studied at Cambridge, prayed for this great preacher's soul. "O God," he pleaded, "I am but 'little Bilney,' and shall never do any great thing for Thee; but give me the soul of that man, Hugh Latimer, and what wonders *he* shall do in Thy most holy Name!"

Bilney continued to listen to Latimer's sermons, and one day, after Latimer had descended the pulpit and was leaving the sanctuary, he passed close by Thomas. "Prithee, Father Latimer," he whispered, "may I confess my soul to thee?" The preacher nodded and motioned him into a private room. There on his knees Thomas poured out his soul, telling the great preacher how he had discovered a passage in the Bible that changed his life. It was a simple message from 1 Timothy 1:15 that suddenly transformed Latimer. He was a good man and had been described as "the honestest man in England," but he now realized that he, too, must be saved.

What followed was one of the great conversion stories in history: "To the astonishment of Bilney, Latimer rises and then kneels beside him. The Father-confessor seeks guidance from his penitent! Bilney draws from his pocket the sacred volume that has brought such comfort and such rapture to his own soul. It falls open at the passage that Bilney has read to himself over and over again: 'This is a faithful saying, and worthy of all acceptation, that Christ Jesus came into the world to save sinners; of whom I am chief.'"

Openly preaching the Reformed faith in England was dangerous business. Bilney was imprisoned and later sentenced to die at the stake. Latimer, too, paid a heavy price for his conversion. He was first confined in the Tower of London, and then with Bishop Ridley, was burned at the stake. They were only two of approximately three hundred Protestant leaders who would be executed under the reign of Queen Mary.[1]

Here is a trustworthy saying that deserves full acceptance: Christ Jesus came into the world to save sinners—of whom I am the worst. But for that very reason I was shown mercy so that in me, the worst of sinners, Christ Jesus might display his unlimited patience as an example for those who would believe on him and receive eternal life. Now to the King eternal, immortal, invisible, the only God, be honor and glory for ever and ever. Amen.

*1 Timothy 1:15–17.*

# "HELD IN SLAVERY BY THEIR FEAR OF DEATH"

Sue Moonsamy and her husband Sam are Baptist missionaries in America to thousands of immigrants from India, Sri Lanka, and Pakistan. Her call to missions came as a young adult, after she had endured a terrifying childhood and an anguishing pilgrimage of faith. She was born in South Africa, where her father was a Hindu businessman and her mother was the daughter of a Hindu priestess. "Everything in our lives revolved around the religion of Hinduism. . . . Daily we offered prayers with regular sacrifices before an illustrious shrine to a multiplicity of deities."

Her uncomplicated childhood suddenly began to unravel, however, when her parents divorced—a rare development in an arranged Hindu marriage. From then on her life was one of poverty and hardship, living in a slum settlement with her mother and younger sister. Among the traumas of her youth, the most terrifying was the aspect of Hindu ritual that included the worship of the live "snake god." Worshipers—sometimes in trances—"were beckoning and earnestly entreating the snake to come out" of its hole, even as this little child prayed it would not.

Life finally became so filled with despair for Sue's mother that she concluded there was only one way to escape. She explained to her daughters "that according to the law of 'Karma,' . . . we were suffering because of sins committed in our past lives. If we died violently and in suffering, we would be born again through reincarnation, the transmigration of the soul, to a higher level of being." She then proceeded to chant to the gods while she poured gasoline over her daughters, and opened a box of matches.

" 'I closed my eyes, knowing that soon we would be engulfed in flames,' recalls Sue. As her little sister began to whimper, her mother suddenly screamed 'Oh, God, help us!' . . At that moment there was the sound of a loud thud on the floor. 'I opened my eyes and saw my mother lying unconscious before me. Quickly searching through her pockets, we found the key and fled to freedom,' " though not free from their mother, who survived the incident.

It was sometime after this that Sue met a blind Christian woman who invited her to a tiny house church. There she committed herself to Christ, despite her mother's threats against her. Sue's involvement with the Christians so upset her mother that she took the girls and moved away to a military transit camp—where she was certain there would be no Christians. She could not have been more wrong. Next door to them was another house church, and three months after they moved in Sue married Sam Moonsamy, the young minister of that church.[2]

Since the children have flesh and blood, he too shared in their humanity so that by his death he might destroy him who holds the power of death—that is, the devil—and free those who all their lives were held in slavery by their fear of death.

*Hebrews 2:14–15.*

# "HELP ME OVERCOME MY UNBELIEF"

Belief comes harder for some people than it does others. For David James Burrell it came with difficulty, but once he committed his life to God he was on the road to becoming the pastor of the Marble Collegiate Reformed Church in New York City, where he served for thirty years during the first decades of the twentieth century. Burrell grew up under the influence of a godly mother who longed to see her son become a minister. He attended Yale, but there he confessed, "I lost all the religion she had taught me." To please his mother, though, he went on to seminary, where he found "all dogma and theory" but "no living Christ." Despite his struggle, he agreed to teach a boys' mission class in New York City, and it was through that experience that he came to *belief* in Christ.

One night a boy in his class asked him to visit his dying father. "I had no comfort to give to a dying man, but I *had* to go," he later wrote. "In a tiny, dirty room of a tenement in the near-by slums the boy showed me his father, lying on a ragged bed. Then began a night of lies."

The man asked him if he believed the Bible. Burrell lied. "I told him I did. I told him I believed that Christ was divine. I told him I believed in every word in the Bible." He quoted verses and asked Burrell if he believed them. "I would have to answer yes," Burrell confessed. " 'Well, make *me* believe it then,' he would say. And I, not believing it at all, would do my best to help him believe it." But after hours of talk, the man was at the point of death and still did not believe. He asked Burrell to pray for him, and during that prayer he died. How incongruous it was that he was praying for someone else to believe when he did not believe himself.

"I decided then and there," Burrell later related, "that I *would* believe. I resolved to take the Bible word for word, without any questioning, and put my faith in every word. I determined to become a fanatic for Christ. And I have been a fanatic ever since." After that decision, Burrell "tossed away dogma and ecclesiasticism" and started a mission in the inner city of Chicago and later became one of America's most powerful preachers, ever lifting up Christ but refusing to "explain" him.[3]

"O unbelieving generation," Jesus replied, "how long shall I stay with you? How long shall I put up with you? Bring the boy to me."

So they brought him. When the spirit saw Jesus, it immediately threw the boy into a convulsion. He fell to the ground and rolled around, foaming at the mouth.

Jesus asked the boy's father, "How long has he been like this?"

"From childhood," he answered. "It has often thrown him into fire or water to kill him. But if you can do anything, take pity on us and help us."

"If you can?" said Jesus. "Everything is possible for him who believes."
Immediately the boy's father exclaimed, "I do believe; help me overcome my unbelief!"

*Mark 9:19–24.*

# "OFFER YOUR BODIES AS LIVING SACRIFICES"

Before he was converted through missionaries with the China Inland Mission, Pastor Hsi was an opium smoker and an opium grower. But his faith in Christ transformed him and he vowed to offer himself as a living sacrifice to the ministry of bringing other opium addicts to Christ. He wanted their minds to be renewed as his had been.

His work began by simply opening a small drug store and treating people with health problems and helping opium addicts overcome their addiction, but as word spread of his success, others called on him to come to their village and treat them. "Soon nineteen men were undergoing treatment. Hsi made frequent visits to this new Opium Refuge, as it was called, and under his ministry many of the patients were led to Christ."

Pastor Hsi supported the ministry through his own earnings and through his wife's sale of her wedding garments and jewels. When their money ran out, support came from Chinese Christians, many of whom had been released from the bondage of opium through the ministry. Soon there were more than forty refuges scattered throughout the region. "Thousands of patients were cured of the opium habit. Hundreds of these were converted. Churches were organized. Whole communities were transformed."

As the work continued to grow, Hsi's life became consumed in the ministry. "He was often away from home for weeks or months together, visiting the refuges and superintending church affairs. On the cover of his cart, as he traveled from place to place, he had the sentence, 'Holy Religion of Jesus,' in large, red characters, to draw attention, and to afford an opening for conversation on spiritual things. For the same reason he often wore across the front of his outer garment the characters: 'Je-su kiang shi kin ren'(Jesus came into the world to save sinners)."

But exhausting work was not his key to success. He relied on prayer above all else. "My wife and I, for the space of three years," he wrote, "seldom put off our clothing to go to sleep, in order that we might be more ready to watch and pray. Sometimes, in a solitary place, I spent whole nights in prayer." His prayers were combined with his creative talents. "He prayed when his own property was spent, and more funds were needed. The answer came when he wrote a prize Christian poem—the first of sixty hymns from his pen, many of which are now used in churches all over China." He died at age sixty, having literally given his body as a living sacrifice to God.[4]

Therefore, I urge you, brothers, in view of God's mercy, to offer your bodies as living sacrifices, holy and pleasing to God—this is your spiritual act of worship. Do not conform any longer to the pattern of this world, but be transformed by the renewing of your mind. Then you will be able to test and approve what God's will is—his good, pleasing and perfect will.

*Romans 12:1–2.*

# "SOME YOU WILL KILL AND CRUCIFY"

Girolamo Savonarola was a prophet who was put to death not by the foreign enemies who despised the Christian faith, but by the leaders of his very own church. These are the kinds of leaders Jesus was speaking of when he lashed out against the Pharisees whom he described as hypocrites, snakes, and vipers.

Savanarola was a fifteenth-century Italian reformer who had turned his back on his medical training to become a Dominican monk. He was a powerful and gifted preacher, and through his sermons, especially those warning of God's coming judgment, he gained wide popularity. He was so popular that he rose to political leadership in Florence. He introduced tax reforms and humanitarian programs for the poor, and he sought to rid the city of its moral corruption. He denounced the Pope as a false prophet, and in 1496, he initiated the "burning of vanities," a ceremony by which people brought their gambling devices, their pornography, their wigs and cosmetics, and threw them into a great fire, thereby renouncing their worldly pleasures.

As with the prophets of moral reform before him, however, his ministry was cut short. His enemies were more powerful than his friends. "Savonarola preached his farewell sermon in the Cathedral of St. Mark, where for years he had thrilled his parishioners with his powerful and eloquent messages. At the end of the service he presented his body to God, saying that he was ready to face death for the cause of truth. Soldiers seized and led him away to be tried.

"His followers deserted him. . . . As the procession left the church, men who had once fawned on him in adulation hurled rocks at his head, brutally kicked him, and all but pulled an arm from its socket."

A simple death sentence was considered too mild a punishment. With the Pope's blessing, his accusers "tied him with ropes and raised him high above the stone floor of the prison, and then released the ropes and watched him fall to the floor." The torture continued for a month until a mock trial was convened at which time he and two friends were condemned to die. His final words summed up his faith: "My Saviour, though innocent, died for my sins, and should I not give up this poor body out of love to Him?"[5]

"You snakes! You brood of vipers! How will you escape being condemned to hell? Therefore I am sending you prophets and wise men and teachers. Some of them you will kill and crucify; others you will flog in your synagogues and pursue from town to town. And so upon you will come all the righteous blood that has been shed on earth, from the blood of righteous Abel to the blood of Zechariah son of Berekiah, whom you murdered between the temple and the altar. I tell you the truth, all this will come upon this generation."

*Matthew 23:33–36.*

# "I HAVE GREAT CONFIDENCE IN YOU"

It is essential that missionaries express confidence, as Paul did, to younger Christians in the faith. Indeed, sometimes an enthusiastic expression of confidence that can accomplish more than anything else to thrust a reluctant believer into productive ministry. This was true of Sappri Turay, a leading evangelist in Sierra Leone.

Sappri did not appear to be destined for greatness. He grew up near the historic American Wesleyan Mission in Kunso, and would often sit for hours on the veranda, hoping to be given a little rice. When the missionaries encouraged him to go home, he ignored them. Although he longed to go to the mission school, he was passed by when missionaries and national leaders recruited children in the region. When he was finally admitted in 1904, at the age of twelve, he still showed little potential for future ministry.

In the years that followed Sappri did not live a consistent Christian life. He "became a member of several secret societies, trusted in charms, smoked, drank excessively, and was involved in serious quarrels." He did, however, excel in linguistic abilities, and after he professed faith in Christ, he was employed as an interpreter. His continued drinking, though, led to his dismissal.

A dream depicting hell led Sappri to renounce his sin. Many missionaries and church leaders were skeptical of his sincerity, but J. E. Cowan, a young missionary, had confidence in him. In 1928, when he was returning to America, he commissioned Sappri to take his place: "Here, I give my walking stick to you. You take my job. I am leaving this to you like Elijah left Elisha his mantle." That show of confidence was just what Sappri needed. "The following twenty-one years of Sappri's life proved the Holy Spirit had done a thorough work in the spiritual nature of this man whose own efforts had previously resulted in repeated sin and failure."

"God gave the young evangelist the joy of seeing a great harvest in his meetings as an awakening among the unevangelized and a revival among the Christians spread from village to village. . . . The striking evidence of a turning to God was the surrender of all idols and charms." Not only did Sappri carry on the work of missionary Cowan, but he went far beyond what his predecessor had done, largely because "he had a wealth of convincing arguments because of his knowledge of the Bible, the Koran, and the tribal customs." When he died in 1949, he left many converts and new Elishas to take up his mantle.[6]

Make room for us in your hearts. We have wronged no one, we have corrupted no one, we have exploited no one. I do not say this to condemn you, I have said before that you have such a place in our hearts that we would live or die with you. I have great confidence in you; I take great pride in you. I am greatly encouraged, in all our troubles my joy knows no bounds.

*2 Corinthians 7:2–4.*

## "OUT OF THE HEART THE MOUTH SPEAKS"

He was a fourth-century Bishop of Constantinople, who was simply known as John, but in the generations since he has become known with the appellation Chrysostom, which means "golden-mouthed." He is called John the Golden-mouthed because his words were very powerful.

On one occasion, after people from his home city of Antioch had taken revenge on some officials of Emperor Theodocius, his dynamic preaching forcefully "moved and melted men to tears. They acted out his every stipulation. In consequence, Theodosius was conciliated and suspended punishment. Such was the power of Chrysostom."

"Job once declared, 'How forcible are right words!' So forcible, indeed, were Chrysostom's that his attendants would often clap hands and stamp their feet while he was preaching. He determined to put a stop to the habit. He delivered a stirring sermon condemning it as irreverent, disgraceful, dishonouring to God. The response was something less than encouraging. His congregation . . . applauded him roundly!"

More than six thousand of his sermons are in print—sermons which "breathe a knowledge of Scripture, devotion, learning, taste, craftsmanship, a passion for beauty, an acquaintance with the Greek classics. He preached to the heart and conscience as well as to the intellect. He delighted to exalt the Christ of God, and to bring to bear on the lives of his beloved people the moral principles of the Bible. Probably he did more to make the pulpit a medium of influence for righteousness than any clergyman in the first Christian millennium."

In his preaching on moral values, John Chrysostom came in direct conflict with Empress Eudocia, and at times he may have gone beyond the bounds of propriety. He spoke against sin in high places and pointed his finger at her, calling her the second Jezebel. She was outraged and demanded that he be deposed. Indeed, "he preached himself right out of the pulpit and . . . into exile," convinced that he was speaking for God. "His influence has extended from the pauper in the street to the ruler in the palace," as he "forgot himself in his cause, and that cause the salvation of souls."[7]

"Make a tree good and its fruit will be good, or make a tree bad and its fruit will be bad, for a tree is recognized by its fruit. You brood of vipers, how can you who are evil say anything good? For out of the overflow of the heart the mouth speaks. The good man brings good things out of the good stored up in him, and the evil man brings evil things out of the evil stored up in him. But I tell you that men will have to give account on the day of judgment for every careless word they have spoken. For by your words you will be acquitted, and by your words you will be condemned."

*Matthew 12:33–37.*

# "BE MERCIFUL TO THOSE WHO DOUBT"

A. Wetherell Johnson, a missionary to China and the founder and director of the world's largest Bible study organization, Bible Study Fellowship, struggled with deep doubts as a young woman. She was raised in Britain and educated in France, where "the heavy study left no leisure for thought or emotional introspection." When she returned to England, she realized how much she had changed: "I had time to recognize that when I gave up belief in the Lord Jesus Christ and the Bible, I had no philosophy to fill the vacuum that remained. Life was utterly without meaning."

It was this doubt that soon after prompted her to cry out in the night, "God, if there be a God, if You will give me some philosophy that makes reasonable sense to me, I will commit myself to follow it." God gave her a philosophy, but not miraculously through a dream or sudden voice from heaven. He had already provided it in the Bible, but she had to search for it. She enrolled in five correspondence courses and continued on in personal Bible study for the remainder of her life.

But it was not enough to keep that philosophy—that knowledge—to herself. In 1936, as a single woman in her late twenties, she sailed for China to serve with the China Inland Mission. There she worked closely with a national "Bible woman" and together they brought that philosophy to people who had never before heard the gospel. Johnson, along with other missionaries, was held in a Japanese internment camp for a time during World War II. After her release and a furlough in England, she returned to China, but fled in 1950, in the face of the increasing terror brought on by the Communist insurgents.

In the years that followed, Johnson was deeply involved in various ministries in the United States, but her most enduring service centered around her vision for Bible study. Her program involves the training of teachers worldwide, and during a twenty year period more than one hundred thousand people had completed the five-year course. Johnson herself has been so highly regarded as a Bible scholar that she was invited to be a member of the sixteen-member council of the International Council on Biblical Inerrancy—the only woman so designated.

Her commitment to Bible study grew out of her doubt as a youth. "Be merciful to those who doubt."[8]

But you, dear friends, build yourselves up in your most holy faith and pray in the Holy Spirit. Keep yourselves in God's love as you wait for the mercy of our Lord Jesus Christ to bring you to eternal life. Be merciful to those who doubt; snatch others from the fire and save them; to others show mercy, mixed with fear—hating even the clothing stained by corrupted flesh.

*Jude 20–22.*

# "I DO NOT PERMIT A WOMAN TO TEACH"

In her years as a missionary to the Balangao people in the Philippines, Joanne Shetler and her partner Anne Fetzer found that progress was slow. The people were not interested in hearing about their God, and they were puzzled as to why these two women were living among them. "They decided among themselves," writes Joanne, "that perhaps we had plans to get rich. Some thought we might sell their language in America, since we were writing it down. Others guessed we were looking for husbands because we didn't have any."

Despite the lack of enthusiasm for their presence, the women went ahead with their work. "We set about to learn to speak Balangao. We'd climb up the bamboo ladders into their smoky, dark little one-roomed houses on stilts, sit by their open fires, eat rice and snails with our fingers and learn about why they sacrifice pigs and chickens to the evil spirits."

During their first term, only two Balangao people believed. Joanne and Anne were frustrated and discouraged when they returned home on furlough in 1967, and Joanne shared this frustration with her prayer supporters, asking them to pray specifically that there would be a breakthrough among the people. When she returned to the Philippines the following year, she was warmly received. Her Balangao father was pleased with the Bible translation she was doing, and invited her to teach the village men, and soon some of them professed faith in Christ.

"Realizing I was responsible for the growth of these new believers," she wrote, "I started to translate the pastoral Epistles with my Balangao father—it seemed like the most logical thing to do for a new church. But I could not persuade these men to teach—even with my help. . . . When we came to the verse in First Timothy where Paul says, 'I don't allow women to teach men,' my Balangao father didn't even make a comment. We just kept going.

"That afternoon after we finished, he asked what we were studying on Sunday. I thought he was just curious, and I told him. On Sunday morning before I could stand and teach, he said, 'My daughter here knows more about this than I do, but we found in the Bible where it says women aren't supposed to teach men, so I guess I'll have to.' That's when the men started to teach in Balangao!"[9]

"I want men everywhere to lift up holy hands in prayer, without anger or disputing.

I also want women to dress modestly, with decency and propriety, not with braided hair or gold or pearls or expensive clothes, but with good deeds, appropriate for women who profess to worship God.

A woman should learn in quietness and full submission. I do not permit a woman to teach or have authority over a man; she must be silent."

*1 Timothy 2:8–12.*

# "OUR STRUGGLE IS NOT AGAINST FLESH AND BLOOD"

"As I walked through the wilderness of this world, I lighted on a certain place where was a Den, and I laid me down in that place to sleep: And as I slept, I dreamed a Dream." This is the opening sentence of one of the most widely-read Christian classics ever written, *Pilgrim's Progress*. The dreamer was John Bunyan and the den that he slept in was the Bedford Prison. The dream was about the Christian's pilgrimage through life—a pilgrimage that sometimes reflected his own struggles.

Bunyan was born near Bedford, England, in 1628, the son of a tinker, a traveling repairman who traded and repaired household and farm implements. It was a lowly vocation, and as was typical in that era, the son followed in the footsteps of his father. Bunyan was well acquainted with grief. As a teenager both his mother and his sister died within a month of each other. In his sorrow, he went his own way, and later commented that he had "few equals . . . for cursing, swearing, lying and blaspheming the holy name of God." His waywardness was challenged, however, after he joined the army, when he encountered a brush with death. Another soldier was ordered to take his place just before battle, and that soldier was killed.

Soon after he was discharged from the army, Bunyan married and settled into his life as a tinker. "We came together as poor as poor might be," he recalled, "not having so much household-stuff as a dish or spoon betwixt us both." During the early years of marriage, he struggled with spiritual doubts and depression, but then one day he was confronted by "three or four poor women . . . sitting at a door, in the sun, talking of things of God." He inquired about their contentment amid poverty, and they shared their faith and introduced him to their pastor. Through this pastor's counsel and through reading Martin Luther's *Commentary on Galatians*, he was converted.

Soon Bunyan became involved in ministry himself, first speaking at tiny house churches and in saloons, but then to large crowds, as word spread about the tinker who was a mighty preacher. With the death of Cromwell in 1658, however, royal rule returned to England, and religious non-conformists like Bunyan were banned from preaching. He stood his ground; he refused to comply. In 1660 he was imprisoned for twelve years—a time of severe suffering and hardship, but also a time of ministry. While in prison, he wrote five books and many treatises. After his release, he was imprisoned again briefly in 1675, at which time he began writing *Pilgrim's Progress*.[10]

Finally, be strong in the Lord and in his mighty power. Put on the full armor of God so that you can take your stand against the devil's schemes. For our struggle is not against flesh and blood, but against the rulers, against the authorities, against the powers of this dark world and against the spiritual forces of evil in the heavenly realms. Therefore put on the full armor of God, so that when the day of evil comes, you may be able to stand your ground, and after you have done everything, to stand.

*Ephesians 6:10–13.*

# "A LONGING FULFILLED IS A TREE OF LIFE"

William Borden grew up with abundance and luxury. He was an heir to a vast fortune, acquired through the giant Borden dairy business. As a youth he was primed for the leadership he would one day assume over this financial empire. He enrolled at Yale for his university education, and graduated in 1909.

But during his years at Yale, his vision for the future had dramatically changed. During his freshman year he was deeply challenged by a Reformed Church missionary who had committed his life to reaching Muslims with the gospel. "He was a man with a map. Charged with facts and with enthusiasm, grim with earnestness, filled with a passion of love for Christ and the perishing, Samuel Zwemer made the great map live, voicing the silent appeal of . . . two hundred millions of our fellow-creatures in the lands colored green on the map—two hundred millions under the sway of Islam."

Zwemer went on to point out that there were "more Moslems in China than there are in Persia; more Moslems in China than in the whole of Egypt; more Moslems in China even than in Arabia, home and cradle of Islam, and *no one* giving himself to their evangelization." He was a powerful speaker and his message penetrated the heart of this wealthy young man. "Who is there tonight who can always see the shadow of the Cross falling upon his banking account? Who is there who has the mark of the nails and the print of his spear in the plans and life, his love and devotion and daily program of intercession? Who is there who has heard the word of Jesus and is quietly, obediently, every day, as He has told you and me, taking up his cross to follow Him?"

Borden's commitment grew stronger in the succeeding years, and upon his graduation he announced that he was donating his inheritance to the cause of world missions and that he was committed to serving overseas. He was determined to serve with the China Inland Mission in order to reach Muslims living in China. He first went to Egypt for Arabic language study, but only four weeks after his arrival he contracted spinal meningitis and two weeks later he was dead. Later a message was found scribbled on a sheet of paper stuffed under his pillow: "No Reserve! No Retreat! No Regrets!"

In one sense his longing was never fulfilled, but through his donated wealth and through his published biography, he left behind a tree of life.[11]

One man pretends to be rich, yet has nothing; another pretends to be poor, yet has great wealth.

A man's riches may ransom his life, but a poor man hears no threat.

The light of the righteous shines brightly, but the lamp of the wicked is snuffed out.

Pride only breeds quarrels, but wisdom is found in those who take advice.

Dishonest money dwindles away, but he who gathers money little by little makes it grow.

Hope deferred makes the heart sick, but a longing fulfilled is a tree of life.

*Proverbs 13:7–12.*

## "DENIAL AND REPENTANCE"

Abdallah and Sabat, two young Arabs, were bound for Mecca, the birthplace of Mohammed, to worship in that most holy city. They were both sons of Arab chiefs, and this trip offered them not only a time to deepen their faith, but also a vacation of sorts. After their visit to Mecca, they headed on eastward toward Kabul in the mountains of Afghanistan.

While there, Abdallah was invited to become an official in the Shah's court. During this time he was given an Arabic translation of the first four gospels. In those pages he found one who was greater than Mohammed. He believed and was baptized. Immediately his life was in jeopardy, so he left the city and fled eastward into Persia to the city of Bokhara, where he hoped he might find safety with Sabat. Word of his conversion, however, preceded him, and Sabat delivered him to the Muslim officials.

Here, Abdallah was offered freedom if he would "spit upon the Cross and renounce Christ and say, 'There is no God but Allah.'" He refused, and with that "a sword was brought forward and unsheathed. . . . Abdallah's hand, cut clean off, fell on the ground, while the blood spurted from his arm." He was given a second chance, but again he refused, and his other hand was cut off. He was given a third chance, and then he was beheaded.

Sabat was tortured by the ordeal of seeing his friend executed. "Nothing that he could do would take away from his eyes the vision of his friend's face as Abdallah had looked at him when his hands were being cut off." He began a life of wandering—wandering that brought him in contact with Christians who gave him an Arabic New Testament, and like his friend Abdallah before him, he found faith in Christ. He, too, met with outrage and hostility but he escaped death and vowed to enter Christian ministry.

His knowledge of the Persian language and his love for the Bible prompted him to seek translation work, and he became an assistant to the great missionary and Bible translator of the early nineteenth century, Henry Martyn. But "Sabat's fiery temper nearly drove Martyn wild." He could not accept criticism, and in a fit of rage, "like St. Peter, the fiery, impetuous apostle, he denied Jesus Christ and spoke against Christianity." When the news was published in a Muslim newspaper, he repented and wrote a letter stating publicly that truly he was a Christian. Later, in an effort to carry the gospel to Sumatra, Sabat was shackled and later thrown off the side of the ship. Though in his Christian walk he had once stumbled, he remained faithful to Christ to the end.[12]

After a little while, those standing near said to Peter, "Surely you are one of them, for you are a Galilean."

He began to call down curses on himself, and he swore to them, "I don't know this man you're talking about." Immediately the rooster crowed the second time. Then Peter remembered the word Jesus had spoken to him: "Before the rooster crows twice you will disown me three times." And he broke down and wept.

*Mark 14: 70b–72.*

# "JESUS THE VERY THOUGHT OF THEE!"

The sacrifice Jesus made for mankind so consumed Bernard, a young man in twelfth-century France, that he turned away from his noble heritage and became a monk. He was born in 1091 in an old castle at Fontaines, where his father and mother "ruled in feudal glory." As a youth he was impassioned by the Crusades for the Holy Land, especially after his own father went forth and never returned.

His conversion precipitated his decision to serve God as a monk. "While riding through bleak moors and tangled forests, he arrived at last at a chapel in the clearing. He suddenly found his heart had turned liquid within him, so he quickly dismounted, fell on his face and poured out his heart to God.

"Immediately following his conversion, Bernard decided to enter the monastery, and with thirty others, whom he won by personal evangelism, began 'preparatory seclusion,'" and after a six-month trial period, he entered the gates of a monastery. Soon after this, he was told to take twelve other monks and go out and start a new community. "Away they went, single file, northward through the wilderness to the headwaters of the River Aube. . . . There in a deep valley, gloomy with heavy forests," the twenty-four-year-old monk— St. Bernard of Clairvaux—and his followers built the Abbey of Clairvaux.

For the next thirty-four years Bernard served the Lord in this region, preaching the gospel, praying, and reaching out to those in need in the surrounding areas. So compelling was he that young women warned their lovers, "Go not near the monastery of Bernard, else he will take the sword from thy hand, and replace it with a Bible!" and "mothers hid their sons, wives their husbands, companions their friends" to prevent them from being brought under his influence.

Bernard's sole motivation was his love of Christ. In an era before the Reformation heart cry of "salvation by faith," Bernard spoke of his deep *love* for Christ, and he recorded that love in verse—verse that lives on. Today in churches we sing his verses that illustrate Christ's death on the cross: "O sacred Head, now wounded; With grief and shame weighed down . . . . Yet, though despised and gory, I *joy to call Thee mine!*" And we also sing his well-known hymn, "Jesus! the Very Thought of Thee."[13]

Surely he took up our infirmities and carried our sorrows, yet we considered him stricken by God, smitten by him, and afflicted. But he was pierced for our transgressions, he was crushed for our iniquities; the punishment that brought us peace was upon him, and by his wounds we are healed. We all, like sheep, have gone astray, each of us has turned to his own way; and the Lord has laid on him the iniquity of us all. He was oppressed and afflicted, yet he did not open his mouth; he was led like a lamb to the slaughter, as a sheep before her shearers is silent, so he did not open his mouth.

*Isaiah 53:4–7.*

# "BEFORE YOU WERE BORN I SET YOU APART"

As a vaudeville actor, he was, in the minds of many of his admirers, the epitome of the bad taste. "Among his props were plumpers which enabled him instantly to look like Henry VIII, with his arctoid jowls, doing a delectable love scene with a court-lady. He possessed an assortment of fearful wads, transforming him at will into a hunch-back . . . cripple. . . . He had, moreover, a line of turbulent sex-patter, so intimate that it would embarrass an Embarcadero stevedore."

It was that "talent" that brought him from his birthplace in Liverpool to San Francisco in 1850, after he had been working at various night spots for some seventeen years. "But to the theatre world of San Francisco he was intolerable," and there he was confronted with great hostility. But in the midst of this rejection, "somewhere in San Francisco's underworld, he entered the ancient mystery of Conviction of Sin. So mightily did the Spirit assault him that he decided to return to Liverpool to visit his family. They might help. They were humble Christians."

He arrived home to find only two older sisters still living. There, through the encouragement and prayers of his sisters, he became convinced that he had not committed the "unpardonable sin," as he had feared, and he was converted. But his conversion did not end his struggle with God. He began having dreams, and in one of those dreams a man was shouting as he walked through the town, "You will find it written in the first chapter of the prophet Jeremiah, and the fifth verse." He arose and read the verse in which God told Jeremiah that before his birth he was ordained a prophet.

With that somber call from God and with the encouragement of his sisters, the vaudeville actor—woefully unprepared for the ministry—set out to preach the gospel. His name, John Hambleton, has been lost in history, but he was a powerful preacher in his day on the streets of Liverpool. And sometimes he did not preach at all. One day while attending the brawling, drunken Yorkshire Fair, he climbed up on a wall and stood silently holding his Bible for more than an hour. "The effect was tremendous. The rowdies came out of the saloon, a great crowd gathered, gazing up at the silent figure. Thereupon street preachers began to address the mob with fiery effect."[14]

**The word of the Lord came to me, saying, "Before I formed you in the womb I knew you, before you were born I set you apart; I appointed you as a prophet to the nations."**

**"Ah, Sovereign Lord," I said, "I do not know how to speak; I am only a child."**

**But the Lord said to me, "Do not say, 'I am only a child.' You must go to everyone I send you to and say whatever I command you. Do not be afraid of them, for I am with you and will rescue you," declares the Lord.**

*Jeremiah 1:4–8.*

# "IF I HAVE CHEATED, I WILL PAY BACK"

The story of Zacchaeus is the story of a converted tax collector, but it bears a strong resemblance in many ways to a story of a converted tax cheater. Even as tax collectors through the centuries have benefited by cheating the taxpayers, taxpayers have responded by cheating the tax collectors. It is often a vicious contest to see who can defraud the other out of the most money. The sympathy, however, lies with the taxpayer, who is often the "little man" who is being oppressed by a heavy-handed political regime through the intimidation of the tax collector.

This cycle of dishonesty is part of life in France, a nation of small shopkeepers whose very livelihood depends on cheating the tax collector. Many of these proprietors keep two sets of accounts—one for their private use and one for the government tax officials. So it was with Jean, a small shopkeeper in Bordeaux, who worked long hours with virtually nothing to show for his labors. Even his best efforts to beguile the Paris tax collector left him very little for his family. His life was depressing and without purpose, until the day when a missionary entered his shop to make a purchase.

Before leaving the shop, this foreigner shared his faith with Jean, and for the first time the shopkeeper realized that there was more to life than he had ever supposed. "In the next few minutes he learned that money was not his greatest need; what he must have was a new birth, a fresh beginning."

As he grew in faith, Jean became convinced that his lifestyle must be radically altered and that he could no longer lie about how much income he was making at his little shop. When the time came to submit his tax forms, he filled them out in full and paid the required amount of taxes. The local tax clerk was stunned, and word spread like wildfire among the shopkeepers. Jean's wife was outraged, and his neighbors were convinced that he had lost his mind. When they inquired about his foolish actions, he could only explain that God had made him a different man.

Not long after this incident, Jean was surprised to receive a check from the local tax collector, who insisted that he adjust Jean's tax bill since the shopkeeper had overpaid. Cheating was part of the system, and the clerk was determined that he would carry out the function even if Jean would not. In the process, however, word had spread far and wide of one simple transformed life.[15]

When Jesus reached the spot, he looked up and said to him, "Zacchaeus, come down immediately. I must stay at your house today." So he came down at once and welcomed him gladly.

All the people saw this and began to mutter, "He has gone to be the guest of a 'sinner.'"

But Zacchaeus stood up and said to the Lord, "Look, Lord! Here and now I give half of my possessions to the poor, and if I have cheated anybody out of anything, I will pay back four times the amount."

*Luke 19:5–8.*

# "DEATH HAS BEEN SWALLOWED UP IN VICTORY"

The year was 1896. The setting was Mboga, deep in the heart of the Congo forest. Here a young man began his missionary career utterly unprepared for the witchcraft and drunkenness and fierce hostility he would encounter in preaching the gospel. But God had called him to this work, and he refused to give up. After two years of difficult labor, he won his first convert, and immediately suffered retaliation. His hut was set on fire while he was in it. He escaped, but refused to flee. Indeed, he began rebuilding while the ground was still smoldering.

"He was ordered to leave the country; he replied that God had sent him and he must stay. He was beaten severely with a whip of hippopotamus hide, and beaten again. But it did not move him at all. He went straight on with his work, teaching the people who gathered round him in the little primitive church. Another beating—the worst and the last. He was left for dead, his body being cast into the bush. Of any life in him, the chief grimly said, the wild beasts would soon make an end."

But the missionary survived. "Mboga was stirred to its depths; everyone flocked to see the dead man who had come to life again, foremost among them the startled chief. . . . He declared with weeping that God had spoken to him. After due teaching he was baptized."

Who was this uncommon missionary who made a center for Christian teaching in the Congo forest? He was Apolo Kivublaya, an African, who had first heard the gospel from Alexander MacKay, the great Scottish missionary to Uganda. He had not forgotten that early teaching during his years of military service in Uganda, and one day, alone in the African bush, he sensed that the hand of the Lord was on him. He began reading his Bible and was baptized, and then, "with little knowledge and few mental gifts, but burning to tell others of his Savior and Lord," set out to reach an unevangelized tribe.

After he established his mission work in Mboga, Apolo penetrated further into the Congo forest. He was the first to offer portions of Scriptures to the Pygmies—his primer being printed by the Bible Society in 1926. The following year he was given special honors for his extraordinary missionary service by the Church Missionary Society during its jubilee celebration.[16]

"Death has been swallowed up in victory."

"Where, O death, is your victory? Where, O death, is your sting?"

The sting of death is sin, and the power of sin is the law. But thanks be to God! He gives us the victory through our Lord Jesus Christ. Therefore, my dear brothers, stand firm. Let nothing move you. Always give yourselves fully to the work of the Lord, because you know that your labor in the Lord is not in vain.

*1 Corinthians 15:54b–58.*

## "THE CHOSEN LADY"

Who was this "chosen lady" to whom the apostle John addresses a letter? Whoever she was, she has been lost in history, as have many other "chosen ladies" through the centuries—including Twyla Ludwig.

From the time she was eleven years old, Twyla had been convinced that God was calling her into the ministry, but her early adult life offered little promise that the calling would be fulfilled. She married an unconverted farmer, who had no interest in Christian service whatsoever. Even after his conversion, he resisted any thought of ministry. He was thirty-six and she was twenty-seven, and he was convinced they were far too old for a new vocation. But her determination was strong, and so it was that she and her husband and their two children set out for Kenya in 1927.

Mamma Ludwig's ministry in Kenya was one that had a powerful impact on the people, as her son later related in a biography of her. She was a strong leader, as is illustrated by an incident her son recalls.

"The missionaries took turns with the native evangelists in speaking at the Kima church. The preacher for a certain occasion was generally determined by the one who felt he had a 'message.' This time Mother announced that she wanted to take her turn.

"Filled to the brim with her concern over the plight of native women, she spoke with tears and deathlike sincerity to the congregation that jammed the little building to the doors. . . . Unfortunately for Dad and me, Mother got so carried away with her defense of the Obunyore women, she forgot that she was supposed to stop at noon. . . . Finally, I could endure it no longer. . . . I got up from my seat on the platform and slipped out the side door. Back at home, I was joined by Dad at one fifteen.

"Mother made her grand entrance at two o'clock. 'So you walked out on me,' she exclaimed. 'You should have stayed with me. Twenty-two people accepted Christ, and all of the men learned what I think of wife-beating.'

"Dad wasn't sure whether Mother was happier about the converts or about what she'd been able to tell the men in regard to treatment of their wives. But he was delighted that it had turned out well, for he always rejoiced in Mother's success and bragged about it wherever he went." Mamma Ludwig was indeed a "chosen lady."[17]

To the chosen lady and her children, whom I love in the truth—and not I only, but also all who know the truth—because of the truth, which lives in us and will be with us forever:

Grace, mercy and peace from God the Father and from Jesus Christ, the Father's Son, will be with us in truth and love.

It has given me great joy to find some of your children walking in the truth, just as the Father commanded us. And now, dear lady, I am not writing a new command but one we have had from the beginning. I ask that we love one another. And this is love: that we walk in obedience to his commands. As you have heard from the beginning, his command is that you walk in love.

*2 John 1–6.*

# "BE SHEPHERDS OF THE CHURCH OF GOD"

The apostle Paul gave very solemn instructions to the elders of the church at Ephesus in his farewell address—instructions that ministers today often neglect. One minister who took these instructions very seriously was the great Puritan preacher of the seventeenth century, Richard Baxter.

Baxter was a master at preparing and delivering sermons. He filled his church to capacity in Kidderminster, England, and then five galleries were added on to accommodate the crowds. Though he was a very sickly man, he preached powerfully—"a dying man to dying men," as he described his ministry. "How few ministers preach with all their might!" he wrote. "There is nothing more unsuitable to such a business than to be slight and dull. What! speak coldly for God and for men's salvation! Let the people see that you are in earnest;—Men will not cast away their dearest pleasures upon a drowsy request."

But more important to him than his public preaching was his private visitation with church members. "We should know every person that belongs to our charge," he wrote, "for how can we 'take heed to the flock of God,' if we do not know them? Does not a careful shepherd look after every individual sheep, and a good physician attend every particular patient? Why then should not the shepherds and the physicians of the church take heed to every member of their charge?"

Baxter did not become involved in visitation initially. He thought it would be too much work for him and that the people would object to him inquiring into their spiritual well-being. But after he initiated the program, he wrote, "I find the difficulties to be nothing to what I imagined, and I experience the benefits and comforts of the work to be such that I would not wish to have neglected it for all the riches in the world. I cannot say that one family hath refused or that many persons have shifted it off."

He soon began involving lay people in this ministry, and its effects were remarkable on the town of Kidderminster: "When I first came there," he wrote, "there was about one family in a street that worshiped God; when I came away there were some streets where there was not one family that did not so."[18]

> "Keep watch over yourselves and all the flock of which the Holy Spirit has made you overseers. Be shepherds of the church of God, which he bought with his own blood. I know that after I leave, savage wolves will come in among you and will not spare the flock. Even from your own number men will arise and distort the truth in order to draw away disciples after them. So be on your guard! Remember that for three years I never stopped warning each of you night and day with tears."
>
> *Acts 20:28–31.*

# "LET US LOVE WITH ACTIONS"

Sam Turner, a young man from the Bronx, had traveled to the Baliem Valley of Irian Jaya for the thrill of adventure and to discover who the people were. He had studied anthropology and was interested in seeing, firsthand, cultures that had not been spoiled by the outside world. He believed that many of the cultures had been ruined, and he had utter contempt for missionaries who introduced new religious ideas and new lifestyles.

After visiting a remote government post in Wamena, Sam began a three-day journey to the valley of Mbuwa. Here he had become so sick from malaria that he languished in a state of delirium and unconsciousness for days, saved only by the tender care of a native nurse and his family from the Nduga tribe. When Sam regained consciousness, he discovered that he was being nursed back to health by a Christian family. They were a family transformed by the gospel of Christ that had been brought to this remote region by dedicated missionaries. Aser was a trained nurse who cared for the health needs of people in the region, and without him, Sam probably never would have survived.

"How it touched him when Aser killed a chicken and a duck from his small supply of animals so that Sam could eat meat to regain his strength. He remembered how the Ndugas had taken him in so wholeheartedly, how the women had given him sweet potatoes when they saw him on the trail, how little children brought cooked sweet potatoes to him in the men's house in the mornings. Everyone did these kind deeds with no idea of asking for pay, just out of the kindness of their hearts."

Despite language barriers, Sam was able to communicate with the people enough to understand that it was their Christian faith that was motivating them to show him kindness. No longer did they seek to kill their enemies or strangers who came uninvited into their village. Their lives had been transformed.

So overwhelmed was Sam with the Christian love of these people that after he left their valley he sought out missionaries on his way to the coast. He requested a New Testament and any other books that could tell him more about the faith of these people who had showed him so much love. Through the act of showing love, the gospel of Christ had been carried from the Baliem Valley to a young man from the Bronx, who otherwise never may have discovered that telling mark of Christianity.[19]

This is how we know what love is: Jesus Christ laid down his life for us. And we ought to lay down our lives for our brothers. If anyone has material possessions and sees his brother in need but has no pity on him, how can the love of God be in him? Dear children, let us not love with words or tongue but with actions and in truth. This then is how we know that we belong to the truth, and how we set our hearts at rest in his presence.

*1 John 3:16–19.*

# "GO NOW TO YOUR COUNTRYMEN IN EXILE"

These verses from Ezekiel, especially the words "Go, get thee to them of the captivity, unto the children of thy people, and speak to them" (KJV), changed the course of life for a young woman, as was evident in 1900 at the International Prison Congress that was convened in the Russian city of St. Petersburg. Attending the conference were dignitaries from around the world, including the Tsar of Russia, who opened the meetings.

One of the speakers was a French sociologist who maintained that hardened criminals were beyond the hope of rehabilitation. Following the address, a small woman rose from her seat and made her way to the platform, unannounced, asking for permission to speak. The startled chairman gave her the floor, and she proceeded to make her challenge to the assembly: "There is, gentlemen, one agency by which every criminal can be transformed, even one who is, as they say, incorrigible. That is the power of God. Laws and systems cannot change the heart of a single criminal but God can. I am persuaded that we ought above all to occupy ourselves with the souls of prisoners, and with their spiritual life."

So convincing was her message that when she was through, the Congress applauded. The woman was not unknown to many of them. She was Mathilde Wrede, a Finnish Baroness, who was known by many as "The Angel of the Prisons."

As a young girl, Mathilde had gone to a revival meeting instead of accompanying her father to a social function. There she was converted, much to the embarrassment of her father. Soon after that, a prisoner was sent to her home on his work assignment. As he was repairing a lock, she struck up a conversation and shared with him her conversion experience. He was impressed with her sincerity and told her she ought to come to the prison and give her testimony to all that were in chains.

She agreed to go, but, due to poor health, did not commit herself to prison work until she was convinced that God was speaking directly to her through his call to Ezekiel. Once convinced, for the next forty years she spent her days—and often nights—in prison. She brought the message of Christ to those with no other hope, and she took ex-convicts into her home and helped them start over. No one else was so loved and admired by Finish prisoners.[20]

"But I will make you as unyielding and as hardened as they are. I will make your forehead like the hardest stone, harder than flint. Do not be afraid of them or terrified by them, though they are a rebellious house."

And he said to me, "Son of man, listen carefully and take to heart all the words I speak to you. Go now to your countrymen in exile and speak to them. Say to them, 'This is what the Sovereign Lord says,' whether they listen or fail to listen."

*Ezekiel 3:8–11.*

# "A MESSAGE ON MARTYRDOM"

John Coleridge Patteson was a missionary to the South Pacific and the first Anglican bishop of Melanesia. He was brought up in wealth and social status and was educated at Eton and Oxford. He was a greatnephew of the famous English poet Samuel Taylor Coleridge and could have enjoyed a life in English high society. Instead he chose to live a solitary life in the islands of the South Seas.

Rather than settling on one island and limiting his ministry to a small population, Patteson—a brilliant linguist—established a school for boys on one island and then sought students from various neighboring islands. He taught boys in twenty different languages and prepared them to return to their islands as evangelists. He loved these boys and despised the European traders who sought to enslave them. He praised their culture and intelligence, and indignantly wrote, "I wonder what people ought to call sandalwood traders and slave masters if they call my Melanesians savages."

Patteson was optimistic about his missionary outreach, but as he continued his work, storm clouds loomed on the horizon. Europeans had migrated to the islands and were developing plantations. The need for labor sparked a new business that was known as *blackbirding*—kidnapping island boys and selling them to plantation owners as slaves. "Gangs of white seamen would go ashore and carry off men and youths at gunpoint."

The reaction of the islanders was, not surprisingly, bitter and revengeful. White men were regarded as the enemy, and no one was safe. Patteson realized the danger, but he continued the ministry, fully aware how closely it resembled blackbirding in the eyes of islanders who might mistake him for a seafaring slaver.

On September 21, 1871, while on one of his tours, Patteson made his final island stop. "That morning he had been teaching some of the schoolboys on the ship, reading them the story of the martyrdom of Stephen concluding by saying: 'We are all Christians here on this ship. Any one of us might be asked to give up his life for God, just as Stephen was in the Bible. This might happen to any one of us, to you or to me. It might happen today.'" It did happen that day. Patteson, the target of revenge, was clubbed to death by angry men who had lost their sons to slave traders.[21]

When they heard this, they were furious and gnashed their teeth at him. But Stephen, full of the Holy Spirit, looked up to heaven and saw the glory of God, and Jesus standing at the right hand of God. "Look," he said, "I see heaven open and the Son of Man standing at the right hand of God."

At this they covered their ears and, yelling at the top of their voices, they all rushed at him, dragged him out of the city and began to stone him. Meanwhile, the witnesses laid their clothes at the feet of a young man named Saul.

While they were stoning him, Stephen prayed, "Lord Jesus, receive my spirit." Then he fell on his knees and cried out, "Lord, do not hold this sin against them." When he had said this, he fell asleep.

*Acts 7:54–60.*

# "BRINGING HER FOOD FROM AFAR"

This familiar passage in Proverbs focuses on the worth of a woman in her home and community, but it can be applied to women everywhere who use their God-given gifts in the Lord's service. This is illustrated in the ministry of Stella Cox, a missionary to Japan, of whom it could be said, "she is like the merchant ships bringing her food from afar."

Stella and her husband Ralph have served in Japan with TEAM since 1952. The idea of offering American cooking classes did not occur to her until two years after they arrived when the wives of some government officials requested that she teach them the Western way of cooking. Soon others heard about her expertise and she began teaching additional classes, working closely with Japanese women to develop recipes that were suitable for that culture. She quickly learned to substitute ingredients that were readily available for those that were not, while maintaining the flavor of the dish.

The classes have been far more than a cross-cultural educational tool. They have provided opportunity for social interaction and for sharing the gospel. Stella spends the first hour of the class demonstrating to the women how to prepare four different recipes, and then, before they eat what has been prepared, she teaches them a Christian song and tells a Bible story. When the women leave, she gives them the recipes of the day, along with a copy of the song, a printed Bible verse, and some Christian literature.

Through this ministry Stella has become one of Japan's "experts" in American cooking and has published her own cookbook, *Aunt Stella's Easy American Cakes*. But far more important than her recipes have been the friends she has made through her ministry and the women she has led to faith in Christ. One woman attended her classes for nine years, hearing the gospel each time, before she committed her life to the Lord. Another woman who was converted through the cooking classes has since become a zealous evangelist herself and has witnessed the fruit of her labors in her own family.

Cooking classes are only one aspect of Stella's ministry. With her husband she is actively engaged in church planting. They have a goal of planting one hundred new churches before the twenty-first century begins, more than twenty of which had been started by 1988.[22]

A wife of noble character who can find? She is worth far more than rubies. Her husband has full confidence in her and lacks nothing of value. She brings him good, not harm, all the days of her life. She selects wool and flax and works with eager hands. She is like the merchant ships, bringing her food from afar.

*Proverbs 31:10–14.*

## "I WILL STRENGTHEN YOU AND HELP YOU"

After eighteen years as a missionary in Italy, Margarita, a Swiss-born missionary, was deeply discouraged. She had made no converts and she began to doubt her effectiveness and her call. Over the years, she had become good friends of the Sottile family, and she longed to win them to Christ, but they were not interested in her religion. When she heard that the evangelist Stephen Olford would be coming to her area, she determined that these meetings would indicate whether or not God's blessing was on her work. She prayed, "God, I'm going to pray that the Sottiles receive the Lord now, because if they don't, I'm going to give up on them, and I'm going to give up on the mission field."

It was out of their love and respect for Margarita that the Sottiles agreed to attend the first meeting. There they heard the gospel preached from a pulpit for the first time. "The whole family was touched by the Word of God, but nobody wanted to admit it," recalled Gaetano Sottile. "We went back each night of the crusade and accepted the Lord on September 23, 1974."

Gaetano found that his life was revolutionized that night. "Instead of wanting to become a professional soccer player or go into the Italian navy, I wanted to preach the Gospel." Through the help of a wealthy businessman, he enrolled at Columbia Bible College, and after graduation returned to Italy with a mission team where he started a Christian radio station and founded a church on Mount Aetna.

Gaetano's greatest success has come in his evangelistic crusades, such as the one he conducted in Naples. "Because the crime rate dropped so dramatically after the crusade, the city of Naples gave the property for a church. Today the church members number 240."

One of the converts at Gaetano's tent crusade in Naples was Franco Balsamo. "So clearly did Sottile communicate the biblical truths that Balsamo realized that his own understanding had been imperfect. Night after night he returned with a yearning for more spiritual truth. One evening he went forward to accept Christ as his Lord and Savior." It was a courageous decision because Franco was the president of the Mormon church in Naples.

God demonstrated his faithfulness to Margarita after eighteen lean years, and she was gloriously reassured that she had not labored in vain.[23]

"I took you from the ends of the earth, from its farthest corners I called you. I said, 'You are my servant'; I have chosen you and have not rejected you. So do not fear, for I am with you; do not be dismayed, for I am your God. I will strengthen you and help you; I will uphold you with my righteous right hand. . . . For I am the Lord, your God, who takes hold of your right hand and says to you, Do not fear; I will help you."

*Isaiah 41:9–10, 13.*

# "REMEMBER THE WONDERS HE HAS DONE"

Pandita Ramabai was one of India's most noted Christian leaders during the early decades of the twentieth century. She was initially hesitant to become deeply involved in the massive responsibility that would come with caring for the needy all around her and she prayed that God would send others to do the work.

"I read the inspiring books, *The Story of the China Inland Mission*, *The Lord's Dealings with George Mueller*, and *The Life of John G. Paton, Founder of the New Hebrides Mission*. I was greatly impressed with the experiences of these three great men, Mr. Hudson Taylor, Mr. Mueller, and Mr. Paton, all of whom have gone to be with the Lord. I wondered, after reading their lives, if it were not possible to trust the Lord in India as in other countries. I wished very much that there were some missions founded in this country which would be a testimony to the Lord's faithfulness to His people and the truthfulness of what the Bible says in a practical way.

"I questioned in my mind over and over again why some missionaries did not come forward to found Faith Missions in this country. Then the Lord said to me, 'Why don't you begin to do this yourself, instead of wishing for others to do it? How easy it is for anyone to wish that some one else would do a difficult thing instead of doing it himself.' I was greatly rebuked by the 'still, small voice' which spoke to me. I did not know then that there were some Faith Missions in India."

It was this call from God and a severe famine that propelled Ramabai into the faith mission work that would become known as the Mukti Mission. The ministry was largely to young widows and orphans who had no means of support. When they were brought into the mission, they were "filthy in the extreme, clad in rags, suffering from sores, and all kinds of ailments."

In many ways Ramabai's mission work exemplified what was best in the work of Taylor, Mueller, and Paton combined. Like Mueller, she focused on humanitarian work for homeless youngsters, and like Taylor and Paton she reached out in evangelistic endeavors. "The vision of the evangelization of India by her own people was an ever expanding one to Ramabai. Such work as that of the Gospel Bands sent out from Mukti . . . became a permanent feature of the work"—a "force of four hundred women ready for service, filled with the Holy Spirit, available to help publish the good news of salvation among the heathen." Ramabai had "remembered the wonders" God had done through others and knew he could do the same through her.[24]

Give thanks to the Lord, call on his name; make known among the nations what he has done. Sing to him, sing praise to him; tell of all his wonderful acts. Glory in his holy name; let the hearts of those who seek the Lord rejoice. Look to the Lord and his strength; seek his face always. Remember the wonders he has done, his miracles, and the judgments he pronounced.

*1 Chronicles 16:8–12.*

# "LOOK AFTER ORPHANS AND WIDOWS IN THEIR DISTRESS"

What is true religion? William A. Passavant, an outstanding leader of the Lutheran church in nineteenth-century America, answered that question, in part, through his personal testimony. "When after tears and strong cryings to God I was reduced to the confession that I could do nothing toward meriting salvation, it pleased God by the foolishness of preaching to work in me the saving trust in Christ. . . . The *consciousness* of personal salvation is the greatest of all consolations, especially to a minister of the Word. It brings him into a new world of life and love. In all the trying experiences through which we poor ministers must pass nothing is more helpful than this experience."

But to Passavant, true religion was far more than a salvation "experience." He was a pastor, an editor, and a traveling missionary. "For fifty years he edited *The Missionary Herald* of his church and through it moulded the life of American Lutheranism." The most extraordinary aspect of his public ministry was his devotion to the needs of orphans and widows and those who needed medical care. "Only when the church goes about doing good," he wrote, "both in preaching the gospel and healing the sick, is she reproducing the life of Christ in the best and holiest form."

According to one writer, "A chance visit to a London orphanage first turned his attention to this form of Christian testimony. He began, himself to save money, omitting a meal or walking instead of riding. A considerable purse accumulated. Out of it came a little hospital with beds for a few sick folk, and from this, in turn, a lovely constellation of charitable institutions."

Wherever he went, Passavant was confronted by needy people. He organized orphan homes, and recruited workers—often with little planning or little assurance that operating funds would be forthcoming. He viewed the work as a venture in faith. He personally cleaned vacant houses to use them as shelters and he met orphans at the train station. So great were the health needs of the immigrants in Chicago that he vowed to establish a hospital.

"We got to Chicago in a drizzling rain," wrote one of his volunteer assistants. "The old house had been painted but not cleaned. . . .As soon as we had warm water we began to clean house. Dr. Passavant put up the beds, and we were ready to open. A Swedish woman brought her little boy, Hermann, who had a crushed foot. . . . Dr. Passavant helped the physician to wash and dress him. The house was soon full of patients." Indeed, this was true religion, and it was an examples for others to follow.[25]

If anyone considers himself religious and yet does not keep a tight rein on his tongue, he deceives himself and his religion is worthless. Religion that God our Father accepts as pure and faultless is this: to look after orphans and widows in their distress and to keep oneself from being polluted by the world.

*James 1:26–27.*

# "SINCE WE HAVE BEEN JUSTIFIED WE HAVE PEACE"

Robert Moffat is remembered as the great pioneer missionary to South Africa. He was not the first missionary to enter that region, but he persevered over the years, despite his sufferings, and developed into a man of character whose life reflected the Holy Spirit's power.

He was born in Scotland on December 21, 1795, and began learning the trade of a gardener as a youth. At eighteen, while attending a Methodist meeting, he sought God for salvation but could find no sense of security. Then one day while studying the Bible he found the assurance he needed in Romans 5:1. "I felt that being justified by faith, I had peace with God through the Lord Jesus Christ," he later testified.

Secure in the knowledge of his salvation, Moffatt sought out training for Christian ministry, and was then commissioned to go to South Africa with the London Missionary Society. In South Africa, he sought permission to travel north to bring the gospel to the unreached tribes there, but confronted one roadblock after another. The governor was suspicious that missionaries were secretly aiding runaway slaves.

Finally permission to travel was granted, and Moffat and two other missionaries headed into a vast territory that was ruled by the fearsome African chief, Afrikaner, who had terrorized the Dutch settlers encroaching on his land. Before Moffat began the journey, stories circulated that Afrikaner had been converted. None of the Dutch settlers believed it, and they were certain that he would be killed by the chief. "He will make a drinking cup out of your skull," they warned.

When Moffat met Afrikaner face to face, he knew immediately that he had truly been converted—that he had been justified through faith. The peace of Christ was evident in his life. He invited the chief to return to Cape Town with him to demonstrate the power of the gospel, but Afrikaner trembled at the thought—he would be an easy target for Dutch settlers who wanted revenge. Finally he was persuaded to come, disguised as Moffat's servant. As they passed through villages, settlers were shocked to see Moffatt. They had heard that he had been killed by the chief. Little did they know that the chief was standing in their presence! In Cape Town, Afrikaner's testimony made a powerful impact on officials, and Moffatt was given permission to plant a mission in the North.[26]

Therefore, since we have been justified through faith, we have peace with God through our Lord Jesus Christ, through whom we have gained access by faith into this grace in which we now stand. And we rejoice in the hope of the glory of God. Not only so, but we also rejoice in our sufferings, because we know that suffering produces perseverance, perseverance, character, and character, hope. And hope does not disappoint us, because God has poured out his love into our hearts by the Holy Spirit, whom he has given us.

*Romans 5:1–5.*

## "SOME TO BE EVANGELISTS"

Evangelism almost seems to come naturally to some people—people to whom grace has been apportioned to be evangelists. After he was converted, Tom Skinner became such an individual. Born and raised in Harlem, he lived a double life as a model student and preacher's son, on the one hand, and as a gang leader, on the other. He was converted in the midst of this duplicity, and immediately he began sharing his faith with others.

The decision to go public with his newfound faith was not easy, as he testified. "You don't just walk up to a gang of fellows that you've been leading around for two years in rioting, looting, fighting and lawbreaking and say, 'Well, guys, it's been nice knowing you. So long.' No one quits a gang. In fact, just two weeks before I had personally broken the arms and legs of two fellows who told me *they* were going to quit. And these fellows got off easy."

But whether or not to tell his gang members about his conversion was not an option for Tom. He had made a promise to God, and he decided to make the announcement in front of the entire gang. "I moved into the smoky room and walked to the front," he later recalled. "There were 129 fellows in that room. Every one of them carried a knife. . . . You could have heard a pin drop. No one spoke. No one even moved. I walked down the aisle and out into the night air, half expecting a knife to come tearing into my back or a bullet to dig into my flesh. But nothing! I walked out without one person raising a hand against me."

Two nights later, Tom led "The Mop"—the "number two man in the gang" to the Lord, and in the weeks that followed several more of his old gang members were converted. Besides personal witnessing, he began preaching on the streets to passers-by. It was on one such occasion that members of the rival "Diablo" gang spotted him. Within minutes they surrounded him, threatening his life. He calmly explained what had happened in his life, and before the encounter was over, he writes, "we led at least twenty-five members of the 'Diablo' gang to Jesus Christ. Many of them prayed openly on the street."

Tom's ministry of evangelism was also effective in the local churches—indeed, so effective that some local pastors feared his ministry would be a threat to their own. His goal, however, was not to start a rival movement, but simply to reach out with the gospel and bring people to Christ.[27]

**But to each one of us grace has been given as Christ apportioned it. . . . It was he who gave some to be apostles, some to be prophets, some to be evangelists, and some to be pastors and teachers, to prepare God's people for works of service, so that the body of Christ may be built up until we all reach unity in the faith and in the knowledge of the Son of God and become mature, attaining the whole measure of the fullness of Christ.**

*Ephesians 4:7, 11–13.*

# "I SING IN THE SHADOW OF YOUR WINGS"

There were many individuals who helped spread the revival fires that swept through Scandinavia during the last decades of the nineteenth century, not the least of whom was a young woman named Lina Sandell Berg. She had grown up in a Christian home; she was the daughter of a pastor, and from the time of her youth enjoyed composing lyrics for hymns. It was only after a devastating tragedy, however, that she released the deepest emotions of her heart in verse. One of those outpourings of her heart became the familiar hymn "Day By Day."

Linda was in her mid-twenties when she accompanied her father on a tragic sea voyage. "The ship gave a sudden lurch and Lina's father fell overboard and drowned before the eyes of his devoted daughter." All three verses of "Day By Day" reflect her deep emotion—especially the third verse: "Help me then in every tribulation so to trust Thy promises, O Lord, that I lose not faith's sweet consolation offered me within Thy holy word. Help me, Lord, when toil and trouble meeting, e'er to take, as from a father's hand, one by one, the days, the moments fleeting, till I reach the promised land."

Lina sang her own hymns, but their great popularity was brought to the people by the beloved Jenny Lind, known as the "Swedish Nightingale," and Oscar Ahnfelt, the composer of the music for "Day By Day." Of him, Lina once said, "Ahnfelt has sung my songs into the hearts of the people."

There was great opposition from the state church to the revivals that were sweeping the Scandinavian countries, and at one point the Swedish monarch King Karl XV was petitioned to outlaw Ahnfelt's singing and preaching. The king demanded that Ahnfelt appear before him to plead his case. Ahnfelt was apprehensive about the meeting, but he was determined to sing his way to the king's heart. He requested that Lina write a special hymn for the occasion, and within days she presented him with a verse opening with the question "Who is it that knocketh upon your heart's door?"

"The king listened with moist eyes. When Ahnfelt had finished, King Karl gripped him by the hand and exclaimed, 'You may sing as much as you desire in both of my kingdoms.' "[28]

I will praise you as long as I live, and in your name I will lift up my hands. My soul will be satisfied as with the richest of foods; with singing lips my mouth will praise you.

On my bed I remember you; I think of you through the watches of the night. Because you are my help, I sing in the shadow of your wings. My soul clings to you; your right hand upholds me.

*Psalm 63:4–8.*

# "REVEALED TO LITTLE CHILDREN"

A simple incident of forgetfulness led to a change in a man's life and opened up an avenue of ministry that would send ripples throughout the country. The setting was nineteenth-century Edinburgh, Scotland, at a time when there was a spiritual renewal in the Scottish churches. E. Payson Hammond, an American seminary student who was reveling in this revival, had, only minutes before, left a church service. He suddenly turned back, realizing that he had forgotten his coat, but by the time he reached the church the door was locked. He shivered in the wind as he pounded on the door.

"Presently the door opened and a little six-year-old girl appeared. Hammond asked for his coat and the little one hurried to get it. Looking inside, the young theologue was surprised to see the vestry full of little girls. They were having a prayer meeting! Furthermore, he noted, there was not a grown-up in the crowd," and "not one of them was more than eight or nine."

When the little girl returned empty-handed, explaining that she could not reach his coat, Payson entered the church. He then actually could hear the words of the prayers. He was dumbfounded.

*What did it mean?* he wondered. *How could little children pray like that? What had brought them together without adult prompting? . . . Of course! They were born again! They were just as thoroughly converted as he had been a dozen years earlier in the Connecticut Valley!*

"That day in Musselburgh, Payson Hammond made a vow. If God would confirm in blessing what seemed to be His clear direction, he would devote his entire life to the winning of children for Jesus Christ! As a result, Hammond was used of God to sweep thousands of children in Britain and the United States to the gates of glory. He was assisted by the winsome genius of a rugged individual named Josiah Spiers, who knew no other world than the merry, uncluttered world of children. Spiers became the founder of the Children's Special Service Mission of England."

Payson was ahead of his time. Dwight L. Moody wrote to him and pleaded with him to come to Chicago to hold evangelistic meetings for children in his congregation. "You do not know," he lamented, "how much infidelity there is in the church in regard to children's conversions."[29]

At that time Jesus, full of joy through the Holy Spirit, said, "I praise you, Father, Lord of heaven and earth, because you have hidden these things from the wise and learned, and revealed them to little children. Yes, Father, for this was your good pleasure.

"All things have been committed to me by my Father. No one knows who the Son is except the Father, and no one knows who the Father is except the Son and those to whom the Son chooses to reveal him."

*Luke 10:21–22.*

# "THE HOPE OF SHARING IN THE HARVEST"

Although the apostle Paul is speaking primarily of financial remuneration in this passage, the admonition not to muzzle an ox, and the reference to the "hope of sharing in the harvest" has broader implications. This freedom and this hope ought to be accessible to all who seek to serve the Lord. That this has not always been the case is evident in the struggles of Mary McLeod Bethune.

Mary was born in a cabin on a tiny farm in Mayesville, South Carolina in 1875. Her parents had both been slaves, and their lives in the post-Civil War South were little different than they had been during the years of slavery. Too poor to afford education for their children, they had little hope of rising above the poverty common to rural blacks who lived in the shadow of the white plantations.

But then one day a new world opened up for little Mary. The Mission Board of the Presbyterian Church had commissioned a Miss Wilson to go to Mayesville and open a school for black children. Mary's father gave the little money that he had saved for her expenses, and she gladly walked the five miles each day for her education.

So exceptional was she in her studies that she was offered a scholarship to continue her education at Scotia Seminary in North Carolina. From there she enrolled at Moody Bible Institute to prepare for missionary work in Africa. At Moody she found an environment in which she could thrive. "There were no feelings of race," she later recalled. "There we learned to look upon a man as a man, not as a Caucasian or a Negro. . . . under this benign influence, including that of Dwight L. Moody, a love for the whole human race, regardless of creed, class, or color, entered my soul and remains with me, thank God, to this day."

When she graduated from Moody, however, she faced rejection that she had not expected. The Presbyterian Board of Missions had no openings for black missionaries in Africa. Her dream was shattered. Mary followed the Board's suggestion that she go instead to Georgia and teach black children there. In the years that followed she went on to become one of America's leading black women of the twentieth century. She founded a black school that later became Bethune-Cookman College. As well as being a leader in educational and women's organizations, Mary was an advisor to President Franklin D. Roosevelt.[30]

Who serves as a soldier at his own expense? Who plants a vineyard and does not eat of its grapes? Who tends a flock and does not drink of the milk? Do I say this merely from a human point of view? Doesn't the Law say the same thing? For it is written in the Law of Moses: "Do not muzzle an ox while it is treading out the grain." Is it about oxen that God is concerned? Surely he says this for us, doesn't he? Yes, this was written for us, because when the plowman plows and the thresher threshes, they ought to do so in the hope of sharing in the harvest.

*1 Corinthians 9:7–10.*

# "HE WAS A TENTMAKER"

The tradition of missionary self-support or "tent-making" that the apostle Paul initiated in Corinth has been carried down through the centuries. Among those who served as "tentmakers" was William Carey, "the Father of Modern Missions," who began his ministry in India in 1793.

Carey's arrival in India was greeted with hostility, and he and his family were forced to live in the interior where they faced privations and disease. He was forced to live on borrowed money, and when he sought the aid of a chaplain from the East India Company, he was sent away "without even . . . refreshment after his long walk." It was a discouraging time. "All my friends are but One," he reflected, "but He is all sufficient."

Carey's fortunes did not turn around until he was able to secure a position as manager of an indigo plantation. In this situation, he "became a well-paid planter with a pleasant home and unrivaled opportunity for getting to know the language, the people, and their customs as he traveled far and wide buying the indigo crop and supervising the processes which turned it into the blue vegetable dye much prized in eighteenth-century Europe. In slack periods he could preach and teach."

In many respects this position was a perfect solution to Carey's financial problems, but that is not how his home missions board—which was sending him insufficient funds—assessed the matter. From them he received a letter deploring the fact that he had taken the position. They reminded him that they had commissioned him to be a missionary.

But in spite of their evaluation of the situation, Carey was indeed a missionary. In contrast to him was George Udny, his employer at the indigo plantation. Udny was a Christian businessman who devoted his time and effort to financial gain. Although he encouraged Carey in his ministry, Udny's primary focus was his indigo. For Carey, the only reason for being in India was to spread the gospel. Any extra money he earned beyond his family needs was devoted to Bible translation. In response to the home board's criticism, he wrote, "I am indeed poor, and always shall be until the Bible is published in Bengali and Hindustani and the people need no further instruction."

This position at the indigo plantation lasted only a few years, but later Carey was able to occupy another tentmaker position as a teacher at Fort William College. Again, like Paul, these occupations were secondary to his call to ministry.[1]

**After this, Paul left Athens and went to Corinth. There he met a Jew named Aquila, a native of Pontus, who had recently come from Italy with his wife Priscilla, because Claudius had ordered all the Jews to leave Rome. Paul went to see them, and because he was a tentmaker as they were, he stayed and worked with them. Every Sabbath he reasoned in the synagogue, trying to persuade Jews and Greeks.**

*Acts 18:1–4.*

# "WILL YOU HIDE YOURSELF FOREVER?"

"It is true that God does not allow himself to be conquered, and that the more one gives, the more one gains; but God sometimes hides himself, and then the Cup is very bitter." These words of Paul Le Jeune were the words of a discouraged missionary. He was not the first missionary, nor the last, who sometimes became so disheartened that he felt God had hidden himself.

Le Jeune, a Jesuit, arrived in French Canada in 1632, and became the first missionary in North America to translate portions of Scripture into the language of the Huron Indians. He lived with the Indians at an outpost more than seven hundred miles from the nearest city; he suffered privations and struggled with the language. "It was a language that often seemed impossible to grasp, not only because it bore no resemblance to his own French tongue, but because his Indian helpers delighted in teaching him obscene words in place of the right ones."

To complicate matters, his Indian language helper was very inconsistent. "I make conjugations, declensions and some little syntax, and a dictionary, with incredible trouble," he wrote, "for I was compelled sometimes to ask twenty questions to understand one word, so changeable was my master's way of teaching."

Le Jeune confessed that when he arrived in Canada, he felt "no particular affection" for the Indians, but that soon changed. "Seeing what I have already seen, I should be touched, had I heart of bronze. Would to God that those who can aid these poor souls and contribute something to their salvation could be here, if only for three days. I believe that a longing to help them would seize powerfully upon their souls."

In the midst of all his discouragement, Le Jeune did encounter times of consolation. He wrote of an Indian who was deeply interested in the gospel: "I instructed him about the Creation of the world, the Incarnation, and the Passion of the Son of God. We talked well into the night, everyone being asleep except him." The Indian later commented, "Oh, how unhappy I am that I am not able to pray to God as you do!" In the years that followed there were converts among the Indians, but many of them were killed when other tribes took advantage of their peaceful nature.[2]

How long, O Lord?
Will you hide
yourself forever?
How long will your
wrath burn like fire?
Remember how
fleeting is my life.
For what futility you
have created all
men! What man can
live and not see
death, or save
himself from the
power of the grave?

O Lord, where is
your former great
love, which in your
faithfulness you
swore to David?
Remember, Lord,
how your servant has
been mocked, how I
bear in my heart the
taunts of all nations,
the taunts with
which your enemies
have mocked, O
Lord, with which
they have mocked
every step of your
anointed one.

*Psalm 89:46–51.*

# "A HOUSE OF PRAYER FOR ALL NATIONS"

Eliza Davis George grew up in Texas in the late nineteenth century. She had been a student at Central Texas College, during the heyday of the Student Volunteer Movement, and as with so many other students, foreign missions captured her imagination. It was at a college prayer meeting during a lengthy prayer, while the leader was "all the way around the world and halfway back again," praying "for India, China, Japan, and Africa, that Eliza's heart was suddenly filled with an overwhelming desire to see her brothers and sisters in Africa. . . . As clearly as if she were there, she saw black people from Africa passing before the judgment seat of Christ, weeping and moaning, 'But no one ever told us You died for us.' "

When Eliza shared her call to missions with others, she received little support. She had two major handicaps in the eyes of many people. She was a woman and she was black. "You don't have to go over there to be a missionary—we have enough Africans over here." But that was only the beginning of the opposition she faced. When she applied to her church, the Southern Baptist Convention, she found no support. Never before had a black woman from Texas become a foreign missionary, and the church leaders "did not believe she was able to take on such pioneering work."

They did, however, allow Eliza an opportunity to present her case at a special meeting. When her presentation was over, she was startled by applause from the board members, and a statement from the chairman: "Miss Davis, your eloquence and sincerity have moved us deeply. I for one can no longer stand in the way of your fulfilling your life's ambition."

Eliza arrived in Liberia in 1914 and began working in the interior, where they established a Bible Industrial Academy. Within two years the school had an enrollment of fifty boys. "Even more thrilling to Eliza was the response to the gospel among the tribal people. Within the year more than a thousand converts had accept Christ in the villages." By 1943 her mission work included four substations in addition to her mission center.

Eliza very effectively carried out missionary work with her African brothers and sisters, despite problems with her mission board back home and a failed marriage. She was forced to retire from the mission at age sixty-five, but she continued on independently for most of the next three decades.[3]

"And foreigners who bind themselves to the Lord to serve him, to love the name of the Lord, and to worship him, all who keep the Sabbath without desecrating it and who hold fast to my covenant—these I will bring to my holy mountain and give them joy in my house of prayer. Their burnt offerings and sacrifices will be accepted on my altar; for my house will be called a house of prayer for all nations."

The Sovereign Lord declares—he who gathers the exiles of Israel: "I will gather still others to them besides those already gathered."

*Isaiah 56:6–8.*

# "YOU TRUSTED IN YOUR BEAUTY"

Although this passage from Ezekiel was written about Jerusalem, it could well have been written about Madame Jeanne Guyon, a well-known seventeenth-century French writer whose work later had a deep influence on John Wesley and other Protestant leaders.

Madame Guyon was born near Paris into a family of French aristocrats. During her early years she spent her life in various convents, and at the age of ten, while residing at a Dominican convent, discovered a Bible. "I spent whole days in reading it," she later recalled, "giving no attention to other books or other subjects from morning to night." But her enthusiasm ended some months later when she returned home from the convent.

At home, her life took on an entirely different character, as she was developing into a beautiful young woman. "Her mother, pleased with her appearance, indulged her in dress. The world gained full sway over her, and Christ was almost forgotten." Her vanity became a controlling force in her life, especially after her family moved to Paris when she was fifteen. "Paris was a gay, worldly, pleasure-loving city, especially in the reign of Louis XIV. . . . The world now seemed to her the one object worth conquering and possessing." The following year she was married into wealth, and her high society life continued.

She could not, however, entirely forget the spiritual hunger of her early childhood, and at the age of twenty had a powerful spiritual experience that gave her assurance of her salvation. Still, though, there was the pull of the world. Her beauty was her downfall. It was a source of pride that kept her from God. Then, "on October 4, 1670, when she was little more than twenty-two years of age, the blow came upon her like lightning from heaven. She was stricken with the smallpox, in a most virulent form, and to a very great extent her beauty was destroyed."

God comforted her in her anguish, and she was convinced that her inward beauty would be strengthened though the unfortunate circumstances. "When I was so far recovered as to be able to sit up in my bed," she later wrote, "I ordered a mirror to be brought, and indulged my curiosity so far as to view myself in it. I was no longer what I was once. It was then I saw my heavenly Father had not been unfaithful in His work, but had ordered the sacrifice in all reality." It was a high price to pay, but the loss of her beauty thrust her into a life of faithful ministry.[4]

'. . . So you were adorned with gold and silver; your clothes were fine linen and costly fabric and embroidered cloth. Your food was fine flour, honey and olive oil. You became very beautiful and rose to be a queen. And your fame spread among the nations on account of your beauty, because the splendor I had given you made your beauty perfect, declares the Sovereign Lord.

" 'But you trusted in your beauty.' ". . .

*Ezekiel 16:13–15a.*

# "I DELIGHT IN MY WEAKNESSES"

Some scholars have speculated on the basis of comments Paul made elsewhere that his "thorn in the flesh" was a problem with his eyesight. Whatever it was, it was apparently what most people would regard as a deterrent in ministry. For Paul, however, it became his strength.

For Fanny Crosby, the thorn in the flesh truly was related to eyesight. She became blind, as an infant, and lived the rest of her life in physical darkness. Yet, even as a child, she recognized the strength she had in weakness. This was a truth she styled in verse:

> How many blessings I enjoy
> That other people don't!
> To weep and sigh because I'm blind
> I cannot nor I won't.

She was convinced that God had permitted her blindness so that she could more faithfully serve him by writing thousands of hymns. Indeed, her hymns have become a priceless treasure of the church: hymns of the Christian life such as "Blessed Assurance" and "I Am Thine, O Lord;" hymns of invitation such as "Pass Me Not, O Gentle Saviour;" and hymns of missionary challenge such as "Rescue the Perishing."

"Rescue the Perishing" was written after Fanny had been moved by the story of a down-and-outer converted at a rescue mission. The second verse of that song illustrates the urgency of the task of reaching such individuals: "Plead with them earnestly, plead with them gently, He will forgive if they only believe." And the third verse offers the glorious new life that can result from such earnest and gentle pleading.

> Down in the human heart, crushed by the
>     tempter,
>   Feelings lie buried that grace can restore;
> Touched by a loving heart, wakened by
>     kindness,
>   Chords that are broken will vibrate once
>     more.

Fanny Crosby's hymns were sung as early as the 1870s at D. L. Moody's evangelistic meetings and have been sung ever since at camp meetings, conferences, and church services. They have strengthened the faith of believers and have opened the way to faith in Christ for those who have not believed.[5]

To keep me from becoming conceited because of these surpassingly great revelations, there was given me a thorn in my flesh, a messenger of Satan, to torment me. Three times I pleaded with the Lord to take it away from me. But he said to me, "My grace is sufficient for you, for my power is made perfect in weakness."

*2 Corinthians 12:7–9a.*

# "ON THE MIGHTY WATERS"

Alexander Duff was one of the great pioneer missionaries to India, who reached out with the gospel to the higher caste Hindus. Although his converts were few, their influence was great. As a brilliant scholar, Duff sought to win the people through education, and many of his converts held positions of prominence in government or education. His top priority, though, was simply presenting the Word of God. His dedication to this priority was intensified on his way to India.

On October 6, 1829, at the age of twenty-three, Duff and his young bride set sail from Portsmouth, England, on the *Lady Holland*, which was bound for India. From the beginning, the voyage was beset with misfortunes. After surviving fierce gale winds off the coast of Portugal, the ship sailed south along the coast of Africa where winds drove it so far off course that it drifted near the coast of South America. By mid-February, the ship was back on course nearing the cape, but then calamity struck.

"It was ten o'clock at night. The lights had been put out, and most of the passengers were in their berths. Duff was half-undressed when he felt a fearful shuddering shock run through the ship. Rushing out he met the captain on the deck and heard him exclaim in an agonized voice, 'Oh, she's gone, she's gone!' The *Lady Holland* had struck a reef over which the waves were dashing with terrible fury. Her back was broken and her fore part settled down between the rocks. Her condition looked hopeless."

During the next terrifying hours, the passengers huddled together, fearing they would be swept away by the pounding waves. Meanwhile, three of the crewmen set out in a small craft in a perilous effort to find land. They returned with good news, and the passengers were taken to a small island inhabited only by penguins. While they were there, some of the wreckage from the ship washed up on shore—including Duff's Bible. Though soaked and stained, he was able to read Psalm 107, the "Traveler's Psalm," to the rest of the passengers. Nearly all of the approximately eight hundred books Duff had brought with him were lost in the sea, but not his Bible. It was a reminder to him that though he was going to India to establish a Christian College, the Bible should always come first.[6]

Others went out on the sea in ships; they were merchants on the mighty waters. They saw the works of the Lord, his wonderful deeds in the deep. For he spoke and stirred up a tempest that lifted high the waves. They mounted up to the heavens and went down to the depths; in their peril their courage melted away. They reeled and staggered like drunken men; they were at their wits' end. Then they cried out to the Lord in their trouble, and he brought them out of their distress. He stilled the storm to a whisper; the waves of the sea were hushed. They were glad when it grew calm, and he guided them to their desired haven. Let them give thanks to the Lord for his unfailing love and his wonderful deeds for men.

*Psalm 107:23–31.*

## "I WILL SING OF THE LORD'S GREAT LOVE"

One of the most touching moments of Ira Sankey's life was when a young girl confessed to him that she had turned her life over to Christ as a result of his singing the gospel song, "Jesus Loves Even Me." To him, that testimony alone was sufficient reward for his services. His father, a state senator from Pennsylvania, was less certain. "I'm afraid that boy will never amount to anything," he lamented. "All he does is run about the country with a hymnbook under his arm!"

Years before, he had realized that God had gifted him with a beautiful voice and a compassion for souls that allowed him to truly "sing from the heart." While working at a bank and later for the Internal Revenue Service, he traveled to nearby cities and sang at various religious functions. It was while he was involved in this type of lay ministry that he encountered Dwight L. Moody. Moody was the featured speaker, and "following a long, sonorous dedicatory prayer," the young man brought the focus of the meeting back to Christ by singing "There Is a Fountain Filled With Blood." The evangelist was as moved, as were the people in the audience.

Following the meeting, Moody sought out the singer, inquiring if he would consider joining him as a song leader for his ministry. He discovered that the young man was Ira Sankey, and that he had no intention of leaving his secure government position for an uncertain future in song leading.

"The next day Moody sent Sankey a note and asked to meet him on a certain street corner. When Sankey arrived, he found Moody setting up a barrel on the sidewalk. Moody called to Sankey to climb up and start singing. Startled, Sankey hardly remembered how, but he found himself on the barrel singing 'Am I a Solder of the Cross?' The crowd of factory workers heading home stopped and stayed for Moody's sermon. One example was worth a thousand arguments to Sankey. He knew he must return home and seriously consider joining Moody in Chicago."

The rest of the story is history. Moody and Sankey became a celebrated team of evangelists—Sankey, no less so than Moody. His "singing from the heart" was "his trademark, a quality he never lost. In later years, men would question the musical quality of his voice or arrangements, but it was his sincerity that brought him before millions of seeking souls." His legacy is far more than his own personal ministry of music. His songs were printed in hymnals that ministered to countless needy souls.[7]

I will sing of the love of the Lord forever; with my mouth I will make your faithfulness known through all generations. I will declare that your love stands firm forever, that you established your faithfulness in heaven itself. . . . Righteousness and justice are the foundation of your throne; love and faithfulness go before you. Blessed are those who have learned to acclaim you, who walk in the light of your presence, O Lord.

*Psalm 89:1–2, 14–15.*

# "I WILL OPEN MY MOUTH IN PARABLES"

Painting word pictures through parables is a teaching style that characterized Jesus' ministry, and it is a model for those who share the gospel with others.

Sophie Muller discovered that this parabolic method was effective in reaching Indian tribes in Colombia, where she began her missionary work with New Tribes Mission in 1944. "As I taught some of the Indians to use illustrations," she wrote, "others easily caught on. Even newer believers gave testimony with lessons they drew from their own daily lives." These homey lessons challenged the listeners with biblical truths, while they provided her with personal insights into the lives and culture of the people she was serving. She could say with all sincerity, "I never tired of hearing the illustrations used by the Christians in their messages."

Pablo, a lay evangelist who had volunteered to take the gospel beyond his tribal boundaries, was particularly effective in his ability to challenge people with homey illustrations. He told how his grandfather had sold fruit to a trader who had come into the tribe. The trader then gave his grandfather a piece of paper, which his grandfather promptly used to make a cigarette, adding his own tobacco. It was not until after he had smoked it that he learned that the green paper was currency and that it amounted to the entire payment for his produce. Pablo went on to relate this mistake to how people reacted to the gift of eternal life—a gift that was often treated as though it were as worthless as cigarette paper.

Stories like these brought the gospel home to people far better than Bible lessons filled with abstract concepts. Sophie had learned this from experience as well as from her early training as an artist. Before becoming a Christian, she had studied art at the National Academy of Design in New York. She had discovered the value of illustrating truths of everyday life in her art work, and she carried that talent with her to Colombia. There she also discovered the power of word pictures. In training native evangelists, Sophie challenged them to paint word pictures to illustrate truth even as Jesus had done.

During her years of ministry Sophie trained dozens of evangelists and preachers who were able to present the gospel in their own style far more effectively than she or some other outsider could have.[8]

He told them still another parable: "The kingdom of heaven is like yeast that a woman took and mixed into a large amount of flour until it worked all through the dough."

Jesus spoke all these things to the crowd in parables; he did not say anything to them without using a parable. So was fulfilled what was spoken through the prophet: "I will open my mouth in parables, I will utter things hidden since the creation of the world."

*Matthew 13:33–35.*

# "GUILTY OF AN ETERNAL SIN"

A. B. Earle was a classic "hell-fire and brimstone" preacher. "I have found by long experience," he testified, "that the severest threatenings of the law of God have a prominent place in leading men to Christ. They must see themselves LOST before they will cry for mercy. They will not escape from danger until they see it. I have reason to believe that a single sermon I have often preached on 'The Sin that Hath Never Forgiveness' (Mark 3:29), has been the means of more than twenty thousand conversions. . . . The wicked never flee from 'the wrath to come' until they are fully satisfied there is a wrath."

During the fifty years of his ministry, beginning in 1830 at the age of eighteen, Earle preached nearly twenty thousand times—"more frequently than any other man living"—and claimed some one hundred and fifty thousand converts. He traveled more than three hundred thousand miles throughout the United States, Canada, and the British Isles.

Although he was a Baptist himself, "he was strongly in favor of union meetings in evangelistic work. He believed that one of the most potent factors in bringing souls to Christ was the sight of Christians of different denominations working together in perfect harmony."

A newspaper reporter once wondered aloud why Earle drew such large crowds and saw so many conversions—as many as fifteen hundred in one city: "His preaching was not eloquent. His delivery was not beyond the average. His voice had no special power. His large angular frame and passionless mouth were decidedly against him. His sermons seemed sometimes as though composed thirty years ago, before we so often heard, as now, the more clear and ringing utterances of free grace, and the name of Jesus in almost every sentence. He expressed his own emotions very simply, and did not often refer to them. His rhetoric was often at fault and sometimes even his grammar. Truly the enticing words of man's wisdom were wanting in his case."

Earle himself insisted that his success was due to the power of the Holy Spirit. "I have observed for nearly forty years past," he wrote, "that the secret of success in promoting revivals of religion is in having our own hearts filled with the Holy Spirit."[9]

"I tell you the truth, all the sins and blasphemies of men will be forgiven them. But whoever blasphemes against the Holy Spirit will never be forgiven; he is guilty of an eternal sin."

He said this because they were saying, "He has an evil spirit."

*Mark 3:28–30.*

# "I DECLARE YOUR POWER TO THE NEXT GENERATION"

When Katharine was fourteen years old she raised her hand at a youth conference to signify her desire to become a Christian, and seven years later she raised her hand at another conference to indicate her willingness to become a missionary. Soon after that she married Phil Howard and they sailed to Belgium to work with the Belgian Gospel Mission. During their first furlough, however, Phil was asked to join the staff of the Sunday School Times, and his acceptance signaled an end to their foreign missionary service. But this was not the end of their commitment to foreign missions. Indeed, the new ministry offered an expanded opportunity for involvement in world missions.

In the years that followed, while they raised their six children, their home became "a cross-road for Christian workers and missionaries," according to Katharine. "The conversation around the dinner table with these people was an eye-opener for our children, as they heard firsthand stories of God's work in far corners of the world. In our guest book are the names of people from forty countries and twenty-four different nationalities."

It was this environment and commitment to prayer that propelled the children into missionary work themselves. Katharine tells how on one occasion a verse kept going over and over in her mind: "Pray ye, therefore, the Lord of the harvest, that he will send forth laborers into His harvest." She vowed to pray for more missionaries. But, she writes, "One day the thought struck me, whose children are you asking God to send? I backed away from the implications, but it was no use. Finally I was willing to pray that he would send my children if that was His will for them."

It was. In the years that followed, one after another of her children became involved in missions and often served in dangerous situations. She later wrote of the result of her prayer: "Our son Phil and his wife [were] in the bush of Canada's Northwest Territories. . . . In that same year, 1958, our daughter Elisabeth Elliot and her three-year-old Valerie went to live with the Auca Indians, the tribe that had killed her husband, Jim. Our second son, Dave, was teaching in the Seminario Biblico in San Jose, Costa Rica. . . . Virginia and her husband [were] in the Sulu Sea of the Philippines, contacting remote villages with the gospel. . . . Tom was criss-crossing the U.S. that year as Foreign Mission Fellowship staff member for Inter-Varsity Christian Fellowship."[10]

I will come and proclaim your mighty acts, O Sovereign Lord; I will proclaim your righteousness, yours alone. Since my youth, O God, you have taught me, and to this day I declare your marvelous deeds. Even when I am old and gray, do not forsake me, O God, till I declare your power to the next generation, your might to all who are to come.

Your righteousness reaches to the skies, O God, you who have done great things.

*Psalm 71:16–19a.*

# "PRECIOUS LORD, TAKE MY HAND"

Having grown up in Georgia, the son of an itinerant preacher, Tom was exposed to gospel messages from an early age, and at thirteen he made a profession of faith. Through the influence of his mother, who was an organist, and his uncle, who was a composer, gospel music quickly became his first love. But the more proficient he became in music, the more he was lured by the financial prospects and glitter of the world. "I began to backslide," he later recalled, "and went on to Chicago, hoping to became a jazz musician. I worked at the theaters, wanting to be around the show folks where things were lively. During the first World War I composed songs for blues singers and began to make money. I put a band together and . . . I wrote over 150 blues songs."

During this period of his life, however, he could not forget his Christian heritage. One night, following a police raid on a bar where he was working, he began to reevaluate his life. The turning point in his life came in 1921, at the National Baptist Convention, when he recommitted his life to God and soon after began writing gospel music.

It was in 1932, following a bitter tragedy, that he wrote his most well-known gospel song. By this time he had become a sought-after musician in black churches, and he had agreed to take part in revival meetings in St. Louis. On the day the meetings were to begin, he slipped out of his home before dawn, leaving his pregnant wife behind, expecting to see her again in a few days. That reunion never took place. Instead, a telegram came saying his wife had died in childbirth, and the following night his baby son died also.

His initial reaction was to lash out at God. "I said, 'God, You aren't worth a dime to me right now.'" But in the weeks that followed, he realized how desperately he needed the Lord, and it was in his grief that Thomas Dorsey wrote the lines to "Precious Lord, Take My Hand." It was a song that soothed his own broken heart, and reached out to others. "My business," he later wrote, "is to try to bring people to Christ instead of leaving them where they are. I write all my songs with a message."

Of all of his 250 gospel songs, this one proved to be the most popular. It was the song that Martin Luther King, Jr., requested of the pianist just before the preacher was shot in Memphis in 1968.[11]

Where can I go from your Spirit? Where can I flee from your presence?

If I go up to the heavens, you are there; if I make my bed in the depths, you are there. If I rise on the wings of the dawn, if I settle on the far side of the sea, even there your hand will guide me, your right hand will hold me fast. If I say, "Surely the darkness will hide me and the light become night around me," even the darkness will not be dark to you; the night will shine like the day, for darkness is as light to you.

*Psalm 139:7–12.*

# "MY SANITY WAS RESTORED"

Next to the Bible itself, one particular book has been, perhaps, the most indispensable book for ministers and biblical scholars. On its flyleaf, Charles H. Spurgeon wrote, "For these ten years this has been the book at my left hand when the Word of God has been at my right. This half-crazy Cruden did better service to the church than half the D.D.'s and L.L.D.'s of all time." It comes as a surprise to many people that *Cruden's Concordance* was compiled by a man—Alexander Cruden—who struggled throughout his life with mental illness. Just as Nebuchadnezzar was able to glorify God, though deranged for a period of time, so it was with Alexander Cruden.

Cruden was born into a strict Calvinistic home in Scotland in 1699. His favorite pastime as a young child was tracing various words through the Bible, and this eventually led to his decision to compile a concordance years later. In the meantime, however, he experienced bouts of mental illness, for which he was confined in an asylum. Three times his confinement was due to failed love affairs. "He first fell in love with a minister's daughter and felt sure that his interests were in the will of God. For her to refuse was to disobey God's sovereign plan." After he was released, he seemed to live a normal life and became a proofreader. He was a skilled proofreader, but he had serious relationship problems and, after he was fired from his job, refused to leave because he believed "it was 'God's will' that he remain."

Cruden's public life was a matter of gossip. Following a second failed romance, he "began to make scenes at church: he would give his responses in loud tones, and occasionally stand up and make dramatic gestures. The congregation was sure the man was out of his mind." Again he was confined in a mental institution. His strange ways continued after he was released, and he became a self-appointed corrector of public morals, manners, and speaking, and actually became involved in brawls to rectify the wrongs. He dubbed himself "Alexander the Corrector."

Aside from his often outrageous public and private behavior, he "had a burden for the lost—especially those in prisons—and he spent much of his own time and wealth trying to help them. He often visited officers and nobles to intercede for the prisoners, and he preached each Lord's Day to the prisoners in Newgate. . . . One evening while returning home from church, Cruden met a man about to commit suicide because of family problems. The man's life and family were saved because of Cruden's interest and sacrifice." God used him in spite of his mental problems.[12]

Immediately what had been said about Nebuchadnezzar was fulfilled. He was driven away from people and ate grass like cattle. His body was drenched with the dew of heaven until his hair grew like the feathers of an eagle and his nails like the claws of a bird.

At the end of that time, I, Nebuchadnezzar, raised my eyes toward heaven, and my sanity was restored. Then I praised the Most High; I honored and glorified him who lives forever.

*Daniel 4:33–34a.*

# "PUT TO DEATH BY THE SWORD"

It's difficult to imagine the incredible torture past generations of Christians have endured for the sake of the gospel. Many such accounts have been lost in history, but some have survived and stand as a memorial to all those who have refused to deny the Lord in times of persecution. One such account is that of Vibia Perpetua, who was martyred on March 7, A.D. 203, in the amphitheater in Carthage, in North Africa.

Perpetua, according to the account of her life and death, was "well born, liberally educated, honorably married, with an infant son at the breast, and was about twenty-two years of age." Nothing is known of her husband, though it is speculated by some that he may have abandoned her after she professed faith in Christ.

She was new to the faith, but that factor offered her no reprieve when Emperor Septimius Severus sent out an edict making Christianity a crime punishable by death. She was imprisoned along with other Christians. "For several days after that I was upset," she confessed, "because, for one thing, I saw that my people were upset about me. Then I obtained permission to have my baby remain in prison with me, and much of my anxiety disappeared. I recovered my health and the prison became a palace to me, so that I would rather have been there than anywhere else."

That tranquility, however, was rudely shattered when her father appeared at the gate begging her to recant her faith. "Put away your pride! Don't ruin us!," he pleaded. When he attempted to rescue her, he was beaten by a guard. "I grieved for my father's plight," she lamented, "as if I had been struck myself."

On the day of the execution, the three men who had been sentenced to death were sent into the arena to be tortured by wild animals, while the crowd enjoyed the spectacle. Perpetua and a slave girl Felicitas were then sent to the arena to face a frenzied heifer that gored them until the crowd demanded the torture cease. Afterwards, on her way to the executioner, Perpetua admonished others to "stand fast in the faith, love one another, and don't let our suffering become a stumbling block to you." Her execution followed. "The clumsy, untrained young gladiator thrust his sword between two bones. She shrieked. When she saw his hand wavering, Perpetua seized it and guided it to her throat." Her faith held firm to the end, and the prison governor was converted that day.[13]

Women received back their dead, raised to life again. Others were tortured and refused to be released, so that they might gain a better resurrection. Some faced jeers and flogging, while still others were chained and put in prison. They were stoned; they were sawed in two; they were put to death by the sword. They went about in sheepskins and goatskins, destitute, persecuted and mistreated—the world was not worthy of them. They wandered in deserts and mountains, and in caves and holes in the ground.

*Hebrews 11:35–38.*

# "AN INFANT SPARED TO GROW UP AND SERVE"

The remarkable story of how God spared Moses from the decree of Pharaoh to kill all the Hebrew baby boys, through the compassion of Pharaoh's daughter, is a familiar Bible story. It reminds us of God's providential plan for every individual. Even as John Wesley was spared from a burning building as a young child, so was Harry A. Ironside spared from death in the delivery room.

Ironside was born dead on October 14, 1876—or so the doctor thought. He set the little corpse aside and turned his efforts to the baby's mother, fearing that she too might die. It was not until forty minutes later that a nurse, handling the newborn, noticed what appeared to be an ever-so-slight pulse. She called for the doctor, and the baby survived.

Growing up under the godly influence of his poor widowed mother, Ironside's interest in spiritual things developed early. At the age of three he was memorizing passages from the Bible, and by the time he was fourteen, he had read the Bible through fourteen times. His faith reached outward as well. When he saw that the children in his neighborhood were being neglected spiritually, he—still a child himself—organized a Sunday school. For accommodations, he and the children collected burlap bags and sewed them together for a tent, and soon the school had an enrollment of sixty.

Despite his apparent faith in God, Ironside lacked assurance of salvation. One night, alone in his bedroom, at the age of fourteen, he asked the Lord to save him. Three days later he attended a Salvation Army street meeting and asked if he could give his testimony. When he was asked if he were saved, he responded in the affirmative, and the captain told him to "fire away!" That experience initiated his preaching career. The next day he returned and led a man to the Lord. Years later, when Ironside became well known, the man fondly referred to him as "my spiritual father."

Today Ironside is remembered as a great evangelist and a prolific writer. He was the president of the Western Book and Tract Company, he did missionary work among the American Indians, he was a popular worldwide Bible conference speaker, he served as pastor of Moody Memorial Church in Chicago for eighteen years, and he wrote more than sixty books. In 1951 he died while preaching in New Zealand. This time his pulse beat truly had stopped—but not until he had served God for more than sixty years.[14]

Now a man of the house of Levi married a Levite woman and she became pregnant and gave birth to a son. When she saw that he was a fine child, she hid him for three months. But when she could hide him no longer, she got a papyrus basket for him and coated it with tar and pitch. Then she placed the child in it and put it among the reeds along the bank of the Nile. His sister stood at a distance to see what would happen to him.

*Exodus 2:1–5.*

# "ASYFEM! LET'S BUILD THE HOUSE OF THE LORD"

Don Richardson's ministry with the Sawi people of Irian Jaya has become well known through his book *Peace Child*. When he and his wife arrived in 1962 they encountered a culture where treachery and trickery were high ideals. Through patient efforts, however, the gospel slowly penetrated the tribe, and by 1972, there were believers in a number of congregations in tribal villages throughout the region.

These people could identify with the story of the Christ child who was sent to earth to bring redemption and peace. Through patient efforts, the gospel slowly penetrated the tribe, and by 1972 a number of congregations of believers had been established in tribal villages throughout the region.

As the gospel spread, there arose a need for suitable meeting places for worship and fellowship between congregations. This need prompted Don to propose the building of a "Sawidome." "Our meeting house," writes Don, "which had already been enlarged twice was again far too small even for regular gatherings and could not accommodate even one-fifth of the people who thronged two or three times a year to our Christian 'love feasts. . . .'"

" 'It should seat at least a thousand people,' I explained to the Sawi church elders. 'And must be circular with a cone-shaped roof. Any other design in a building so large will be too weak for monsoon storms, considering the kind of materials we have to work with.' . . . The decision was entirely theirs to make— the structure would be their property, not mine. They would need to gather and prepare thousands of poles, tens of thousands of sago leaves for thatch, hundreds of yards of tying vines and other jungle materials for the project. . . ."

Don, who was very familiar with the Sawi's intricately-built treehouses, was confident of their building skills, and with his encouragement, the people agreed to take on the project. The following Sunday, all the native Christians were urged to attend a congregational meeting. The building project was presented as a house of peace. "The response was immediate. A swelling cry of 'Asyfem! Asyfem! Let's build it! Let's build it!' rose on all sides." As in the days of Ezra, the people had spoken, within months this massive dome building was dedicated to the Lord.[15]

With praise and thanksgiving they sang to the Lord: "He is good, his love to Israel endures forever." And all the people gave a great shout of praise to the Lord, because the foundation of the house of the Lord was laid. But many of the older priests and Levites and family heads, who had seen the former temple, wept aloud when they saw the foundation of this temple being laid, while many others shouted for joy. No one could distinguish the sound of the shouts of joy from the sound of weeping, because the people made so much noise. And the sound was heard far away.

*Ezra 3:11–13.*

# "AARON'S STAFF SWALLOWED UP THEIR STAFFS"

Part of Joy Johnson's ministry as a missionary with the African Evangelical Fellowship in South Africa has been to conduct crocheting classes for Asian women. These classes are combined with Bible study. One woman who showed particular interest in the Bible study was Sita, a Hindu. Following the class one day she asked Joy if she would come to her house and visit her.

When Joy arrived, she found Sita troubled, and after the usual pleasantries, Sita confessed her problem: "I've invited you to my house today to ask you a question. . . . I've been praying to my goddess a lot these past days, even this morning I prayed to her . . . for hours. I've been summoning the spirit but it will not come and I don't know what to do."

How long had this been going on, Joy wondered. "All my life," Sita answered. "My mother taught me to pray to them when I was a little girl. And my grandmother worshipped snakes before that. I guess for generations our god has been the Snake goddess. When my grandparents came here to Africa from India they brought a picture of her with them."

At her invitation, Joy followed Sita to the end of a narrow hallway, where the altar to this snake goddess was located. Amid bowls and trays and a vase of flowers was an ornate picture of a woman with two large cobras entwined around her body. "When I pray these snakes come off the picture and slither down the table onto the floor and finally they come to me and wrap themselves all around me," Sita told her. "They make me feel good . . . like I have the power to do anything. . . . But in the past months they've been acting different. And then this morning, no matter how hard I tried, they refused to come."

Sita had thought that she could be involved in Bible study and worship her snake goddess at the same time, but she now feared that was not so. What should she do? Joy shared with her how Aaron's rod that turned into a snake ate the magician's snakes. God's power, she assured Sita, is stronger than the power of the Evil One. God was showing Sita that she should worship him alone. Sita was troubled. She wanted to worship Jesus and put his picture alongside her snake goddess. She could not give up—at least for now— her altar and her incense and her snake goddess, but she did want to continue hearing about Jesus at the Bible study.[16]

The Lord said to Moses and Aaron, "When Pharaoh says to you, 'Perform a miracle,' then say to Aaron, 'Take your staff and throw it down before Pharaoh,' and it will become a snake."

So Moses and Aaron went to Pharaoh and did just as the Lord commanded. Aaron threw his staff down in front of Pharaoh and his officials, and it became a snake. Pharaoh then summoned wise men and sorcerers, and the Egyptian magicians also did the same things by their secret arts: Each one threw down his staff and it became a snake. But Aaron's staff swallowed up their staffs.

*Exodus 7:8–12.*

# "SEARCH FOR IT AS FOR HIDDEN TREASURE"

Viggo Olsen is known best for his widely read autobiography, *Daktar*, that details his ministry as a medical doctor in Bangladesh with the Association of Baptists for World Evangelism. He was serving in that war-torn country during its struggle for independence, and when others fled to safety, he risked his life to continue his medical care to those who most needed it. His devotion was not forgotten. Following independence, the new nation assigned him visa number one "in recognition of service to our country." In assessing his contribution as a missionary, the New York Times ranked him "in the tradition of Livingstone and Schweitzer."

Who was this man who turned his back on the promise of a beautiful home and a prestigious career to serve in one of the poorest nations in the world? He was an agnostic in medical school, and was regarded by a Christian acquaintance as "the most unlikely candidate in our class to become a Christian." His future career was foremost in his thinking when he graduated cum laude from the University of Nebraska College of Medicine and he "regarded religion unnecessary and irrelevant to life."

The story of Viggo's conversion is one of an amazing pilgrimage in search for God. Following his graduation, he and his wife Joan headed for Brooklyn, to begin his internship. Along the way they stopped to visit Joan's family in Toledo. Her parents had become Christians after she went away to college, and it was in their home that Viggo was forced to seriously confront the claims of Christ for the first time in his life. To avoid family discord, he respectfully discussed the issues and attended church, but inwardly he was ridiculing their beliefs. In deference to them, he agreed to study the matter for himself and visit a church in Brooklyn that they recommended.

Convinced that he could prove the Bible wrong through a philosophical study of it, he first laid out his presuppositions. "With little difficulty we assembled a number of agnostic arguments: because no man has ever seen God, there is no assurance of His existence. Man, frightened by inevitable death, merely manufactures God for his own comfort. Either God cannot prevent human suffering, in which case He is powerless; or He can prevent suffering and does not, in which case He is evil."

The journey to faith was filled with obstacles, but praying friends, a concerned pastor, well-reasoned books, and the power of the Bible itself combined to turn an agnostic rationalist into a confident believer.[17]

My son, if you accept my words and store up my commands within you, turning your ear to wisdom and applying your heart to understanding, and if you call out for insight and cry aloud for understanding, and if you look for it as for silver and search for it as for hidden treasure, then you will understand the fear of the Lord and find the knowledge of God. For the Lord gives wisdom, and from his mouth come knowledge and understanding.

*Proverbs 2:1–6.*

# "LIVING STONES"

To be a "living stone" is the prayer of officer Torres, who has been forced to confront the stark reality of street life in Lima, Peru. The crime problem there, as in other teeming world-class cities, is heightened due to the large population of juvenile delinquents. Many of these are young children, as the officer quickly discovered. "I never realized before," writes Torres, "that on the streets of Lima there were children sleeping in the parks at night, in doorways; that every day, newborn babies were abandoned and left in the garbage or in hospital bathrooms.

"I remember a case where a mother had lost her mind and kept her children in their little shack. As I entered the place, I found an insane woman who wouldn't let her children out. In her own way, she was protecting them. We took the children away, but they began to cry. . . . After all, that woman who mistreated them was their mother."

Torres often felt overwhelmed with the massive societal problems that presented themselves every day. How could they be more effectively dealt with? She, studying psychology at the local university, and enrolling in "an unceasing race of seminars, courses, and conventions," did not offer a solution. "I wanted to learn more and more, but I felt very alone; something was missing."

When Torres's mother and sister became Christians, Torres felt a sense of outrage. "I turned away. I would cover up my ears, throw the Bible aside, and scream, 'You're talking foolishness. You've been brainwashed. You're crazy.' . . . But as time passed, I could see the change in my mother, from a bitter, angry woman who screamed all day to a woman of hope, my friend. Monica, my sister, who had been timid and introverted, became sociable. Her face glowed with the love of the Lord.

At the invitation of Monica, Torres attended a church service—not knowing it was an evangelistic campaign, and that night, October 18, 1987, "went forward, crying and asking God to forgive my sins."

Since then, officer Torres, known as Elizabet by her friends and family, has resigned her position on the police force and has become a full-time missionary, ministering to the abandoned street children of Lima."[18]

"As you come to him, the living Stone—rejected by men but chosen by God and precious to him—you also, like living stones, are being built into a spiritual house to be a holy priesthood, offering spiritual sacrifices acceptable to God through Jesus Christ. For in Scripture it says:

See, I lay a stone in Zion,
a chosen and precious cornerstone,
and the one who trusts in him
will never be put to shame."

Now to you who believe, this stone is precious. But to those who do not believe,

"The stone the builders rejected has become the capstone," and,

"A stone that causes men to stumble and a rock that makes them fall."

*1 Peter 2:4–8a.*

## "BEHOLD, THE LAMB OF GOD"

The ministry of Charles Haddon Spurgeon was controversial from the beginning. He was no more than a teenager when he entered the pastorate, and by his early twenties he was drawing crowds of thousands that could not be contained in the church sanctuary. The congregation moved to a temporary location while the church was expanded, but by the time the expansion was completed, the crowds had already outgrown the space. Once again the congregation moved to another location—this time to Surrey Music Hall in London where the massive crowds could be accommodated.

It was while in this location on October 19, 1856, that tragedy struck. More than ten thousand people packed the overcrowded hall, and thousands more stood outside. The service had only begun a few minutes earlier when someone in the crowd yelled out, "Fire! The galleries are falling!" Although there was no fire, beginning with that shout there was bedlam, and a terrible stampede. Before it was over, seven people were dead and many others severely injured. In the weeks that followed, Spurgeon was "in tears by day, and dreams of terror by night."

False reports about Spurgeon abounded, and he endured ridicule and criticism from leading ministers, but was convinced that God had laid his hand on him. He would continue to proclaim God's Word. The crowds kept coming to hear him preach, and soon Metropolitan Tabernacle was built to accommodate them. Even before it was built, however, Spurgeon had moved to the Crystal Palace, where attendance reached nearly twenty-four thousand.

In preparation for his sermons in that huge enclosure, the preacher went alone one afternoon to test the acoustics. There, not thinking of who might be listening, he shouted out in his preaching voice, "Behold the Lamb of God which taketh away the sin of the world." It was simply a test to see how well his voice carried and whether there were echoes. It was only later that he learned the result of that short sermon. "A workman in a high gallery heard the voice, was smitten with conviction, put down his tools, went home, and after a season of spiritual struggle, found peace and life by beholding the Lamb of God."[19]

**The next day John saw Jesus coming toward him and said, "Look, the Lamb of God, who takes away the sin of the world! This is the one I meant when I said, 'A man who comes after me has surpassed me because he was before me.' I myself did not know him, but the reason I came baptizing with water was that he might be revealed to Israel."**

***John 1:29–31.***

# "BE FAITHFUL, EVEN TO THE POINT OF DEATH"

When the apostle John received the Revelation on the Island of Patmos, he could not have known that his own dear disciple Polycarp would be involved in at least one aspect of the fulfillment of the prophecy to the church in Smyrna.

Polycarp was an early church leader, who, according to tradition, was a disciple of the apostle John. He was known as a kindly pastor and a defender of orthodox doctrine, and in later life he became the Bishop of Smyrna. The threat of persecution was very real to him, as it was to those in the churches he served, and this is very evident in his letter to the church at Philippi. Here he reminds believers that "Christ endured for our sins even to face death," and he exhorts them to "Pray for emperors, magistrates, rulers, and for those who persecute and hate you."

It was during an athletic festival in Smyrna (approximately A.D. 155), when the words of Polycarp's teacher, "Be faithful even to the point of death" must have reverberated in his ears. Christians who refused to worship the emperor were threatened with the death penalty—a threat that was carried out randomly. In this instance, the people wanted Polycarp—perhaps hoping that he might deny the faith and be a disgrace to Christianity.

Polycarp's friends warned him and provided a hiding place outside the city, but authorities found him and he was brought back into the city to face execution. But his death was not what they wanted. The chief of police begged him to simply cooperate: "What harm is there to say 'Lord Caesar,' and to offer incense?"

The Proconsul also pleaded with him to spare his own life by simply cursing Christ and taking an oath to Caesar, but Polycarp did not flinch. "For eighty-six years I have served Him," he testified, "and He never did me wrong. How can I blaspheme my King Who saved me?" When he was threatened with fire and wild beasts, he replied, "The fire you threaten burns but an hour and is quenched; you do not know the fire of the coming judgment and everlasting punishment laid up for the impious." His age offered him no mercy. The flames burned his body, but through the centuries his testimony has lived on: Polycarp, a martyr for the faith.[20]

"To the angel of the church in Smyrna write: These are the words of him who is the First and the Last, who died and came to life again. I know your afflictions and your poverty— yet you are rich! I know the slander of those who say they are Jews and are not, but are a synagogue of Satan. Do not be afraid of what you are about to suffer. I tell you, the devil will put some of you in prison to test you, and you will suffer persecution for ten days. Be faithful, even to the point of death, and I will give you the crown of life."

*Revelation 2:8–10.*

# "SEEK THE LORD, ALL YOU HUMBLE OF THE LAND"

These words of the Lord were spoken by the Jewish prophet Zephaniah hundreds of years before Christ, but they might well have been spoken by another Jewish prophet, Solomon Ginsburg, who warned the people of Brazil of God's judgment in the late nineteenth and early twentieth centuries.

Following his conversion to Christianity in London, this Polish Jew witnessed to his fellow Jews, to ghetto youngsters, and to anyone else who would listen to him. He encountered fierce persecution, but time and again God spared his life—a sign, he was convinced, that God had a divine mission for him. As he prayed about ministry, Brazil "seemed to loom up with outstretched arms." With the financial help of a woman who had previously served as a missionary in Brazil, he secured his passage, and was then commissioned by a group of ministers, including Hudson Taylor of the China Inland Mission.

Once in Brazil, Ginsburg quickly became involved in ministry, selling Bibles and tracts and preaching—sometimes attracting as many as five thousand people. Like Jewish prophets before him, his words were often focused on people who had a form of religion but not a religion of the heart. Once again he encountered intense opposition—often from Roman Catholic leaders who believed he was infringing on their turf.

In 1891, Ginsburg joined the Southern Baptists, and two years later he and his wife began a church planting ministry in Campos. They began their work with thirty believers, and in the decades that followed hundreds of congregations and preaching places were established in the region. But success only invited further opposition. More than once assassins were hired to take his life, but they failed to carry out their assignments.

One such assassin was Captain Antonio Silvino, a notorious bandit. One night he knocked at Ginsburg's door. Convinced that this was the end, he whispered a final prayer and went to the door, only to discover that the hired bandit who had planned to kill him while he was preaching, had been so convicted by the message he was unable to do so. Now he was at the door to seek God's mercy. Again Ginsburg had been spared. Later a letter came from a women's prayer group in Americus, Georgia, saying they had been praying for him that day—the very day that Silvino came to be converted rather than to kill God's Jewish prophet.[21]

Gather together, gather together, O shameful nation, before the appointed time arrives and that day sweeps on like chaff, before the fierce anger of the Lord comes upon you, before the day of the Lord's wrath comes upon you. Seek the Lord, all you humble of the land, you who do what he commands. Seek righteousness, seek humility, perhaps you will be sheltered on the day of the Lord's anger.

*Zephaniah 2:1–3.*

# "MARY WAS GREATLY TROUBLED"

Mary was greatly troubled. Who would believe that she could be pregnant without ever having had sexual relations with a man? A virgin birth is simply not believable. Yet, it was only through the Virgin Birth that Jesus could be fully God and fully human. For skeptics, however, the doctrine of the Virgin Birth remains unbelievable, and it was this very issue that broke up an engagement between a young minister and his fiancée, Sarah, and eventually led to the conversion of a criminal who would later become a great evangelist.

The minister and his fiancée were walking one evening in Washington D.C., when the minister confessed that he did not believe in the Virgin Birth. Sarah was upset with the disclosure, and an argument ensued. As the quarrel intensified, he flung his copy of the New Testament down on the pavement and she returned her engagement ring. He walked away in a rage and she was left alone to retrieve the New Testament.

Some time later Sarah fell in love with Samuel and married him. When she learned he had a brother who had repeatedly been arrested for thefts and burglary and drug-related crimes, she immediately wanted to reach out to him. Though she herself had never made a personal commitment to Christ, she decided to send him the New Testament that she had kept ever since the night she had picked it up off the street.

When Anthony Zeoli was handed the book in his cell in the Eastern State Penitentiary in Philadelphia, his immediate reaction was that he was too sinful even to read it. Then his eyes fell on Matthew 24:35: "Heaven and earth shall pass away, but my words shall not pass away." He closed the book, but he could not forget those words. The next day he encountered another prisoner with a Bible. Through his counsel, Anthony returned to his cell and turned his life over to God. In the flyleaf of his New Testament, he wrote "SAVED OCT. 22 1920 3PM."

"That night, as I lay on the bed, I took the New Testament, kissed it, and squeezed it tightly with great emotion," he recalled. "I valued the book so highly, because it was through this little volume that God had revealed to me the plan of salvation." Anthony later became known as "the walking Bible," and served as a nationally-known evangelist and radio preacher. Where would his life of crime have taken him, had it not been for one young woman's belief in the Virgin Birth?[22]

Mary was greatly troubled at his words and wondered what kind of greeting this might be. But the angel said to her, "Do not be afraid, Mary, you have found favor with God. You will be with child and give birth to a son, and you are to give him the name Jesus. . . " "How will this be," Mary asked the angel, "since I am a virgin?"

The angel answered, "The Holy Spirit will come upon you, and the power of the Most High will overshadow you. So the holy one to be born will be called the Son of God."

*Luke 1:29–31, 34–35.*

# "THE WISDOM OF THIS WORLD IS FOOLISHNESS"

What appears to be foolish in the eyes of society is often that which is most effective in the work of the kingdom. The ignorant, the uneducated, the despised of the world are sometimes God's choicest servants. So it was with Sophie "the scrubwoman" Lichtenfels, "whose sermons rose not from an exalted podium or pulpit but from callused hands and knees and with the rhythm of a lowly washtub and scrub brush."

Sophie was a German-born house maid, who found faith in Christ at the New York Gospel Tabernacle under the preaching of A. B. Simpson. She spoke with a thick accent, and her appearance was often comical. "In her work clothes she appeared like a character from a comic valentine—wearing an oversize bonnet profusely trimmed with red flowers, a dress of the waterfalls style of bygone days with a well-worn shawl across her shoulders." Her testimony was simple.

"God called me to scrub and preach. I was born a preacher, but since I was poor I had to work. My work is good and I can be trusted, so they want me. But if they have me, they must hear me preach. No preach, no work. I scrub as unto the Lord and I preach to all in the house. When I am out of work I tell my father. He is the best employment office. You don't have to pay or wait.

"How many in my family? Four—Father, Son, the Holy Ghost and me. Once I saved up 300 dollars but a rascal learned about it and talked me into marrying him. Foolishly, I did. In three weeks I lost both my man and money. Good riddance. Guess I got off cheap at that. . . .

"Sometimes we pray so foolish. For 12 years I prayed the Lord make me a foreign missionary. One day I prayed like that and my Father said, 'Stop Sophie. Where were you born?' 'In Germany,' I replied. 'And where are you now?' 'In America.' 'Well, aren't you already a foreign missionary?' Then He said to me, 'Who lives on the floor above you?' 'A family of Swedes.' 'And above them?' 'Some Swiss.'

" 'Yes, and in back are Italians, and a block away Chinese. You have never spoken to them about My Son. Do you think I'll send you a thousand miles away when you've got foreigners, even heathen, all around you?' "[23]

Do not deceive yourselves. If any one of you thinks he is wise by the standards of this age, he should become a "fool" so that he may become wise. For the wisdom of this world is foolishness in God's sight. As it is written: "He catches the wise in their craftiness"; and again, "the Lord knows that the thoughts of the wise are futile." So then, no more boasting about men! All things are yours, whether Paul or Apollos or Cephas or the world or life or death or the present or the future—all are yours, and you are of Christ, and Christ is of God.

*1 Corinthians 3:18–23.*

# "TAKE IT; THIS IS MY BODY"

The Reformed Presbyterian Church of Scotland advertised for a missionary to serve in the South Sea islands known as the New Hebrides. No one offered to go—with good reason. Indeed, when John Paton accepted the challenge in 1857, he was forced to defend his call against strong opposition.

"Amongst many who sought to deter me, was one dear old Christian gentleman, whose crowning argument always was, 'the cannibals! you will be eaten by cannibals!' At last I replied, 'Mr. Dickson, you are advanced in years now, and your own prospect is soon to be laid in the grave, there to be eaten by worms; I confess to you, that if I can but live and die serving and honouring the Lord Jesus, it will make no difference to me whether I am eaten by cannibals or by worms.'"

Although Paton was not eaten by cannibals, he did face grave dangers during his years of missionary service—dangers that paled into insignificance when compared to the joys of bringing these cannibals to Christ. His delight in his ministry was never more evident than on the occasion of his first communion service on the island of Aniwa on October 24, 1869, preceded by a baptismal service:

"Then beginning with the old chief, the twelve came forward, and I baptized them one by one. Solemn prayer was then offered, and in the name of the Holy Trinity the Church of Christ on Aniwa was formally constituted . . . and then, after the prayer of Thanksgiving and Consecration, administered the Lord's Supper—the first time the Island of Aniwa was heaved out of its coral depths! . . . .

"The whole service occupied nearly three hours. The islanders looked on with a wonder whose unwonted silence was almost painful to bear. Many were led to inquire carefully about everything they saw, so new and strange. . . . At the moment when I put the bread and wine into those dark hands, once stained with the blood of cannibalism, but now stretched out to receive and partake the emblems and seals of the Redeemer's love, I had a foretaste of the joy of Glory that well-nigh broke my heart to pieces. I shall never taste a deeper bliss till I gaze on the glorified face of Jesus Himself."[24]

While they were eating, Jesus took bread, gave thanks and broke it, and gave it to his disciples, saying, "Take it, this is my body."

Then he took the cup, gave thanks and offered it to them, and they all drank from it.

"This is my blood of the covenant, which is poured out for many," he said to them. "I tell you the truth, I will not drink again of the fruit of the vine until that day when I drink it anew in the kingdom of God."

*Mark 14:22–25.*

# "WHO SINNED THAT HE WAS BORN BLIND?"

The question of cause and effect relating to sin and physical disability can have devastating implications for some people. This was particularly true for Kwei-Mei Wu, a young Chinese woman living in Taiwan, who was convinced that she was being punished for past sins. Following her marriage to a young medical student, she had nine late-term miscarriages and gave birth to a son who was discovered to be severely brain-damaged—so much so that he would never be able to care for himself or walk normally.

In despair, Wu consulted fortune-tellers who told her, "You came into conflict with the white tiger star the day you married . . . as soon as you conceive, the white tiger eats the child." *Could she overcome this doom?* she wondered, as she went from place to place to worship Buddhas.

In disgrace, Wu wrote a letter to her husband's family, apologizing that in her ten years of marriage she had not been able to bear her husband a normal child and promising them she would "leave their household without any complaints" if she did not bear a healthy child within a year. But in the next two years she gave birth to two healthy children. She should have been happy. She was a doctor's wife, and she now had the children she wanted. But her life was miserable. Her husband was consumed with his work, and her life was consumed in caring for her handicapped child.

Finally she despaired to the point of suicide—not just suicide, but double suicide. "Buddha said this is repayment for previous wrong doing; if her son died, the next generation would be normal and they would not be scorned like this, nor would they go through these sufferings," she reasoned, and then to her son she said, "What if I made you die first, then I killed myself and we died together?" With his garbled words, he dissuaded her. Another time she was in the process of drowning her son and herself, when he pleaded, "Mama, I don't want to, I don't want to!"

In the midst of her hopelessness, Wu found Christ. Her sister had been converted through a Billy Graham Crusade, and her vibrant faith and testimony and the faith of others combined to reach Wu's heart when nothing else met her desperate need. In the Bible she found what she had never found in Buddhism—especially the story of the blind man, who was born that way so that God might be glorified. Her greatest joy was the baptism of her children, especially her disabled son, who was the one who, initially, objected most strenuously to her turning her back on Buddha.[25]

As he went along, he saw a man blind from birth. His disciples asked him, "Rabbi, who sinned, this man or his parents, that he was born blind?"

"Neither this man nor his parents sinned," said Jesus, "but this happened so that the work of God might be displayed in his life. As long as it is day, we must do the work of him who sent me. Night is coming, when no one can work. While I am in the world, I am the light of the world."

*John 9:1–5.*

# "I AM OBLIGATED BOTH TO GREEKS AND NON-GREEKS"

The obligation that the apostle Paul felt to reach out to people from other cultures has been felt by people around the world in the generations since. Indeed, it was Paul's confession, "I am obligated both to the Greeks and the non-Greeks," that constituted Pham Van Nam's call to ministry. Like Paul, he was hindered in his effort to reach out cross-culturally, but eventually he reaped a harvest.

Nam was the son of a prosperous businessman in the Mekong Delta of South Vietnam. He hoped to follow in his father's footsteps, but those aspirations changed after missionaries entered the area in 1930. He professed faith in Christ, and through Romans 1:14, dedicated his life to ministry. After Bible school studies, Nam and his new bride returned to the Mekong Delta, where they planted a number of churches. But Nam was convinced that God was calling him to cross-cultural missions, and in 1941 he and his wife went to work among the Koho tribe near Dalat. Due to illness, however, that ministry was short-lived, and they returned to their home.

The burden for the Koho tribe, though, did not diminish. In 1947, Nam and his wife were reassigned to that area with other missionaries. "Adversity, hardship, difficulty and danger followed them during those years from 1947 to 1960, but the power of God was manifested. Thousands of Koho were reclaimed from darkness to light, from Satan to God, from savagery, superstition and idolatry to truth and the worship of the living God as His true children."

During the 1960s Nam accepted a call to serve on the faculty of the Biblical and Theological Institute in Nhatrang, where he was able to multiply his dream of cross-cultural ministry. Through him, "scores of students who came through the school were able to catch a vision of missions, a zeal for witnessing and a love for the Lord Jesus that would influence them for their years of ministry ahead."

In 1975, Nam headed the Evangelism-Deep-and-Wide program and was instrumental in making this "aggressive program of evangelism . . . responsible for the great harvest of people won to Jesus Christ prior to that time when foreign missionaries were withdrawn from the country and activities of the churches were severely curtailed." Nam and his family escaped their homeland in 1975, in a pilfered Air Force C-130 flown by his son. Nam has since ministered to Vietnamese communities in America.[26]

I do not want you to be unaware, brothers, that I planned many times to come to you (but have been prevented from doing so until now) in order that I might have a harvest among you, just as I have had among the other Gentiles.

I am obligated both to Greeks and non-Greeks, both to the wise and the foolish. That is why I am so eager to preach the gospel also to you who are at Rome.

*Romans 1:13–15.*

## "A CUP OF WATER IN MY NAME"

Giving a cup of water in the name of the Lord may seem like a terribly insignificant deed in light of the sacrificial acts of kindness that great saints have performed throughout history. Yet, Jesus said that even such seemingly insignificant service will have its reward. Mildred Hughes, a Lutheran missionary to Liberia, gives examples of this.

She tells the story of an old woman and her grandchild who would sometimes visit her. Despite the fact that they could not speak each other's language, writes Mildred, "she would come to the door and we'd 'talk' a few minutes in gestures—grandmotherly gestures of approval of the little boy—and in a short time she'd smile and go. I might give them each a cookie if I had any; one time I took their picture with our 'quick service' (Polaroid) camera and sent her home cackling with delight."

The old woman was comfortable with Mildred, and no doubt that is what brought her again during her deepest grief. Her only son had been killed in a car accident the day before. "She just came in quietly and sat down; her face was bland and her eyes were dead," writes Mildred. "There was nothing I could do but be there. She made a couple of grief noises in her throat and after sitting a short while she looked around and spied the camera which had been left out on the table. She pointed to it and to herself, indicating that she wanted me to take her picture. I did, and that empty, stunned face was the classic picture of grief in any culture. When the picture was dry she took it, rose slowly to drag herself home. She looked at the picture once, then tucked it into her lappa at her bosom. As she walked out the door, she said what were probably the only two English words she knew: 'T'ank you.' How the picture helped her in her anguish I'll never know, but I'm glad it did."

Mildred tells another, unrelated, story of a small gesture of love that will surely have its reward. Some young boys had come to visit her one day while she was busy, and after a short time she told them they would have to leave but that she had something to give them—a small picture of Jesus. Very soon they were back, however, with a little friend. He came up to her window, "peered in bashfully, and in a soft, husky voice, asked, 'Gi' me Jesus?'

"That scene, and that question . . . seemed to me symbolic of the role of all missionaries and all Christians everywhere."[27]

"Teacher," said John, "we saw a man driving out demons in your name and we told him to stop, because he was not one of us."

"Do not stop him," Jesus said. "No one who does a miracle in my name can in the next moment say anything bad about me, for whoever is not against us is for us. I tell you the truth, anyone who gives you a cup of water in my name because you belong to Christ will certainly not lose his reward."

*Mark 9:38–41.*

# "THOROUGHLY EQUIPPED FOR EVERY GOOD WORK"

It is the teaching of the Scripture that makes an individual thoroughly equipped for every good work, and it was with that objective in mind that the Sunday school movement was born—a movement that used the Bible rather than the catechism as its basic curriculum

If there is a "Father" of the Sunday school movement, Robert Raikes, an Englishman, is deserving of the recognition, though in many ways he was an unlikely candidate for such an appellation. In 1757, at the age of twenty-two, he succeeded his father as the editor of the *Gloucester Journal*. Because of his prim and proper attire, he earned the nickname "Buck Raikes, the dandy." Yet, he had compassion for the poor—a compassion that often found its way into his editorial comments.

One day, walking through the slum district of Gloucester seeking a gardener to care for his lawns, he was taunted and jostled by a group of young boys. "You ought to see them on Sunday," commented an observer, "when the factory is closed and they have nothing to do but get in trouble." This incident sparked his concern for children in the slum districts, and he immediately recruited his pastor to help in a venture to reach them with the gospel.

Their efforts to recruit young boys for a Sunday Bible study program frequently met with a bitter response from the parents, but after visiting many homes, they managed to bring together a small group of boys who met in the kitchen of Mrs. Meredith. She was the first teacher, the pastor served as superintendent, and Raikes was the recruiter. He went to the boys' homes and brought them to the class. "If some did not have sufficient clothing to come, he bought it for them. What was the price of a pair of shoes or a pair of trousers, when the investment netted a life in return?"

It was through his newspaper, however, that Raikes had his greatest influence. After three years, he was convinced the concept of Sunday Bible schools was valid. He wrote an enthusiastic article in his paper, telling how slum children were being transformed by the Word of God. The response was immediate—people pleaded for him to start Sunday schools all over England. The movement grew rapidly, and was officially organized in 1785 as the Society for the Support and Encouragement of Sunday Schools Throughout the British Dominions. By 1830, more than one million children were enrolled.[28]

But as for you, continue in what you have learned and have become convinced of, because you know those from whom you learned it, and how from infancy you have known the holy Scriptures, which are able to make you wise for salvation through faith in Christ Jesus. All Scripture is God-breathed and is useful for teaching, rebuking, correcting and training in righteousness, so that the man of God may be thoroughly equipped for every good work.

*2 Timothy 3:14–17.*

# "HE WHO COMES TO GOD MUST BELIEVE THAT HE EXISTS"

"You must picture me alone in that room at Magdalen, night after night, feeling, whenever my mind lifted even for a second from my work, the steady, unrelenting approach of Him whom I so earnestly desired not to meet. That which I greatly feared had at last come upon me. In the Trinity Term of 1929 I gave in, and admitted God was God, and knelt and prayed: perhaps, that night, the most dejected and reluctant convert in England."

Those words are the testimony of Clive S. Lewis, one of the twentieth century's literary giants, also known as the foremost Christian apologist in modern times. He went on to say, "I did not see then what is now the most shining and obvious thing; the Divine humility, which will accept a convert even on such terms."

The terms by which Lewis offered himself to God were certainly not those of a confident believer. They might better be described as those of an offender who had finally been apprehended. For some time he had felt "that God, if there was a God, was almost ruthlessly following him." He had "the odd sensation that *he* was the prey, and was being quietly remorselessly hunted, and that God was closing in on him."

As a child, Lewis had believed in God, but God had dealt him a severe blow. When he was ten, his mother became ill. Although he fervently prayed for her, his prayers were not answered. Day after day, his beloved mother languished in pain. "At last, late in the night, as if in a nightmare, he saw his father come into the room in tears. This horrified him. It was as if the foundations of his life were crumbling away. Presently his father told him the unbelievable and terrible news. His mother was dead."

In the years that followed, as Lewis matured into a brilliant student and scholar, he began to view Christianity as a legend. But he could not shake the influence it had on him. Some of the writers and poets whom he admired the most, among them George McDonald, were Christians. Indeed, he was being pursued by God, though he hardly recognized it at first.

Following his "conversion" in 1929, Lewis began attending church and seeking God. That search was ended when he found God in Jesus Christ in 1931. "Here and here only God was made man. The myth had become fact, and the Everlasting Word had become flesh for him." He was now a confident believer.[29]

Now faith is being sure of what we hope for and certain of what we do not see. This is what the ancients were commended for.

By faith we understand that the universe was formed at God's command, so that what is seen was not made out of what was visible.... And without faith it is impossible to please God, because anyone who comes to him must believe that he exists and that he rewards those who earnestly seek him.

*Hebrews 11:1–3, 6.*

# "PROMINENT WOMEN RECEIVE THE GOSPEL"

It is significant that "prominent Greek women" accepted the gospel in Berea, as they had in Thessalonica. There, Luke writes that "not a few prominent women" were persuaded to believe (Acts 17:4). These women were an asset to early Christianity, not only because of their influence and wealth, but it would seem—at least in Berea—because of their devotion to the truth and their eagerness to examine the Scriptures.

Prominent women have had important roles in the church throughout its history—from the early centuries, to the medieval period, and during the Reformation. This was particularly true during the Wesleyan revival in England, when one woman, Selina, the Countess of Huntingdon, rose to an extraordinary level of leadership—a level previously unknown to women.

Selina came to faith in Christ during a time of illness through another prominent woman, Lady Margaret Hastings. Selina's husband was so upset by her Methodist conversion that he called in an Anglican Bishop to restore his wife to a "saner" mind. But her resolve to follow the Lord only became stronger. She did not hesitate to share her faith with her aristocratic friends, and she worked closely with George Whitefield and the Wesleys, while conducting an independent ministry of her own.

"She sold all her jewels and by the proceeds erected chapels for the poor. She relinquished her aristocratic equipage, her expensive residences and liveried servants. . . . She purchased theaters, halls, and dilapidated chapels in London, Bristol, and Dublin, and fitted them up for public worship. New chapels were also erected by her aid in many places in England, Wales and Ireland. Distinguished Calvinistic clergymen, Churchmen as well as Dissenters, cooperated with her plans, and were more or less under her direction. . . . She mapped all England into six districts or circuits, and sent out six 'canvassers' from among her most successful adherents, to travel them, and preach in every community.'" Selina also established a preachers' college to train young men to serve in her chapels and on the circuit and she was deeply involved in doctrinal affairs, particularly the Calvinist-Arminian controversy that separated Whitefield and the Wesleys. Though a Calvinist herself, she was able to bring reconciliation between them, thus averting further public scandal. Indeed, she was a major force in the Evangelical revival in England.[30]

As soon as it was night, the brothers sent Paul and Silas away to Berea. On arriving there, they went to the Jewish synagogue. Now the Bereans were of more noble character than the Thessalonians, for they received the message with great eagerness and examined the Scriptures every day to see if what Paul said was true. Many of the Jews believed, as did also a number of prominent Greek women and many Greek men.

*Acts 17:10–12.*

## "HIS EYE IS ON THE SPARROW"

When she entered the world on October 31, 1896, she had more than two strikes against her. Her twelve-year-old mother was alone in a run-down Philadelphia slum dwelling when she went into labor, and would have delivered the baby by herself, had not her cries been heard by a neighbor. She did not want the baby, who had been conceived when she was brutally raped at knife point. Her pregnancy had been a disgrace, and she was rejected by her church.

From her earliest memories little Ethel (who was actually bigger than most children her age) knew only a life of crime and poverty and rejection. "I never belonged," she recalled. "I never got the affection I so desperately wanted." She never knew a stable home life or what it was like to have plenty to eat. When she was nine, however, her life took a turn for the better. Her grandmother enrolled her in a Catholic school, and there she found an atmosphere of love and concern.

At the age of twelve, she attended a Methodist Quarterly meeting motivated by the hope of getting a free meal. She returned the following nights, convinced that God could not accept her, but by the end of the week she had given her life to the Lord, but living a Christian life, was not easy. When Ethel was thirteen, she married a man ten years her senior. The marriage soon failed, and she was on her own again, struggling to earn a living as a chambermaid, while dreaming of becoming a star.

Her break into show business came when she was invited to sing in a Philadelphia nightclub. In the years that followed, Ethel slowly moved into the limelight and became a popular attraction for both black and white audiences. She soon became widely known through her vocal recordings. In 1929, she made her first movie with Warner Brothers, in 1933, she sang with Irving Berlin on Broadway, and in 1939, she became the first black woman to appear in a Broadway drama. During the 1940s and the 1950s opportunities came her way, but she was not happy. She still felt rejected.

Then, during the 1957 Billy Graham Crusade in Madison Square Garden she rededicated her life to God. No longer did she feel rejected. Her life radiated the love of Jesus, and she became a regular feature at the Graham crusades in the years that followed. She is best remembered for singing—as no one but Ethel Waters could sing—a song with a message that rang true to her own life, "His Eye Is On The Sparrow."[31]

"I tell you, my friends, do not be afraid of those who kill the body and after that can do no more. But I will show you whom you should fear: Fear him who, after the killing of the body, has power to throw you into hell. Yes, I tell you, fear him. Are not five sparrows sold for two pennies? Yet not one of them is forgotten by God. Indeed, the very hairs of your head are all numbered. Don't be afraid, you are worth more than many sparrows.

*Luke 12:4–7.*

# "BAPTIZED BY ONE SPIRIT INTO ONE BODY"

The apostle Paul made it very clear to believers that the gospel could not be compromised by discrimination—by denying fellowship on the basis of rank or social standing in society. John Clough courageously upheld this principle during his missionary service to India, even though it dashed his hopes for reaching some of his most promising inquirers.

As a youth living on the Iowa frontier, Clough gave no thought to serving as a missionary. Rather his thoughts were on earning money, and at the age of seventeen he became a surveyor for the United States government. By the time he was twenty he had become a deputy surveyor with fifteen men working under him. He saved his money and enrolled at Burlington College in 1857, intending to study law. There he was converted through the influence of his college roommate, and some months later a missionary to Burma challenged him to devote his life to missions.

Following his college years he sold Bibles door-to-door in Iowa. Then in 1864, he was called to serve as a Baptist missionary for the Lone Star Mission among the seventeen million Telugus who lived in southern India. "There had been thirty years of almost fruitless toil. Twice the Board in Boston talked of giving up this barren field. But the pioneers of the mission . . . held on." On one occasion they and some native workers met at sunrise for prayer on a hill overlooking the region, praying that God would reach these people—not knowing that a surveyor in Minnesota would one day come and be the instrument for a great harvest of souls.

After Clough and his wife arrived in India, they began reaching out to all segments of society, including some high-caste Brahmans who showed genuine interest in the gospel message. Their interest quickly waned, however, when a group of Madigas—"poor, despised, ignorant" outcast Pariahs, "abhorrent to the caste people"—believed. Clough anticipated the consequences, but he knew he had no alternative. "The Pariahs were baptized and the Brahmans withdrew. The die was cast."

For the first ten years of his ministry, there was a steady growth of the church among the Madias, but then in in 1878, following a famine, a great revival spread through the area. The Cloughs and other missionaries had offered famine relief, but when supplies ran out, the people came by the thousands, pleading, "Baptize us . . . We want to die as Christians." Clough asked them penetrating questions about their faith, and many were turned away, but in the space of three days, 3,536 were baptized—baptized into a faith that utterly rejected caste barriers.[1]

> The body is a unit, though it is made up of many parts; and though all its parts are many, they form one body. So it is with Christ. For we were all baptized by one Spirit into one body—whether Jews or Greeks, slave or free—and we were all given the one Spirit to drink.
>
> *1 Corinthians 12:12–13.*

# "THUS THE HEAVENS AND THE EARTH WERE COMPLETED"

The creation-evolution debate that has filled columns of newspapers, torn apart local school boards, and split churches is not of recent origin. Ever since Charles Darwin published his *Origin of Species* in 1859, it has been a controversial issue. In 1925 the issue captured headlines in America when the flamboyant populist politician and presidential candidate William Jennings Bryan took center stage at the celebrated Scopes "Monkey Trial" in Dayton, Tennessee.

Although Bryan technically won the case, it was in many ways a setback for him as a dedicated and successful Christian layman. During the trial Clarence Darrow, the defense attorney, called Bryan himself to the witness stand. Bryan confidently accepted the challenge, convinced that with his knowledge of the Bible he could debunk evolution once and for all. But after the two hours of questioning were over, he was perceived by many to be a narrow-minded bigot. And in the process of defending creation, he alienated many of his fundamentalist friends because he did not claim to necessarily hold to a literal-six-day creation account.

In many respects the mockery of the trial was a discredit to the Christian faith and to Bryan himself, who died five days after the trial was over. And in the generations since, Bryan has been remembered far more for that two-week trial than for wide-ranging influence as a Christian layman.

Throughout his lifetime, Bryan taught Sunday school and was active in working with the YMCA—even though the latter involvement created some tension between him and his wife Mary. She resented the amount of time he spent in this Christian ministry, and would have preferred that he spend more time with the family.

As his political and legal career was winding down, he and Mary moved to Florida for health reasons. Here "he became a substitute teacher in a small room in the church. Soon the class grew so large that it had to move to the church auditorium. Then, when the class outgrew the church, he took his students to a nearby ballpark. The attendance fluctuated between two and five thousand. When Florida vacationers asked to receive copies of his lessons throughout the year, he began to syndicate them in a hundred newspapers across the nation."[2]

God saw all that he had made, and it was very good. And there was evening, and there was morning—the sixth day.

Thus the heavens and the earth were completed in all their vast array.

By the seventh day God had finished the work he had been doing; so on the seventh day he rested from all his work. And God blessed the seventh day and made it holy, because on it he rested from all the work of creating that he had done.

*Genesis 1:31–2:3.*

# "I HAVE OTHER SHEEP THAT ARE NOT OF THIS SHEEP PEN"

The words on his tombstone have inspired others for more than a century: "Other sheep I have which are not of this fold: them also I must bring, and they shall hear my voice." One young man, discouraged and depressed, knelt at the tomb and recommitted his life to work in Africa. He promised God he would return to Africa and lay down his life, if necessary. He returned, and fourteen months later he was dead, but the commitment Peter Cameron Scott made at that tomb of David Livingstone in Westminster Abbey paved the way for the founding of the Africa Inland Mission, which today sponsors hundreds of missionaries serving throughout Africa.

David Livingstone had dreamed of being a missionary when he was a youngster working in the mills in his hometown of Blantyre, Scotland. He had begun working at the age of ten, and during his long days of labor between 6 a.m. and 8 p.m. he often daydreamed about faraway places and adventure. He had heard about the ministry of Karl F. A. Gutzlaff, who was smuggling gospel tracts and testaments into the port cities of China. He vowed that he too would go to China, but was prevented from doing so with the outbreak of the Opium War.

At the very time that the door to China closed, another door opened. Young Livingstone attended a missionary meeting where the featured speaker was Robert Moffat, the great missionary patriarch from Kuruman in Southern Africa. His appeal was gripping: "There is a vast plain to the north where I have sometimes seen, in the morning sun, the smoke of a thousand villages where no missionary has ever been." Within weeks, Livingstone was on his way to Africa.

Livingstone's exploits in Africa are well-known. He was mauled nearly to death by a lion and his life was often threatened by hostile tribesmen and African fever as he sought to find a suitable waterway from the interior of Africa to the coast. He struggled with loneliness and guilt as he pondered the fate of his family living in hardship without him. Yet, he persevered—dedicating his entire life to ending the slave trade and seeking to improve the lot of the Africans through commerce and Christianity.

Like his hero, Karl Gutzlaff, David's failures were as pronounced as successes. Both of them, however, were committed to reaching out to "other sheep," and through their dedication inspired a host of others. Gutzlaff deeply influenced Hudson Taylor, and David Livingstone's influence touched scores of individuals, who, like Peter Cameron Scott, dedicated themselves to reaching Africa no matter what the cost.[3]

"I am the good shepherd; I know my sheep and my sheep know me—just as the Father knows me and I know the Father—and I lay down my life for the sheep. I have other sheep that are not of this sheep pen. I must bring them also. They too will listen to my voice, and there shall be one flock and one shepherd."

*John 10:14–16.*

# "I WILL COME BACK AND TAKE YOU TO BE WITH ME"

What would prompt a young woman to abandon "the bright lights and gay life" of New York City for an ant-infested mud hut in a "dark corner" of the world? For Johanna Veenstra, the answer was simple. God had called her to Nigeria and she joyfully accepted the challenge. "There has been no sacrifice," she wrote, "because the Lord Jesus Himself is my constant companion."

Johanna grew up in Paterson, New Jersey, and was active in the Christian Reformed Church. At the age of fourteen, after two years of training, she took a job as a stenographer in New York City, in order to help her widowed mother with household expenses. Although the bright lights of the city attracted Johanna, she knew God had a higher calling for her than a career in the business world and a pleasure-seeking social life. So at nineteen, she enrolled at the Union Missionary Training Institute in New York City. She continued her studies at Calvin College, where she became the first woman member of the Student Volunteer Board.

In 1919, at the age of twenty-five, she set sail for Africa with the Sudan United Mission—she was one lone woman seeking to bring the gospel of Christ to people who had never before heard the message. There was opposition and hardship as she lived and worked with the people in primitive conditions. "I took one trek through the hills, walking from place to place for nine days," she wrote. "We planned to stay over Sunday at a certain village but it proved that we were not welcome. . . . Rain hindered the people coming to the meetings. I sat at the hut door, with an umbrella to keep me dry, while the people were huddled together inside the hut about the fire. . . . The rain came down in torrents. The hut where I camped was a grass-walled one and the rain came rushing in until the whole place was flooded."

Despite the hardships, Johanna established an effective medical and educational work among the people, and was dearly loved by them. It was with great sadness, then, that they received word of her untimely death in 1933. She had entered a mission hospital for surgery and died unexpectedly. She had left her African hut to live in a mansion in glory, which paradoxically was reflected in a letter that arrived home after her death. Although it was referring to an African Christian who had died, it had a fitting title for Johanna herself: "From a Mudhut to a Mansion on High."[4]

"Do not let your hearts be troubled. Trust in God; trust also in me. In my Father's house are many rooms; if it were not so, I would have told you. I am going there to prepare a place for you. And if I go and prepare a place for you, I will come back and take you to be with me that you also may be where I am. You know the way to the place where I am going."

*John 14:1–4.*

## "JEWELS FROM THE DEVIL'S JUNKPILE"

The banner on the wall of Mickey Evans's dining hall at Dunklin Memorial Camp in the swamplands near Lake Okeechobee, Florida, reads "Jewels From the Devil's Junkpile." Below it are "pictures of men, many smiling and proudly posing with a wife and children. These are men of all walks of life. Men like Tim McGinnis, a former alcoholic who once lived under a bridge in Orlando. After going through Evans's program, he joined Youth With A Mission and led a group of missionaries to the kibbutz in Israel.

"And men like Hugh Murrow. He grew up in a home with alcoholic parents who both eventually died from alcoholism. Murrow used to live in the gutters of a North Carolina city. Now he leads his own 'overcomers' ministry for alcoholics and addicts in Florida."

For twenty-five years, Evans has been a missionary to what he calls the "Fourth World"—the millions of "American social outcasts who are bound in chemical abuse, homosexuality, prostitution and the like." Prior to that he was a pastor in the First Baptist church in Indiantown, Florida. "We had a nice little social club," he recalls. "It was the spring of 1963. We had built a new church building and a new parsonage. Our little flock was happy and content. But my own dad was dying of alcoholism. . . . Our church wasn't touching them [alcoholics]. All we were doing was holding nice Sunday services for nice people—while the real world was going to hell all around us."

Evans could not escape the remorse he felt for his own failure to reach out to those in need. Finally, convinced God was leading him, he purchased a "320-acre tract of alligator-infested swamp." He and his wife left their comfortable parsonage and moved into a "swamp shack." "Our friends thought we were crazy," his wife recalls. "They would say, 'Why in the world would you leave a church of nice, respectable people to go out there with a bunch of drunks?' " Since those early days the camp has increased in size and been modernized to meet the needs of the residents.

"While it is not required that only Christian men enter the program, it's mandatory that the addict be open to change. . . . Nearly without exception, men emerge from the program as dedicated believers in Christ."[5]

And we pray this in order that you may live a life worthy of the Lord and may please him in every way: bearing fruit in every good work, growing in the knowledge of God, being strengthened with all power according to his glorious might so that you may have great endurance and patience, and joyfully giving thanks to the Father, who has qualified you to share in the inheritance of the saints in the kingdom of light. For he has rescued us from the dominion of darkness and brought us into the kingdom of the Son he loves in whom we have redemption, the forgiveness of sins.

*Colossians 1:10–14.*

# "ANGERED WITH THEIR WORTHLESS IDOLS"

Should godly citizens obey a ruler who compelled idolatry and outlawed true Christianity? John Knox, the great Scottish Reformer, put this question before John Calvin when he visited him in Geneva. It was a serious inquiry that required a thoughtful response.

John Knox became a Roman Catholic priest following his studies at St. Andrews University in 1536, but the Reformed doctrine being taught by George Wishart captured his heart, and he volunteered to serve as his bodyguard. George Wishart was taken prisoner, however, and shortly thereafter was executed.

Despite the dangers, Knox picked up the mantle and carried on the tradition of his mentor. He was banned from preaching on Sunday morning, but he lectured during the week, and "a great number of the town openly professed Reformed doctrine." But like his predecessor, Knox was a marked man. He and some of his countrymen were taken prisoner and forced to serve as galley slaves for some eighteen months before they were released.

Life during those months was grim. "Food and clothing were scant and coarse. . . . The galleymen were 'chained by the neck in couples,' and were so bound to the benches that they could 'neither sit nor stand upright,' nor yet 'lie down at full length.' At night they slept under the benches closely packed together, 'on a little straw gnawed by rats and mice.' They were sometimes obliged to row ten or twelve hours without interruption; and their labours were stimulated by frequent strokes of the cowhide whip."

One incident during this time as a galley slave stands out. During a religious ritual, "a painted wooden image of the Virgin was brought to be devoutly kissed." Knox "refused to touch what he called 'an idol accursed.' The 'painted brod' was then violently thrust in his face and put between his hands; whereupon the indignant Protestant threw the image into the Loire [River], exclaiming, 'Let our Lady now save herself.'"

Following his imprisonment and a time of exile in Europe, Knox returned to his beloved Scotland. There, despite royal opposition, he courageously led the Reformed movement—the infant Presbyterian church.[6]

The Lord saw this and rejected them because he was angered by his sons and daughters. "I will hide my face from them," he said, "and see what their end will be, for they are a perverse generation, children who are unfaithful. They made me jealous by what is no god and angered me with their worthless idols. I will make them envious by those who are not a people, I will make them angry by a nation that has no understanding. For a fire has been kindled by my wrath, one that burns to the realm of death below.

*Deuteronomy 32:19–22.*

# "SHOULD WE STRIKE WITH OUR SWORDS?"

Jesus made it clear that there was no place in his kingdom for those who would strike with swords to defend him. Yet, down through the centuries, nations and individuals have fought religious battles to defend Jesus. Andrew Gih, who later became a great Chinese evangelist, met a man who struggled with his desire to use violence to defend his Lord.

One of Gih's earliest converts was a man by the name of Wang; he was a bandit whose days were spent plundering the countryside in West Shantung. Wang had first met Gih when he had visited an outlying village "in the hope of finding some spoil. But there was Gih telling the story of the prodigal son to a crowd who had gathered to hear him. Wang was astounded. 'How did this man know my story,' he puzzled. When Gih gave the invitation to repent and believe in Jesus, Wang did just that.

"His transformation bore instant fruit. He went home, knelt before his wife and begged her forgiveness. Then searching out his aged parents, he asked them to forgive him too. His next journey took him to the pastor of the district in which he lived. He became a loyal member of the congregation there and used every opportunity to testify of his newfound faith."

But Wang still struggled with his old ways. That was evident one day when a scoffer jeered at him, " 'If a gangster can preach the gospel, then this bloke Jesus must also . . .' " Wang flew into a rage. He "was on him in a moment and bit off one of his ears. Spitting it out he wiped the blood from his mouth." Convinced he had done right, he calmly told the man, " 'You can insult me as much as you like, but you're not going to insult Jesus while I'm around.' "

Wang shared this incident with his pastor, who reminded him of the story of Peter. " 'You have done exactly the same,' he told him. 'When Peter was filled with the Holy Spirit later on, he no longer acted like that.' " It was a difficult message for Wang to hear. He was so sure that he had served his Master well. But this passage of Scripture spoke to him and "Wang repented and asked God to fill him with the Holy Spirit."[7]

While he [Jesus] was still speaking a crowd came up, and the man who was called Judas, one of the Twelve, was leading them. He approached Jesus to kiss him, but Jesus asked him, "Judas, are you betraying the Son of Man with a kiss?"

When Jesus' followers saw what was going to happen, they said, "Lord should we strike with our swords?" And one of them struck the servant of the high priest, cutting off his right ear.

But Jesus answered, "No more of this!" And he touched the man's ear and healed him.

*Luke 22:47–51.*

## "HE WHO WINS SOULS IS WISE"

She was refreshed and she thrived like a green leaf as she invested her life for the souls of others. Her reward was not riches, but a tree of life bearing the many names of people who had come to Christ through her ministry. She was Maggie Newton Van Cott, the first woman in the United States licensed to preach by the Methodist Episcopal Church. So effective was her ministry that she was called "the female Wesley" and compared to Dwight L. Moody.

Following the death of her husband, Maggie became actively involved in ministry, first in city mission work and then itinerant evangelism. After one year of evangelistic outreach, she offered a report of her labors: 335 sermons preached (averaging one hour in length), three thousand miles traveled, five hundred converts who went on to join Methodist churches, $735.35 in money received.

She was described in a newspaper article as "possessing very superior power as a preacheress, . . . considerably above the middle height, and very stout, weighing over two hundred pounds." Another reporter wrote: "This lady is a marvel, considering her power of physical endurance. How she can hold three or four meetings daily, as she has done almost without interruption for the last three years, and not break down, is a wonder, and yet she never feels tired. . . . She has been entreated . . . to quit preaching, and use her dramatic powers in reading or lecturing, which would return her a larger income . . . but no argument will induce her to relinquish her calling, for money."

In the spring of 1870, she conducted meetings in Wilbraham, Massachusetts, where "night after night the altar was thronged by scores and hundreds of souls, mourning on account of their sins. The whole community was shaken to the center. . . . Never had Wilbraham witnessed such a scene as this."

"Do we endorse her?" asked a Chicago minister, who was noncommittal in his response. "We are dumb in the presence of the fact that hundreds come to Christ when she calls. . . . The questions of her relations to our ministry, whether she is to be admitted to Conference, or whether she is to be ordained, are matters to be decided by those to whom application is made, but whether she can win souls to the Cross is beyond all question."[8]

---

A generous man will prosper; he who refreshes others will himself be refreshed.

People curse the man who hoards grain, but blessing crowns him who is willing to sell.

He who seeks good finds good will, but evil comes to him who searches for it. Whoever trusts in his riches will fall, but the righteous will thrive like a green leaf.

He who brings trouble on his family will inherit only wind, and the fool will be servant to the wise.

The fruit of the righteous is a tree of life, and he who wins souls is wise.

*Proverbs 11:25–30.*

# "LOVE YOUR ENEMIES"

"Love your enemies" is a motto often referred to in situations involving neighborhood or workplace strife, and rightly so. If a supervisor is spiteful or if a neighbor is inconsiderate, the Lord's admonition is appropriate. But the command becomes more significant when it applies to actual physical enemies, such as the enemies of jungle tribes.

The Ayores were known as the fiercest of the Indian tribes in the Bolivian jungles, and their enemies consisted of anyone outside their tribe. This included the five American missionaries from the New Tribes Mission, who were brutally slain when they sought to enter their territory in 1943. Even while grieving, the surviving New Tribes missionaries refused to give up on the mission effort, and through a slow, tedious process of leaving gifts for them, the missionaries finally persuaded the Ayores to come out of the jungle to meet their benefactors. As a result, many were converted to Christ.

Years later, the Ayores were involved in a missionary effort of their own. They were seeking to reach the Pig People for Christ. Led by Cadui and Dejabi, they were fully aware of the dangers involved. Many years earlier the Ayores had massacred almost the entire Pig People tribe. They had pretended they were coming in peace, but then, with no warning, suddenly attacked the people and killed them with their own weapons. Since that time surviving babies had grown into fierce warriors, and Cadui and Dejabi knew they would be prepared to avenge the treachery of long ago. But the urgency of the gospel was more powerful than the fear of death.

As they approached the village, they were spotted by an old woman, who let out a piercing scream to warn the village. It was too late to turn back. Warriors armed with spears and knives quickly surrounded them. Cadui and Dejabi explained that they were on a mission of peace and that they were unarmed and had come with gifts, but the Pig People were not about to be fooled again. They attacked without mercy. In the mêlée, Cadui was wounded but he managed to wrestle his attacker to the ground and grab his spear. Raising the spear over his head, he insisted again that he was on a mission of peace. Only then did the Pig People believe him—only after five of his comrades lay dead, including his own brother.

The Pig People accompanied the Ayores back to their village. It was a somber time. The Ayores had paid a heavy price—even as the New Tribes missionaries had—but it was a first step in reaching out with the gospel to their most vengeful enemies.[9]

"But I tell you who hear me: Love your enemies, do good to those who hate you, bless those who curse you, pray for those who mistreat you. If someone strikes you on one cheek, turn to him the other also. If someone takes your cloak, do not stop him from taking your tunic. Give to everyone who asks you, and if anyone takes what belongs to you, do not demand it back. Do to others as you would have them do to you."

*Luke 6:27–31.*

## "I WAS EYES TO THE BLIND"

William Henry Jackson was a sickly baby, who was blind due to health complications before he was two years old. His mother, however, treated him no differently from her eight other children. He enrolled in a school for the blind and quickly became a student leader, excelling in swimming, gymnastics, carpentry, and journalism. After completing his training there he went on to Wedham College, Oxford, where he graduated with honors in history and theology.

Following his graduation he became a curate in the Catholic church. Here he conducted the usual parish duties, but was particularly taken up with the ministry of the boys' club. On one occasion, he "enraptured the boys by giving a diving display, which included every sort of trick and accomplishment, from 'swallow' dives and 'somersault' dives to 'fire' dives, in which he had cotton-wool lighted on his back and jumped into the water a mass of flame."

During his ministry as a curate his brother-in-law, a missionary with the Society for the Propagation of the Gospel, challenged him about the need for missionaries to work with the blind in Burma. It sounded like an exciting prospect for ministry, but how could he, a blind man, begin a new missionary venture facing so many culture and language barriers? But Father Jackson had risen above obstacles before, and in the fall of 1917, he set sail for Burma, studying the language en route.

Very soon after he arrived, Jackson indicated in a letter the style of his missionary outreach: "I have gone into Burmese costume, and lived and slept and talked and played with only the Burmese children. So important do I consider the rapid acquisition of the language and of an insight into the racial characteristics that I have rigidly cut myself off from English work, and have refused six invitations to European functions."

Through his own triumph over blindness, he was ideally suited to work with the blind. By examining native craftsmanship, he learned how to construct cane furniture, taking it apart piece by piece and putting it back together, then teaching his students. He put the Burmese language into phonetic form and transcribed it into braille, and then punched the script into tin cans to be used with an old printing press. Nothing, it seemed, was beyond his capability. During his fourteen years of ministry he made such an impact on Burma that he was given a gold medal and when he died, the Governor paid his respects. He was remembered as "Big Father," a man who preached the gospel with his life and his words.[10]

"Whoever heard me spoke well of me, and those who saw me commended me, because I rescued the poor who cried for help, and the fatherless who had none to assist him. The man who was dying blessed me, I made the widow's heart sing. I put on righteousness as my clothing, justice was my robe and my turban. I was eyes to the blind and feet to the lame. I was a father to the needy."

*Job 29:11–16a.*

# "THE LORD IS SLOW TO ANGER AND GREAT IN POWER"

The prophet Nahum introduces his prophecy with a description of God that emphasizes both his wrath and his caring concern. It is a balanced portrait—not a one-sided view of God that is often presented by preachers and Bible teachers. This balanced view was part and parcel of the Salvation Army in its early years, especially as it is reflected in the preaching and outreach of Catherine Booth, the cofounder and "mother" of the Salvation Army.

In response to her critics for her bold preaching, Catherine responded, "Oh! people say, you must be very careful, very judicious. You must not thrust religion down people's throats. . . . Then I say, you will never get it down. What! Am I to wait till an unconverted godless man wants to be saved before I try to save him?" Her critics preferred a more one-sided view of God, and they opposed her preaching on the wrath of God and the damnation of the lost. But Catherine did not shy away from opposition. In fact, she regarded it as a sign of true Christianity: "Opposition! It is a bad sign for the Christianity of this day that it provokes so little opposition. If there was no other evidence of it being wrong I should know it from that."

Catherine also placed great emphasis on the caring concern of God and how that could be demonstrated in ministry to the needy. She was deeply involved in city mission work—reaching out to the poor and reclaiming the prostitutes. She and her husband and the Army volunteers who worked with them offered assistance to the urban poor, and their ministry soon spread out worldwide. Despite all these humanitarian efforts, however, the opposition continued and Salvation Army workers were often the victims of assaults.

Catherine refused to be silenced whether by the threats of street rowdies or the ridicule of sophisticated churchmen. She continued in the work until she died of cancer in 1890 at the age of sixty-one. She had devoted her final years to preaching and mission work, a ministry that served as a model for those who would follow. She refused to compromise her message, and her contemporaries and history have vindicated her. Of her thirty years of preaching in England, Norman Murdoch writes, "Many agree, no man of her era exceeded her in popularity or spiritual results, including her husband." Catherine's ministry has served as a model for those who followed.[11]

"The Lord is a jealous and avenging God, the Lord takes vengeance and is filled with wrath. The Lord takes vengeance on his foes and maintains his wrath against his enemies. The Lord is slow to anger and great in power, the Lord he will not leave the guilty unpunished. His way is in the whirlwind and the storm, and clouds are the dust of his feet. . . . The Lord is good, a refuge in times of trouble. He cares for those who trust in him.

*Nahum 1:2–3, 7.*

## "WE MUST OBEY GOD RATHER THAN MAN"

Peter's bold declaration to his accusers that his responsibility to obey God was higher than his obligation to submit to man-made laws, has been quoted through the centuries by Christians who have found themselves in similar circumstances. One such individual was another Peter—Peter Waldo, a wealthy twelfth-century merchant who lived in Lyons, France.

Waldo was frustrated by the corruption of the Roman Catholic church of his day and by its failure to emphasize the Scriptures and inner spirituality. Finally he sought out the Word of God for himself, employing priests to translate the Gospels. He memorized passages of Scripture and began to share his faith with others, circulating portions of the Bible for others to study and memorize.

The church leaders perceived Peter's activity as a threat— especially as more and more people began to approach him instead of the priests for spiritual counsel. When he refused to stop distributing Scriptures and sharing his faith, he and his followers were excommunicated from the church.

In 1173, Waldo committed himself wholly to the work. "He distributed his wealth in three parts: one part was given to his family, who did not follow him, the second part, to the poor in the city of Lyons, and the third part, to pay for the translation of the New Testament." He and his followers became known as the Poor Men of Lyons and later the Waldenses.

An opponent of Waldo, Friar Steven de Borbonne, gave the following account of the situation: "A rich man in the said town, called Waldensis, hearing the Gospels, and having a little learning, desirous to know their contents, made a bargain with these priests, that one should translate the Gospels into the vernacular language, and the other should write under the dictation of the first. . . . Now the same citizen, after reading those writings and learning them by heart, resolved to keep evangelical perfection as the Apostles did. . . . So he succeeded in gathering together men and women, and teaching them the Gospels, induced them to do the same. . . . They were called to account by the Bishop of Lyons, named John, who commanded them not to dare to explain the Scriptures nor to preach any more. They defended themselves with the answer of the Apostles: 'It is necessary to obey God rather than man, God commanded the Apostles to preach the Gospel to every creature.' "[12]

**Peter and the other apostles replied: "We must obey God rather than men! The God of our fathers raised Jesus from the dead—whom you had killed by hanging him on a tree. God exalted him to his own right hand as Prince and Savior that he might give repentance and forgiveness of sins to Israel. We are witnesses of these things, and so is the Holy Spirit, whom God has given to those who obey him."**

*Acts 5:29–32.*

# "BUILDING BRIDGES CROSS-CULTURALLY"

There is a bond among people who treasure their livestock, and an awareness that not everyone shares their love for animal husbandry. This was true when Joseph's family fled to Egypt during a time of famine. They quickly learned that Egyptians detested the occupation and lifestyle of cattle herding.

It is imperative that missionaries seek to identify with the people to whom they minister, as Ann Croft discovered during her years in Nigeria. She had gone to serve as a teacher, but her acquaintance and subsequent friendship with the family of one of her students sparked her interest in the nomadic Fulani people of Northern Nigeria. She was fascinated by their rich traditions and their folklore, and she was burdened for them spiritually. They were Muslims who were unfamiliar with the gospel of Christ.

The more her friendship grew with these people the more she learned about their customs, lifestyle, and the importance they placed on their cattle. As she shared with them the truths of the Bible she told them stories of Abraham, Jacob, and Esau other great patriarchs who shared their love for cattle and the nomadic life. But simply sharing these stories was not enough. Ann became involved herself and demonstrated her own love for animal husbandry in a very personal way.

She took it upon herself to help upgrade the Fulani's veterinary medicine and supply them with vaccines. "On one occasion she help a Fulani elder get tuberculosis medicine for his son and worm medicine for himself. But it was not until she gave him medicine for his cows that he said, 'Now I know you *really* love us!'"

Through her participation in the Fulani peoples' lives, Ann was able to encourage them to participate in an evangelistic conference. At the close of the meetings, "the chief of the area said to Ann that he wanted his people to become part of the Christian community."[13]

Then Joseph said to his brothers and to his father's household, "I will go up and speak to Pharaoh and will say to him, 'My brothers and my father's household, who were living in the land of Canaan, have come to me. The men are shepherds; they tend livestock, and they have brought along their flocks and herds and everything they own.' When Pharaoh calls you in and asks, 'What is your occupation?' you should answer, 'Your servants have tended livestock from our boyhood on, just as our fathers did.' Then you will be allowed to settle in the region of Goshen, for all shepherds are detestable to the Egyptians."

*Genesis 46:31–34.*

## "WERE YOU A SLAVE WHEN YOU WERE CALLED?"

One of the great missionary stories of the post-apostolic age is that of Saint Patrick, a fifth-century Christian who was neither Irish nor Roman Catholic. Little is known of his early life, except what he himself reveals in his *Confession*: "I, Patrick, a sinner, the rudest and least of all the faithful, and most contemptible to very many, had for my father Calpornius, a deacon, the son of Potitus, a priest who lived in Bonnaven Taberniae . . . where I was taken captive when I was nearly sixteen years of age."

Patrick was captured along with other young Britons by Irish invaders who brought him to Ireland and sold him into slavery as a sheepherder. During this nearly seven-year period of captivity he came back to God: "There the Lord opened my heart to a sense of my unbelief, and taught me to remember my sin, and to be converted to Him with all my heart."

Eventually Patrick escaped and returned to his family, where he was welcomed as a child who had returned from the dead. So overwhelmed was he with the renewed family ties that he vowed never to leave home again. But that was before his visionary missionary call: "There verily I *saw in the night visions* a man, whose name was Victorious, coming as it were from Ireland with countless letters. And he gave me one of them, and I read the beginning of the letter, which was entitled, 'The Voice of the Irish', and while I was reading aloud the beginning of the letter, I thought that at that very moment I heard the voice of them who lived beside the wood of Foclut which is nigh unto the western sea. And thus they cried, as with one mouth, 'We beseech thee, holy youth, to come and walk among us once more.' "

Patrick was deeply moved by the vision. "I was exceedingly broken in heart, and could read no further. And so I awoke. Thanks be to God that after very many years the Lord granted to them according to their cry."

There was great sorrow when Patrick announced to his family that he would be returning to the very people who had enslaved him. But he was convinced of God's call. "God directing me, I consented to no one, nor yielded to them," he testified. "So I went to Ireland to preach the Gospel." And a mighty preacher he was. "He baptized more than ten thousand persons and built more than three hundred churches."[14]

> Each one should remain in the situation which he was in when God called him. Were you a slave when you were called? Don't let it trouble you—although if you can gain your freedom, do so. For he who was a slave when he was called by the Lord is the Lord's freedman, similarly, he who was a free man when he was called is Christ's slave. You were bought at a price, do not become slaves of men.
>
> *1 Corinthians 7:20–23.*

# "I AM THE WAY AND THE TRUTH AND THE LIFE"

Peter Tibi was born in 1964, the son of Christian parents who lived in southern Sudan. In 1967, during a time of intense civil strife, his parents were killed, and he was cared for by neighbors until a relative moved him into exile in northern Uganda and became his guardian. He had endured severe trauma in his short life, and now he would have a sense of security again. The three-year-old could not know what awaited him in the all-encompassing world of Islam.

Peter's guardian, Abdallah, was a well-known Muslim religious leader who earned his living as a healer and an Arabic school teacher. Peter was eager to please him and excelled in his study of Arabic and the Koran—indeed, so much so that he was honored with a new name, Abdallah, the name of his guardian.

The turning point in Peter's life came in 1979, when he was fifteen years old. He returned to Sudan to continue his secondary schooling. Here he was the only Muslim in the school, and he was suddenly confronted with Christianity. He had read about Jesus in the Koran, but that was certainly not the same Jesus of whom the Christians spoke. He argued with them and vehemently rejected their efforts to convert him, but as time passed he realized that the truth of their message was penetrating his heart.

Peter fought against the idea of converting to Christianity, but then one night as he was looking through the Koran for a passage to recite, he was frustrated to find nothing that brought him peace. He then opened the Bible, and there read John 14:6: "I am the way and the truth and the life. No one comes to the Father except through me." After reading the passage, he went to bed without saying his prayers to Allah. He fell into a restless sleep. The verse kept going over and over in his mind. Finally, torn between Jesus and Islam, he got up and took out his Bible and began searching for more truth. He kept reading until the tears began to flow down his cheeks and he committed himself to the Lord and to Christian service.

When Peter returned to Uganda to spend a holiday with his guardian, he reluctantly admitted that he had become a Christian. "This made him react bitterly and beat me," writes Peter, "and I was forced to sleep outside in the cold night." A Christian pastor opened his home to him, and in the years since, Peter has been involved in tract distribution and in further education at Moffatt College of Bible in Kijabe, Kenya.[15]

Thomas said to him, "Lord, we don't know where you are going, so how can we know the way?"

Jesus answered, "I am the way and the truth and the life. No one comes to the Father except through me. If you really knew me, you would know my Father as well. From now on, you do know him and have seen him."

*John 14:5–7.*

## "IN ALL THINGS GOD WORKS FOR GOOD"

It is difficult to imagine any good coming out of the Boxer Rebellion in China in 1900. Scores of missionaries and hundreds of national Christians were tortured and killed, and most of the missionaries in the interior who managed to escape the terror were forced to leave the country. It was one of the most tragic periods in all of missions history. Yet, during the time of evacuation, ministries were initiated elsewhere that may have never otherwise developed. The lives of Solomon and Maria Bergstrom illustrate this truth.

Solomon was recruited for missionary service by Fredrik Franson (founder of The Evangelical Alliance Mission) when he came to Sweden in 1892. He was eager to go immediately to China, but since he was unable to obtain financial support from his own countrymen, Franson suggested he visit the United States. There he found his base of financial and prayer support. In 1894, he and several other new recruits set sail for China.

In China, he and his American bride quickly became involved in evangelism while learning the language. Maria worked with the women, and Solomon started a boys' school. They hoped to spend their lives in China and build a church in Hingping, Shensi, to reach out into the surrounding area. But storm clouds were gathering on the horizon. In 1900, with the onset of the Boxer uprising, their work in China suddenly came to a halt. Fearing for their lives, they left the country. But God brought good out of what seemed to be a devastating setback in their ministry.

"The Bergstroms spent the next two years in Thief River Falls, Minnesota, where God blessed the community with revival, a congregation was organized, and a church erected."

The results of this revival renewed their enthusiasm for the work back in China. When they returned to China they found only one of the eight believers they had left behind. But in the years that followed the tiny church that they established grew. Again they witnessed revival and had the joy of leading hundreds of people to faith in Christ. Among those was a Confucian scholar, a man whom Solomon visited more than one hundred times before he made a profession of faith.[16]

In the same way, the Spirit helps us in our weakness. We do not know what we ought to pray for, but the Spirit himself intercedes for us with groans that words cannot express. And he who searches our hearts knows the mind of the Spirit, because the Spirit intercedes for the saints in accordance with God's will.

And we know that in all things God works for the good of those who love him, who have been called according to his purpose.

*Romans 8:26–28.*

# "IF YOU SUFFER FOR WHAT IS RIGHT, YOU ARE BLESSED"

Through the centuries, a countless number of innocent people have suffered for the sake of the gospel. Scripture affirms that those who suffer for what is right are blessed, but is there any way for men and women to respond to unjust punishment? One way mentioned in the text is to shame the persecutor through good behavior and thereby check further persecution. It was with this intent that one of the most widely-read classics in history was written. John Wesley believed this book, *Foxe's Book of Martyrs*, more than any other Christian classic, belonged in the libraries of his preachers.

John Foxe was born in 1516, and despite the fame he would receive from his book during his lifetime, he would live his entire life on the edge of poverty. His writing was a labor of love—a monument to the faith and devotion of those who had suffered wrongly and a monument to the shame of those who had committed infamous injustices. Though faulty in spots, the book has long outlived its critics.

Foxe had a reputation for being a Christian "holyman" or a Christian version of Robin Hood. "He not only gave away his own money but that of his merchant friends, so that there came to him from every quarter deserving beggars and impostors. There is the story of how he left the house of his friend Aylmer, Bishop of London and found the poor waiting for him, so went back and borrowed five pounds which he bestowed cheerfully and graciously and then completely forgot. Some months later the bishop reminded his friend of the money. 'Oh,' said Foxe, 'I have laid it out for you and have paid it where you owed it, to the poor people that lay at your gate.'"

Foxe also acquired fame for having the gift of healing of both mental and physical illnesses, and he was known as a powerful preacher. "One of his sermons, which resulted from his converting a Spanish Jew, was so famous that Sir Francis Walsingham, then in bed, sent to him and ordered a repeat and private performance in his bedroom."

But above all else, Foxe was committed to offering his countrymen a record of the history of martyrdom and the terrible persecution that sent hundreds of his fellow believers to the flames beginning in 1555, with the reign of Queen Mary. This record thereby challenged those who would continue the persecution.

Foxe was a Protestant stalwart, but he was ahead of his time in his commitment to justice and toleration in his loud condemnation of the persecution of Roman Catholics and sectarians.[17]

Who is going to harm you if you are eager to do good? But even if you should suffer for what is right, you are blessed. "Do not fear what they fear; do not be frightened." But in your hearts set apart Christ as Lord. Always be prepared to give an answer to everyone who asks you to give the reason for the hope that you have. But do this with gentleness and respect, keeping a clear conscience, so that those who speak maliciously against your good behavior in Christ may be ashamed of their slander. It is better, if it is God's will, to suffer for doing good than for doing evil.

*1 Peter 3:13–17.*

## "WHERE YOUR TREASURE IS, THERE YOUR HEART WILL BE"

What did Jesus mean when he warned his followers not to store up treasures on earth? Many of his first-century followers took the command literally, and in the centuries since, this passage and others have prompted believers to demonstrate in a tangible way that their only real treasures were those stored in heaven.

Material wealth had been a high priority for Lettie Cowman. She was the daughter of a prosperous banker, and her husband Charles was a successful manager who had worked his way up through the ranks of the Western Union Telegraph Company. They lived in a beautiful home and enjoyed an active social life. But then they were converted—Lettie first, then her husband.

Less than a year later, Lettie and Charles attended a missionary convention at Moody Church in Chicago. A. B. Simpson, the founder of the Christian and Missionary Alliance, was the featured speaker. Following his dynamic message, an offering was taken for missionary work. So moved was Charles that he contributed "a roll of bills that represented a month's salary."

"Then as the enthusiasm mounted higher, people wanted to give their jewelry and even watches. At the announcement of this second offering, Charles disentangled his solid gold watch and chain, and looked down at the large diamond in Lettie's engagement ring, as if to say: 'Surely you are going to come along with me in this, aren't you?'"

Lettie did come along. She came along on a journey through life that would focus on treasures in heaven rather than treasures on earth. She and Charles volunteered for missionary service in Japan and went on to found the Oriental Missionary Society. It was a faith mission in the truest sense of the word. Funds were often low, but new recruits were admonished to be willing to sacrifice all for the cause of the gospel.

After Charles died, Lettie served as the director of the mission. Her goal was to spread worldwide the "Every Home Crusade" that they had initiated in Japan. She began an exhaustive traveling schedule, always challenging her listeners to reach out with the gospel to every home. The ideas and stories she gathered in her travels eventually found their way into her widely acclaimed devotional books, *Streams in the Desert*. Her one ambition in life was to lay up treasure in heaven.[18]

"Do not store up for yourselves treasures on earth, where moth and rust destroy, and where thieves break in and steal. But store up for yourselves treasures in heaven, where moth and rust do not destroy, and where thieves do not break in and steal. For where your treasure is, there your heart will be also.

*Matthew 6:19–21.*

# "HE RENEWED HIS COVENANT TO FOLLOW THE LORD"

King Josiah is remembered as the king who was faithful to God. He did not hesitate to lead his people in worship and to set an example before them by following the Lord. King George was another such king. He was the first Christian king in the United Kingdom of Tonga, who took "his turn as a local preacher in common with the others," according to a missionary observer. "He preached with great plainness and simplicity, and in strict accordance with the teaching of God's word."

George Tupou was born in the late eighteenth century, at a time when cannibalism and bloody warfare were still rife in the South Sea islands. Indeed, as a little child, he "witnessed violence almost continuously. When he was only two, the murder of his grandfather set off a civil war, which continued off and on for many years. Boys of his own age were taught to torture wounded prisoners."

When his father died in 1820, George became the new king. It was a time of change in the island world. Protestant missionaries had arrived, but they often found that they could not meet the demands of the tribal groups and chiefs. In 1829, King George himself visited the Methodist mission on Tonga to ask for a missionary. He was insulted when they offered Peter Vi, a native missionary. He left in anger, but a terrible storm on the way to his island convinced him that God was displeased with him. He thus returned to the mission and brought Peter Vi with him. Two years later he was baptized.

King George was a powerful evangelist—and three years after his baptism, there was a revival among his people. Missionaries reported that "it was found necessary to give up the schools for a week or two, and to hold six prayer-meetings every day." The revival affected the king personally, and from then on he insisted on sitting in church on the same level with the people rather than on his traditional elevated platform.

The revival in Tonga was so powerful that its impact spread beyond the natives. A sailor who was marooned there "found nothing going on but singing and praying. . . . He could not understand a single word, but he knew well what they were doing. . . . Forgotten words came back to his memory—words learned in a Sunday school. . . . His hard heart was melted. The English sailor knelt down among the Islanders of the Pacific."[19]

Then the king called together all the elders of Judah and Jerusalem. He went up to the temple of the Lord with the men of Judah, the people of Jerusalem, the priests and the prophets—all the people from the least to the greatest. He read in their hearing all the words of the Book of the Covenant, which had been found in the temple of the Lord. The king stood by the pillar and renewed the covenant in the presence of the Lord—to follow the Lord and keep his commands, regulations and decrees with all his heart and with all his soul.

*2 Kings 23:1–3a.*

## "HOW THE JAILER AT PHILIPPI WAS CAUGHT"

When in 1880 Dwight L. Moody was conducting evangelistic meetings in St. Louis, Missouri, the editors of the *Globe-Democrat* recognized the intense local interest and decided to print each evening's sermon in the next day's edition of the paper. "One night," Moody later recalled, "I preached on the Philippian jailer, and the next morning the paper came out with the sensational headline: 'How the Jailer at Philippi Was Caught.' A copy of the paper was carried into the city jail and fell into the hands of a notorious prisoner named Valentine Burke.

"This man was one of the worst characters known to the St. Louis police. He was about 40 years old at that time, had spent about 20 years in jail, and was then awaiting trial on a serious charge.

"As Burke glanced over the morning paper, the headline caught his eye. Thinking that it was some jail news, he began to read it; he was anxious to see how the jailer was caught. He thought he had once passed through a town called Philippi in Illinois.

After reading the article, "Burke wondered what had happened to the *Globe-Democrat* and looked at the date. It was that morning's paper all right. He was disgusted, but he could not shake off the text: 'Believe on the Lord Jesus Christ, and thou shalt be saved.'"

The following Sunday during a jail service, Valentine Burke made a profession of faith. From then on he was a changed man. "The sheriff thought he was playing the 'pious dodge' and had no confidence in his professed conversion," but once Burke was freed, the sheriff changed his mind and invited him to come back to the jail to work. He explained why. "I have had you shadowed ever since you left jail. I suspected your religion was a fraud. But I am convinced that you are sincere, as you've lived an honest life. I have sent for you to offer you a deputyship under me. You can begin at once."

Moody noted that: "Valentine Burke lived an active, consistent Christian life and maintained his position until God called him home in 1895."[20]

Suddenly there was such a violent earthquake that the foundations of the prison were shaken. At once all the prison doors flew open, and everybody's chains came loose. The jailer woke up, and when he saw the prison doors open, he drew his sword and was about to kill himself because he thought the prisoners had escaped. But Paul shouted, "Don't harm yourself! We are all here!"

The jailer called for lights, rushed in and fell trembling before Paul and Silas. He then brought them out and asked, "Sirs, what must I do to be saved?"

They replied, "Believe in the Lord Jesus, and you will be saved—you and your household."

*Acts 16:26–31.*

# "GOD DEMONSTRATES HIS OWN LOVE FOR US"

This passage of Scripture—especially Romans 5:8, in the King James Version, was instrumental in lighting the spark that ignited the fires of the great Welsh Revival in 1904, a revival that soon spread worldwide. During a routine revival meeting, evangelist Seth Joshua was aware that his message was not reaching the hearts of the people. As he concluded, he cried out to God in anguish, "Bend us—bend us—bend us, O Lord!" That appeal, combined with the realization of God's love for sinners, had a powerful impact on Evan Roberts, a young man in the congregation, as he later testified:

"I would have burst if I had not prayed. What boiled me was that verse, 'God commending His love,' I fell on my knees with my arms over the seat in front of me, and the tears and perspiration flowed freely. I thought blood was gushing forth. For about two minutes it was fearful. I cried, 'Bend us! Bend me! Bend us! . . . What bent me was God commending His love (Romans 5:8), and I not seeing anything in it to commend. After I was bent a wave of peace came over me. . . . Henceforth the salvation of souls became the burden of my heart."

For the next thirteen months, Roberts pleaded with God to send a spiritual awakening to Wales. Finally, he sensed that God wanted him to reach out with the gospel. He returned to his home town, and asked to speak to the youth of his church. The meeting lasted until midnight, and marked the beginning of a continuous revival. "The chapel was not closed afterward night or day for many months."

From there the revival spread like wildfire, and soon the only "entertainment" to be found was spiritual in nature. "The Devil had not really disappeared, nor had he been destroyed by that revival, but that he had been soundly defeated was undeniable! Theater-going dropped drastically. . . . In one village the entire football team disbanded because its members had been converted. Soccer and rugby matches were cancelled or rescheduled. Dance halls in area after area were completely deserted. . . . In a few months seventy thousand to one hundred thousand were said to have been saved, baptized and added to the churches.

"Probably one of the greatest transformations was seen in the speech of the Welsh miners. These men . . . marked by their profanity and blasphemy . . . were converted to Christ and their profanities gave way to paeans of praise sung or spoken to the glory of God in the lilting beauty of the Welsh brogue."[21]

**You see, at just the right time, when we were still powerless, Christ died for the ungodly. Very rarely will anyone die for a righteous man, though for a good man someone might possibly dare to die. But God demonstrates his own love for us in this: While we were still sinners, Christ died for us.**

*Romans 5:6–8.*

## "IT IS WELL WITH MY SOUL"

Sometimes the worst of life's tragedies turn into unexpected triumphs. Even the death of loved ones—the most bitter grief known to mankind—can lead to blessings. Such were the blessings H. G. Spafford experienced in 1873 when he penned the lines to one of the church's most moving hymns, "It Is Well With My Soul."

Spafford was a businessman who had lost much of his fortune in the Chicago fire in 1871, but that loss was not a "drop in the ocean" compared to the loss he would suffer two years later. In the fall of 1873 he bid farewell to his wife and four daughters—Maggie, Tanetta, Annie, and Bessie—and they left for Europe aboard the French passenger ship S.S. *Ville du Havre*. He was planning to join them after completing some necessary business transactions in Chicago. That reunion, however, never took place.

"At two o'clock on the morning of November 22, 1873, when the luxury liner was several days out, and sailing on a quiet sea, she was rammed by the English iron sailing vessel, the *Lochearn*. In two hours the *Ville du Havre*, one of the largest ships afloat, settled to the bottom of the ocean, with a loss of some two-hundred twenty-six lives, including the four Spafford children. Nine days later when the survivors landed at Cardiff, Wales, Mrs. Spafford cabled her husband these two words, 'Saved alone.'"

Spafford was comforted in his deep grief by his strong faith in God. That was evident as he sailed to join his wife. As the ship passed by the area where his daughters lost their lives, he once again committed his sorrow to God. "That night he found it hard to sleep. But faith soon conquered doubt, and there, in the mid-Atlantic, out of his heart-break and pain, Mr. Spafford wrote five stanzas, the first of which contained these lines:

"When peace like a river attendeth my way,
When sorrows like sea-billows roll,
Whatever my lot, Thou has taught me to say,
'It is well, it is well with my soul!'"

Further tragedy would soon be associated with this great hymn. The well-known composer, Philip P. Bliss, who put the words to music soon after Spafford wrote it, died with his wife in a train crash only three years later at the age of thirty-eight. For friends and relatives, the pain was almost too much to bear, but they, like succeeding generations of Christians, took comfort in their faith and in the words and music of "It Is Well With My Soul."[22]

Unless the Lord had given me help, I would soon have dwelt in the silence of death. When I said, "My foot is slipping," your love, O Lord, supported me. When anxiety was great within me, your consolation brought joy to my soul.

*Psalm 94:17–19.*

# "HE HAS MADE EVERYTHING BEAUTIFUL IN ITS TIME"

The fateful day was November 23, 1961—the day before Thanksgiving. The small twin-engine aircraft was just getting airborne, after having been delayed for a night by a blinding blizzard. Almost without warning one engine failed, and then the other. The pilot desperately tried to return to the runway, but to no avail. The plane went down in a pine forest and burst into flames.

"I opened my eyes and all I could see were flames," he later recalled. "I groped for the door, ripped off my seat belt and staggered away. How I got to the highway, I don't know. But when I made it that far, some men, whom I had been having a cup of coffee with just minutes before, and who had heard the explosion, came to help. They got me into the car, and I laid down in the back seat as they rushed me to a hospital."

As he lay in the hospital bed, even those closest to him never could have identified him as the Merrill Womach they had known. His face was charred beyond recognition, and his wife turned away in horror when she saw him the day after the accident. "Oh God," she prayed, "don't let that creature be my husband." After ten weeks in the hospital and dozens of operations over the following years, Merrill once again had a face. Indeed, it was a beautiful face that helped Merrill testify to God's work in his life.

At the time of the accident Merrill was returning home from singing engagements. He had used his voice in Christian ministry since he was six years old, and had become known on the west coast of the United States because of his frequent concerts. Such a tragedy would surely put an end to that, his friends thought. But, instead, it opened the door to ministry. "God has given me a face that people never forget," he insists. "Once they see me, they never forget me . . . and once they have heard what I have to say to the glory of the Lord, they never forget the face of the man who said it."

Following the accident, Merrill continued singing, but, as he has pointed out, his ministry expanded greatly as he was invited to simply tell his story. "I do more speaking for non-Christian groups than for church-related gatherings. I appear at a lot of conventions, some of them national affairs. . . . In telling my story, I can relate a personal experience with a personal God who is Jesus Christ."

Though deeply scarred, Merrill's face had a beauty that radiated the love of Jesus.[23]

What does the worker gain from his toil? I have seen the burden God has laid on men. He has made everything beautiful in its time. He has also set eternity in the hearts of men; yet they cannot fathom what God has done from beginning to end. I know that there is nothing better for men than to be happy and do good while they live. That everyone may eat and drink, and find satisfaction in all his toil—this is the gift of God. I know that everything God does will endure forever; nothing can be added to it and nothing taken from it. God does it so that men will revere him.

*Ecclesiastes 3:9–14.*

## "A HEART OF WISDOM"

One of the most brilliant scientists of the seventeenth century was Blaise Pascal; he was "one of the first and most significant mathematicians and physicists of the modern world." He "not only introduced calculus; he created the hydraulic press and did pioneering work in atmospheric pressure and the principle of the vacuum. He also invented the computer, but more important was his work on probability—the bet on God's existence."

Pascal was a Frenchman and a Jansenist—a follower of Cornelius Jansen, who had sought to reform Roman Catholicism by emphasizing the biblical concepts of man's sin and God's grace. Pascal's sister Jacqueline was a nun and a Jansenist, and he was deeply influenced by her. Indeed, so much so that on the night of November 23, 1654, he experienced what he referred to as his "night of fire." During this two-hour experience, he described his feelings in verse. He wrote that there was "Fire inside burning away doubt and distress," bringing "certitude" and a "forgetfulness of the world and of everything except God." It was an experience that changed his life. "Jesus Christ, Jesus Christ," he wrote, "let me never be separated from Him."

Pascal's "night of fire" changed his thinking. He continued his scientific research, but no longer was he depending exclusively on the reasoning of the mind. He had come to realize that there was more to life than brilliant scientific accomplishments. If he were to number his days aright, he would need a wisdom of the heart.

It was because he possessed this heart wisdom that Pascal developed what has become known as the "wager" of faith. This celebrated wager was a philosophical argument that he posed to his non-believing colleagues. It simply challenged them to gamble their lives on the possibility that Christianity might be true. Since the existence of God cannot be proven in a scientific laboratory, he dared skeptics: "Let us weigh the gain and the loss in wagering that God is. . . . If you gain, you gain all; if you lose, you lose nothing."

Through his wisdom of the heart, Pascal has had a powerful influence on skeptics and doubters in the centuries since his death. Of him, T. S. Eliot wrote: "I can think of no Christian writer . . . more to be commended than Pascal to those who doubt."[24]

The length of our days is seventy years—or eighty, if we have the strength; yet their span is but trouble and sorrow, for they quickly pass, and we fly away.

Who knows the power of your anger? For your wrath is as great as the fear that is due you. Teach us to number our days aright, that we may gain a heart of wisdom.

*Psalm 90:10–12.*

## "I HAVE SET BEFORE YOU LIFE AND DEATH"

Matthew Rice, a missionary with Overseas Crusades in West Germany, focuses on people in the prayer letters he sends to supporters back home. Most of these people are Germans with whom he has shared the gospel, but sometimes he includes others who have come into his life in unexpected ways, as he relates in one of his letters.

" 'Beer Can Stan' died in a barroom brawl 15 years ago in Denver. He'd been drinking beer that night, a lot of beer, when suddenly the guy standing next to him said something that cut him to the quick. So he pushed the guy. That sounded just like Stan. He'd done it to me too, but only in jest. You know, one of those affectionate gestures common between rowdies. But he'd also do it to people who irritated him, as a warm-up to a good fight. Well, the guy didn't like it, and he pulled out a gun and killed Stan right on the spot. So I was told.

"Stan's home life had been bad. He had an alcoholic father who would often go into brutal frenzies, yelling and hitting whoever was in the way. Because of this, Stan looked for self-worth by being rough, crass and propagating an image as an unbeatable drinker. But I knew Stan. Underneath that tough outer shell were hints of nobler qualities, partially dormant, sometimes active. Stan was brave. He'd once told the state golden-gloves boxing champ to leave me alone, because I was his friend. He was loyal. He'd have done anything for me in a pinch. And deep down there was a certain honor within him, like with the knights of old. I'd have trusted him with my baby sister.

"I grieved when I heard of Stan's death, because you see, I'd just become a believer in Jesus Christ. After years of aimless wandering I'd finally come home where I belonged. And I wanted Stan to come home too. But now it was too late. He was dead. . . ."

What a shock it was to Matt when he received a letter from Stan, saying that he was an Army sergeant and stationed close by in Germany. The story of his death had been greatly exaggerated! They immediately renewed their friendship, and the following Thanksgiving, Stan invited Matt and another friend of his for dinner—a dinner that would change their lives. "After a scrumptious Thanksgiving Day feast . . . my old buddy kneeled down on his living room floor, along with another sergeant friend of his, and both men gave over control of their lives to Jesus Christ!" God had set before him life and death, and he chose life.[25]

This day I call heaven and earth as witnesses against you that I have set before you life and death, blessings and curses. Now choose life, so that you and your children may live and that you may love the Lord your God, listen to his voice, and hold fast to him. For the Lord is your life, and he will give you many years in the land he swore to give your fathers, Abraham, Isaac and Jacob.

*Deuteronomy 30:19–20.*

# "THIS DAY IS SACRED TO THE LORD"

After five years of marriage, Sarah Hale was left a widow with five little children. She opened a millinery shop to support her family, and somehow she found time to write as well. In 1823, she published her first book, which told of her grief, and soon after that she wrote a novel, *Northwood*, written "literally with my baby in my arms." The success of her writing opened up the field of editing. In 1837, after successfully editing a smaller women's magazine, she was invited to edit *Godey's Lady's Book*. Under her leadership, subscriptions rose from 10,000 to nearly 150,000 in 1863.

*Godey's* was a secular magazine, but Hale did not hesitate to inject religious issues and to campaign for causes she deemed worthwhile. She was an Episcopalian and a committed Christian, and she had become convinced that America, as a nation, must set aside at least one day of the year to offer thanks to God. Indeed, for thirty-six years it was her single-minded mission to establish Thanksgiving as a national holiday. She wrote to congressmen, governors, and presidents, and by 1859, the governors from thirty states had agreed to a common day for celebration, but still there was no national holiday.

In 1863, she wrote to President Lincoln pleading her cause. As the editor of the nation's most popular women's magazine, he could not ignore her. She had strongly appealed for a Thanksgiving holiday on the basis of Scripture, emphasizing particularly Nehemiah 8:10, and called on the President to do what would give honor to God. He complied. On October 3, 1863, Lincoln read the proclamation, the last paragraph of which explicitly stated the purpose of the holiday.

"I do, therefore, invite my fellow citizens in every part of the United States, and also those who are at sea and those who are sojourning in foreign lands, to set apart and observe the last Thursday of November next as a day of thanksgiving and praise to our beneficent Father who dwelleth in the heavens."

For Mrs. Hale, the long campaign was over. At last, she "could relax and turn her editorial attention to other issues that were on her heart, such as women medical missionaries and the spiritual role of women for their children and their children's children."[26]

Then Nehemiah the governor, Ezra the priest and scribe, and the Levities who were instructing the people said to them all, "This day is sacred to the Lord your God. Do not mourn or weep." For all the people had been weeping as they listened to the words of the Law.

Nehemiah said, "Go and enjoy choice food and sweet drinks, and send some to those who have nothing prepared. This day is sacred to our Lord. Do not grieve, for the joy of the Lord is your strength."

*Nehemiah 8:9–10.*

# "WITH THE LORD OUR GOD THERE IS NO INJUSTICE"

The advice that Jehoshaphat gave the judges he appointed should still be heeded today—especially the absolute statement of fact that "with the Lord our God there is no injustice or partiality or bribery." How then should Christians respond to leaders and governments that foster injustice and partiality? Albert Luthuli, a black opponent of apartheid in South Africa gave an answer that is characteristic of his Christian testimony:

"But the struggle goes on, banishments, deportations, gaol [jail] or not. We do not struggle with guns and violence, and the Supremacist's array of weapons is powerless against the spirit . . . and every time cruel men injure or kill defenseless ones, they lose ground. The Supremacist illusion is that this is a battle of numbers, a battle of race, a battle of modern armaments against primitives. It is not. It is right against wrong, good against evil, the espousal of what is twisted, distorted and maimed against the yearning for health. They rejoice in what hurts the weak man's mind and body. They embrace what hurts their own soul."

Luthuli was raised in a Christian family, and served as a teacher before he was elected to be the chief of the Abase Makolweni Tribe in 1935. In 1952, because of his strong anti-apartheid stance, the government dismissed him from that role and began harassing him. "My only painful concern at times is that of the welfare of my family," he confessed, "but I try even in this regard, in a spirit of trust and surrender to God's will as I see it, to say: 'God will provide.' It is inevitable that in the working for Freedom some individuals and some families must take the lead and suffer: The Road to Freedom is via the Cross."

After Luthuli was confined in prison, he continued to serenely trust the Lord, confident that in the end justice would prevail. "I do not remember my cell as a place of boredom. It became, in fact, a place of sanctuary, a place where I could make up for the neglect of religious meditation occasioned by the hurly-burly of public life. There was time, there was quietness, there was comparative solitude. I used it. Frail man that I am, I pray humbly that I may never forget the opportunity God gave me to rededicate myself . . . and above all to be quiet in His Presence. My whitewashed cell became my chapel, my place of retreat."[27]

Jehoshaphat lived in Jerusalem, and he went out again among the people from Beersheba to the hill country of Ephriam and turned them back to the Lord, the God of their fathers. He appointed judges in the land, in each of the fortified cities of Judah. He told them, "Consider carefully what you do, because you are not judging for man but for the Lord, who is with you whenever you give a verdict. Now let the fear of the Lord be upon you. Judge carefully, for with the Lord our God there is no injustice or partiality or bribery."

*2 Chronicles 19:4–7.*

## "DEAR FRIENDS, LET US LOVE ONE ANOTHER"

For John Fawcett, a poor pastor in a little Yorkshire village, the call to a new church had been a dream come true. He had been converted through the ministry of George Whitefield and had served faithfully in a tiny Baptist parish for seven years. But his income of less than two hundred dollars a year was simply not adequate to comfortably support his growing family. The invitation to serve at the Carter's Lane Baptist Church in London was an honor and an opening for enlarged opportunities. He was to succeed Dr. Gill, a well-known and much loved minister who had recently died.

Excited by the prospect of a new field of ministry, Fawcett accepted the invitation and announced his decision to his congregation the following Sunday. It was a difficult announcement because he and his wife had developed a deep love for the dear friends in their parish—a love that was reinforced on the day of parting. The wagons were loaded and the people had come to bid a tearful farewell. Their sorrow and pain was evident in their faces.

"Finally the wife could bear it no longer. 'Oh, John,' she said. 'I know not how to bear this. I know not how to go.' 'Nor I, either,' replied her husband, 'nor will we go. Unload the wagons and put everything back where it was before.'"

It was a hasty and emotional decision, but it was firm. Fawcett continued in that pastorate until he died fifty-four years later. His ministry extended far beyond the bounds of that tiny parish—he opened a school for training pastors and wrote books and essays. Today, however, he is best remembered not for his preaching or scholarship, but for one hymn—a hymn reflecting on his and his wife's inability to part with his beloved parishioners.

> Blest be the tie that binds
> Our hearts in Christian love,
> The fellowship of kindred minds
> Is like to that above.[28]

Dear friends, let us love one another, for love comes from God. Everyone who loves has been born of God and knows God. Whoever does not love does not know God, because God is love. This is how God showed his love among us: He sent his one and only Son into the world that we might live through him. This is love: not that we loved God, but that he loved us and sent his Son as an atoning sacrifice for our sins. Dear friends, since God so loved us, we also ought to love one another. No one has ever seen God, but if we love one another, God lives in us and his love is made complete in us.

*1 John 4:7–12.*

# "HE HAS NOT LEFT HIMSELF WITHOUT TESTIMONY"

Missionaries to China have faced many obstacles in their work, but one of the most difficult has been that of language. Accustomed to relatively simply alphabets, they were often overwhelmed by the Chinese writing system of more than two hundred symbols or "radicals," which when combined in various ways, form some forty thousand word pictures called ideographs.

Some missionaries may have wondered why God in his sovereignty allowed this language barrier to slow down the progress of bringing the gospel to those who had never heard.

"One day, however, one of the missionaries stopped complaining. He was studying a particular Chinese ideograph, the one which means 'righteous.' He noticed that it contained an upper and lower part. The upper part was simply the Chinese symbol for *lamb*. Directly under the lamb was a second symbol, the first person pronoun *I*. Suddenly he discerned an amazingly well-coded message hidden within the ideograph: *I under the lamb am righteous!*"

When he challenged his Chinese friends with his finding they were amazed and more eager to hear the gospel message. Other missionaries began looking for spiritual meaning hidden within the word pictures. They found that the Chinese word for *boat* pictures a craft with eight people—a spiritual symbol of the eight people spared in Noah's ark during the flood.

"The radical meaning 'man' is a figure shaped like an upside down *y*. The ideograph meaning *tree* is a cross with the symbol for *man* superimposed upon it! And the symbol for *come* calls for two other smaller symbols for *man* to stand on either side of the tree with the greater man superimposed upon it. Some students of Chinese writing claim that the two smaller human figures collectively mean *mankind*. If so, the ideograph meaning *come* seems to carry a code that says: 'Mankind come to the man on the tree.'"

A missionary challenged a Chinese soldier with some of these spiritual messages he had found in the Chinese language. The soldier was amazed. "I was told that Christianity was a foreign devil's religion!" he insisted. "Now you show me that the writing system of my own country preaches it."[29]

But when the apostles Barnabas and Paul heard of this, they tore their clothes and rushed into the crowd, shouting: "Men, why are you doing this? We too are only men, human like you. We are bringing you good news, telling you to turn from these worthless things to the living God, who made heaven and earth and sea and everything in them. In the past, he let all nations go their own way. Yet he has not left himself without testimony."

*Acts 14:14–17a.*

# "YOUR ASTROLOGERS CANNOT EVEN SAVE THEMSELVES"

Contemporary Americans sometimes assume the phenomenon of astrology originated in California and has since spread nationwide—even into the White House during the Reagan Administration. But long before it became a western religion, astrology was an eastern religion, a fact that Anand Chaudhari could readily attest to.

Chaudhari was raised in a Brahman family in India, and at a young age began training to follow his father into the priesthood. In 1942, at the age of twelve, he moved to Bombay for secular schooling, and in 1950, he enrolled at the University of Bombay. Although he continued to perform ritual priesthood duties, his interests shifted, first to the ideals of Mahatma Gandhi and later to communism. Then he met Joseph, a Catholic studying at the university, who introduced him to Christianity.

Through his influence, Anand began reading the gospel of Matthew. He was gripped by the story of Jesus. One night while he was meditating along the sea shore, he began praying for Jesus to reveal himself to him. He later described the moments that followed: "Somehow I felt the real presence of Christ there. Someone holy just touched me and surrounded me. . . . I was really committed to Christ." Not surprisingly, Anand's commitment to Christ devastated his family. It was seen as prompting the wrath of the gods that caused his parents' death.

The year was 1954, and the setting was the Ganges River. Anand's parents had made a pilgrimage for the Kumbh Mela festival to bathe in the holy waters. "Each year pundits and astrologers determined the most propitious moment to enter the water, according to the phases of the moon, and the alignment of the sun, moon, and the planet Jupiter. . . . In 1954 . . . a series of conditions had come together which occurred only once in 144 years." As a result millions of people thronged the area all seeking to bathe at the opportune moment. Tragically, hundreds were trampled to death, Anand's parents included.

Although he was brokenhearted by his parents' death, the tragedy only increased his dependence on his newfound faith. After hearing a Christian radio program, he enrolled in Bible school, and in later years Anand became the president of Rajasthan Bible Institute.[30]

All the counsel you have received has only worn you out! Let your astrologers come forward, those stargazers who make predictions month by month, let them save you from what is coming upon you. Surely they are like stubble, the fire will burn them up. They cannot even save themselves from the power of the flame. Here are no coals to warm anyone, here is no fire to sit by. That is all they can do for you—these you have labored with and trafficked with since childhood. Each of them goes on in his error, there is not one that can save you.

*Isaiah 47:13–15.*

# "WHATEVER HE DOES PROSPERS"

At the age of seventeen, the only word he could read was *cat*. At the time of his death, he had an eight-thousand volume library and could read in Greek and Hebrew, as well as English. Unfortunately, this remarkable man has been forgotten by the history books.

Charles A. Tindley was born a slave on a Maryland plantation. After his mother died when he was five, he was separated from his father and sold to a man who wanted to make sure his investment remained passive and hardworking. Recognizing the boy's intelligence, he forbade him to attend church or learn to read. He did not want him to acquire any notions about racial equality.

After winning his freedom following the Civil War, Tindley was determined to get an education. He worked long days in the fields, as he had previously, but he was a free man in the evenings. Night after night he walked fourteen miles to classes for a basic elementary education. But Charles learned far more than any teacher could offer him. He sacrificed necessities to buy books and spent his spare time reading. His thirst for knowledge also led him to church, where his call to ministry followed soon after his conversion. On his own he began studying for the ministerial exams to enter the Methodist ministry, and when he sat for the exam, he rated second highest in the class.

Tindley began his ministry at a tiny black church in Cape May, New Jersey, but soon he received a call from another church—a dingy storefront mission in Philadelphia. The opportunities of a big city challenged him, and before long his congregation purchased a building that would accommodate six hundred people. The building soon had to be enlarged, and when it no longer held the crowds, the congregation acquired a vacant church seating fifteen hundred. Over the years the congregation continued to grow, and by 1924, it had to be enlarged to seat more than three thousand.

Tindley was ever a humble man. Once while speaking before a large audience of ministers and educators, he opened with the prayer: "Father, speak through me as if I were a telephone, and when you are through hang up." This humble spirit was also evident in the gospel songs he wrote, which included "Take Your Burden to the Lord and Leave it There," and "Nothing Between"—a song that has long stirred the hearts of Christians: "Nothing between my soul and the Savior, Naught of this world's delusive dream, I have renounced all sinful pleasure, Jesus is mine, let nothing between."[1]

Blessed is the man who does not walk in the counsel of the wicked or stand in the way of sinners or sit in the seat of mockers. But his delight is in the law of the Lord, and on his law he meditates day and night. He is like a tree planted by streams of water, which yields its fruit in season and whose leaf does not wither. Whatever he does prospers.

*Psalm 1:1–3.*

# "DIFFERENT GIFTS ACCORDING TO THE GRACE GIVEN US"

Out of necessity sometimes Christians develop more than one spiritual gift. Indeed, on rare occasions they demonstrate virtually all of those that the apostle Paul lists in Romans 12. Mary Slessor was one such individual. Born in Scotland in 1848, she was often physically abused by her drunken father, and was required to work long hours. The influence of her devout Christian mother propelled her into Christian ministry—first as a volunteer in the city slums and then, at the age of twenty-eight, as a missionary to Africa.

Her work in Africa has been described by many contemporary observers and biographers, but perhaps the most telling portrayal of her came from an unbelieving journalist, Mary Kingsley, who traveled to Africa in 1893 and later wrote of her findings in *Travels in West Africa*. The journalist had no sympathy for the message of the gospel, but of Mary Slessor, she wrote, "she gave me some of the pleasantest days of my life." They talked together for hours about spiritual matters, and the visitor confessed, "I would give anything to possess your beliefs, but I can't, I can't; when God made me He must have left out the part that one believes with."

But what the journalist failed to comprehend on a spiritual level, she grasped very readily on a practical level—especially as she described Mary Slessor's work and the amazing gifts she demonstrated with the Africans.

"This very wonderful lady has been eighteen years in Calabar; for the last six or seven living entirely alone, as far as white folks go, in a clearing in the forest near to one of the principal villages of the Okoyong district, and ruling as a veritable white chief over the entire district. Her great abilities, both physical and intellectual, have given her among the savage tribe a unique position, and won her, from white and black who know her, a profound esteem. Her knowledge of the native, his language, his ways of thought, his diseases, his difficulties, and all that is his, is extraordinary, and the amount of good she has done, no man can fully estimate. Okoyong, when she went there alone ... was given, as most of the surrounding districts still are, to killing at funerals, ordeal by poison, and perpetual internecine wars. Many of these evil customs she has stamped out. . . . Miss Slessor stands alone."[2]

Just as each of us has one body with many members, and these members do not all have the same function, so in Christ we who are many form one body, and each member belongs to all the others. We have different gifts, according to the grace given us. If a man's gift is prophesying, let him use it in proportion to his faith. If it is serving, let him serve; if it is teaching, let him teach; if it is encouraging, let him encourage; if it is contributing to the needs of others, let him give generously; if it is leadership, let him govern diligently; if it is showing mercy, let him do it cheerfully.

*Romans 12:4–8.*

# "TEACH THEM TO YOUR CHILDREN"

"A child of five, if properly instructed, can as readily believe and be regenerated as anyone." This statement could not be true, the pastor reasoned—even if it did come from the pen of the great preacher and evangelist, Charles Haddon Spurgeon.

The pastor was Jesse Irvin Overholtzer. He had only recently come to accept the belief in salvation by faith alone, and now to think that this salvation experience could be enjoyed by young children was beyond his comprehension. He had nine children of his own, and he always assumed that a decision as important as one's personal faith could be made only by a mature individual. But the more he thought about Charles Spurgeon's statement, the more troubled he became. If Spurgeon was right in his assessment, then he himself was overlooking a large segment of his congregation, as well as his family, in his evangelistic ministry.

As Overholzer struggled with the issue, he decided to put the evangelist's assertion to the test. He approached two youngsters in his church—not his own nor children of members, because he feared opposition. Rather, he spoke to children who attended school, who came from non-Christian homes. One was a nine-year-old boy, the other a ten-year-old girl. In both instances the children readily accepted the gospel and professed faith in Christ. His victory prompted him to speak to other children, and soon twenty of them had made professions of faith.

But were these professions real, or were they induced by the power of persuasion that an older person has over a child? His answer to that question came during a series of revival meetings. When the invitation was given, the first person to respond was the mother of two of the girls who had been converted through his *child evangelism*. He had sought to lead her to the Lord previously, but she had resisted the gospel. What had changed?

"Her reply shook from him any doubts he had held about the credibility of conversions among little children. 'I came,' she replied, 'because of the changed lives of my two little girls.'" From that point on Overholzer's burden for children grew. In the years that followed he spoke at churches and conferences, always presenting the need to reach children. Then, in 1937, at the age of sixty, "Mr. O," as he was affectionately called, founded Child Evangelism Fellowship, an organization that would focus on his deepest concern—children. He would direct this organization for the next fifteen years.[3]

Only be careful, and watch yourselves closely so that you do not forget the things your eyes have seen or let them slip from your heart as long as you live. Teach them to your children and to their children after them. Remember the day you stood before the Lord your God at Horeb, when he said to me, "Assemble the people before me to hear my words so that they may learn to revere me as long as they live in the land and may teach them to their children."

*Deuteronomy 4:9–10.*

## "REJOICING OVER ONE SINNER WHO REPENTS"

The aspect of Billy Graham's evangelistic ministry that draws the most attention from the media and outside observers is the crusades, when hundreds of people respond to the invitation at the end of the service. But as important as these mass meetings are, the months of preparation and follow-up are even more crucial. During these times the gospel goes out not to crowds of thousands, but to people one by one. This is illustrated by the Brazilian crusade held in Rio in 1974.

"The Christian Life and Witness course, as in many other cities when a crusade is in preparation, had the effect of beginning the evangelism long before Billy Graham's arrival. Thus at one church a married woman believer, Dona Zerda, inspired and taught by the classes, began to speak of Christ to her neighbors. The woman next door, Dona Helza, a backslider, returned to her faith. Soon Dona Helza's three daughters and two nieces, all living in the house, were converted, followed by Dona Zerda's youngest son.

"Dona Zerda's husband, Senhor Serafim, was the leader of a spiritist center. Practicing black magic (macumba) with its blood offerings of sacrificed chickens, it promoted hatred and fear. Through the prayers of his son and the church, and the witness of his wife, Serafim abandoned macumba and accepted Christ. His first convert was Jaedemilto, fiancé of one of their daughters, who later brought in several of his own family."

The chain reaction continued on and on—months before the crusade had even begun. The most widely-known individual to come to Christ through personal evangelism during this period of crusade planning was Darlene Gloria, "Brazil's favorite film and television star . . . who had recently received an award as best actress of the year for her part in a film written by Brazil's equivalent of Tennessee Williams, *All Nudity Will be Punished.*"

Following her conversion, Darlene abandoned her acting career and joined a Presbyterian church. When the actual crusade came to the city, she sang in the choir all five nights. After the crusade, "she devoted herself to work among the very poor in the shanty settlements near Brasilia. As with each of the others in the chain reaction after Dona Zerda's commitment to the Lord, there was surely rejoicing in heaven for Darlene Gloria—one sinner who repented.[4]

"Or suppose a woman has ten silver coins and loses one. Does she not light a lamp, sweep the house and search carefully until she finds it? And when she finds it, she calls her friends and neighbors together and says, 'Rejoice with me, I have found my lost coin.' In the same way, I tell you, there is rejoicing in the presence of the angels of God over one sinner who repents."

*Luke 15:8–10.*

# "IT IS GOOD FOR THEM TO STAY UNMARRIED, AS I AM"

The effectiveness of the apostle Paul's ministry was apparently due in part to his unmarried status, and his encouragement to others to emulate him has influenced many Christians down through the centuries. Often for these people there had been the opportunity for marriage, but the call to ministry has been stronger. This was the case with Henrietta Mears, who founded Gospel Light Publishing Company and served with distinction for many years as the Christian Education minister at Hollywood Presbyterian Church. When she began her work at that church in 1928, there were fewer than five hundred enrolled in the Sunday school. Two years later the enrollment had increased to over four thousand. Her first love was her large college class, and she dedicated her life to this ministry in a way that she could not have done were she married.

"Henrietta modeled singleness to thousands of college students. She insisted that choosing a mate was one of life's greatest decisions. When collegians asked why she had not married, she answered because she had not lived in the same dispensation as the apostle Paul. Moreover, she had never found anyone, in this age, to match him, although she kept looking."

Years earlier, on a spring night in Minnesota, she had faced the difficult decision of whether or not to marry. The young man was a banker who had many things to offer, but he was not fully committed to God. "Lord," she prayed, "You have made me the way I am. I love a home, I love security, I love children, and love him. Yet I feel that marriage under these conditions would draw me away from You. I surrender Lord, even this, and I leave it in Thy hands. Lead me, Lord, and strengthen me. You have promised to fulfill all my needs. I trust in Thee."

Did God fulfill all her needs? She was certain he had: "The marvelous thing has been . . . that the Lord has always given me a beautiful home; He has given me thousands of children; the Lord has supplied everything in my life and I've never felt lonely. . . . I've never missed companionship."

Henrietta's single status gave her influence and authority that she may never have had were she married. She was a strong woman and was accepted as such. On one occasion she angrily interrupted a testimony meeting: "This has been the most ridiculous testimony time I think I have ever heard. All we have been talking about is silly little things that don't amount to a hill of beans! Have we lost sight of why we are here? There hasn't been one word about winning the nations for Christ."[5]

I wish that all men were as I am. But each man has his own gift from God; one has this gift, another has that.

Now to the unmarried and the widows I say: It is good for them to stay unmarried, as I am. But if they cannot control themselves, they should marry, for it is better to marry than to burn with passion.

*1 Corinthians 7:7–9.*

# "THE BELOVED PHYSICIAN"

Luke, the author of the gospel by that name and the Acts of the Apostles, was truly "the beloved physician" (KJV). He serves as a role model for physicians of all generations to reach out with the gospel, as Paul admonished, to "pray that God may open a door for our message" and to "make the most of every opportunity." A physician in more recent times who demonstrated this kind of evangelical zeal was Howard A. Kelly, the "beloved physician of Baltimore."

Kelly studied at the University of Pennsylvania Medical School and then went on to found the Kensington Hospital in that state. He was quickly recognized by his colleagues as a brilliant physician and in 1889, at the age of thirty-one, was invited to help found Johns Hopkins Medical School in Baltimore. "There he was catapulted to world fame." Indeed, he pioneered in two areas of medicine: "A large amount of modern urology bears upon work that he did many years ago. His work in kidney surgery alone would stamp him as one of the greatest authorities in modern urology. . . . His work in physics and radium makes him unquestionably the one to receive credit for introducing radium to the medical profession." During his career, he wrote more than a dozen textbooks and hundreds of articles.

But Kelly, like Luke, was far more than a physician. He was a member of the Mount Vernon Methodist Episcopal Church, a frequent contributor to the *Sunday School Times*, and an active supporter of the YMCA and the China Inland Mission. He was known for wearing a little blue lapel pin with a question mark on it. When asked about it, as he frequently was, he said it symbolized the most important question that could be asked. Inevitably that answer roused even more curiosity, and then the doctor would ask, "What think ye of Christ?"

Kelly was convinced that "the only way you can keep your Christian faith is to give it away," and he was motivated by his belief that "the only excuse I have for insisting on breaking through the reserves of every man I meet is that Jesus Christ died for him as well as for me, and I want him to know it." On one occasion while riding with a friend in a cab, he asked the driver when he stopped at a red light, "When you get to the gate of heaven, will there be a red light or a green light?" When the driver responded that he hoped it would be green, Kelly asked if he would like to make sure. When the driver responded in the affirmative, they pulled off the road with the meter still running, and he committed his life to Christ.[6]

**Devote yourselves to prayer, being watchful and thankful. And pray for us, too, that God may open a door for our message, so that we may proclaim the mystery of Christ, for which I am in chains. Pray that I may proclaim it clearly, as I should. Be wise in the way you act toward outsiders; make the most of every opportunity. . . . Our dear friend Luke, the doctor, and Demas send greetings.**

*Colossians 4:2–5, 14.*

# "ALWAYS DOING GOOD AND HELPING THE POOR"

What a tribute to Dorcas that after she had died, it would be said of her that she "was always doing good and helping the poor." Because of her concern for others—especially the poor—Dorcas has been a role model for women of all cultures down through the ages. China has had its Dorcas in the person of Mother Soong, the wife of a Methodist preacher and Bible publisher.

Mother Soong was born into an illustrious family and carried on her family's tradition with her own children. She was a descendant of Wen Ting-Kung, an acclaimed prime minister of the Ming Dynasty, who was converted in 1601, through the missionary outreach of Matthew Ricci, a Jesuit priest. Her own children grew up in the Christian faith and were influential in high places. One daughter became the wife of Sun Yat-sen, the father of the Republic of China; another daughter married Chiang Kai-shek, the famous general who fought against Mao Tse-tung; and a son served as a finance and foreign minister for his country.

But the Soong heritage was more than one of public government service. Wen Ting-Kung's daughter, Candida, founded hospitals and churches in seventeenth-century China, and Mother Soong maintained that legacy. She was compelled to share her wealth with the less fortunate. She was known far and wide for her loving generosity. "Poor mothers came to her with their sick babies, and often they went away restored by her gifts and prayers and Bible stories."

Her daughters followed her example in their outreach to the needy, particularly Chingling who was married to Sun Yat-sen. "During the period of Japanese invasion and occupation from 1937 to 1945, Mme. Sun also went forth to gather 'guerrilla babies'—children in the isolated mountain region of northwest China, whose fathers were in guerrilla bands or the regular army and whose mothers were in war work. She established a dozen or more schools for these nearly-abandoned youngsters. She also induced three friends to join her in giving eighty thousand dollars to equip a hospital, and organized a drive to finance a small one." And so the Dorcas legacy lived on in China.[7]

**In Joppa there was a disciple named Tabitha (which, when translated, is Dorcas), who was always doing good and helping the poor. About that time she became sick and died, and her body was washed and placed in an upstairs room. Lydda was near Joppa; so when the disciples heard that Peter was in Lydda, they sent two men to him and urged him, "Please come at once!"**

**Peter went with them, and when he arrived he was taken upstairs to the room. All the widows stood around him, crying and showing him the robes and other clothing that Dorcas had made while she was still with them.**

*Acts 9:36–39.*

## "WE ARE MORE THAN CONQUERORS"

"The Lord bless you and guide you, and as for us, may God be glorified whether by life or by death." These were some of the last words that John Stam wrote to his mission board, the China Inland Mission, before he and his wife Betty were executed on December 8, 1934. They had been married only fourteen months and had just moved with their two-month-old baby to their new station in the province of Anhwei.

They were aware of the unrest in this area due to the Communist insurgents, but they had been assured that the government forces of Chiang Kai-shek could hold them back. Their uneasy sense of security was broken suddenly on December 6, while Betty was bathing little Helen. The insurgents plundered the town, and the Stams were taken hostage.

"As part of John and Betty's torture, the captors discussed whether they would kill the infant immediately to save trouble. But an unexpected protest arose from an onlooking Chinese farmer, who had been released from prison when communists sacked the town. He stepped forward to plead that the baby had done nothing worthy of death."

How dare he challenge them! "Then it's your life for hers!" they sneered. The man acquiesced. "He was chopped to pieces." The Stams were then marched under guard to another town, where they had previously worked.

"The next morning, John and Betty were summoned and led outside. Painfully bound with ropes and stripped of their outer garments, they passed down the street where John had ministered to many. . . . Like their Master, they were led up a little hill outside the town."

When a Chinese Christian pleaded they be spared, he was dragged away and slain. "John began to speak to the crowd, probably a Christian testimony, but the executioner cut his throat. Betty quivered. Still bound, she fell on her knees beside him. A quick command and the flash of a sword from behind reunited them for eternity."

In the meantime, baby Helen was left in a deserted house until she was discovered thirty hours later by a Chinese Christian who carried her to safety in a rice basket. Her rescue became a symbol of God's grace to countless Christians throughout the world. She was spared; her parents were not. "May God be glorified, whether by life or death."[8]

As it is written: "For your sake we face death all day long; we are considered as sheep to be slaughtered."

In all these things we are more than conquerors through him who loved us. For I am convinced that neither death nor life, neither angels nor demons, neither the present nor the future, nor any powers, neither height nor depth, nor anything else in all creation, will be able to separate us from the love of God that is in Christ Jesus our Lord.

*Romans 8:36–39.*

## "THE LEAST OF THESE BROTHERS OF MINE"

Thomas and Cynthia Hale, a team of medical doctors who served as missionaries in Nepal, discovered that there were many cross-cultural adjustments to make when they first arrived in that exotic land. How to deal with the stream of beggars that knocked at their door was just one of those adjustments. As middle-class Americans they had never before been confronted with this social phenomenon.

One particular beggar known by the villagers as Laato became a daily nuisance to the Hales. He "was an unpleasant young fellow who used to put his nose up to the living room window and stare inside for minutes on end, trampling all over Cynthia's flowers to get a better view. He was invariably dirty and unkempt. . . . Only after several visits did we realize that he was deaf and dumb. . . . When he wasn't watching through the window, he would sit for hours on our doorstep waiting to be fed. He would grunt and grimace, pointing comically to his supposedly empty stomach."

One day while on his way to the hospital and, only minutes after the Hales had given Laato a dish of rice, Thomas spotted him at another house eating a bowl of rice there, and when he returned home not long after that, Laato was at still another house eating rice that he had begged from the householder. "He gave me a sly grin, happy to let me in on his little secret. He couldn't have been more pleased with himself."

Thomas was—not surprisingly—irritated with Laato. But God's Word reprimanded him for these feelings. "One day seeing Laato again with his nose flattened against the window pane, I remembered afresh what Jesus had said about those who fed the hungry and invite in the stranger and clothe the naked: '. . . whatever you did for one of the least of these brothers of mine, you did for me.' I began to see Laato in a new light and no longer resented his intrusions. His visits occurred less frequently after that, as if, having taught me my lesson, he was no longer needed."9

"Then the righteous will answer him, 'Lord, when did we see you hungry and feed you, or thirsty and give you something to drink? When did we see you a stranger and invite you in, or needing clothes and clothe you? When did we see you sick or in prison and go to visit you?'

"The King will reply, 'I tell you the truth, whatever you did for one of the least of these brothers of mine, you did for me.'"

*Matthew 25:37–40.*

# "IMPRESS THEM ON YOUR CHILDREN"

Sharing the gospel should not be construed as a one-time proposition. Even as the children of Israel were instructed to repeat the commands of God over and over again, so ought contemporary Christians to talk about the Lord as they walk along the road and as they lie down and get up.

This was the conviction of Katherine Hankey, a nineteenth-century English woman whose family was active in the evangelical wing of the Anglican church. She longed to be able to preach, but her church barred her from having any official preaching ministry. She refused, however, to let any such restrictions stop her from sharing the gospel. Her "congregation" was made up of the children who attended her Sunday schools located throughout London.

So forceful was she that many of her pupils went on to become influential Christian leaders. She wrote material for her classes and books of verse, donating the royalties to missions. Her view of ministry was summed up in the treasured legacy she left for the church: her testimony in verse which became one of the church's best-loved hymns. It speaks of telling the story "for those who know it best," but also to those who have never heard:

> I love to tell the story—'Tis pleasant to
> repeat
> What seems, each time I tell it, more
> wonderfully sweet;
> I love to tell the story, for some have never
> heard
> The message of salvation from God's own
> holy Word.

Another hymn she wrote with a similar message, but from the hearer's viewpoint, was her much loved "Tell Me the Old, Old Story." For her, Christian ministry was simply sharing the gospel with others— to those who have heard it before and to those who have not..[10]

Hear, O Israel: The Lord our God, the Lord is one. Love the Lord your God with all your heart and with all your soul and with all your strength. These commandments that I give you today are to be upon your hearts. Impress them on your children. Talk about them when you sit at home and when you walk along the road, when you lie down and when you get up.

*Deuteronomy 6:4–7.*

# "CLEANSING CONSCIENCES THAT LEAD TO DEATH"

James O. Fraser, a missionary with the China Inland Mission for many years among the Lisu people of northwest China, was often in anguish over the behavior of the converts in the region. He became discouraged with Christians who reverted back into their sinful ways, and he struggled with the slow progress his converts often made in recognizing wrong behavior or in accepting his ethical standards. An example of this was their involvement in opium production and trade.

In one area converts welcomed him with delight, sharing the good news of their flourishing opium trade. There was anger in their voices, however, when they told him that the Chinese government had planned to send in the military to destroy their crops. But they took action to protect themselves. "We had a prayer-meeting," they explained, "and asked God to protect our opium. We got knives and poisoned arrows ready to fight the soldiers if they came. But they didn't turn up, and we've made more money than ever on our opium this year, praise God!"

"They know my position," Fraser wrote to his supporters, "and I am telling them plainly that I cannot baptize anyone directly connected with the growth, use or sale of opium. Still, we must, I think, have broad enough sympathies to recognize genuine faith, even when it is accompanied by an almost untutored conscience. We must remember how, among ourselves, John Newton never had a conscience against the slave traffic but 'enjoyed sweet communion with God,' as he tells us, even when on his slave-raiding expeditions."

"There is such a thing as exercising faith for others," Fraser had written previously. "When others are weak and we cannot be with them in person, God may be calling us to stand with and for them in spirit. He is able to quicken into life the very feeblest spark of desire for Him, or to use for their blessing the smallest amount of truth they may have apprehended. Indeed I have seen this before now, among the Lisu. They may know, often what we call next to nothing; yet, if in any measure the grace of God is in them, they remember the little they do know, and it seems to sustain them. . . . Let us all be imbued with the spirit of the Apostle who, though he had never seen the Roman converts, truly longed after them, that he might 'impart unto them some spiritual gift,' and so far from absolving himself from responsibility, felt himself to be a debtor, 'both to the Greeks and to the barbarians, both to the wise and to the foolish.'"[11]

The blood of goats and bulls and the ashes of a heifer sprinkled on those who are ceremonially unclean sanctify them so that they are outwardly clean. How much more, then, will the blood of Christ, who through the eternal Spirit offered himself unblemished to God, cleanse our consciences from acts that lead to death, so that we may serve the living God!

*Hebrews 9:13–14.*

## "DO NOT BE ASHAMED TO TESTIFY ABOUT OUR LORD"

He was a public figure whose name had been in the newspaper headlines for weeks. The last thing he wanted people to hear about was his personal religious commitment. But the media was relentless in its search for any tidbit of interest, and the report of a religious conversion gave the perfect twist to the story. One such write-up, entitled "Conversion," began with a caustic sentence: "Of all the Watergate cast, few had a reputation for being tougher, wilier, nastier or more tenaciously loyal to Richard Nixon than one-time Presidential Adviser Charles W. Colson."

As much as he abhorred the ridicule that he knew would be heaped upon him, deep down Charles Colson realized that such publicity could reinforce his fragile faith. He was now "locked completely into a new life, no falling back into my old ways." He had no choice but to admit that the rumors were true. "Not to verify the story would be almost to deny the reality of what had happened to me," he confessed. "There was no other way, I concluded, no way to modify it, condition it, or call it something else, no socially acceptable middle ground."

Colson had come to faith in Christ because a friend had not been ashamed to share openly what Christ had done for him. The friend was Tom Phillips. He testified how he had been converted at a Billy Graham Crusade in Madison Square Garden, and how his life had changed. Phillips went on to share how pride, as C. S. Lewis argued, was the "great sin" that kept people from God. "It is Pride," wrote Lewis, "which has been the chief cause of misery in every nation and every family since the world began. . . . Pride always means enmity—it *is* enmity. And not only enmity between man and man, but enmity to God."

Those words cut deeply, as Colson painfully recalled how pride had driven him and controlled him as he had clawed his way to the top. He recognized his need, and that night, driving from his friend's home, he pulled off the road and prayed his "first real prayer"—"God, I don't know how to find you, but I'm going to try! I'm not much the way I am now, but somehow I want to give myself to You. *Take me. Take me. . . .*" Colson did find God, and in the years that followed, after serving a prison sentence for his Watergate involvement, he went on to develop a far-reaching prison ministry and to speak and write openly about his faith in God.[12]

So do not be ashamed to testify about our Lord, or ashamed of me his prisoner. But join with me in suffering for the gospel, by the power of God, who has saved us and called us to a holy life—not because of anything we have done but because of his own purpose and grace. This grace was given us in Christ Jesus before the beginning of time, but it has now been revealed through the appearing of our Savior, Christ Jesus, who has destroyed death and has brought life and immortality to light through the gospel.

*2 Timothy 1:8–10.*

## "WE ARE GOD'S FELLOW WORKERS"

The desire to preach God's Word almost seemed to be in his blood. He preached his first sermon in 1876, at the age of twelve, and when he died in 1945, he left behind four sons who were preachers and he "was known throughout the English-speaking world as the 'prince of expositors.'" Although he never took any formal Bible school or seminary training, his name— G. Campbell Morgan—has become known throughout the world. He wrote books and published sermons that have been used often to train other pastors.

Morgan's commitment to Bible exposition developed in his early adult years after he had gone through a period of doubt. He studied many books, but they offered him no certainty of belief. Finally, he became so troubled that he locked his books in a cabinet, purchased a Bible, and vowed to read it until the matter was settled. "If it *be* the Word of God, and if I come to it with an unprejudiced and open mind," he insisted, "it will bring assurance to my soul of itself." He discontinued his preaching ministry and spent hours and days poring over the Bible until he could say, "the Bible found me." No longer did he feel compelled to defend the Bible; he simply preached its message.

Despite his early success in itinerant preaching, Morgan met with failure when he first sought a settled pastorate. His "trial sermon" before the congregation at the Lichfield Road Church in Birmingham was an utter failure. He wired his father a single word: "Rejected!" His father responded in six: "Rejected on earth—accepted in heaven."

Morgan went on to serve in pastorates, but he had a style of ministry that was sometimes criticized. Except for a twelve-year pastorate at Westminster Chapel in London, he served churches for short periods of time. So much of his time was spent in study and sermon preparation that he had little time for pastoral visitation. He preached devotional rather than doctrinal messages—focusing on the four Gospels. As he moved on from his earlier ministry of an evangelist, he simply concentrated on preaching the Word.

As such, Morgan seemed to be in the right place at the right time. He "came on the scene in Britain just after the great Moody-Sankey meetings, when there were thousands of new converts who needed to be taught the Word of God. Morgan met that need." Apollos watered. So also did Morgan.[13]

**What, after all, is Apollos? And what is Paul? Only servants, through whom you came to believe—as the Lord has assigned to each his task. I planted the seed, Apollos watered it, but God made it grow. So neither he who plants nor he who waters is anything, but only God, who makes things grow. The man who plants and the man who waters have one purpose, and each will be rewarded according to his own labor. For we are God's fellow workers; you are God's field, God's building.**

*1 Corinthians 3:5–9.*

## "FLEE AND FIND REFUGE"

How do missionaries explain to people of vastly different cultures what Christianity is all about? How do they describe who Jesus really is and how he can transform lives? How do they define the meaning of true faith and the peace and security it offers? There are no easy answers, but missionaries learned long ago that it requires more than simply translating biblical concepts word for word into a new language—if, indeed, the language has words that even remotely fit the concepts.

Most missionaries realize that in order to explain the gospel effectively, they must investigate the culture as they learn the language, and seek to discover traditional practices and beliefs. One way of using traditional practices to help explain the gospel is to employ "redemptive analogies." Don Richardson demonstrated their use in his work with tribal groups such as the Yali of Irian Jaya.

After his missionary colleague, Stan Dale, died at the hands of the Yali, Richardson traveled to that region of Irian Jaya. He wanted to investigate the situation and seek to find ways to more effectively present the gospel to the Yali people. In his research, he discovered that the Yali, regarded as a thoroughly ferocious and warlike people, had a tradition that seemed to run counter to their reputation as brutal killers.

While talking with a young Yali man about tribal life, he was suddenly transfixed when he learned for the first time about the *Osuwa*. Two Yali men, the story went, had suddenly been ambushed by their enemies. One was speared, but Sunahan, the other man, managed to escape to the *Osuwa*, a small area encircled by a stone wall. Richardson was amazed to learn that "if the raiders had shed one drop of Sunahan's blood while he stood within that wall, their own people would have punished them with death when they reached home. Likewise, although Sunahan held weapons in his hands, he dared not release an arrow at the enemy while standing within that wall."

For Richardson, this tradition in Yali culture was very significant. He later pointed out to Kusaho, a Yali Christian, that the Yali place of refuge was not only similar to the ancient Jewish cities of refuge, but that it was also similar to the refuge Christ offers the believer—except that "Christ was man's perfect Refuge . . . one that could be around you in any geographical location—one that could deliver you from spiritual as well as physical danger." Suddenly the gospel took on new meaning to Kusaho, and he was better equipped to explain it to others.[14]

**Then Moses set aside three cities east of the Jordan, to which anyone who had killed a person could flee and find refuge if he had unintentionally killed his neighbor without malice aforethought. He could flee into one of these cities and save his life. The cities were these: Bezer in the desert plateau, for the Reubenites, Ramoth in Gilead, for the Gadites, and Golan in Bashan, for the Manassites.**

*Deuteronomy 4:41–43.*

# "THE LORD WILL COME LIKE A THIEF IN THE NIGHT"

Andrew P. Stirrett was a successful, unmarried thirty-seven-year-old Canadian pharmacist, who sold his business in 1902, donated his property to the Sudan Interior Mission, and then offered himself as a missionary. His motive was simple—his anticipation of Christ's return. "A quiet, gentle, and determined little man, he crossed to England on a cattle boat to save money, leaving on such short notice he did not have time to say good-by to his relatives. In Liverpool he enrolled in a course in tropical medicine while the bewildered mission Council wrestled with the problem of whether to accept him."

The mission board did accept him, as he later reflected "on suspicion rather than on probation," and he sailed for Africa with four others. Within a year after they began making their way five hundred miles into the interior, one of the four had died and the remaining two became so ill that they had to be sent home. Stirrett remained and served as the senior missionary as other recruits arrived.

"Physically, Stirrett proved to be as tough as he was small. Spiritually he was utterly committed to winning men and women to Christ. It became his unalterable practice to preach the gospel or speak to someone each night before he retired, no matter what the circumstances. His constant visits to traders' camps, his earnest personal witness and his acts of kindness spread his name along the caravan routes long before his first term ended." During his missionary tenure, it is estimated that he had preached "not less than 20,000 times, and was heard by at least one and one-half million people." He kept a rigid schedule of rising each day at 3:45 a.m. for prayer, and of setting aside whole days for prayer and fasting for the Africans whom he loved dearly.

What some people might find unusual is that Stirrett spent forty-one years in Africa faithfully serving God, but without a missionary call. "I never had a call," he told friends and colleagues, and he challenged others not to wait for a call either. "Come," he pleaded, as he spoke before young men and women. "The Lord is coming very soon and you will surely have to meet Him. Do you want Him to find you in your easy chair?"

His own commitment to missions was simple. "What finally brought me to my senses was a sermon on the return of our Lord. There came up before me more vividly my great sin of omission, my failure to tell those who know not the gospel. The question was insistent: 'Will Jesus be pleased if He comes, to find me behind the counter?' "[15]

Now, brothers, about times and dates we do not need to write to you, for you know very well that the day of the Lord will come like a thief in the night. While people are saying, "Peace and safety," destruction will come on them suddenly, as labor pains on a pregnant woman, and they will not escape.

But you, brothers, are not in darkness so that this day should surprise you like a thief. You are all sons of the light and sons of the day. We do not belong to the night or to the darkness. So then, let us not be like others, who are asleep, but let us be alert and self-controlled.

*1 Thessalonians 5:1–6.*

357

## "A TEARFUL REUNION"

The last time Paul Chang (Chang Bao Hwa) had seen his family in China was thirty years earlier in 1949, just before he had fled the country as a refugee. He was seventeen years old at that time, and he left not knowing what would happen to his family in his absence. His father was a pastor, who had founded Tai Tung Seminary to train university students for the ministry.

The decision for him to leave the country had been prompted by the increasing Communist activity in the region. "Son, we're not running anymore," his father told him. "We can't move the school anymore—there are no safe places left. . . .Your older brothers have families, and they have chosen to stay here. . . . But you are seventeen and a strong Christian, and I believe God wants to use you in his work. When this is all over, China will need men of God trained in His Word and able to teach others. Therefore, we've decided to send you to Hong Kong."

Paul had expected to be reunited with his family in a year or two, never dreaming that his exile would extend to thirty years. During that time his family suffered through the Cultural Revolution, when "thousands of Christians were imprisoned, tortured, and killed." For six years he lost contact with them and only later learned that his father had been sentenced to prison and to hard labor, where he died after three years.

In the meantime, Paul traveled from Hong Kong to the United States for further education in biblical studies and music, with the help of an organization known as Christian Nationals Evangelism Commission. He then went on to minister as an evangelist and vocalist through concerts and on records. So much had happened since he had last seen his family. As he approached his family home, after thirty years, he was tingling with excitement—especially to be reunited with his eighty-one year old mother.

"My mother was waiting for me near the kitchen door. We couldn't say anything for a long time. We both just cried. Then she prayed and thanked the Lord for bringing her son back and for guiding and using him as His servant. This had been my mother's prayer over those many years. . . . Those days together were precious—we had family prayer and studied the Bible together. We sang many of our old, old songs that my parents taught us." Paul later returned to Hong Kong, where he has since served as the Southeast Asia coordinator for Christian Nationals Evangelism Commission.[16]

Now Jacob sent Judah ahead of him to Joseph to get directions to Goshen. When they arrived in the region of Goshen, Joseph had his chariot made ready and went to Goshen to meet his father Israel. As soon as Joseph appeared before him, he threw his arms around his father and wept for a long time.

Israel said to Joseph, "Now I am ready to die, since I have seen for myself that you are still alive."

*Genesis 46:28–30.*

# "SPARE MY PEOPLE"

One can only wonder if Esther's comment about slavery wasn't tongue-in-cheek. Surely she did not view the enslavement of Jews lightly, and she could not have forgotten the Jewish heritage of slavery in Egypt, and their miraculous deliverance. Indeed, after the king granted her request to spare her people, she went on to make sure their rights as citizens were guaranteed.

Esther's courage has inspired countless people in the generations since. Not the least of these were Sarah and Angelina Grimke. The Grimke sisters grew up in the antebellum South, the daughters of a South Carolina slaveholder and state Supreme Court justice who had drafted a law forbidding anyone to teach slaves to read. But Sarah and her younger sister Angelina could not accept the injustice of slavery. When she was four, Sarah witnessed a slave being whipped, and that ugly incident was the beginning of her road to abolitionism.

Although a young women, both Sarah and Angelina were slaveowners themselves—beneficiaries of a family inheritance—they were determined to treat their slaves differently. Sarah invited slaves into her room late at night when her parents were in bed, and secretly taught them how to read. Angelina taught a Sunday school class for black children and vehemently argued that they must be taught to read the Bible.

The sisters refused to attend their own Presbyterian church in Charleston, because of its defense of slavery, and instead joined with the Quakers. For them Christianity and abolitionism were inseparable. How could they reach out with the gospel to people they could not affirm as free and equal? They were convinced that slavery not only violated human law and the Declaration of Independence, but that it was diametrically opposed to the teachings of Jesus. So persuaded were they of their convictions that they began speaking out publicly—in an era when it was regarded a disgrace for women to speak in front of men.

Their lecturing took them from state to state. Sometimes they spoke in barns and sometimes before state legislatures, as was the case in 1838, when they spoke to the Massachusetts State Legislature. The sisters always encountered opposition because of their sex—sometimes only verbal, but other times taking the form of rotten eggs and tomatoes. When challenged about ignoring propriety, Angelina would simply respond: "What about Queen Esther?"[17]

**Then Queen Esther answered, "If I have found favor with you, O king, and if it pleases your majesty, grant me my life—this is my petition. And spare my people—this is my request. For I and my people have been sold for destruction and slaughter and annihilation. If we had merely been sold as male and female slaves, I would have kept quiet, because no such distress would justify disturbing the king."**

*Esther 7:3–4.*

## "WE DO NOT WAGE WAR AS THE WORLD DOES"

In April, 1982, the Falkland Islands off the coast of South America suddenly became the focus of international attention. Argentina, bolstered by its long-standing opposition to British control, invaded the islands. Great Britain responded by sending in the navy gunners with ground and air support. Many lives were lost in this "little" war, and tensions remained high until Argentina surrendered two months later.

It was not the first time that a British naval officer had led an attack on the Falklands. In 1850, another war had been waged. On that occasion, however, the weapons were "not the weapons of the world." The invasion was led by Allen Francis Gardiner, a Commander of the royal English fleet.

Gardiner was raised in a Christian family, but he neglected his spiritual life while he pursued his military career—until a near-fatality brought him back to God. Later, "as he knelt at the deathbed of his devoted wife, he promised to give himself wholly to God and His service."

In his desire to serve God, Gardiner began by focusing his attention on the unreached tribes in South America. He pleaded with the Church Missionary Society to begin missionary work among the Indians there, but there was little interest. Though he had no missionary or theological training, he determined to bring the message himself if no one else would. When his efforts were rebuffed by tribal chiefs, he wrote to a friend: "My thoughts are now turned toward the Falkland Islands."

Again he sought assistance from the Church Missionary Society and was turned down. "He was encouraged, however, by a gift of thirty-five dollars from a Christian lady and by the offer of six young men to accompany him as missionaries to the Indians."

On December 18, 1850, Gardiner and the six volunteers went ashore on one of the islands. Their ship continued on, with the promise that another ship would bring supplies in six months. That ship did not come, and in the meantime most of their supplies were confiscated by the Indians. The men survived on roots and bark for a time, but by late August, eight months after they had arrived, Gardiner wrote in his diary, "Our strength is exhausted. By the time the ship arrived in late October, all seven had died—but not in vain. The mission Gardiner had founded continued, and the gospel was preached to the Indians on the Falkland Islands.[18]

> For though we live in the world, we do not wage war as the world does. The weapons we fight with are not the weapons of the world. On the contrary, they have divine power to demolish strongholds. We demolish arguments and every pretension that sets itself up against the knowledge of God, and we take captive every thought to make it obedient to Christ.
>
> *2 Corinthians 10:3–5.*

# "I WILL FULFILL MY VOWS TO THE LORD"

Sometimes the death of a loved one has mighty consequences. So it was with a fifteen-year-old pawnbroker in nineteenth-century England. He was awakened one night to be told his father was dying. He rushed to his father's side, and there, together with his mother and sisters and an Anglican priest, he heard his father make a death-bed confession of faith. In that room, he vowed to turn his life over to God. He began attending a Wesleyan chapel, where his commitment was reinforced when he heard a sermon entitled, "A Soul Dies Every Minute." He publicly professed faith in Christ and determined that he would devote his life to bringing others to Christ.

Initially, the young man's commitment launched him into revolutionary political activity. Outraged by the neglect of the poor, he determined to serve God through political protest. But then an American evangelist, James Caughey, challenged him to preach the gospel. He took up the challenge and preached his first sermon at age seventeen.

"He preached on street corners, still plying his trade as a pawnbroker. On Sundays he would round up his ragtag, ragamuffin group of drunkards, wife-beaters, and bring them to the chapel, often leading many of them forward for prayer and penitence. But the elders of the chapel, repelled by the sight and stench of products of his street evangelism, expelled him from the membership."

Without a church home, the young man went on to conduct tent evangelism. Later, with the help of his wife and loyal supporters, he established the Christian Mission. By 1869, "the Christian Mission was on firm financial ground: there were 14 preaching stations, some soup kitchens, 140 services indoors and outdoors each week."

The ministry kept growing and soon spread worldwide. Of this ministry, Josiah Strong testified: "Probably during no one hundred years in the history of the world have there been saved so many thieves, gamblers, drunkards and prostitutes as during the past quarter of a century through the heroic faith and labors of the Salvation Army."

The young pawnbroker who dedicated himself to God at the time of his father's death was William Booth. He and his wife founded that worldwide missionary outreach that still continues today.[19]

Precious in the sight of the Lord is the death of his saints. O Lord, truly I am your servant, I am your servant, the son of your maidservant, you have freed me from my chains.

I will sacrifice a thank offering to you and call on the name of the Lord. I will fulfill my vows to the Lord in the presence of all his people, in the courts of the house of the Lord—in your midst, O Jerusalem. Praise the Lord.

*Psalm 116:15–19.*

## "I COMMEND TO YOU OUR SISTER"

Many of those who served faithfully with the apostle Paul were women—women who often worked behind the scenes and did not receive the recognition accorded his closest male associates. Who were these women mentioned at the end of his letter to the Romans—Phoebe, Priscilla, Mary, Junia, Tryphena, Tryphosa, Persis, Julia, and Olympas? What service did they render? We know most of them only through a single reference to their names. It is left to our imagination to envision a ministry so important that their names would forever become part of Scripture itself.

Perhaps they served faithfully as Mary Webb did, whose name surely would have been included had she served some eighteen centuries earlier. Mary is recognized for organizing "the first woman's missionary society in the world." In 1800, at the age of twenty-one, she and three other women formed the Boston Female Society for Missionary Purposes.

Her ministry was all the more remarkable because she had been disabled since the age of five and was confined to a wheel chair—a handicap which in that era generally precluded public ministry, particularly for a woman. But Mary used the disability to her own advantage, knowing that a church leader would appear very unmanly, and perhaps even cruel, if he were to denounce her for overstepping her bounds as a woman.

Mary served for fifty years as the secretary-treasurer of the society, but her influence was felt far beyond one organization in Boston. The Boston female Society for Missionary Purposes served as a model for other women, and similar societies were formed elsewhere in various other denominations. She corresponded with leaders offering advice and encouragement.

But Mary's contributions were not limited to society. Through her leadership, several other organizations developed out of the first, "such as the Female Cent Society in 1803, the Children's Cent Society . . . in 1911, the Corban society, in 1811, to raise money to help educate young ministers, the Fragment Society, 1812, to provide clothing and bedding for needy children, the Children's Friend Society, to provide day care for young children of working mothers, and a Penitent Females' Refuge. . . . She also founded societies to minister to immigrants, blacks, and Jews. No wonder Mary Webb was described as a 'society within herself.' " She had no time for self-pity, as she tirelessly served others.[20]

I commend to you our sister Phoebe, a servant of the church in Cenchrea. I ask you to receive her in the Lord in a way worthy of the saints and to give her any help she may need from you, for she has been a great help to many people, including me.

Greet Priscilla and Aquila, my fellow workers in Christ Jesus. . . . Greet Mary, who worked very hard for you. . . . Greet Tryphena and Tryphosa, those women who work hard in the Lord. Greet my dear friend Persis, another woman who has worked very hard in the Lord.

*Romans 16:1–3, 6, 12.*

# "FOR TO US A CHILD IS BORN"

Frank Ringsmuth was the editor and publisher of a Bohemian newspaper that circulated throughout the United States. It was newspaper that, in his own words, "was soaked in infidelity." It was Christmas week 1891, and amid the bustle of activity, he had forgotten to write his regular weekly article. When his assistant came to collect the copy, he hurriedly grasped at ideas, vowing to have the article done in time to run it in the paper.

With no other subjects coming to mind, his focus seemed transfixed on one theme. "Against my will," he confessed, "I resolved to say something of the birth of Christ. I did not know what I was writing. There was a power which drove me on. I wrote of His birth in poverty and of His life of suffering. The central point of the article was the argument that those who are blaspheming Christ now are of the same character of those who crucified Him—the most miserable creatures of earth. . . . As I wrote my tears flowed like a flood. My assistants looked on and wondered."

When his assistant brought back the proofs that afternoon, he was alarmed, and questioned Ringsmuth as to whether he really intended to publish it. "I answered that I did intend to do so, and added, 'What I write goes in.' When I read the proof I was astonished. For the first time I realized what I had written. I thought it was impossible to print the article. I would lose subscriptions. It was just at the time for renewals. But I was ashamed to go back on my words to the assistant. So the article was printed.

"Within twenty-four hours of the paper's issue there were three hundred and sixty-five stops. Some of my best friends said they felt greatly insulted, and at least thirty Bohemian newspapers attacked me." Amazingly, however, news of the Christmas story spread throughout the Bohemian communities, and soon the paper had gained twice as many subscriptions as it had lost.

But the article had a far greater effect than simply increasing subscriptions. It was the beginning of Ringsmuth's search for God. For more than twenty years he had not attended church, but he had convinced himself in that Christmas article that his life was missing something. Through his search, he found his way to faith in Christ and eventually into Christian service as an evangelist to the Bohemians.[21]

**For to us a child is born, to us a son is given, and the government will be on his shoulders. And he will be called Wonderful Counselor, Mighty God, Everlasting Father, Prince of Peace. Of the increase of his government and peace there will be no end. He will reign on David's throne and over his kingdom, establishing and upholding it with justice and righteousness from that time on and forever. The zeal of the Lord Almighty will accomplish this.**

*Isaiah 9:6–7.*

## "A NEW UNDERSTANDING OF CHRISTMAS"

The Christmas story has become so familiar that we often forget how difficult it is to fully understand. The idea of God's becoming a baby and being born in a stable is beyond human comprehension. How can we even begin to identify with such an experience? An answer was revealed to Bernie May many years ago, before he became the U.S. Director of Wycliffe Bible Translators.

It was three days before Christmas and he was on a flight to deliver emergency medical supplies to a remote Indian tribe. He had been serving for fewer than three years as a missionary pilot with his family in the Amazon jungle of South America, and was anxious to complete his mission and return to his family.

The five-hour flight into the region had been uneventful, and he had landed his pontoon plane safely on the river. After bringing his cargo to the village, he settled down to sleep in a makeshift shelter between two trees, hoping to wake rested for his flight home. During the night, however, a steady rain began to fall and it continued through the next day and night. There he was, without his family in the jungle, wallowing in self-pity.

"It was Christmas Eve and night was descending on the jungle. There was no way I could get back home. Back in Pennsylvania, my folks would have returned from church and Mother would be getting the turkey ready. Outside, the snow would be falling past the window. The big tree, with the star on top, would be standing as always in its corner.

"In Yarinachcha, six hours away, Nancy and the boys would be sitting at home alone. They knew by now, because I had been able to radio back, that I was stuck in the jungle. I would not be with them for Christmas.

"'Oh God,' I moaned, 'I'm in the wrong place.' . . . That night, under my mosquito net I had a visitation from God—something like those shepherds must have had on the hills of Bethlehem. There were no angels, and no bright light. But as I lay there in my hammock, desperately homesick, I felt I heard God say: 'My son, this is what Christmas is all about. Jesus left heaven and on Christmas morning He woke up in the "wrong place"—a stable in Bethlehem. Christmas means leaving home, not going home. My only begotten Son did not come home for Christmas—He left His home to be with you.'"[22]

So Joseph also went up from the town of Nazareth in Galilee to Judea, to Bethlehem the town of David, because he belonged to the house and line of David. He went there to register with Mary, who was pledged to be married to him and was expecting a child. While they were there, the time came for the baby to be born, and she gave birth to her firstborn, a son. She wrapped him in cloths and placed him in a manger, because there was no room for them in the inn.

*Luke 2:4–7.*

# "THEY OPENED THEIR TREASURES"

Gift giving at Christmas, which began with the Magi, is most honorable when gifts are given in the name of the Lord to those who have no means to return the favor. This is what Lisbeth Piedrasanta, a Christian worker in Guatemala, envisioned when she contemplated a special Christmas project for the dump dwellers who lived on the outskirts of the city.

Lisbeth had been deeply concerned for the dump-dwelling people, knowing that many of them did not have even a blanket to wrap themselves in at night when the temperature dropped and the air became chilly. Her dream was to raise funds for one thousand blankets, but so overwhelming was the response that she was able to purchase more than two thousand blankets as well as many toys and meals.

On December 23, she and her helpers went out to the dump to invite people to the celebration the next day. Each person invited was asked to have a finger dyed red, so that they would be eligible to come for the feast and receive their blanket. "Even though I was walking over reeking garbage and dead animals," Lisbeth later recalled, "it was like walking in heaven because I was doing God's will."

The celebration began at 8:00 a.m. on December 24th. Soon hundreds of children and adults began arriving. It was an amazing sight. "Lisbeth could hardly believe the change! They were freshly washed and dressed in the best they could find. She knew the nearest cold water tap was five blocks away. A bucket poured over the head was the only possible shower, so people rarely took the trouble to wash themselves."

The honored guests that day were the dump dwellers—the poorest of the poor—but the real celebration was for Lisbeth and her helpers. "This has been a life-transforming experience for all of us," she confessed. "Twenty-three adults responded to the invitation—and most of the children. At the end of Christmas Day when we were all praising the Lord, I felt that Jesus was surrounding us. We felt His love poured out for these people."[23]

After they [the Magi] had heard the king, they went on their way, and the star they had seen in the east went ahead of them until it stopped over the place where the child was. When they say the star, they were overjoyed. On coming to the house, they saw the child with his mother Mary, and they bowed down and worshiped him. Then they opened their treasures and presented him with gifts of gold and of incense and of myrrh. And having been warned in a dream not to go back to Herod, they returned to their country by another route.

*Matthew 2:9–12.*

## "SAVIOR, LIKE A SHEPHERD LEAD US"

It was Christmas Eve, 1875. The setting was a steamboat that was slowly making its way up the Delaware River. Many of the passengers were out on the deck enjoying the night air and contemplating this holy season of the year. It was the perfect setting for a Christmas carol, and it just happened that in the crowd was Ira Sankey, the well-known singer whose music stirred the hearts at Dwight L. Moody's evangelistic campaigns. Someone asked him to sing, and as usual, he was eager to accommodate.

"He stood leaning against one of the great funnels of the boat, and his eyes were raised to the starry heavens in quiet prayer. Mr. Sankey intended to sing a Christmas song, but somehow he was driven almost against his will to sing the 'Shepherd Song':"

> Savior, like a shepherd lead us,
> Much we need Thy tender care;
> In Thy pleasant pastures feed us,
> For our use Thy folds prepare:
> Blessed Jesus, Blessed Jesus
> Thou has bought us, Thine we are.

After he had finished all four verses, there was a stillness that pervaded the night, and then a man in the crowd approached the singer. He knew he had heard that voice and that song before, but he wanted to make sure. He asked Sankey if he had served in the Union Army, and if so, where and when. Further questions confirmed that Sankey had, indeed, not only served but had been assigned to picket duty one night in 1862. The moon was bright and this Confederate soldier was in the shadows nearby ready to take aim with his musket. But as he lifted the gun to his shoulder, Sankey lifted that same song heavenward.

"I heard the words perfectly: 'We are Thine; do Thou befriend us. Be the Guardian of our way.' Those words stirred up many memories. I began to think of my God-fearing mother. . . . When you finished the song it was impossible for me to take aim. . . . Since that time I have wandered far and wide . . . Now I wish you may help me find a cure for my sick soul." It was a Christmas Eve that Sankey would never forget, as he led to the Lord this man who had come so very close to taking his life.[24]

The Lord is my shepherd, I shall not be in want. He makes me lie down in green pastures, he leads me beside quiet waters, he restores my soul. He guides me in paths of righteousness for his name's sake. Even though I walk through the valley of the shadow of death, I will fear no evil, for you are with me; your rod and staff, they comfort me.

You prepare a table before me in the presence of my enemies. You anoint my head with oil; my cup overflows. Surely goodness and love will follow me all the days of my life, and I will dwell in the house of the Lord forever.

*Psalm 23.*

# "A QUECHUA CHRISTMAS STORY"

For people who have grown up in "Christian" countries such as the United States, the Christmas story is familiar. It is sung in Christmas carols, portrayed on Christmas cards and in nativity scenes, and acted out in dramas. But for people who have never been a part of this festive season of the year, the Christmas story is often obscure and difficult to remember.

Melanie and Rick Floyd, working with Wycliffe Bible Translators in Peru, had told the story of Jesus many times to the Quechua Indians with whom they worked, and some had become Christians. But the Floyds were never fully sure how much the people understood. The Bibles they used in the church services were Spanish, and most of the people could neither speak or read Spanish.

It was exciting, then, for the Floyds, when they completed their first portion of Scripture for these people in their own Huanca Quechua dialect. They had translated the Christmas story from the first two chapters of Matthew, hoping to distribute it in tract form before the Christmas season. In preparation for this, Rick tested it for accuracy with some of their Quechua friends—including Grandma Julia.

"He read about Mary and Joseph and the angel of the Lord, then Jesus' birth in Bethlehem, and King Herod's decree, about the star in the east, the Magi, their gifts and worship of their King Jesus."

Rick's plan was to test for accuracy, not bring a new message. But to Grandma Julia, the story suddenly came alive. This familiar passage had a new meaning now that it was being read in her own tongue. When Rick stopped to ask if it made sense, she insisted that he continue on so that she could find out what happened next and how the story would end. For her and for many others, Christmas would have new meaning that year when for the first time they would be able to hear the story of that first Christmas in their own language.[25]

This is how the birth of Jesus Christ came about. His mother Mary was pledged to be married to Joseph, but before they came together, she was found to be with child through the Holy Spirit. Because Joseph her husband was a righteous man and did not want to expose her to public disgrace, he had in mind to divorce her quietly. But after he had considered this, an angel of the Lord appeared to him in a dream and said, "Joseph son of David, do not be afraid to take Mary home as your wife, because what is conceived in her is from the Holy Spirit. She will give birth to a son, and you are to give him the name Jesus, because he will save his people from their sins."

*Matthew 1:18–21.*

## "TRAIN A CHILD IN THE WAY HE SHOULD GO"

A childhood accident left John Pounds with a severe limp and an unpleasant personality. He had intended to be a dock worker, but his disability led him into shoe-making, and he eventually established his own shop in a run-down tenement house. Medical treatment in eighteenth-century England was not highly advanced, and he grudgingly accepted the fact that he would endure a life of pain and physical limitation.

At age thirty-eight, Pounds was unmarried and unhappy, but then his life suddenly changed in a way that allowed him to radiate the love of Christ. His concern for a disabled nephew prompted him to open his home to the youngster and fit him with corrective shoes, giving him a chance to run and play with other children. "What has gotten into John Pounds?" neighbors inquired. "He used to always be grieving over something. Now, he's the happiest man in Portsmouth!"

When his nephew became old enough for schooling, Pounds decided to teach the boy himself. He soon became convinced that a child learns better with other children, so he invited a poor neighborhood boy, whose parents could not support him, to live with him as well. Soon there were other street children who moved in with him, and those he could not house in his tiny tenement shoe shop were invited to come for schooling only.

Pounds always took his "family" to church on Sunday, and he "led practically all of his boys to Jesus." Many of these boys grew up to become influential citizens in government and business. He lived his life essentially unnoticed but he would be forever memorialized in a grand oil painting.

On Christmas Day in 1938, when he was seventy-two years old, he was invited to a wealthy friend's home—a man who had admired John's dedication to the unwanted street boys. There he was ushered into the luxurious drawing room where "on the wall was a magnificent oil painting, executed by the famous British artist, Shief. . . . The subject of the wall-wide oil was *John Pounds*! John Pounds in the narrow room . . . surrounded by his boys!"

In the years after his death, it was not unusual "to see men of affairs resort to a little monument in the Portsmouth Cemetery . . . shamelessly weep a while; quickly brush the tears away, and depart." They were John Pounds's boys.[26]

In the paths of the wicked lie thorns and snares, but he who guards his soul stays far from them.

Train a child in the way he should go, and when he is old he will not turn from it.

The rich rule over the poor, and the borrower is servant to the lender. He who sows wickedness reaps trouble, and the rod of his fury will be destroyed.

A generous man will himself be blessed, for he shares his food with the poor.

*Proverbs 22:5–9.*

# "NOT TRYING TO PLEASE MEN BUT GOD"

In his single-minded commitment to evangelism, Paul avoided flattery and putting on a mask, seeking only to please God. Throughout his life, R. A. Torrey, "the successor to D. L. Moody," tried to emulate Paul's style. Unlike Moody, who was poorly educated, Torrey "held degrees from Yale University and Divinity School and did postgraduate work in the Universities of Leipzig and Erlangen in Germany." But like Moody, evangelism was his highest priority:

"I would rather win souls than be the greatest king or emperor on earth; I would rather win souls than be the greatest general that ever commanded an army; I would rather win souls than be the greatest poet, or novelist, or literary man who ever walked the earth. My one ambition in life is to win as many as possible. Oh, it is the only thing worth doing, to save souls; and, men and women, we can do it!"

This evangelist's extraordinary success in winning souls was rooted in his determination not "to please men but God." He "was sometimes brusque and always direct. While he tried to avoid offense and make a wholesome impression, yet there is no record that he ever tried to win people to himself first as a means of winning them to Christ." Nor did he seek personal credit for soul-winning; rather, he trained others in his church to do the work, while serving as a role model himself.

Reflecting back on his pastoral ministry, Torrey testified that he started out in each church "by going to work on my own people to be intelligent soul-winners, so that if a revival ever should come, I would have people ready to lead others intelligently to an acceptance of Christ. . . . Since the first year of my ministry, I have had a perpetual revival, and that has been due largely to the fact that I have trained membership."

Torrey conducted large evangelistic campaigns and wrote books on evangelism. He held many prestigious positions, serving as the President of Moody Bible Institute and the pastor of Moody Church. But he always viewed personal evangelism as paramount. "He believes thoroughly in doing personal work," wrote a contemporary, "not merely in the meetings but on the streets, in street cars, on buses, on trains and steamers—everywhere. Many of the most striking parts of his sermons are the stories of his experiences in soul-winning in all parts of the world."[27]

**For the appeal we make does not spring from error or impure motives, nor are we trying to trick you. On the contrary, we speak as men approved by God to be entrusted with the gospel. We are not trying to please men but God, who tests our hearts. You know we never used flattery, nor did we put on a mask to cover up greed—God is our witness. We were not looking for praise from men, not from you or anyone else.**

*1 Thessalonians 2:3–6.*

## "BE PREPARED IN SEASON AND OUT OF SEASON"

For John Vasser, who was simply known as "Uncle John," there was no off-season for evangelism, there were no limitations on whom he would approach with the gospel. President Ulysses S. Grant and Brigham Young both heard the plan of salvation from him, as did thousands of Civil War soldiers and people on the street and in the work place.

Uncle John was converted while he was working in a brewery in Poughkeepsie, New York. He began witnessing to his fellow workers and became so successful in his personal ministry that pastors began calling upon him to help out during revival campaigns. He continued working at the brewery in order to support his family, but after a series of tragic illnesses that took the lives of his two sons and his wife, he dedicated himself to full-time ministry. In 1850, he was commissioned as a missionary with the American Tract Society at a salary of one hundred and fifty dollars a year.

A. J. Gordon, the great pastor, educator, and missionary statesman, later wrote about Vasser's "in season and out of season" ministry: "He travelled from Maine to Florida, from the Atlantic coast to the Pacific, on foot, on horseback, by rail, and by steamer, resting not in summer or in winter, in the one intense, eager pursuit of souls; and wherever you found him there was the same burning zeal speaking out in his looks and in his words."

During the Civil War Uncle John traveled behind the battle lines to bring the gospel to soldiers, often working from sixteen to eighteen hours a day and witnessing to as many as one hundred men. So powerful was his preaching that some feared he would interfere with the outcome of the war. After he was captured by Confederate forces, General Steward released him with an order: "Take this man's promise that he will not tell of our whereabouts for twenty-four hours, and let us see him out of our lines, or we will have a prayer-meeting from here to Richmond."

Uncle John never sought ordination or recognition as an evangelist. He viewed himself simply as a worker whose duty it was to evangelize people wherever he found them and assist pastors in building up their churches. "He loved to pray, exhort, sing, visit and do personal work while others did the preaching."[28]

Preach the Word; be prepared in season and out of season; correct, rebuke and encourage—with great patience and careful instruction. For the time will come when men will not put up with sound doctrine. Instead, to suit their own desires, they will gather around them a great number of teachers to say what their itching ears want to hear. They will turn their ears away from the truth and turn aside to myths. But you, keep your head in all situations, endure hardship, do the work of an evangelist, discharge all the duties of your ministry.

*2 Timothy 4:2–5.*

# "BUT THE GREATEST OF THESE IS LOVE"

Demonstrating love can be a powerful asset in evangelism, and failure to show love can discredit the gospel. Florence Allshorn discovered this when she went to Uganda as a missionary in 1920. She was well aware of many of the risks such a venture would include. Many missionaries before her had sacrificed their lives to that deadly climate within a few short months or several years after their arrival. What she did not anticipate was the struggle she would face in living in harmony with coworkers—especially with one woman whom Florence found difficult to work with and impossible to love.

Despite the disharmony with her coworker, Florence was outwardly successful in her work at her girls' school. Yet, as she preached the love of Christ to her students, she was well aware that love was not evident in her relationship with her colleague—a problem she was convinced was not of her own making. Then, one day while crying in dejection, an elderly African woman challenged her about her own life. She pointed out to Florence that she was not showing the love that she herself so often preached.

This admonition had a powerful impact on Florence, and she began making changes in her attitude. It was not easy, but her daily pattern of Bible reading aided the process. She determined that for one year she would read the love chapter—1 Corinthians 13— each day, and live with those verses fresh on her mind as she carried out every task that was before her. It became a pattern that changed the course of her life, and the Africans were the first to notice the change not only in her but also in her colleague.

Florence later returned to England due to health problems, but her ministry was not over. She was convinced that God could change other lives even as he had hers, and on that basis she founded a community known as St. Julian's. Here students and missionaries found a place where they could renew their relationship with God and could focus on that one area of life most difficult to fully demonstrate—not faith or hope, but love.[29]

If I speak in the tongues of men and of angels, but have not love, I am only a resounding gong or a clanging cymbal. If I have the gift of prophecy and can fathom all mysteries and all knowledge, and if I have a faith that can move mountains, but have not love, I am nothing. If I give all I possess to the poor and surrender my body to the flames, but have not love, I gain nothing.

Love is patient, love is kind. It does not envy, it does not boast, it is not proud. It is not rude, it is not self-seeking, it is not easily angered, it keeps no record of wrongs. Love does not delight in evil but rejoices with truth. It always protects, always trusts, always hopes, always perseveres.

Love never fails. . . .

And now these three remain: faith, hope, and love. But the greatest of these is love.

*1 Corinthians 13:1–8a, 13.*

# "HERE AM I, SEND ME"

This passage is commonly associated with the ultimate call to foreign missionary service. But it also applies to those who have been called to awaken believers from their lethargy to the unfinished task of world evangelism. An individual who has responded to both challenges in an extraordinary way is Donald McGavran.

McGavran began his missionary career in India with the Disciples of Christ in 1923. A highly-educated third-generation missionary, he was well prepared to serve as a mission educator, but soon became disillusioned with the emphasis on education and the neglect of evangelism.

The neglect of evangelism hit McGavran very suddenly one day when he met a woman on the mission compound and learned that she and her extended family were not Christians because no one had ever taken the time to explain the gospel to them. "That went through me like a knife," he recalls. Despite his hectic schedule, he vowed to devote one night a week to this woman's family and caste. He began challenging other missionaries to change their priorities, but with little success. He was not reelected as field secretary. Instead he was sent to work in a remote area.

"For the next seventeen years—until the early 1950s—this Yale-educated Ph.D. was found among the illiterate peasants of small, rural villages. He covered a vast area, often by bicycle or on foot, struggling along with a team of Indian evangelists and pastors to start a people movement among the Satnami caste." His work resulted in converts and the church grew, but his "dream of seeing his own people movement never came true."

McGavran made observations and developed strategies in his work that eventually became the basis for his classic *The Bridges of God*. This controversial and pragmatic volume focused on reaching people groups—not by traditional methods of evangelism rooted in Western individualism. In the years that followed, he slowly began to alert mission and church leaders in America to the vast need to reach people groups worldwide. When he was sixty-seven, McGavran was invited to develop the School of World Missions at Fuller Theological Seminary—an opportunity that has allowed his scholarship to have a lasting impact on contemporary missiology.[30]

Then I heard the voice of the Lord saying, "Whom shall I send? And who will go for us?"

And I said, "Here am I. Send me!"

He said, "Go and tell this people: 'Be ever hearing, but never understanding; be never seeing, but never perceiving.' Make the heart of this people calloused; make their ears dull and close their eyes. Otherwise they might see with their eyes, hear with their ears, understand with their hearts, and turn and be healed."

*Isaiah 6:8–10.*

# "CAN THESE BONES LIVE?"

Twenty-nine years after his death in 1384, they dug up his bones and burned them because he was deemed a heretic, but one of his contemporaries felt differently. This contemporary penned a tribute to the dry bones that were turned to ashes—bones that would indeed "live" and thereby proclaim the glory of God: "They burnt his bones to ashes and cast them into the Swift, a neighborhood brook running hard by. Thus this brook hath conveyed his ashes into Avon, Avon into Severn, Severn into the narrow seas, they into the main ocean. And thus the ashes of Wycliffe are the emblem of his doctrine, which now is dispersed the world over."

John Wycliffe's enemies were as numerous when he was living as after his death. At the time of his death, a Catholic leader wrote a scathing indictment of him: "That instrument of the devil, that enemy of the church, that author of confusion to the common people, that image of hypocrites, that idol of heretics, that author of schism, that sower of hatred, that coiner of lies, being struck with the horrible judgment of God, was smitten with palsy and continued to live till St. Sylvester's Day [New Year's Eve] on which he breathed out his malicious spirit into the abodes of darkness."

What had Wycliffe done to deserve such denunciation? As a Professor of Divinity at Oxford, he "had dared to assail the mendicant friars, a sizeable army of strolling monks infesting England, hawking indulgences, foisting superstitious fetishes on the public, padding their purses with coins extracted by fraud. They further disgraced the Church with a manner of life marked by laziness, ignorance, prodigality, and indifference to human suffering. . . . He went on to question the doctrine of the Mass, calling transubstantiation idolatry and a fable. The Communion bread represented the body of Christ, he said; but it was not His true physical body. And the Bible, not Church law, should be the rule of faith. . . . And to prove that he was not only interested in defending evangelical doctrines but also in spreading them, he organized a band of evangelists known as Lollards and sent them ranging over the island to preach Christ."

His greatest contribution to the Christian church, however, was his translation of the Bible into English—the first such translation. Church officials were outraged that mere lay people should have access to the Scripture. Wycliffe had a ready response: "The Clergy cry aloud that it is heresy to speak of the Holy Scriptures in English, and so they would condemn the Holy Spirit, who gave tongues to the Apostles of Christ to speak the Word of God in all languages under heaven."[31]

**The hand of the Lord was upon me, and he brought me out by the Spirit of the Lord and set me in the middle of a valley; it was full of bones. He led me back and forth among them, and I saw a great many bones on the floor of the valley, bones that were very dry. He asked me, "Son of man, can these bones live?"**

**I said, "O Sovereign Lord, you alone know."**

*Ezekiel 37:1–3.*

# NOTES

## JANUARY

[1] John T. Faris, *The Book of God's Providence* (New York: George H. Doran, 1913), 121–127.

[2] Robert Harvey, *Best-Loved Hymn Stories* (Grand Rapids: Zondervan, 1963), 79–81.

[3] Colin Whittaker, *Seven Guides to Effective Prayer* (Minneapolis: Bethany, 1987), 137–145.

[4] Aggie Hurst, *One Witness* (Old Tappan: Revell, 1986), 106–109.

[5] Festo Kivengere, *I Love Idi Amin* (Old Tappan: Revell, 1977), 1.

[6] Corrie ten Boom with Jamie Buckingham, *Tramp for the Lord* (Old Tappan: Revell, 1974), 56.

[7] Dongo Pewee, interview with author, Reformed Bible College, Grand Rapids, 12 September 1988.

[8] Samuel H. Moffat, *The Christians of Korea* (New York: Friendship Press, 1962), 39.

[9] Joni Eareckson Tada, "Disabling Attitudes in the Church," *World Vision* (August/September 1988): 21–22.

[10] Raymond Edman, *They Found the Secret* (Grand Rapids: Zondervan, 1960), 125–130.

[11] Karen Burton Mains, *Open Heart, Open Home* (Elgin: David C. Cook, 1976), 21–22.

[12] John T. Seamands, *Pioneers of the Younger Churches* (Nashville: Abingdon, 1967), passim.

[13] Clarence W. Hall, *Miracle on the Sepik* (Costa Mesa: Gift, 1980), passim.

[14] James D. Knowles, *Memoir of Mrs. Ann H. Judson* (Boston: Lincoln and Edmands, 1829), 37–41, 58.

[15] John T. Faris, *The Book of God's Providence* (New York: George H. Doran, 1913), 116–120.

[16] Glenn D. Kittler, *The Woman God Loved: The Life of Blessed Anne-Marie Javouhey* (Garden City: Hanover House, 1959), 16.

[17] Ken Williams, "A Church That Continues," *In Other Words* (April/May 1987): 1–2.

[18] Maria Nilsen, with Paul H. Sheetz, *Malla Moe* (Chicago: Moody Press, 1956); Alan H. Winquist, "Scandinavian-American Missions in Southern Africa and Zaire," unpublished paper delivered at the Billy Graham Center, Wheaton, Illinois, June 1986.

[19] Steve Estes, *Called to Die* (Grand Rapids: Zondervan, 1986), 193–196.

[20] Hal Olsen, *African Heroes of the Congo Rebellion* (Kijabe, Kenya: Africa Inland Mission, 1969), 15–18.

[21] Kari Torjesen Malcolm, *Women at the Crossroads* (Downers Grove: InterVarsity Press, 1982), 22–23.

[22] Terry D. Bilhartz, ed., *Francis Asbury's America: An Album of Early American Methodism* (Grand Rapids: Zondervan, 1984), 26, 46, 82.

[23] Leroy Fitts, *Lott Carey: First Black Missionary to Africa* (Valley Forge: Judson Press, 1978), passim.

[24] Henri Nouwen, "Adam's Peace," *World Vision* (August/September 1988): 4–7.

[25] Jeanne Guyon, *The Autobiography of Madame Guyon*, trans. Thomas Allen (New Canaan, Conn.: Keats, 1980), passim.

[26] Carl F. H. Henry, *The Pacific Garden Mission: A Doorway to Heaven* (Grand Rapids: Zondervan, 1942), 47–50.

[27] Interview with Socheth Na, Reformed Bible College, Grand Rapids, 13 December 1988.

[28] Judy Downs Douglass, "Guess Who's Coming to Dinner?" *Worldwide Challenge* (June 1988): 18–19, 24–25.

[29] Kathy Long, "The Evangelicals' Uneasy Conscience," *Worldwide Challenge* (June 1988): 52–53.

[30] Sandra Contreras, verbal testimony as a student, Reformed Bible College, Grand Rapids, 4 October 1988.

[31] Henri Daniel-Rops, *The Heroes of God* (New York: Hawthorn, 1959), 194.

## FEBRUARY

[1] George Beverly Shea with Fred Bauer, *Then Sings My Soul* (Old Tappan: Revell, 1968), 22, 82, 83.

[2] Olive Rogers, "The Ministry of Women in the Church," *In God's Community: Essays on the Church and Its Ministry*, ed. David J. Ellis and W. Ward Gasque (Wheaton: Harold Shaw, 1978): 62–63.

[3] Brian H. Edwards, *God's Outlaw: The Story of William Tyndale* (Grand Rapids: Evangelical Press, 1976), 163–164.

[4] John T. Seamands, *Pioneers of the Younger Churches* (Nashville: Abingdon, 1967), 142–162.

[5] Corrie ten Boom with John Scherrill, *The Hiding Place* (Old Tappan: Revell, 1971), 202–203.

[6] Thomas Hale, *Don't Let the Goats Eat the Loquat Trees* (Grand Rapids: Zondervan, 1986), 76–77.

[7] J. Herbert Kane, *Life and Work on the Mission Field* (Grand Rapids: Baker, 1980), 151.

[8] Dorothy Clarke Wilson, *Climb Every Mountain: The Story of Granny Brand* (London: Hodder and Stoughton, 1976), 76–77.

[9] Constance Padwick, *Temple Gairdner of Cairo* (London: S.P.C.K, 1929), 221–222.

[10] Craig Nimmo, "Seven Graves to Freedom," *Power for Living* (May 4, 1980): 2–3.

[11] "Veteran Missionary Absolved of Drug Charges," *Moody Monthly*" (February 1983): 111.

[12] Thomas J. Bach, *Pioneer Missionaries for Christ and His Church* (Wheaton: Van Kampen, 1955), 73–76.

[13] Eusebius Pamphilus, *The Ecclesiastical History* (Grand Rapids: Baker, 1984), 257–259.

[14] Dorothy R. Pape, *In Search of God's Ideal Woman* (Downers Grove: InterVarsity, 1976), 237–239.

[15] Interview with John Peshlakai, Grand Rapids, April 23, 1989.

[16] Dr. and Mrs. Howard Taylor, *Hudson Taylor's Spiritual Secret* (Chicago: Moody, 1932), 33–37.

[17] Alan Burgess, *Daylight Must Come: The Story of a Courageous Woman Doctor in the Congo* (New York: Dell, 1975), 45.

[18] Hale, *Don't Let the Goats Eat the Loquat Trees,* , 240–247.

[19] James and Marti Hefley, *By Their Blood* (Milford, Mich.: Mott, 1979), 203.

[20] Martin Jarrett-Kerr, *Patterns of Christian Acceptance: Individual Response to the Missionary Impact* (London: Oxford, 1972), 78–86.

[21] Mildred Larson and Lois Dodds, *Treasure in Clay Pots* (Dallas: Person to Person Books, 1985), 203–226.

[22] Stan Telchin, *Betrayed* (Grand Rapids: Zondervan, 1981), 117–18.

[23] Roland H. Bainton, *Women of the Reformation in Germany and Italy* (Minneapolis: Augsburg, 1971), 69.

[24] Billy Graham, *Facing Death and the Life After* (Waco: Word Books, 1987), 113–14.

[25] Amy Carmichael, *Toward Jerusalem,* (London: Society for Promoting Christian Knowledge, 1936), 106.

[26] Daniel J. Boorstin, *The Americans: The Colonial Experience* (New York: Vintage Books, 1964), 39–40.

[27] Hall, *Miracle on the Sepik,* 33–34.

[28] Corrie ten Boom, *Father ten Boom: God's Man* (Old Tappan: Revell, n.d.), 10–11, 148–151.

## MARCH

[1] Alan Burgess, *The Small Woman* (New York: E. P. Dutton, 1957), 29.

[2] Eileen Crossman, *Mountain Rain: A New Biography of James O. Fraser* (Southampton, UK: Overseas Missionary Fellowship, 1982), 101–102.

[3] John Wesley, *Journals*, 5th ed., (October, 27, 1783).

[4] Eugene M. Harrison, *Missionary Crusaders for Christ* (Glendale, Calif.: The Church Press, 1967), 56–57.

[5] Dee Jepsen, *Women Beyond Equal Rights* (Waco: Word Books, 1984), 52–53.

[6] Michael Haynes, "Three Minutes to Midnight: The Evangelical and Racism," *Evangelical Missions Quarterly* (Fall 1968): 2–3.

[7] Helen Barrett Montgomery, *Helen Barrett Montgomery: From Campus to World Citizenship* (London: Fleming H. Revell, 1940), 78.

[8] K. P. Yohannan, *The Coming Revolution in World Missions* (Altamonte Springs, Fla.: Creation House, 1986), 23–25.

[9] Louis Bobe, *Hans Egede: Colonizer and Missionary of Greenland* (Copenhagen: Rosenkilde and Bagger, 1952), 16–29, 162—172.

[10] V. Raymond Edman, *They Found the Secret*, 44–49.

[11] Ibid., 78–81.

[12] Ibid., 105–113.

[13] Ruth A. Tucker, *From Jerusalem to Irian Java: A Biographical History of Christian Missions* (Grand Rapids: Zondervan, 1983), 234–239.

[14] Betty Lee Skinner, *Daws: The Story of Dawson Trotman, Founder of The Navigators* (Grand Rapids: Zondervan, 1974), 66–68.

[15] Bruce Olson, *Bruchko* (Carol Stream: Creation House, 1973), 152–153.

[16] William Deal, *John Newton* (Westchester, Ill.: Good News Publishers, 1974), 61–66.

[17] Ruth A. Tucker, *Guardians of the Great Commission: The Story of Women in Modern Missions*, (Grand Rapids: Zondervan, 1988), 152–154.

[18] Warren W. Wiersbe, "Two Giants of Bible Interpretation," *Moody Monthly* (February 1974): 61–63.

[19] Fred Barlow, *Profiles in Evangelism* (Murfreesboro, Tenn.: Sword of the Lord, 1976), 82–85.

[20] K. P. Yohannan, *The Coming Revolution in World Missions* (Altamonte Springs, Fla.: Creation House, 1986), 49–50.

[21] Kurt Koch, *The Revival in Indonesia* (Grand Rapids: Kregel, 1970), 111–114.

[22] Bruce Olson, *Bruchko*, 147–151.

[23] J. C. Pollock, *Moody: A Biographical Portrait of the Pacesetter in Modern Mass Evangelism* (New York: Macmillan, 1963), 188–189.

[24] Jeanne A. Dunn, "From Cynic to Saint: The Extraordinary Life of Malcolm Muggeridge," *Possibilities* (January/February, 1988): 21–14.

[25] J. C. Pollock, *Moody: A Biographical Portrait of the Pacesetter in Modern Mass Evangelism*, 188–189.

[26] C. Stephen Evans, "A Misunderstood Reformer," *Christianity Today* (September 21, 1984): 26–29.

[27] James E. Davey, "The Praying Man of Pittsburgh," *The Alliance Witness* (January 7, 1987): 20, 22.

[28] Dr. and Mrs. Howard Taylor, *Hudson Taylor's Spiritual Secret* (Chicago: Moody, 1932), passim.

[29] Richard Ellsworth Day, *The Shadow of the Broad Brim: The Life Story of Charles Haddon Spurgeon* (Valley Forge: Judson Press, 1934), 47–48.

[30] Frank Houghton, *Amy Carmichael of Dohnavur* (London: Society for the Propagation of Christian Knowledge, 1954), 62.

[31] Lillian Dickson, *These My People* (Grand Rapids: Zondervan, 1958), 7–8, 20–21.

## APRIL

[1] E. Stanley Jones, *Along the Indian Road* (New York: Abingdon, 1939), 19–20.

[2] Courtney Anderson, *To the Golden Shore* (Grand Rapids: Zondervan, 1972), 41–44.

[3] Robert Harvey, *Best-Loved Hymn Stories*, 43–45.

[4] Ernest Gordon, *A Book of Protestant Saints* (Grand Rapids: Zondervan, 1940), 9–14.

[5] Betty Fletcher, "Jake DeShazer: Man With Two Missions," *Christian Herald*, (April 1982): 57–60.

[6] Richard Gehman, *Let My Heart Be Broken* (New York: McGraw-Hill, 1960), 7–14.

[7] K. P. Yohannan, *The Coming Revolution in World Missions* (Altamonte Springs, Fla.: Creation House, 1986), 19–20.

[8] Josef Tson, "Thank You for the Beating," *Christian Herald* (April 1988).

[9] Roland H. Bainton, *Here I Stand: A Life of Martin Luther* (New York: American Library, 1950), 34, 49–50.

[10] Pearl S. Buck, *The Exile* (New York: Reynal & Hitchcock, 1936), 77–78, 83, 90–92, 191–192, 264.

[11] Noriko Suziki, "Thank You for Your Prayer," *Light of the World*, trans. from Japanese by Nobuaki Ishihara (April 1987).

[12] Faris Daniel Whitesell, *Great Personal Workers* (Chicago: Moody, 1956), 165–179.

[13] Charles Partee, "Unpublished Letters of Donald McClure," (Pittsburgh Theological Seminary 1988): 238.

[14] Ernest Gordon, *A Book of Protestant Saints* (Grand Rapids: Zondervan, 1940), 14–25.

[15] Dorothy Clarke Wilson, *Ten Fingers for God* (New York: McGraw-Hill, 1965), 142–144.

[16] Eunice V. Pike, *An Uttermost Part* (Chicago: Moody, 1971), 153–154.

[17] Robert P. Evans, *Transformed Europeans* (Chicago: Moody, 1963), 8–9.

[18]Joan Jacobs Brumberg, *Mission for Life: The Story of the Family of Adoniram Judson* (New York: The Free Press, 1980), 68–69.

[19]Dana L. Robert, "The Legacy of Adoniram Judson Gordon," *International Bulletin of Missionary Research* (October 1987): 176–181.

[20]Ruth Hitchcock, *The Good Hand of Our God* (Elgin: David C. Cook, 1975), 14–15.

[21]J. C. Pollock, *Moody: A Biographical Portrait of the Pacesetter in Modern Evangelism* (New York: Macmillan, 1963), 13–14.

[22]Marjorie H. Tiltman, *God's Adventurers* (London: Harrap, 1933), 278–298.

[23]Raymond Davis, *Fire on the Mountains* (Grand Rapids: Zondervan, 1978), 38–47.

[24]S. Pearce Carey, *William Carey* (London: The Carey Press, 1934), passim.

[25]Colin Whittaker, *Seven Guides to Effective Prayer*, 32–35.

[26]Correspondence between the cited missionaries and Joseph R. Showalter, Trinity Evangelical Divinity School, 1985–1986.

[27]Stephen Kwok, personal files, Trinity Evangelical Divinity School, 1988.

[28]B. Bishop, "Florists for the Maasai," *World Christian Magazine* (January/February, 1985): 14–16.

[29]Eileen Crossman, *Mountain Rain: A New Biography of James O. Fraser* (Southampton, UK: Overseas Missionary Fellowship, 1982), 60–61, 88. 5FN [30]Charles C. Creegan, *Pioneer Missionaries of the Church* (New York: American Tract Society, 1903), 64–75.

**MAY**

[1]Marshall Broomhall, *The Jubilee Story of the China Inland Mission* (London: Morgan and Scott, 1915), passim.

[2]Russell T. Hitt, *Jungle Pilot* (Grand Rapids: Zondervan, 1973), 213–215.

[3]Charles Ernest Scott, *Answered Prayer in China* (Philadelphia: The Sunday School Times, 1923), 9–20.

[4]Charles Partee, "Unpublished Letters of Donald McClure," (Pittsburg Theological Seminary, 1988) 243.

[5]Robert P. Evans, *Transformed Europeans* (Chicago: Moody, 1963), 11–14.

[6]Mabel Francis, *One Shall Chase A Thousand* (Harrisburg, Pa.: Christian Publications, 1968), 84–85.

[7]Denis Masson, "The Devil Spoiled His Head," *In Other Words* (September 1987): 5.

[8]Mildred Morehouse and Bertha Neufeld, *A Branch Made Strong: A Short History of FEGC/SEND Japan: 1945–1985* (Tokyo: SEND International, 1987), 32–33.

[9]Basil Miller, *Charles Finney* (Grand Rapids: Zondervan, 1941), 36–38.

[10]Andrew Dong-sup Chung, personal testimony, Deerfield, Ill., March 6, 1983.

[11]Dorothy Clarke Wilson, *Ten Fingers for God*, 112–115.

[12]Ernest Gordon, *A Book of Protestant Saints* (Grand Rapids: Zondervan, 1940), 33–40.

[13]Jay Gary, "Come With Me," *World Christian* (July/August 1986): 31–33.

[14]Elisabeth Elliot, *A Chance to Die: The Life and Legend of Amy Carmichael* (Old Tappan: Revell, 1987), 37–38.

[15]Russell T. Hitt, *Cannibal Valley: The Heroic Struggle for Christ in Savage New Guinea* (New York: Harper & Row, 1962), 112, 119.

[16]David Otis Fuller, ed., *Valiant for the Truth: A Treasury of Evangelical Writings* (New York: McGraw-Hill, 1961), 359–360.

[17]E. Stanley Jones, *A Song of Ascents: A Spiritual Autobiography* (Nashville: Abingdon), 109–110.

[18]Philip Harnden, "Mission to the Missionary," *The Other Side* (December 1986): 7–13.

[19]Charles Partee, "Unpublished Letters of Donald McClure," 352.

[20]Richard Ellsworth Day, *Beacon Lights of Grace* (Grand Rapids: Eerdmans, 1917), 67–75.

[21]Kurt Koch, *The Revival in Indonesia* (Grand Rapids: Kregel, 1970), 54–55.

[22]Glenn Kendall, "Rejected Priesthood Candidate Becomes Pastor," *Impact* (August 1986): 2–3.

[23]James and Marti Hefley, *Unstilled Voices* (Chappaqua: Christian Herald, 1981), 105–107.

[24]James Gilchrist Lawson, *Deeper Experiences of Famous Christians* (Anderson: Warner Press, 1970), 116–120.

[25]Edith Deen, *Great Women of the Christian Faith* (New York: Harper & Row, 1959), 365–367.

[26]Salim Sulamane, "Marked for Execution," *Alliance Witness* (21 May 1986): 14–15.

[27]E. Stanley Jones, *A Song of Ascents: A Spiritual Autobiography*, 352–355.

[28] David J. Hesselgrave, "Tell Us the Way," *Sunday School Times* (Summer Quarter, 1985): 20–21.

[29] John N. Shannon, *A History of the Christian and Missionary Alliance in Argentina* (D.Miss. Dissertation, Trinity Evangelical Divinity School, June 1989), 164–165.

[30] Dorothy Clarke Wilson, *Ten Fingers for God* (New York: McGraw-Hill, 1965), 156–159).

[31] Marie Drown, "Chief Tsantiacu," *The Gospel Message* 1 (1986): 8–9.

## JUNE

[1] Peter Kingston, "One Verse To Go," *In Other Words* (April/May 1987): 6.

[2] Carole Carlson, *Corrie ten Boom* (Old Tappan: Revell, 1983), 11–14.

[3] Christiana, Tsai, *Queen of the Dark Chamber* (Chicago: Moody, 1953), 67, 68, 71–72, 184.

[4] Paul Brand and Philip Yancey, *In His Image* (Grand Rapids: Zondervan, 1984), 43–46.

[5] Elliott Wright, *Holy Company: Christian Heroes and Heroines* (New York: Macmillan, 1980), 21–23.

[6] Myra Scovel, *Richer By India* (New York: Harper & Row, 1964), 93–95.

[7] Day, *The Shadow of the Broad Brim*, 197–201.

[8] Edith Deen, *Great Women of the Christian Faith*, 164–171.

[9] Lillian Fleischmann, "In Search of Forgiveness," *In Other Words* (March 1984): 6.

[10] Elliott Wright, *Holy Company: Christian Heroes and Heroines*, 85–87.

[11] Ruth Slifer, "Christian Chattels," *With Love, From Missionaries Around the World*, ed. Paul Baranek (Kutztown, Pa.: Lutheran Church in America, 1987): 6.

[12] J. I. Packer, "David Martyn Lloyd-Jones," *Chosen Vessels*, ed. Charles Turner (Ann Arbor: Servant Publications, 1985): 109–123.

[13] J. Johnston Walsh, *A Memorial of the Euttebourb Mission and Her Martyred Missionaries* (Philadelphia: Joseph M. Wilson, 1859), 157–190.

[14] Deloris Sunda, "We Have Souls, Too," *Alliance Life* (November 23, 1988): 16–17.

[15] E. B. P. Pusey, ed., *The Confessions of St. Augustine*, (London: J. M. Dent & Sons, 1907), passim.

[16] Elliott Wright, *Holy Company: Christian Heroes and Heroines*, 154–158.

[17] Richard Gehman, *Let My Heart Be Broken* (New York: McGraw-Hill, 1960), 159–163.

[18] Ibid., 159–160.

[19] Joyce Prettol, "A White Robe for Asha," *In Other Words* (March 1986): 5.

[20] John T. Seamands, *Pioneers of the Younger Churches* (Nashville: Abingdon, 1967), 164–180.

[21] Colin Whittaker, *Seven Guides to Effective Prayer*, 32–35.

[22] Karen Lewis, "When the Book Came to Balangao," *In Other Words* (Summer 1983): 7–11.

[23] Todd Poulter, "If I Pay You Today I Can't Greet You Tomorrow," *In Other Words* (March 1987): 5.

[24] Carl F. H. Henry, *The Pacific Garden Mission: A Doorway to Heaven*, 25–28.

[25] Hipolito Alvarez with Fran Olson, "Terror on the Bridge," *In Other Words* (April/May 1986): 6.

[26] W. Harold Fuller, (*Mission-Church Dynamics* (Pasadena: William Carey Library, 1980), 226.

[27] Ken Taylor with Virginia Muir and Matt Price, "Tayloring the Scriptures," *Worldwide Challenge* (June 1988): 34–35, 43–44.

[28] Hal Olsen, *It Happened in Africa* (Kijabe, Kenya: Kesho, 1975), 95–101.

[29] Jamie Buckingham, *Daughters of Destiny: Kathryn Kuhlman . . . Her Story* (Plainfield, N. J.: Logos International, 1976), 259–260.

[30] George Walker, *Miracle In Moccasins* (Phoenix: Phoenician Books, 1969), 9–11, 33–34.

## JULY

[1] Helen Roseveare, "Stir Me To Go," Lecture at Wheaton College, Mission in Focus Conference, 1984.

[2] Hugh Steven, *Good Broth To Warm Our Bones* (Westchester: Crossway, 1982), passim.

[3] A. Stephen, "Saved from Death . . . Sent to Preach," *The Quiet Miracle*, (January/February 1986): 10–11.

[4] Louis I. King, "In The Presence of the King," *The Alliance Witness* (April 15, 1987): 22, 25.

[5] Rosalind Goforth, *Climbing* (Chicago: Moody, n.d.), 113–116.

[6] Heidi Coombs, "Our Heads Aren't Tired!," *In Other Words* (September 1986): 5.

[7]Donald E. Demary, *Pulpit Giants: What Made Them Great* (Chicago: Moody, 1973), 43–46.

[8]Andrew Coe, "Heaven Help Us," distributed by Manhattan Bible Church.

[9]David Lazell, *Gipsy Smith* (Chicago: Moody, 1973), 25–38.

[10]John T. Faris, *The Book of God's Providence* (New York: George H. Doran, 1913), 95–97.

[11]D. G. Hart, "At the Front': The World War 1 Experiences of J. Gresham Machen," *Decision* (November 1988): 12–13.

[12]Margaret E. Burton, *Comrades in Service* (New York: WCTU, 1915), 79–99.

[13]Jeannie Lockerbie, "The Effect of Literature Can Make a Full Circle," *The Quiet Miracle* (Fall 1985): 15.

[14]Ruth John Jay, *Christians You Should Know* (Lincoln: Back to the Bible, 1960), 45–50.

[15]H. Clay Trumbull, *Old Time Student Volunteers* (New York: Revell, 1902), 34–39.

[16]Victor Landero, as told to Bob Owen with David M. Howard, *The Victor: The Victor Landero Story* (Old Tappan: Revell, 1979), passim.

[17]J. Harry Haines, *Ten Hands for God* (Nashville: The Upper Room, 1982), 27–39.

[18]James Gilchrist Lawson, *Deeper Experiences of Famous Christians* (Anderson: Warner Press, 1970), 166–172.

[19]Grace B. Cutts, "Wooden-eyed Bill," *The Alliance Witness* (December 10, 1986): 44–45.

[20]Margaret Burton, *Comrades in Service* (New York: WCTU, 1915), 25–43.

[21]H. Clay Trumbull, *Old Time Student Volunteers* (New York: Revell, 1902), 34–39.

[22]Norman Rohrer, *The Indomitable Mr. O: The Story of J. Irvin Overholtzer, Founder of Child Evangelism Fellowship* (Grand Rapids: CEF, 1970), passim.

[23]James Gilchrist Lawson, *Deeper Experiences of Famous Christians* (Anderson: Warner Press, 1970), 186–194.

[24]Tom Skinner, *Black and Free* (Grand Rapids: Zondervan, 1968), passim.

[25]Dorothy C. Haskin, *In Spite of Dungeon* (Grand Rapids: Zondervan, 1962), 11–18.

[26]James Gilchrist Lawson, *Deeper Experiences of Famous Christians*, 195–202.

[27]James and Marti Hefley, *By Their Blood* (Milford, Mich.: Mott Media, 1979), 35–37.

[28]Warren W. Wiersbe, *Listening to the Giants: A Guide to Good Reading and Great Preaching* (Grand Rapids: Baker, 1980), 201–209.

[29]Carl F. H. Henry, *The Pacific Garden Mission: A Doorway to Heaven*, 41–46.

[30]Roy Guinness, *Mrs. Howard Taylor: Her Web of Time* (London: China Inland Mission, 1949), 89–95.

[31]Della Olson, *A Woman of Her Times* (Minneapolis: Free Church Press, 1977), 53–54.

## AUGUST

[1]Timothy Kituo, testimony taped by Bud Berends, Kijabe Kenya, September 1988.

[2]*The Journal of John Wesley* (Chicagao: Moody, n.d.), 100–103.

[3]Violete Lopez-Gonzaga, "Crisis, Poverty, and Survival in the Phillipines: One Woman Finds Hope," *Missiology* (July 1987): 357–363.

[4]Alan Rosenberg, "The 101-year-old Evangelist," *Alliance Life* (1 February, 1989): 10–11.

[5]Kenneth W. Osbeck, *101 Hymn Stories* (Grand Rapids: Kregel, 1982), 227–229.

[6]Gladys Hunt, *Does Anyone Here Know God?* (Grand Rapids: Zondervan, 1967), 137–142.

[7]Annie Shau Bernsten with Katherine Shang Vee Sui, *Trials of Glad Tidings in Shan Xi*, English title of Chinese book, story translated by Man Chee Kwok (Hong Kong: Haven of Hope Evangelistic Fellowship, 1985), 133–134 .

[8]"What God Hath Joined Together," *TEAM Horizons* (January/February 1989): 5.

[9]Theodore J. Kleinhans, *Martin Luther: Saint and Sinner* (London: Marshall, Morgan & Scott, 1959), 31–35.

[10]Stephen Neill, *A History of Christian Missions* (New York: Penguin, 1964), 157–161, 412–413.

[11]Charles Ernest Scott, *Answered Prayer in China* (Philadelphia: The Sunday School Times, 1923), 26–39.

[12]Frank T. Hoadley and Benjamin P. Browne, *Baptists Who Dared* (Valley Forge: Judson, 1980), 23–26.

[13]Carl F. H. Henry, *The Pacific Garden Mission: A Doorway to Heaven*, 31, 60, 82.

[14]Keith J. Hardman, *The Spiritual Awakeners: American Revivalists from Solomon Stoddard to D. L. Moody* (Chicago: Moody, 1983), 31–38.

[15] Sallie Chesham, *Born to Battle: The Salvation Army in America* (New York: Rand McNally, 1965), 86–87.

[16] Charles Ernest Scott, *Answered Prayer in China* (Philadelphia: The Sunday School Times, 1923), 21–25.

[17] Sallie Chesham, *Born to Battle: The Salvation Army in America*, 104–106.

[18] H. K. W. Kumm, *African Missionary Heroes and Heroines* (New York: Macmillan, 1917), 43–57.

[19] Carl F. H. Henry, *The Pacific Garden Mission: A Doorway to Heaven*, 31, 60, 82.

[20] Richard K. Curtis, *They Called Him Mister Moody* (Grand Rapids: Eerdmans, 1962), 66–69.

[21] Basil Mathews, *The Book of Missionary Heroes* (New York: George H. Doran, 1922), 86–91.

[22] Ibid.

[23] Dongo Pewee, interview with author, Reformed Bible College, Grand Rapids, Mich., 12 September 1988.

[24] Keith J. Hardman, *The Spiritual Awakeners: American Revivalists from Solomon Stoddard to D. L. Moody* (Chicago: Moody, 1983), 84–90.

[25] Basil Miller, *How They Were Won* (Kansas City: Beacon Hill, n.d.), 44–46.

[26] Eileen Crossman, *Mountain Rain: A New Biography of James O. Fraser* (Southampton, UK: Overseas Missionary Fellowship, 1982), 107–108.

[27] Velura Kinnan, "Two Graves on Mt. Meru," in *With Love, From Missionaries the World*, ed. Paul Baranek (Kutztown, Pa.: Lutheran Church in America, 1987): 6.

[28] Carl F. H. Henry, *The Pacific Garden Mission: A Doorway to Heaven*, 30, 39, 57, 59, 113.

[29] George Fry, "Isaac Watts: Minstrel of Missions," *Missionary Monthly* (October, 1985): 3–6.

[30] Basil Mathews, *The Book of Missionary Heroes* (New York: George H. Doran, 1922), 186–195.

[31] David Otis Fuller, ed., *Valiant for the Truth: A Treasury of Evangelical Writings* (New York: McGraw-Hill, 1961), 383–384.

## SEPTEMBER

[1] Peter F. Gunther, comp., *A Frank Boreham Treasury* (Chicago: Moody, 1984), 9–15.

[2] Sue Monnsamy, "Through Fire, Snakes and Persecution," *The Baptist Bulletin* (November 1986): 11–12, 35–36.

[3] William G. Shepherd, *Great Preachers As Seen By a Journalist* (New York: Revell, 1924), 13–26.

[4] John T. Faris, *The Book of God's Providence* (New York: George H. Doran, 1913), 166–172.

[5] David Otis Fuller, ed., *Valiant for the Truth: A Treasury of Evangelical Writings* (New York: McGraw-Hill, 1961), 99–100.

[6] Marie Lind, *Dramatic Stories for Missionary Programs* (Grand Rapids: Baker, 1972), 15–31.

[7] David Otis Fuller, ed., *Valiant for the Truth: A Treasury of Evangelical Writings*, 32–33.

[8] A. Wetherell Johnson, *Created for Commitment* (Wheaton: Tyndale House, 1982), 40–43.

[9] Joanne Shetler, "Then Things Began to Change," *Decision* (April 1968): 29–30.

[10] Leslie K. Tarr, "Progress of a Pilgrim," *Decision* (September 1988): 13–14.

[11] Mrs. Howard Taylor, *Borden of Yale* (Chicago: Moody, n.d.), passim.

[12] Basil Matthews, *The Book of Missionary Heroes* (New York: George H. Doran, 1922), 213–223.

[13] Day, *Beacon Lights of Grace*, 31–39.

[14] Day, *Beacon Lights of Grace*, 43–53.

[15] Robert P. Evans, *Transformed Europeans* (Chicago: Moody, 1963), 83–89.

[16] Georgina A. Gollock, *Sons of Africa* (New York: Friendship Press, 1920), 173–178.

[17] Charles Ludwig, *Mamma Was A Missionary* (Grand Rapids: Zondervan, 1963), 112–113.

[18] Albert H. Currier, *Nine Great Preachers* (Boston: The Pilgrim Press, 1912), 113–129.

[19] Mary Frances Owen, "A Skeptic Discovers Love," *Alliance Witness* (April 1, 1987): 19.

[20] Ernest Gordon, *A Book of Protestant Saints* (Grand Rapids: Zondervan, 1940), 103–118.

[21] Graeme Kent, *Company of Heaven: Early Missionaries in the South Seas* (Nashville: Thomas Nelson, 1972), 138–55.

[22] Stella Cox, "Cookies, Salads, and the Gospel," *TEAM Horizons* (November/December 1988): 11.

[23] Jean Schilla, "Sicilian Evangelist Accomplishes the Unthinkable," *Partners*, 24–25.

[24] Helen S. Dyer, *Pandita Ramabai* (London: Pickering & Inglis, n.d.), 45–60, 115–116.

[25] Ernest Gordon, *A Book of Protestant Saints* (Grand Rapids: Zondervan, 1940), 75–85.

[26] Charles Ludwig, *Their Finest Hour* (Elgin: David C. Cook, 1974), 57–62.

[27] Tom Skinner, *Black and Free* (Grand Rapids: Zondervan, 1968), 65–72.

[28] Kenneth W. Osbeck, *101 Hymn Stories*, 57–59.

[29] Norman Rohrer, *The Indomitable Mr. O: The Story of J. Irvin Overholtzer, Founder of Child Evangelism Fellowship* (Grand Rapids: CEF, 1970), 11–14.

[30] Walter R. Bowie, *Women of Light* (New York: Harper & Row, 1963), 119–127.

## OCTOBER

[1] John Pollock, *Victims of the Long March* (Waco: Word, 1970), 11–19.

[2] Daniel Scalberg and Joy Cordell, "A Savage With the Savages," *Moody Monthly* (April 1987): 55–61.

[3] Lorry Lutz, *Born to Lose, Bound to Win: The Amazing Journey of Mother Eliza George* (Irvine: Harvest House, 1980), passim.

[4] James Gilchrist Lawson, *Deeper Experiences of Famous Christians* (Anderson: Warner Press, 1970), 69–79.

[5] Bernard Ruflin, *Fanny Crosby* (n.p.: United Church Press, 1976), passim.

[6] Basil Mathews, *There Go the Conquerors* (New York: Round Table Press, 1936), 31–44.

[7] Eric J. Fellman, "Ira Sankey: The Gospel in Song," *Moody Monthly* (January 1986): 49–51.

[8] Sophie Muller, *His Voice Shakes the Wilderness* (Sanford, Fla.: New Tribes Mission, 1988), passim.

[9] James Gilchrist Lawson, *Deeper Experiences of Famous Christians* (Anderson: Warner Press, 1970), 211–221.

[10] Katharine Howard, "Lord, Send My Children," *Moody Monthly* (October 1978): 63–68.

[11] Thomas A. Dorsey, "Precious Lord, Take My Hand," *Moody Monthly* (April 1976): 44–46.

[12] Warren W. Wiersbe, "Cruden: 'Alexander the Corrector,' " *Moody Monthly* (September 1975): 125–131.

[13] Sherwood Wirt, "God's Darling," *Moody Monthly* (February 1977): 57–60.

[14] Ruth Johnson Jay, *Christians With Courage* (Lincoln: Back to the Bible, 1973), 24–33.

[15] Don Richardson, *Peace Child* (Ventura: Regal, 1974), 272–280.

[16] Connie Griffith, "Conversation with a Snake Worshiper," Unpublished manuscript, Boone, N.C., 1988.

[17] Viggo Olsen, "The Agnostic Who Dared to Search," *Moody Monthly* (November 1973): 34–35, 70–71, 100, 109.

[18] Elizabet Torres, "She Saw Children in the Streets," *TEAM Horizons* (May/June, 1989): 8–9.

[19] Day, *The Shadow of the Broad Brim*, 94–98.

[20] James C. Hefley, *Heroes of the Faith*, (Chicago: Moody, n.d.), 7–14.

[21] Eugene M. Harrison, *Missionary Crusaders for Christ* (Glendale, Calif.: The Church Press, 1967), 56–75.

[22] Anthony Zeoli with Gerald S. Strober, *Free Forever: The Autobiography of Anthony Zeoli* (Old Tappan: Revell, 1980), passim.

[23] David J. Fant, Jr., "Sophie—The Scrubwoman," *Alliance Witness* (November 19, 1986): 20–23.

[24] James Paton, ed., *The Story of Dr. John G. Paton's Thirty Years with South Sea Cannibals* (New York: George H. Doran, 1923): 179–180.

[25] Su Sui-Feng, *Softly Falling Tears: The Confession of a Doctor's Wife* (Taipei: Campus Evangelical Fellowship, 1986), passim.

[26] Spencer T. Sutherland, "Fifty Years of Ministry," *The Alliance Witness* (18 February, 1987): 12–13.

[27] Mildred Hughes, "Photos of Faith," in *With Love, From Missionaries Around the World*, ed. Paul Baranek (Kutztown, Pa.: Lutheran Church in America, 1987): 18–19.

[28] "Sunday School: A Colorful History," *Charisma & Christian Life* (February 1989): 77–79.

[29] Anne Arnott, *The Secret Country of C. S. Lewis* (Grand Rapids: Eerdmans, 1975), 23–24, 85–95.

[30] Abel Stevens, *The Women of Methodism* (New York: Carlton & Lanahan, 1869, reprinted in New York: Garland, 1987), 145–173.

[31] Twila Knaack, *Ethel Waters: I Touched A Sparrow* (Waco: Word, 1978), passim.

## NOVEMBER

[1] Charles C. Creegan, *Pioneer Missionaries of the Church* (New York: American Tract Society, 1903), 213–224.

[2] William J. Petersen, *Catherine Marshall Had A Husband* (Wheaton: Tyndale, 1986), 85–118.

[3] Basil Mathews, *Livingstone the Pathfinder* (New York: Missionary Education Movement, 1912), passim.

[4] Ruth A. Tucker, *From Jerusalem to Irian Jaya: A Biographical History of Christian Missions*, 246–249.

[5] Brian Peterson, "The Sobering Crusade of Mickey Evans" *Charisma & Christian Life* (November 1988): 42–49.

[6] Henry Cowan, *John Knox: The Hero of the Scottish Reformation* (New York: G. P. Putnam's Sons, 1905), 59–85.

[7] Kurt Koch, *The Revival in Indonesia* (Grand Rapids: Kregel, 1970), 64–65.

[8] John O. Foster, *Life and Labors of Mrs. Maggie Newton Van Cott* (New York: Garland, 1987), 326–337.

[9] Tom Taylor, "The Martyrs of Campo Loro," *Moody Monthly* (April 1988).

[10] Marjorie H. Tiltman, *God's Adventurers* (London: Harrap, 1933), 278–298.

[11] Ruth A. Tucker and Walter L. Liefeld, *Daughters of the Church: Women and Ministry from New Testament Times to the Present* (Grand Rapids: Zondervan, 1987), 263–267.

[12] Thomas J. Bach, *Pioneer Missionaries for Christ and His Church* (Wheaton: Van Kampen, 1955), 26–28.

[13] Fatima Mahoumed, "Ann Croft and the Fulani," *Perspectives on the World Christian Movement*, ed. Ralph D. Winter and Steven C. Hawthorne (Pasadena: William Carey Library, 1981): 720–721.

[14] Thomas J. Bach, *Pioneer Missionaries for Christ and His Church* (Wheaton: Van Kampen, 1955), 19–22.

[15] Peter Tibi, "From Islam to Christianity," unpublished paper, Moffat College of Bible, Kijabe, Kenya, June 1987.

[16] Thomas J. Bach, *Pioneer Missionaries for Christ and His Church* (Wheaton: Van Kampen, 1955), 105–108.

[17] Gordon Rupp, *Six Makers of English Religion, 1500–1700* (London: Hodder and Stoughton, 1957), 53–73.

[18] B. H. Pearson, *The Vision Lives: A Profile of Mrs. Charles E. Cowman* (Grand Rapids: Zondervan, 1961), passim.

[19] Martin Jarrett-Kerr, *Patterns of Christian Acceptance: Individual Response to the Missionary Impact* (London: Oxford, 1972), 171–188.

[20] D. L. Moody, "A Change of Heart for Valentine Burke," *Moody Monthly* (February 1986): 120.

[21] Fred Barlow, *Profiles in Evangelism* (Murfreesboro, Tenn.: Sword of the Lord, 1976), 150–153.

[22] Ernest K. Emurian, *Living Stories of Famous Hymns* (Grand Rapids: Baker, 1955), 66–67.

[23] Roger Williams, "Triumph From Tragedy," *Christian Life* (April 1976): 28–29, 37, 77.

[24] Elliott Wright, *Holy Company: Christian Heroes and Heroines* (New York: Macmillan, 1980), 183–187.

[25] Matthew L. Rice, Missionary Correspondence, West Germany, February 1988.

[26] Harold Ivan Smith, "The Woman Who Brought Us Thanksgiving," *Charisma & Christian Life* (November 1988): 95–101.

[27] Francis M. DuBose, ed. *Classics of Christian Missions* (Nashville: Broadman, 1979), 409–419.

[28] Robert Harvey, *Best-Loved Hymn Stories*, 25–27.

[29] Don Richardson, *Eternity in Their Hearts*, rev. ed. (Ventura, Calif.: Regal, 1981), 128–130.

[30] Lorry Lutz, *Destined for Royalty* (Pasadena: William Carey Library, 1985), passim.

## DECEMBER

[1] Charles Ludwig, *Their Finest Hour* (Elgin: David C. Cook, 1974), 13–19.

[2] W. P. Livingstone, *Mary Slessor of Calabar: Pioneer Missionary* (London: Hodder and Stoughton, 1915), 142–143.

[3] Norman Rohrer, *The Indomitable Mr. O: The Story of J. Irvin Orerhollzer, Founder of Child Evangelism Fellowship* (Grand Rapids: CEF, 1970), 11–14.

[4] John Pollock, *Billy Graham: Evangelist to the World* (New York: Harper & Row, 1979), 222–223.

[5] Harold Ivan Smith, *Movers and Shakers* (Old Tappan: Revell, 1988), 166–187.

[6] Bernard R. DeRemer, "Howard A. Kelly: Beloved Physician of Baltimore," *Fundamentalist Journal* (December 1988): 34–35.

[7] Edith Dean, *Great Women of the Christian Faith* (New York: Harper & Row, 1959), 275–279.

[8] Mrs. Howard Taylor, "Whether by Life or by Death," *Moody Monthly* (December 1984): 119–121; Marie Lind, *Dramatic Stories for Missionary Programs* (Grand Rapids: Baker, 1972), 15–31.

[9] Hale, *Don't Let the Goats Eat the Loquat Trees*, 68–69.

[10] Kenneth W. Osbeck, *Singing With Understanding* (Grand Rapids: Kregel, 1979), 143–144.

[11] Eileen Crossman, *Mountain Rain: A New Biography of James O. Fraser* (Southampton, UK: Overseas Missionary Fellowship, 1982), 98–99.

[12] Charles W. Colson, *Born Again* (Old Tappan, N.J.: Revell, 1976), passim.

[13] Warren W. Wiersbe, "G. Campbell Morgan: Prince of Expositors," *Moody Monthly* (December 1974): 67–71.

[14] Don Richardson, *Lord s of the Earth* (Glendale: Regal, 1977), 132–134, 363–364.

[15] Kerry Lovering, "The Pioneer Who Never Had a Call," *SIM NOW* (Nov/Dec 1985).

[16] Allen Finley and Lorry Lutz, *The Family Tie* (Nashville: Thomas Nelson, 1978), 17–31.

[17] Harold Ivan Smith, "A Time to Speak Out," *Charisma & Christian Life* (March 1988): 73–78.

[18] Thomas J. Bach, *Pioneer Missionaries for Christ and His Church* (Wheaton: Van Kampen, 1955), 49–53.

[19] Fred Barlow, *Profiles in Evangelism* (Murfreesboro, Tenn.: Sword of the Lord, 1976), 27–32.

[20] Leon McBeth, *Women in Baptist Life* (Nashville: Broadman, 1979), 76–78.

[21] John T. Faris, *The Book of God's Providence* (New York: George H. Doran, 1913), 121–127.

[22] Bernie May, "The Wrong Place for Christmas," *In Other Words* (December 1984): 8.

[23] "Guatemalan Christmas Blanket Project Exceeds Wildest Dreams," *Partners*, (January/February/March 1988): 23.

[24] I. M. Anderson, "When Sankey Sang the Shepherd Song," *Moody Monthly* (February 1986): 77–81.

[25] Melanie Floyd, "Understanding Christmas," *In Other Words* (December 1988): 1–2.

[26] Day, *Beacon Lights of Grace*, 157–166.

[27] Faris Daniel Whitesell, *Great Personal Workers* (Chicago: Moody, 1956), 56–71.

[28] Faris Daniel Whitesell, *Great Personal Workers* (Chicago: Moody, 1956), 26–40.

[29] Eleanor Brown, "The Legacy of Florence Allshorn," *International Bulletin* (January 1984): 24–28.

[30] Tim Stafford, "The Father of Church Growth," *Christianity Today* (February 21, 1986): 19–23.

[31] David Otis Fuller, ed., *Valiant for the Truth: A Treasury of Evangelical Writings* (New York: McGraw-Hill, 1961), 70–71.

# SUBJECT INDEX

# SCRIPTURE INDEX